BLOOD RICH

First Edition

Library of Congress Cataloging-in-Publication Data

Wolfe, Jane, 1957-
    Blood rich: when oil billions, high fashion, and royal intimacies are not enough / Jane Wolfe. —1st ed.
        p.   cm.
    Includes bibliographical references (p.   ) and index.
    ISBN 0-316-95092-0
    1. Sakowitz Department Store—History.   2. Family-owned business enterprises—Texas—History.   3. Business failures—Southwestern States—History.   4. Scandals—Texas—History.   5. Sakowitz, Robert. 6. Businessmen—Texas—Biography.   7. Wyatt, Lynn Sakowitz. I. Sakowitz, Robert.   II. Wyatt, Lynn Sakowitz.   III. Title.
    HF5465.U6S248   1993
    381'. 141'09764—dc20   93-15356

10 9 8 7 6 5 4 3 2

MV-NY

Published simultaneously in Canada by Little, Brown & Company (Canada) Limited

Printed in the United States of America

BLOOD RICH

Also by Jane Wolfe

The Murchisons

BLOOD RICH

When Oil Billions, High Fashion, and Royal Intimacies Are Not Enough

JANE WOLFE

Little, Brown and Company

Boston   New York   Toronto   London

First Edition

Library of Congress Cataloging-in-Publication Data

Wolfe, Jane, 1957-
    Blood rich: when oil billions, high fashion, and royal intimacies are not enough / Jane Wolfe. —1st ed.
        p. cm.
    Includes bibliographical references (p.   ) and index.
    ISBN 0-316-95092-0
    1. Sakowitz Department Store—History. 2. Family-owned business enterprises—Texas—History. 3. Business failures—Southwestern States—History. 4. Scandals—Texas—History. 5. Sakowitz, Robert.
6. Businessmen—Texas—Biography. 7. Wyatt, Lynn Sakowitz.
I. Sakowitz, Robert. II. Wyatt, Lynn Sakowitz. III. Title.
HF5465.U6S248 1993
381' . 141'09764—dc20   93-15356

10 9 8 7 6 5 4 3 2

MV-NY

Published simultaneously in Canada by Little, Brown & Company (Canada) Limited

Printed in the United States of America

For
Jane Culver King

BLOOD RICH

1

LYNN WYATT was as strong as she was beautiful. Her strength, as much as her beauty, had helped her become one of the most glamorous, most photographed women in the world. But when she left Houston in July 1987 for her villa at St.-Jean-Cap-Ferrat, she did not feel strong. She was being torn apart, devastated, by a gut-wrenching decision that her husband was forcing upon her.

Oscar Wyatt demanded that she choose between her love for him and her love for her brother, Robert Sakowitz. Of course, Oscar did not put it that way, but Lynn was no fool. She knew what he wanted. He wanted her to take her brother to court, to sue him, to punish and expose him publicly. It was a horrendous situation, to be caught between these two men, and Lynn knew she must find an escape from it.

Lynn had been going to the French Riviera for more than two decades. She had built her international reputation in this part of the world — as the close friend of Princess Grace of Monaco and as the hostess of the legendary La Mauresque, the villa made famous by British novelist Somerset Maugham, whose wickedly witty guests and lavish parties had been the talk of society on both sides of the Atlantic.

Confounding the skeptics, Lynn had proved herself Maugham's equal at bringing celebrities and titled Europeans, the rich and the powerful, to Mauresque. Here, every July, she opened the Riviera's season with a birthday party in her honor. There was no more desirable invitation. Every year, who really was who (and who was not) was defined by Lynn's guest list. Shorter than the Social Register or the Almanach de Gotha and more important, her list usually numbered fewer than eighty. This was Lynn's triumph.

Beautiful since birth, in barely two decades she had made herself into an international icon of style. Although she was dressed by Paris's top couturiers, her fabulous clothes were almost an insignificant part of what had made her. She understood better than anyone the difference between style and fashion. Her family had made its money selling fashion, but style was not for sale at Sakowitz or Saks Fifth Avenue or even at Saint Laurent. Lynn's style was not something she put on like a cape. It was her self.

Her large green eyes, her wide slash of a smile, her ballerina's body, and her trademark mane of golden hair were her physical self, and all contributed to her international image as a beauty. But what set her apart more even than her seductive beauty was her Texas charm, an area in which even her most envious enemies admitted she was unsurpassed. What she said, how she listened, and how she laughed were the most essential elements of her self.

Because she was often covered in expensive clothes and expensive jewels, and photographed at fashionable places, it was easy to assume she was superficial. She was not. And while there were richer and more beautiful women on the Riviera, here, every July, she reigned.

Jutting precipitously into the Mediterranean, halfway between Nice and Monte Carlo on the Côte d'Azur, Cap Ferrat is one of the most opulent oases in the world. Its 580 acres, terraced and cantilevered up the steep pre-Alps, have long been the exclusive preserve of the rich and royal who each season inhabit the grand villas that dot the hillside secreted behind monolithic, perfectly clipped hedges and iron gates.

Malbousque, the villa to which Lynn fled in 1987 — having sold La Mauresque a few years earlier — is situated halfway up a hill, perfectly placed amid wind-whipped sea pines and lush poplars. Salmon-colored, with a red tile roof and long white shutters thrown open to a broad terrace, the villa has an exuberant Italian flair. Inside, it is bright, airy, and almost formal, with yellow-and-white-checked marble floors and sienna walls, elaborately carved mantels and high, white ceilings. Two six-foot painted blackamoors stand in the front foyer, before the swirling, suspended stairway that seems to float gracefully up to the sky. Billowy, soft, Mediterranean light pours through the open double windows and doors of each room; it plays on the blue-and-white porcelain in the dining room and on the white marble mantel in the drawing room. Malbousque is a Gatsbyesque background for its star.

From the terrace, which spans the entire length of the villa and is bordered by a marble balustrade, Lynn could look out over the tops of the trees and see the cobalt blue sea that gives the Côte d'Azur its name. Just below the terrace, a rectangular stone-bottomed swimming pool casts a greenish reflection, like a Roman bath. Seagulls fly and call overhead, and the scents of jasmine and orange blossoms fill the air.

This spectacular setting, which is only more glamorous and mysterious at night, was the perfect backdrop for the theme Lynn had chosen for this year's party: romance. But as always, more important than the theme was Lynn's guest list, which through the years had ranged from Henry Ford II, the Aga Khan, Princess Grace, and Prince Rainier, to Joan Collins, Mick Jagger, and Andy Warhol. It was these and other star players at her birthday bash that attracted the attention of the international press, which had come to expect from Lynn a better show every year and was never disappointed.

But this year it was impossible for Lynn to focus her attention and imagination on her party when the problem of Oscar's pressure to expose and punish Robert was unresolved. She was terrified of the predictable public reaction to a courthouse catfight. She had brilliantly and tirelessly made herself the darling of the international press, but she knew they would not spare her once they smelled the blood of a feral family fight over the only things worth fighting for — money and ego.

She had once been close to her brother, very close, but no longer. Oscar charged that Bobby had run the eighty-three-year-old Sakowitz store into bankruptcy while cheating his family and making himself rich. Lynn was not sure whether he had done all those terrible things, and even if he had, she did not want to hear it. The store's bankruptcy two years earlier had been devastating enough. For Oscar now to demand that she attack Robert publicly was more than she could face.

At first she had refused to listen to Oscar's accusations of her brother. When he brought up the subject, she walked out of the room. But Oscar was relentless. He seemed obsessed with what he called Bobby's "plunder."

Some of her friends believed that Oscar's burning hatred of Bobby was motivated by vengeful jealousy. Bobby had looks, elegance, background, and manners. Oscar, the son of a brutal drunk who made a meager living in a small Texas town, had had none of the privileges Bobby had growing up, a fact that seemed to enrage Oscar, even now, when he controlled a $9 billion oil corporation, when he could go wherever he wanted, do whatever he wanted, live however he wanted.

Before leaving for Europe, Lynn had told her mother that she was considering resigning her directorship at the store and turning her interest in her father's estate over to her four children. Ann Sakowitz objected strongly. If Bernard Sakowitz had wanted his grandsons to have that stock now, he would have said so in his will, Ann argued.

But Lynn was caught in a terrible bind. She did not want to sue her brother, but neither could she continue to be torn apart by Oscar's relentless berating of Bobby. And she had only to reflect on her success since marrying him to know how important he was to her. It was Oscar, not Robert or her mother, who had helped her become a social star.

The more she thought about it, alone in the tranquil surroundings of the villa, the more the stock assignment to her sons appealed to her. It would take her out of Oscar's firing line — he could then put pressure on her sons, instead of her, to investigate her brother — and she could hold herself above the brutal fight and avoid sullying her reputation.

The task, she decided, must go to Douglas, her second son by her first marriage, whom Oscar had adopted, along with Douglas's older brother, Steve, when Oscar and Lynn married. She would make her decision known to Douglas when he arrived for her birthday party.

But Douglas, a handsome and eligible twenty-nine-year-old Houston lawyer, surprised her. He refused the stock assignment. No, he said, he did not want to become involved in the fight between his father and his uncle.

The birthday party provided Lynn with temporary relief from her painful dilemma, especially when photographer Helmut Newton arrived in drag, wearing a long, golden Rapunzel wig, and jumped up on the terrace's balustrade to expose his high heels and knee-high black silk stockings. Safely surrounded by her own millionaire Mafia, Lynn laughed her smoky, sexy Texas laugh, an undulating mix of innocent fun and bawdy sexuality, flirted with Monaco's Prince Albert, and gave each guest, female as well as male, a few moments of her you-are-the-most-significant-to-me-of-anyone-here treatment that seduced the members of her court. Douglas was locked in serious gossip with Christina Onassis on a sofa in the living room, and Oscar, clutching a short drink, held the rapt attention of one of the world's top bankers, Michel David-Weill of Lazard Frères.

After the party Douglas told his mother that he had reconsidered and would accept the stock assignment, acting as trustee for himself and his brothers. He was the lawyer in the family, and he said he felt it was his duty to do what she wanted regarding his grandfather's estate.

Once she had elicited Douglas's agreement, Lynn moved very quickly. Rather than wait until she returned to Houston to tell Sakowitz's board that she was resigning her directorship, she immediately scribbled her resignation by hand on a blank sheet of paper. She also handwrote the three-page document assigning her share of the family trust to her sons. She then hurriedly took the papers to be notarized in the neighboring town of Beaulieu-sur-Mer, another of the Côte d'Azur's sunny jewels.

Finally, she had rid herself of the heartrending problem that had been torturing her for more than two years. But there was an irony to what she had done. The one thing she wanted most to avoid, a public, internecine fight, she had, in fact, made possible.

What was most astonishing about Lynn, Robert, and Oscar was how alike they were. This was not obvious on the surface. Oscar was as rude and rough as Robert was elegant and refined. Lynn had an extraordinary ability to charm others, while Robert seemed chiefly charmed with himself.

But the dominant characteristic all three shared was an iron will. Brains and hard work had played a role in the success of each, but the major element that had catapulted Robert and Lynn and Oscar to the tops of their respective fields was relentless determination.

It was easy to find fault with them as they battled each other, to complain that they should be grateful for their extraordinary good fortune and should love and support one another. But Oscar had not built a $9 billion corporation, Lynn had not made it to the top of international society, and Robert had not put his store on the world fashion map, by giving up or giving in. They were competitors of the fiercest kind. This competition, this rivalry, explained why now, even as Lynn assigned her stock to Douglas at her villa in the south of France, Robert was fighting an even bigger battle back in Houston, a battle for the store's life — long after most would have resigned themselves to defeat.

Following the bankruptcy of Sakowitz two years earlier, the store's creditors were threatening to force liquidation if Robert did not invest a substantial sum into the desperately ill company. Robert was scrambling to find a buyer, and he was losing the battle. The store that he had touted brilliantly to the international press and where he had courageously introduced the first designer boutiques in America was dying, and no matter how hard he tried there was little Robert could do to save it.

Anyone who had watched Robert's ascent, who had followed his successes at Harvard and in his early years at the store, now wondered how he had gotten into so much trouble. He had wanted to be America's premier merchant prince, the next Stanley Marcus, and for several years he came close. Slight but muscular, he could have been the actor James Dean's twin, with deep-set hazel eyes, a low, rectangular forehead, a small, straight nose, long vertical dimples, and skin so fair and clear it looked almost feminine. His smile, revealing just the right amount of perfect teeth, was simultaneously mysterious and inviting. By 1987, the passing of time and his business experiences had matured his face and made it even more handsome.

Like James Dean, Robert had a mythical aura; there was something of a legend about him. It was obvious from the way the press followed him, from the way he broke new ground in fashion, from the way he lived. In his twenties, he was "Bachelor Bob"; at thirty, his wedding to the wealthy New York debutante Pamela Zauderer was splashed across an entire half-page of the *New York Times*; at thirty-two, he was among the first men ever named to the International Best-Dressed List.

As with Lynn, Robert's greatest genius had been publicity. But where had it gone now? Instead of receiving the usual glowing stories long associated with the prince of fashion, he was taking a beating in the press. HOW BOBBY SAKOWITZ TOOK AN ESCALATOR TO THE BASEMENT, trumpeted *Business Week*.

By the late summer of 1987, Robert's situation had become so desperate that the store's creditors finally imposed a September 16 "drop-dead date," a date by which he must have an investor for the store or face liquidation. But then, some luck fell his way, as it had so many times before. On September 8, Robert received a call from the president of the American retail arm of the Australian real estate conglomerate L. J. Hooker Corp. After Robert explained that he had a drop-dead date, Hooker's executives raced to Houston and negotiated with him through the weekend. At the final moment, Hooker agreed to inject $10 million into Sakowitz, which would bring the store out of bankruptcy.

As Robert sighed with relief over the last-minute merger, his nephew Douglas Wyatt was scrambling to block it. Under the terms of the merger, the new company would be owned 80 percent by Hooker and 20 percent by Robert, while Sakowitz's other shareholders — including Lynn, Ann, and the Bernard Sakowitz trusts — had their ownership stake reduced to nothing.

If Lynn's stock assignment to Douglas had made a courthouse battle possible, Robert's deal with Hooker made it inevitable. On the evening of October 13, 1987, Robert was at home celebrating his forty-ninth birthday with his wife and four children when the doorbell rang. When Robert opened the door, a process server slapped him with a lawsuit from Douglas. The suit alleged that Robert had violated his fiduciary duties in the Hooker merger, and it demanded that he be removed as executor of the Bernard Sakowitz estate and as trustee of the family trusts.

Robert was certain that Oscar was the instigator of Douglas's suit. Oscar had already filed his own lawsuit against Robert a year earlier, and it was clear that he had a hand in this suit too. Robert believed that Oscar wanted to prove that whereas Lynn's father, Bernard Sakowitz, and Robert had once wielded the power in the family, Oscar was in charge now. Robert believed that Oscar could not stand to see Robert win because if Robert won, in Oscar's mind that meant Oscar lost.

Robert telephoned Lynn and pleaded with her to intervene in Douglas's lawsuit. She must talk with Douglas and tell him the suit was wrong, Robert insisted. But Lynn refused to be pulled into the conflict. If Robert had anything further to say on the matter, he should talk with Douglas, not her, she told her brother.

Robert was shattered by Lynn's snub. How could his only sibling — with whom he had once been so close, to whom he had thought himself more like an older brother than a younger brother — do this to him?

Robert's recollection of their childhood could not have differed more from Lynn's. He saw himself as the protective and loving brother, but she recalled him as the favored child on whom her parents showered most of their attention. Like all children, Lynn needed help when she was young in creating her own identity. Her family had both the money and the business vehicle to support her obvious interest and talent for fashion, to help her become an important figure in that world. But, instead, her parents had devoted their time and energy and resources to their son.

Of all the opportunities that lay ahead for Oscar to bring down his brother-in-law, the quickest during the fall of 1987 was to block the Hooker merger. So on the Friday before Monday, November 16, the day the court would rule on whether to confirm the merger, Oscar, as a creditor, filed court objections to it. He cited twenty-one conditions that had to be met before the merger could go through.

If Oscar could stop the court's confirmation, it would be virtually impossible in just two weeks to work out anything that would prevent liquidation by the store's creditors. It seemed clear to Robert that liquidation was what Oscar really wanted. He was not going to let up until Robert was destroyed. He had Robert convinced of that, whether it was true or not.

But Oscar's last-minute objections were overruled by the judge, and the merger went through. Robert had won a round.

It was hard to imagine how paunchy, long-faced Oscar Wyatt, with his tiny, cruel eyes and a trophy set of wattled jowls, could have attracted Lynn Sakowitz. Of course, many assumed the answer was money — and money alone. But that was the response of those who had not seen Lynn and Oscar together, had not seen the way Oscar captivated her with his brilliant mind, the way the aura of his strength absorbed her.

Oscar was the quintessence of brute force. His nature had not changed since he was an uncontrollable two-hundred-pound tackle in high school. He was smarter and richer now, but at sixty-two he was still as rough as he had been on the Navasota football team, as tough as when he had laid irrigation pipe in the cotton fields during Texas's blistering summers.

It was both his physical and mental prowess that Lynn loved, now and when they first married. In the early 1960s, at a time in her life when she seemed most vulnerable, when she was newly divorced and with two young children, Oscar had rescued her. He had taken her and her two boys from her parents' home and installed them in Houston's most famous mansion. He had lavished his money on her, made it possible for her to become whatever she wanted.

As much as he protested that he hated Lynn's jet-setting and the money she spent on clothes, the opposite seemed true. Oscar was too smart not to recognize how much his wife's contacts with royalty and movie stars and the rich women who were married to the world's major industrialists benefited his business. He knew how much her beauty and stardom helped his image in Texas and abroad.

But when it came to her brother, Oscar had the last word. Bobby pinched a nerve in Oscar, and it was not just because French words and the names of fine wines rolled off Bobby's tongue. There were shrewd observers who believed that what Oscar hated about his brother-in-law was that Bobby confirmed Oscar's worst fear about himself — that someday, somehow, he too would lose all his money. Robert was Oscar's worst nightmare.

Whatever Oscar's motivation, one thing appeared certain long before *Wyatt v. Sakowitz* ever went to trial. The family lawsuit would result in one of Texas's most bitter and notorious courtroom battles. Less certain, in fact impossible to predict, was which of its determined, competitive, ambitious players would win.

2

THE MERCHANTS SAKOWITZ began in America in 1887 with the arrival of Robert Sakowitz's great-grandfather, Leib Shaikevitch. Having made a poor living as a teacher in his native Korosteschev, Russia, a small town near Kiev, Leib hoped he could do better in America. But after working for some time as a fruit peddler on the streets of New York, he lost the small amount of money that he had arrived with, money that he had planned to increase in order to bring his wife, Leah, and four young children to America.

Even before she learned that her husband was virtually penniless, Leah grew tired of waiting for him to send for the family and raised the passage money herself. Leah was prescient, as well as practical, and more than once was the catalyst behind an important family move. Years later, it was she who insisted that her two youngest sons relocate from Galveston to Houston, a move that was crucial to their success.

When Leah arrived in New York and found her husband living in poverty, she ordered him to pack up his few belongings. They would leave New York at once. Happily, a means of leaving was available.

Because the number of Jews in America was infinitesimal in colonial times and the early days of the republic, there was very little anti-Semitism. But with the sizable immigration of Western European Jews to America from 1840 until 1880, anti-Semitism increased in New York, Boston, Philadelphia, and the other eastern cities where the newcomers congregated. With the flood of Eastern European Jews in the 1890s, the earlier arrivals — particularly the most successful of them, epitomized by New York banker Jacob

Schiff — feared that dangerous anti-Semitism would result if the new arrivals remained in the already crowded ghettos in the East.

Therefore, Schiff and other influential German Jews subsidized what they called the Galveston Plan, intended to distribute Jews throughout America's Southwest and West. Agents in Europe persuaded emigrating Jews to sail for Galveston. Also, a substantial number of Jews in America's ghettos passed through a "Removal Office" in New York, which put them on a boat for Galveston.

The Shaikevitch family journeyed from New York to Galveston on a dirty, crowded, cattle boat that made Leah wonder whether America was just as grim as the world they had left behind. After the murder of Czar Alexander II in 1881, official policy in Russia was to get rid of all Jews in any of three ways: force them to convert to Christianity; force them to emigrate; or kill them — either by starvation or by massacres that ranged from small Cossack amusements to the Christ Night bloodbath of 1881, the worst such butchery in the three hundred years since the St. Bartholomew's Day massacre of the Huguenots in France.

Just as the earlier German Jews had feared, the new flood of Eastern European Jews diminished the social acceptance of the earlier Jewish arrivals. Soon, Americans saw the stereotypical Jew as a pale, weak, bespectacled, crouching tailor, terrified lest he offend the sweatshop owner. The German Jews, to express their contempt for these ragged new arrivals whose names often contained *k* sounds, coined an insulting name for them: "kikes." It was a bitter irony that the new deprecation was soon applied to all Jews by American non-Jews.

At the port in Galveston, the Shaikevitch name was changed to Sakowitz. Instead of moving farther west, Leib and Leah decided to make their home in Galveston, which, by the 1890s, had become Texas's major port and second-largest city after San Antonio.

Leib, Leah, their eldest son, Sam, and youngest son, Simon, went to work in a cotton gin. It was dirty, back-breaking work, a step down even from Leib's work peddling apples and bananas. But the woman who ran the gin liked the family, especially three-year-old Simon. Because he was so small, she allowed him to hide behind one of the big machines and sleep during work hours.

Leib and Leah also had another son, Tobias, who was the second-oldest, next to Sam. Tobe, as he was called, had remained in Russia with his paternal grandfather, who wanted an heir and insisted that the family leave behind a son. Many years later, Tobe still remembered crying and clinging to the wagon wheels to try to stop the departure of his mother and his siblings. The grandfather was kind to Tobe and wanted him to become a rabbi, but when he died, Tobe was left in the care of his grandmother, who was cruel to him. At the age of nine, Tobe left his grandmother's house and supported himself, first as an apprentice to a bookbinder and later as a paperhanger and stencil painter. He saved his money for the day when he would sail to America and rejoin his family.

Meanwhile, Leah did well at the mill and was soon in charge of a number of workers, but Leib had trouble with his tender hands. He quit and tried peddling again, this time selling work clothes to seamen on Galveston's wharves. Leah supplemented the family income by taking in boarders in a large house they had rented on the courthouse square.

In 1896, at the age of fifteen, Tobe finally arrived in America and moved into his mother's house, where he paid for his room and board. He got his first job washing windows in a Galveston dry-goods store, then worked his way up to clerk and stayed for five years, until 1901, when he was offered $15 per week by a local men's clothing store, a raise of $2.50 above his current salary. Tobe accepted the new job, but at the last minute, the man whose job he was supposed to take decided not to leave the store. Tobe was too proud to ask for his old job back.

During the five years Tobe had been working, Leah had put aside $750 from what he paid for room and board, and now she offered it to him. The money helped Tobe open his own store, and he asked his younger brother, Simon, to join him.

Tobe made the important decision to locate the store not on the wharves, where Leib now had a store, but on the courthouse square. The center of town was a better location than the wharves, Tobe believed, because his and Simon's store would offer high-end merchandise and solicit the business of Galveston's affluent. Choosing a store's location is often the most important business decision a merchant makes. Throughout his life, Tobe had a nose for making the right one.

In 1902, the same year that the Sakowitz brothers opened their one-room store with an investment of $1,250, the Straus brothers in New York completed their enormous new store, Macy's. Built at an astounding cost of $4.5 million and covering virtually an entire block at Herald Square between 34th and 35th streets, Macy's became the largest and most famous store in the world, the symbol of what the immigrant Jew could do.

Rather than hire employees, Tobe and Simon ran their store, which they named The Globe, alone. While one of the brothers clerked in the store, the other rode a bicycle around the town, soliciting orders. They got their merchandise — hats, shirts, ties, coats, and suits — on credit from wholesalers, who typically made their decisions on how much credit to extend based on the storekeeper's character. When men in the business of extending credit said they were interested in a man's *character,* they were not really concerned whether he coveted his neighbor's wife or maidservant or ox or whether he kept or broke the other commandments. What they meant by character was that a man be scrupulously truthful to his creditor and put his promise to a creditor first among his obligations. The fact that Tobias and Simon lived at their mother's house, even though they were both in their twenties, was a sign of frugality recognized by the town's wholesalers and bankers.

A financial statement in 1904, two years after The Globe opened, listed Tobias and Simon's net worth at $2,000 and stated, "They are apparently doing a fair business, are economical, industrious and attentive and their prospects for making something over expenses are believed fairly good."

Living at home, however, had its drawbacks. Leib and Leah Sakowitz were Orthodox Jews who did not allow their sons to work on the Sabbath. So their store was closed on Saturdays, the busiest day of the week downtown. As a result, not many years later Simon converted to Reformed Judaism, the most liberal form of Judaism.

As the store grew, Simon traveled with trunks of goods as far as New Orleans, and on one such trip he met his wife to be. Clara Bowsky was the beautiful daughter of a successful New Orleans dry-goods merchant. Clara, who had been educated at Sophie Newcomb College and had grown up in a refined household, pushed Simon to rid himself of his Eastern European ways. She saw to it that he lessened his thick Russian accent, and soon his voice contained barely a trace of his birthplace. Tobe never lost his accent, which was so heavy that many employees had difficulty understanding him.

Simon, with his light skin and straight, light brown hair, also looked more Anglo-Saxon than Tobe, who had swarthy skin, thick lips, and wavy black hair. Simon was tall and lean; Tobe short and stocky. But there was a strong resemblance in the two men — both had large, protruding eyes and wore serious expressions.

Before Simon married Clara in 1909, he and Tobe decided that the store was not adequate to support two families. Five years earlier, Tobe had married Matilda "Tillie" Littman, who was born in Amsterdam as her parents made their way to America from their native Poland. So the brothers decided they would open another store, this fifty miles inland, in Houston. With $10,000 cash and an unpaid balance due in ninety days, Tobias and Simon acquired an existing store, at 308 Main Street in the center of downtown Houston, and renamed it Sakowitz Bros.

In later years, Tobe would often remind his son, Bernard, that he and Simon were easily able to pay off the balance without borrowing any money. In fact, the brothers made it a practice never to take on long-term debt; it was a basic tenet of their business philosophy.

There is no doubt that shrewd business foresight caused the Sakowitz expansion to Houston, but it was the unpredictable element of nature — a hurricane that struck Galveston Island in 1915 — that resulted in their abandoning Galveston forever and making Houston their base. Tobe's younger son, Alexander, recalled, "One of my earliest memories was the 1915 storm. I remember being on the second floor in my grandmother's house and looking down and seeing the water coming up the steps of the house. My father came in from the store and his fingers were burnt from matches that he had lit, trying to see to get merchandise off the floor of the store which was under water."

An earlier and much more severe hurricane in 1900 had leveled the island and killed more than five thousand people. Although Tobe and Simon did not own their own store in 1900, they had witnessed the total destruction of all of Galveston's stores, businesses, and homes. Simon vividly remembered clinging to a rooftop to survive the 1900 hurricane. Like so many immigrants in Galveston, the brothers had not survived the difficult journey to America and built up a business only to be wiped out by a violent hurricane — the kind that had struck twice in fifteen years and was certain to strike again. Leah urged Tobe not to rebuild the Galveston store but instead to join Simon in Houston.

Tobe took his mother's advice, and in 1917 he and Matilda moved to Houston, where the brothers expanded the existing store at 308 Main. The new 7,500-square-foot store was well located, just two blocks from the luxurious Rice Hotel and the town's two largest banks.

Houston was a city on the move, and the linchpin to its commercial development was the just-opened Houston Ship Channel, a partially man-made waterway one hundred feet wide and eighteen feet deep. As Will Rogers said, the channel permitted Houston "to bring the sea to its door." In fact, access to the Gulf of Mexico had been the reason behind the city's founding fifty miles inland from Galveston, on Buffalo Bayou, a stream that had a healthy tide from Galveston Bay.

Although a city ordinance in 1841 created the Port of Houston, the bayou was considerably less navigable than the city's founders had promised. It was almost impassable in the antebellum period, with collisions, explosions, and groundings on sandbars. Meanwhile, Galveston, with its hegemony in shipping seemingly secure, looked down on Houston's brash attempts to compete. After shipper Sampson Heidenheimer lost six barges of salt in the bayou, the *Galveston News* jeered: HOUSTON AT LAST A SALT-WATER PORT; GOD ALMIGHTY FURNISHED THE WATER; HEIDENHEIMER THE SALT.

But Houston's city fathers were not to be discouraged. In 1899, they convinced the United States Congress to approve deepening the channel to twenty-five feet. Some Texans, who even this early were masters of exaggeration, claimed that it was a project approaching in importance the Panama Canal. And when no Eastern financiers stepped up to put money into the reckless scheme, the bankers of Houston did it themselves.

If the maturation of the ship channel did not assure Houston's future, the devastating hurricane that ripped through Galveston in 1900 did. In 1902, for the first time, Houston surpassed Galveston as the largest city in Texas; by 1910, Houston was twice as large and growing.

Houston's population boom meant much more business for Sakowitz Bros. For the first time, the new store at Main and Preston offered ready-to-wear clothing in sizes "fat, lean and medium." Many storekeepers still scoffed at the idea of ready-to-wear clothes, but Sakowitz proved that ready-to-wear could be acceptable. The brothers sold the best lines, from Stetson hats to Hickey-Freeman and Louis Roth suits.

Once Sakowitz became synonymous with prestige, a story,

probably apocryphal, circulated about two men standing together on Galveston's wharves. One says to the other, "How d'ya like this Stetson hat I'm wearin'?"

The other takes the hat, examines it inside and out, then hands it back to his friend and says, "That ain't no Stetson."

"What d'ya mean?" says the other. "Here's the signature right in the sweatband."

"Cheap imitation."

"Why do you say that?" pleads the hat's owner.

"Can't you see? It ain't got Sakowitz Brothers' name in it."

The fabulous growth and the ultimate death of America's great independent department stores is in that anecdote. For the first fifty years of this century, the imprimatur of the local merchant — Filene's, Marshall Field, B. Altman — was what counted for the customer. The name of the manufacturer, no matter how prestigious, was secondary. But in the last half of the century, as independent stores were absorbed into chains and lost their uniqueness, the manufacturer's name — Bill Blass, Ralph Lauren, Yves Saint Laurent — came to mean more than the store's.

A 1916 article in the *Houston Chronicle* explained that the Sakowitz brothers' success was due to exceedingly hard work. "They studied buying," the *Chronicle* reported, "when other clerks were giving swimming lessons to fair maidens in the surf." This information could only have come from interviewing one of the brothers, whose obvious pride seems not unmixed with wistful regret.

Simon was in charge of merchandise while Tobe handled all financial responsibilities. Such work as checking inventory, inspecting for quality, bookkeeping, and paying bills was done before the store opened or after it closed. While it was open, store owners in those days were expected to be "on the floor." There they supervised salespeople to make certain that they gave the proper service, and the owners made many sales themselves, often to customers who would have considered themselves insulted had they not been waited on by "the boss."

It was frequently a cause of wonder that well into the 1920s and 1930s, long after their little shops had developed into enormous establishments, these first-generation merchants spent so many hours every day standing on the first floor greeting customers. The store's owner was his own greatest asset.

Sakowitz Bros. had some of the highest prices in town, but customers believed Simon Sakowitz when he told them that the merchandise was of the highest quality and warranted the price. He was a fair man whose continued success, he knew, was based on satisfying the customer with every sale.

Until near the end of the nineteenth century, American store-keepers, like those all over the world, marked their merchandise only with a secret coded price incomprehensible to the customer. But this merely established a minimum below which they would not sell; they and their salespeople started by asking a higher price and bargained for as much over the minimum as possible. This meant that, on every item, the customer must beat down — or "Jew down" as it was called — the salesperson. Under this system, many customers left the store wondering whether they got a bargain or might have done better with more time and harder trading. One of the chief reasons for the success of Rowland Macy's huge depart-ment store in New York, before he sold it to the Straus family, was that he marked his merchandise clearly with one price and refused to budge from it. "By adopting one price and never deviating," Macy advertised, "a child can trade with us as cheap as the shrewdest buyer in the country."

Sakowitz Bros. had made a profit every year since it had opened, and as the 1920s roared into Texas, the brothers saw every reason to be optimistic about their future. They believed that if they moved cautiously, they could continue to expand and grow richer with the city and the country. Their biggest gamble came on the eve of the stock market crash of 1929, when a local millionaire real estate developer, Jesse Jones, convinced them to move into his brand-new skyscraper, the Gulf Building.

The thirty-two-story building was the tallest and most elegant in Houston, and, with the move, the new Sakowitz Bros. — whose 70,000 square feet on five floors was almost ten times larger than its previous space — became the most elegant store in town. On the first floor, intricately carved art deco columns supported a twenty-foot ceiling. Beautiful polished-wood cases and a sleek marble floor were lighted by enormous chandeliers. The store's interior was compared with that of a bank — the ultimate compliment of the day.

On April 13, 1929, two days before the long-planned opening of the Gulf Building store, Houston's streets were flooded and traffic paralyzed by the heaviest rainfall recorded up to that time. Despite the weather, however, more than 40,000 Houstonians — nearly one-sixth of the city's population — showed up for the opening.

A story that lives in Sakowitz mythology is the time Tobe visited the office of Jesse Jones following the stock market crash of 1929. Tobias handed Jones the keys to the store and said, "You are now in the retail business. We can no longer afford the rent." Legend has it that Jones handed the keys back to Tobias and said he would carry the brothers until times improved.

In fact, because Tobe and Simon never had long-term debts and had not invested in the stock market, and because their oil-rich customers did not disappear even during the crash, the Sakowitzes were never in serious danger of losing the store, a fact that would make Tobe proud for the rest of his life.

The Gulf Building store marked Sakowitz's entry into the women's clothing business. But because Simon had had no experience in women's clothes, he leased the women's departments to a merchant who did. Still, for at least the next two decades, Sakowitz Bros. remained very much a man's store.

In the early part of this century, Sakowitz built its reputation on impeccable service, as did so many of the top specialty stores. Philadelphia storekeeper John Wanamaker invented the motto "The customer is always right," and it was a practice that would lead to the huge success of stores all across America. Simon became a master at making the customer feel important. By the mid-1930s, Sakowitz Bros. employed more than sixty clerks and buyers, which required Tobe to spend more time in the office, but Simon continued to spend most of each day walking the floors and greeting customers. Tall, erect, and elegantly dressed, Simon had a commanding presence; he looked and acted the role of merchant prince. Despite his almost regal manner, he was approachable. If a customer had a problem, or even if she didn't, she did not hesitate to talk to Simon.

Despite the brothers' prosperity and their love for their new country, during the 1930s, Tobe was not convinced that something similar to Hitler's persecution of Jews could not happen in America. He became so concerned, in fact, that instead of reinvesting all his profits in his growing store, he bought a small farm about eight miles from downtown Houston. As with almost every single investment the brothers made, they owned the farm equally.

Tobe felt safer having the farm, knowing that if his big downtown business were seized, he might still be able to feed and protect his family on the farm. It was a precaution similar to the Jewish man's practice of sewing a few coins or pieces of jewelry in the hem of his wife's skirt against the day they had to flee for their lives.

3

DURING WORLD WAR II, there was a shortage of merchandise because the armed services took so much of what could be produced. The result was that demand for retail goods far exceeded supply. At the same time that shoes and other items were rationed, consumers coming out of the Great Depression had money to spend from their wartime jobs. When the war ended, all this pent-up demand for goods that had either not been available or had been rationed created a retail boom. Sakowitz Bros. predicted the boom and was determined to profit from it.

By 1945, the store had outgrown the five floors of the Gulf Building and its owners had grown tired of rearranging stock to eke out a bit more space. So they decided to build a new store, one in a building all its own. As always, Tobe was shrewd in choosing its location.

His store would go up across the street from the gargantuan department store Foley Bros., an eight-story, windowless brick structure covering an entire city block. Foley's did such a big business that its owner, George Cohen, liked to say that each time a hearse passed by the store, Foley's had lost a customer. Although they were competitors in a broad sense, Foley's was a full-line department store, while Sakowitz had built its reputation as an expensive specialty store.

Simon and Tobe, now both in their sixties, were no less aggressive than when they had opened in Houston thirty-six years earlier. They wanted to expand their business. Encouraging their desire to grow was the next generation, led by Tobe's thirty-eight-year-old son Bernard, the store's very serious and very ambitious general manager. While Simon and Tobe imagined a store that would be the finest in Houston, Bernard talked of a store that, while located in Houston, would be the envy of store owners throughout America.

"Bernard was very aggressive," recalls Bernard's younger brother, Alex. "More than anything else, he liked the idea of expanding and being bigger and bigger. At one point he even talked about Sakowitz buying Bergdorf Goodman on Fifth Avenue in New York. That was the degree of his ambition."

Bernard was born on January 12, 1907, in Galveston, the first child of Tobias and Matilda. Four years later, in 1911, Matilda had her second and last child, Alexander, called Alex. When Bernard was ten, the family of four moved to Houston and into a comfortable house on the edge of downtown. Business was booming at Sakowitz, and when Bernard and Alex were not in school they were helping out at the store.

In 1923, Bernard was a sixteen-year-old cadet at Fishburn Military School in Virginia when he learned that his mother had died. It was a blow that he and Alex would never get over. In fact, it seemed to Clara and Simon that Tobias and his sons were having such a difficult time coping with Matilda's death that they invited Tobias and Alex to come live with them. Tobias tried this arrangement for a year and then moved into Houston's grand Rice Hotel located only a few blocks from the store.

A few years after Matilda died, Tobias became very fond of a woman who worked as a saleswoman at the store. "My father said she was very warm and friendly," says Tobias's granddaughter, Margaret Sackton Rosan. "My grandfather enjoyed his money, but he also was a simple man. He did not put a lot of stock in people's rank in society."

But when Simon and Clara and other family members learned that Tobias was considering marrying the employee, a woman they considered socially inferior, they pressured him not to marry her. Instead, he married Ruth Cohn, who may have been more socially acceptable than the Sakowitz clerk but was hardly the quiet, refined woman that Clara was.

Nevertheless, Ruth was accepted by the family — or at least by most of the family except Bernard, who learned about his father's remarriage after the fact. "Bernard came home from school, and his father said, 'This is your new mother,'" says a longtime store employee. "It came as a total surprise, and he immediately resented the idea of someone taking the place of his real mother."

Adjusting to a stepmother was very difficult for both boys, says Alex. "I think Father did want us to and expect us to call her Mother, which I did for a short time, but then I asked her if I could call her Aunt Ruth."

Ruth was amusing and energetic, the "Auntie Mame" of the family, with an ageless quality that enabled her to put herself on the boys' level. Ruth took dance lessons at the Arthur Murray studio in Houston and loved to give dance parties at her home. Every Christmas — which was also Tobe's birthday — Ruth had the family to a buffet lunch at home. "During the lunch, Ruth would turn on the record player and we'd all get up and dance," recalls a family friend. "Tobe would just sit there and watch her. He was fascinated by her."

Ruth also had a habit of making indiscreet remarks without realizing it. An acquaintance of Ruth's recalls, "Once Ruth told a group of ladies at a tea, 'It's the funniest thing about Tobe. Every morning when he wakes up his little thing is standing straight up.'"

The other ladies winced.

The only things not genuine about Ruth were her long false eyelashes and platinum blond hair, which were a sharp contrast against her olive skin and dark eyes. "People respectfully called Simon's wife 'Mrs. Simon' or 'Mrs. Clara,' but Ruth was just 'Ruth,'" says a friend of Clara's.

Ruth adored Alex, and Alex loved her, but family and friends say Bernard never grew to love, or even like, her. "Bernard didn't like Ruth because she was a threat," confides a family member. "She wasn't his mother, and he feared his father would leave much of his money to Ruth, which he did."

Unlike Alex, who grew up unsure whether he wanted a career in retailing, Bernard knew exactly what he wanted. For years — from the first summer he worked at Sakowitz Bros., when he was still a boy and the store was still in its original Houston location at 308 Main — Bernard had been anticipating the day he would take control of the business. After receiving a degree from the University of Pennsylvania's Wharton School and spending a year in Macy's executive training program in New York, Bernard joined the store in 1929, the same year that it opened in Jesse Jones's skyscraper.

Tobe welcomed his son into the company but warned him that he would have to start small and learn the business literally from the ground floor up. Bernard was put in charge of the first-floor

women's accessories department. Although all women's departments were new to Sakowitz Bros., and Tobe and Simon considered
them a challenge for everyone at the store, Bernard thought the
position beneath him. He also thought his salary was less than it
should have been.

Bernard was always interested in positions of power, says
Alex: "As a student at the University of Pennsylvania, he was
active in student politics, and when elections were held he became
the controlling voice for all the votes in his fraternity. As a result,
he won appointment to what seemed like prestigious positions.
The main recognition and goal was a distinctive 'key' to hang on
one's watch-chain."

Although Bernard's ascent within the company was not as
swift as he expected, in 1931 something happened that accelerated
his success not only in business but, even more, socially. He met
blond and beautiful Ann Baum.

Ann was born in 1913 in San Antonio, the last of six children
of Sara Rosenman and Victor Baum and the only one of their children born in America. Victor had changed his surname from von
Birnbaum when he emigrated from Prussia to the United States two
years before World War I began.

Although the well-educated Victor spoke seven languages and
his family, according to one of his daughters, "had been in the banking business in Prussia," his occupation in America was considerably less grand. When Victor and Sara and their son and four
daughters settled in San Antonio, he opened a small dry-goods
store. Ann was born a few years later.

Like her sisters, Ann was very fair and blond and a striking
beauty. Victor perceived his daughters' beauty as their dowry, and
to protect his investment, they were forbidden to leave the house
without a hat to protect their fair skin from the Texas sun.

When Ann was a teenager and her siblings were grown, Victor
died and Ann and her mother went to live in Mercedes, a town of
3,000 just a few miles from the Mexican border, where Ann's
brother had opened a store. Despite living in the struggling town of
Mercedes, and without a father, Ann was optimistic about her
future, says her sister Dora Baum Axelrod.

"We blocked out of our minds what we didn't like," insists
Dora. "I won't let things get me down, and Ann is the same way.
We're very strong, gutsy women."

Ann was eighteen and a student at Rice University in Houston when she was invited to a party where she met the twenty-four-year-old Bernard Sakowitz. He was considered a good catch, but when Ann first met him she was not immediately attracted to him. But she continued to see him and decided that because they got along well she would marry him.

Ann Sakowitz was the antithesis of her serious husband. "She was a great storyteller, and she would always tell jokes in Yiddish. She was very unpretentious, very funny, and a lot of fun," recalled a close family friend. "She was so attractive and so full of personality and so different from Bernard. No one knew why she married him, except for the money."

Despite their many differences, they obviously had one thing in common. Both were intensely, almost fiercely, ambitious. They may have started out small — in a modest house on Sunset Boulevard near Rice University — but they had big dreams for themselves and their children, the first of whom was born on July 16, 1935. The baby girl, named Martha Lynn Sakowitz, would become one of the most beautiful and most frequently and widely photographed women in the world.

Blond like both parents and with large green eyes, Lynn possessed an obvious sense of style from the time she was a very little girl. When she was barely old enough to talk, her mother was braiding Lynn's hair over the top of her head when Lynn interrupted the process. "Mommy, let me do it this way and see how it looks," she begged, styling her hair differently. Ann Sakowitz looked at her daughter and agreed that the new hairstyle was much prettier.

As much as her parents seemed to adore Lynn, Bernard and Ann were anxious for a son, a merchant prince to carry the retail dynasty into the next generation. It was unthinkable that a woman could run such a business. They got their wish on October 13, 1938. They named their son Robert Tobias Sakowitz.

Not long after the baby was born, Bernard enlisted in the Air Force. Tobias headed Houston's draft board at the time, and although Bernard was exempt from the service because he had a wife and two children, he confessed years later that he felt "very self-conscious knowing that my dad was drafting my friends' and customers' sons."

Bernard, always eager to become a leader, rose to the rank of Air Force Captain.

Alex Sakowitz, like his brother and many sons of America's retail families, attended Wharton. But after graduating, he decided he did not want to join the store. He wanted to continue his education. After taking an honors degree in English at Cambridge, he decided to make teaching English his profession. His first job, in 1934, was at Texas A&M, which was not a top school, but, Alex thought, a good enough place to start. Two years later he took a PhD at Harvard, but when he again applied at the nation's top universities, again only Texas A&M would take him.

"I had a friend whose name was Joseph Prescott. We wrote to the same places, writing almost the same letters, and he was accepted but I wasn't. It was clear that there was a prejudice against a foreign name," he recalls, "so my father suggested I change it." Alex changed his last name to Sackton and in 1946 became a professor of English at the University of Texas in Austin, where he taught for more than forty years.

Because Alex had chosen not to enter the store and because Simon had no sons, only two daughters, Bernard viewed himself as heir to the enterprise. However, in 1938, when Simon's younger daughter married, Bernard suddenly found himself sharing power with his cousin Louise Sakowitz's new husband. Louise was a junior at Rice University in Houston when she married Gaylord Johnson, a strapping redhead twenty-two years older than she. Gaylord ran Rice's athletic department, taught chemistry, and ran a drugstore called The Gables, a popular college hangout in the thirties. Despite his various jobs, he had not accumulated much money. Clara Sakowitz said that her son-in-law "came to the marriage with a little suitcase and a few books."

While not rich, Gaylord was something of a legend at Rice, so it was surprising when, after returning from the service in 1945, he quit the university, sold The Gables, and joined Sakowitz Bros. "He went to work at the store because Simon and Tobe were getting up in age and the store had gotten enormous," says Gaylord Johnson, Jr. "They needed people to help them run it."

Both Gaylord and Bernard were made vice presidents of the store, but they were never the team that the first generation was. Not only did they lack the talent of Simon and Tobe, but theirs was an acrimonious relationship. Gaylord, the son of an Irish immigrant railroad worker, was born poor and had worked his way up by being friendly and eager to learn; Bernard had been born rich, liked his position in life, and thought himself answerable to no one. Bernard saw Gaylord as a threat to his eventual domination of the store. Gaylord viewed Bernard as arrogant and not very bright.

One of the few ideas Gaylord and Bernard agreed on was the need for the store to upgrade its technology in ticketing, taking inventory, and printing sales slips. Gaylord tried to introduce an early computer that would simplify bookkeeping and help in pricing and ticketing, but the newfangled machines and equipment were objected to vehemently, not only by longtime salespeople but also by Tobe.

A classic retail-family story is repeated in cities across America — always told as though it were unique to that storekeeping family. The founder grandfather or father, visiting his store on Sunday, sees an inventory in progress, with very complicated methods and printed forms devised by very costly accountants. "What's all this expensive *mishmash*?" demands the Patriarch.

"It's an inventory," explains the New Generation.

"What's it for? Who needs it? All these people cost money and they're not *selling* anything!"

"But it's necessary," the New Generation explains patiently. "We must do this regularly or we can't know what our profit is."

Thereupon the Patriarch takes the New Generation by the sleeve and guides him to the Patriarch's office, where he unlocks a desk drawer that the New Generation has never seen unlocked before. From the drawer the Patriarch takes out an old, worn, dirty, canvas pack, and from the pack he removes and spreads on the desk a few dozen spools of thread, papers of pins, darning needles, and sets of buttons.

"This," explains the Patriarch, pointing to the pack's pitiful contents, "is the inventory." And then, with a gesture that encompasses all the floors of the enormous store and all the millions of dollars of merchandise the store contains, the Patriarch intones: "Everything else — that's the profit."

As stores throughout America grew larger, it became increasingly difficult for the founders to oversee personally everything that went on. But an incident at Marshall Field, which resulted in a motto for great stores everywhere, proved how important it was that the owner continue to keep an eye on what was happening on the floor.

One day when the white-gloved, stiff-backed Marshall Field was walking through his great Chicago emporium, he came across one Lindsay T. Woodcock, an assistant manager who was in the midst of a heated conversation with a female customer.

"What are you doing, sir?" demanded the furious Field.

"I am settling a complaint," offered the unfortunate Woodcock.

"No, you are not, sir," snapped Field. *"Give the lady what she wants!"*

Until the latter half of the twentieth century, many if not most department store owners, like most small business owners, felt a paternal obligation toward their employees and often toward the employees' families. Time off, small loans, advice on legal matters were available, often from the boss himself or his lawyer or his doctor. The result was that employees truly felt that they were part of an extended family. Employees were usually delighted to have a son or daughter join the same team, and nepotism, enthusiastically practiced by the owner's family, was acceptable and even encouraged at every level.

Such loyalty from the top down, of course, inspired the same feeling from the bottom up, and if the business was the best in town or the biggest in town or the oldest in town, genuine pride complemented the loyalty. Outside the store, Sakowitz employees were delighted at any opportunity to say, "I work at Sakowitz," which usually prompted the listener to open his or her coat and say, with much of the same pride, "Look, look, this is from Sakowitz."

"Because it was a family-owned store, you always had this feeling that you were being protected," says a buyer who was with Sakowitz from 1951 until 1970. "You worked for the family and you had become part of that family. And you stayed that way.

"Gentlemen did not come to work in those days without a hat, but one day I left mine at home and Mr. Simon saw me. I told him the truth, but Mr. Simon thought that, in fact, I didn't own a hat, so he said, 'If you don't have a hat, I'll buy you one.'"

It was a tiny gesture, but it was the kind of gesture Simon and Tobias made dozens of times a day to dozens of their employees.

Neither Simon nor Tobias knew when his birthday was because their mother had not kept careful records and because Russia's Julian calendar differed from the West's Gregorian calendar. They knew only that they were born about two years apart, both near the end of the year. So, not long after opening their store in Galveston, Simon and Tobe each chose a date to celebrate his birthday. Tobe chose December 25 and Simon chose January 1, days when they knew the store would always be closed.

But even though their birthdays fell on store holidays, Tobias and Simon celebrated with the "employee family" on Christmas Eve day and New Year's Eve day. "Mr. Simon or Mr. Tobe would wait by the employee entrance and everyone would line up coming in and out of the store to wish him a happy birthday. There was tremendous loyalty and love for the two founders. Each man was like a father to many of us."

These feelings were reciprocated. Tobias and Simon always put the store's interests above their own.

"My grandfather felt he had a lot of obligations to his customers and to the employees who worked for him," says a grandson of Tobias, Toby Sackton. "He lived in tremendous debt to these people."

The sense of debt Tobias and Simon felt at the store carried over into the community and typified the successful Jewish immigrant. In the years from just before the Civil War to shortly after World War II, Jewish storekeeping families played a vital role in America, a role that far exceeded the relative size of their fortunes and a role almost inconceivable today. Storekeepers helped determine the economic climate of their towns. Where they chose to locate their stores dramatically affected real estate values. They were among the largest bank depositors, often the largest, and so they frequently sat on the bank's board and influenced who received loans and who did not. How many employees they hired or fired was felt throughout the community. It was common for the storekeeper to serve on the boards of civic, educational, and charitable organizations. Even in the largest cities — Boston, New York, Philadelphia — where the economic influence of the Jewish storekeeper was not crucial, his role as a philanthropist was enormous — Edward Filene, the Strauses, Benjamin Altman, and the Gimbels are all examples.

There was no mandatory retirement age at Sakowitz, and Simon helped institute a similar policy at the University of Houston. The university was only a few years old when Simon joined the board, and it was having trouble employing top professors. Simon believed that the university could get some of the best professors from around the country by hiring them when they were forced out of other universities because of their age. Sakowitz Bros. was filled with men and women who were well into their seventies and were selling as much as they ever had. What worked at the store often worked for the local symphony or university.

Despite the strong influence of the Jewish storekeeper in his community, by the 1940s a virtually absolute line of demarcation had been drawn. Jews across America were not invited to join the clubs of non-Jews and in many cases were excluded from living in the upper-class suburbs established by rich Gentiles. This had happened in Houston. Ironically, only forty years earlier, a prominent Jewish department store owner and his brother were two of the founders of the Houston Country Club but now Jews were no longer admitted.

There had been relatively little anti-Semitism in the first century of this country's existence. This was especially true among America's richest citizens. Jew and Gentile, they founded and supported the same clubs and traveled to the same resorts, just as they invested in each other's businesses and served on each other's boards of directors. In 1877, when Jewish New York banker Joseph Seligman was excluded from the Grand Union Hotel in Saratoga, it was reported and discussed nationally because it was so surprising. It quickly became, however, a practice widely copied.

Because of anti-Semitism in America, until the latter half of the twentieth century Jews were largely excluded from the professions and from many major businesses. As a result, many Jews went into business for themselves. Retailing was often a logical choice for the immigrant Jew because his chance of success depended largely on how hard he was willing to work. More important, it did not require lengthy specialized education or a high initial investment. A peddler could carry on his back all the goods he needed to get started in business — as the Sakowitzes had.

In February 1951, Sakowitz Bros. opened its $10 million showplace at 1111 Main Street. Five and one-half tall stories covering almost an entire city block, the store was the most elegant establishment in the city. The exterior's solid facade of perfectly matched Vermont marble made the building look like a classic Greek temple, especially as it glistened in the bright Texas sun. Determinedly self-important, it was so impressive that Simon and Tobe found themselves having to play down its grandness, explaining that it was "the same store, merchandised in the same price ranges by the same people."

In deciding what kind of store design they wanted, Bernard and Tobias had traveled from coast to coast looking at other great stores. They copied fixtures, cases, floors, walls, and other details. Any well-traveled salesman or storekeeper or customer immediately recognized Sakowitz's exterior as a close copy of the new I. Magnin store in Los Angeles.

For several months after it opened, a steady stream of women and men, spectators as well as customers, crowded into the new store. Not all of them would have rushed downtown to visit a new musuem or church, but they were curious and excited to see what kind of glamorous temple of luxury those Sakowitz brothers had given Houston. Visitors marveled at the terrazzo floors, ten-foot antiqued mirrors hung in gilt frames, gigantic custom-built chandeliers, and burled-wood and red lacquer walls.

More than anything else, what consciously or unconsciously gave customers a feeling of luxury was the store's lavish waste of space — the twenty-foot ceilings and the second-, third-, and fourth-floor rooms so large and uncluttered that a woman trying on an evening gown could swirl and turn on fine beige carpeting in an area bigger than her own living room. The store felt even more spacious than its 225,000 square feet.

The new store marked Sakowitz Bros.' first significant push into women's fashion — and it was an immediate success. Houston women arrived in large numbers to buy coats and suits and dresses by Traina Norell, Pauline Trigère, Maurice Rentner, and Nettie Rosenstein.

It was a time when a woman going shopping dressed up in her best suit, gloves, hat, and jewelry. When she arrived at the store she received in every department the attention, the flattery, the cosseting, the ego-building interest that she had come to town for, as much as she had to make a purchase. In Sakowitz's Sky Terrace, she was served a perfectly composed shrimp salad by perfectly trained black waiters in starched white jackets and spotless white gloves. It was a lunch that seemed more luxurious than what she experienced at home, regardless of the size of her own staff, because she had not expended the slightest effort in order to enjoy it.

No detail was too small to make the customer feel that her needs and her wants were considered. If a customer left a package or a pair of gloves on one of the upstairs floors and realized it only as she was leaving the store, Sakowitz had red telephones on the first floor that she could use to have the item brought to her.

The crucial customers in such stores as Sakowitz and Neiman-Marcus in those postwar years were middle-aged and older women, most of them well beyond the days when their husbands romanced them. When Bernard Sakowitz spent his valuable time showing an expensive mink coat to one of these women or Stanley Marcus explained how an emerald-and-diamond necklace enhanced her beauty, the woman experienced a sense of romance. The magical climate of luxury and service and effortless sensuality created by the Sakowitz family are as long gone and almost as forgotten as the lovely, languid social life on the great pre–Civil War southern cotton plantations. It was another time in America.

4

B Y THE TIME the new downtown store opened, the family was already grooming its next merchant prince. The small, hazel-eyed, brown-haired boy had been working at the store on weekends, during holidays, and during summers since the age of nine. He put price tags on shirts, helped out in the loading and receiving areas, and did odd jobs around the store. He was paid just ten cents an hour, but he worked as hard as a $50-a-week saleslady bucking for a $2 raise.

He was so cheerful that employees — many of whom considered themselves part of the family — could not help but pat his head as he sat marking shirts. When he passed them on the floor, employees greeted him as "Bobby," a nickname meant to be affectionate but that, as he grew older, he would come to hate.

Bernard, Ann, and their two young children had moved just a few miles southeast of downtown, to MacGregor Way, a street of mansions built at the turn of the century. The Sakowitz home, an old, rambling, white colonial, was elegantly decorated and well maintained by both an upstairs and a downstairs maid, a cook, and a chauffeur. Surrounding the property were acres of land ideal for hunting, fishing, and climbing trees. The outdoors fascinated Lynn, who was an indomitable tomboy as a little girl. A crack shot, she loved to hunt with her father and play football with the neighborhood boys. Her greatest passion, however, was painting. In her bedroom on an easel, there was always at least one painting in progress.

The MacGregor property included a chicken coop, which gave young Bobby his first retail idea. He decided to collect the eggs laid by the chickens and deliver them by bicycle to the neighbors. Naturally, his were high-end eggs; he marked them up two cents over the local grocer's price, explaining that his customers were paying extra for fresh-laid quality and door-to-door service. His business quickly boomed, and when he could no longer fit all his customers' eggs into his bicycle basket, Ellis, the family chauffeur, drove him on his deliveries.

While other wealthy Houstonians built or moved into River Oaks estates in the 1930s and 1940s and sent their children to private school or to public school in River Oaks, the Sakowitzes continued to live on MacGregor Way even though the area was falling out of fashion. In those days, the very fashionable and exclusive neighborhoods of River Oaks did not admit Jews. When it came time for Lynn to enter high school, she went to public school, the neighborhood San Jacinto High.

Robert, however, was enrolled in 1950 in seventh grade at the private St. John's preparatory school. Founded just four years earlier and located in River Oaks, the coeducational St. John's numbered among its enrollment the sons and daughters of Houston's rich. The fact that Bobby Sakowitz was one of very few Jewish students at St. John's in the fifties was not always easy for him. At times, classmates called him anti-Semitic names, behind his back and to his face.

To defend himself, he learned to box by joining the Golden Gloves. Although he never won, he participated in several Golden Gloves tournaments and became very strong and very fast on his feet.

In addition to the disadvantages of being Jewish at an almost all-WASP school, Robert was haunted with doubts about whether his friends and classmates used him for his name. "It's very interesting growing up and not knowing whether you have any friends," he said in 1992, "because your name is on a big store and your name is in the newspaper every day and they want something from you."

"When he was little," says Robert's first wife, Pam Bryan, "he overheard some girls talking about him, and one said to the other, 'Wouldn't it be nice to be married to him? Just think of all the dresses you would get.'"

The store was so much a part of young Robert's life that when it came time for show-and-tell at school, his presentation was on the new store at 1111 Main. At home each evening, dinner table discussion inevitably revolved around the store. These discussions, night after night, year after year, almost certainly had a greater effect on both Robert and Lynn than school or their experiences with contemporaries.

To Robert it became clear that his obligation, his burden, was someday to run an important, complicated business enterprise, and that to prepare for the job, he must learn a wide variety of skills.

To Lynn it became clear that if she were to have a career, a life other than that of an attractive and educated society woman, or if she were to enjoy position and power, she would have to reach these goals on her own. There was no question that the excitement, the visibility, and the power connected with the store would automatically go to her brother, not her, precisely as he had been sent to private school and she had not.

The injustice of this situation must have been obvious to Lynn. She was not less intelligent than her younger brother, not less determined, not less attractive, not less charming, but she was a female. But this injustice, instead of destroying her, appeared to make her more patient and even more determined.

Lynn let her mother know that she felt her parents favored Robert. But Ann denied that this was the case. "There were times when she thought we were more partial to [Robert], but we loved them both," she testified under oath in 1991.

While Lynn may have resented the greater attention paid to Robert, she did not take her unhappiness about it out on him. The two were very close. He called her "Ski," short for an earlier nickname, "Lynnski," and she called him "Bub." So close were they that when they fought, as all children do, and Lynn hit him, he could not bring himself to hit her back. "In many ways she was my baby sister," he says. "I looked out for her all my life."

By his own account, he also helped her with her homework, but there is no evidence that he helped her in areas more substantial. Save for the occasional math problem, Lynn, as a girl, got very little help from her brother or anyone else in the family.

Among the many things Lynn discovered about herself at an early age was the edge she had over others when she was outside Texas, simply because she was a Texan. It happened first one summer at camp in Maine when she noticed that the other campers were fascinated to learn that Lynn came from a mythic land of cowboys and cattle and oil and millionaires. Her Texas roots would never stop giving her an edge. Years later, in New York and Paris and Rome, she was always careful to play up her accent, and just as the other girls had at her camp, international society found her carefully maintained Texas drawl not the least of her charms.

By the time she entered San Jacinto High, many of her most attractive traits were already developed. "In high school she had the exact same type of personality that she carried into her adult years," says Jackie Pope Aldredge, who was a cheerleader with Lynn and one of Lynn's closest friends during their senior year. "She had a very outgoing, winning personality, and even though she was so precious-looking and so much more glamorous than the rest of us, she made everyone immediately comfortable with her."

Lynn's remarkable ability to charm others by showing interest in them is often described today as her chief asset. It is not surprising, considering that she had mastered the talent in high school, at a time when most boys and girls are their most self-centered.

"She revealed nothing about herself, even to her closest friends, and yet she had a marvelous way of getting you to talk about yourself, which I thought was extremely mature for someone of such a young age," recalls Jackie Aldredge.

Few students at San Jacinto High had a car, but Lynn had a convertible. Naturally, she wore the prettiest clothes of anyone in school, and she was cast in the most glamorous role in the school's 1953 drama, *Evening Star.* A photograph of Lynn in the play, dressed in high heels, a mink stole, and sunglasses, could be any photograph of her thirty years later, in *Paris Vogue, Harper's Bazaar,* or *W.*

Lynn's ability to expand her wide circle of friends around the world today was also a talent she developed and honed in high school. In the late 1940s and early 1950s, the social line of demarcation was still strong in Houston, but Lynn crossed the Jewish boundary with great ease. "There was always a group of beautiful Jewish girls, but I don't remember Lynn ever allowing herself to be known as part of the Jewish group or the Gentile group," says Jackie Aldredge. "She was able to be friends with everyone, an incredible politician at such a young age.

"She just got the whole picture socially, the dynamics of what was going on. During football season, she dated a really cute football player, but when football season ended, he was quickly eliminated."

In 1983, when Lynn attended her thirty-year high school reunion, she went for the day's festivities but declined the evening party. When she explained the reason — that she was entertaining

Donald Trump at her house that night — few of her friends from the 1950s were surprised. The most glamorous girl at San Jacinto had not changed a bit.

Robert, like his older sister, by the time he entered high school also cut a high profile. If he continued to feel used by his friends because of his name or alienated because he was Jewish, he did not let it show. By his senior year, he involved himself in virtually every high school extracurricular activity — from drama and debating to sports, from student government to editing the newspaper and yearbook. The list of accomplishments next to his senior photograph in St. John's 1956 yearbook was longer than that of any other student in the class, and no other student's photograph appeared more often than his. Even then, he had a flair for publicity. Of course, the frequent appearance of his photograph in the book may have been related to the fact that he was the yearbook's editor. Nonetheless, it was fitting that his fellow senior classmates elected Bob Sakowitz "Most Likely to Succeed."

In the fall of 1953, when Bobby was a freshman at St. John's, Lynn left home for college. She chose Bennington in Vermont, a school widely recognized for its arts programs. Lynn majored in commercial design, and as part of her curriculum she did an internship at the New York studio of then top fashion designer Adele Simpson.

"She was a beautiful young girl, with a flair for clothes like no one else on this earth," recalls a friend of the Sakowitzes with whom Lynn stayed for a short time in New York.

That same year, Lynn met a very wealthy New Yorker named Robert Steven Lipman. He had dark eyes, a mass of thick dark hair that fell over his low forehead, and a nose so large and ugly that it was handsome. What was most striking about him was his height. He was six feet six in his socks, and he walked very erect, with his chin up.

Robert Sakowitz did not like Lipman from the moment he met him. "He was different than Oscar," says Robert, "but he was one of the stereotypical New Yorkers who knows everything and makes you feel as though you know nothing. [He] was sort of condescending."

The fact that her brother did not care for Lipman apparently had no effect on Lynn. After her first year at Bennington, she decided not to return to college but instead to marry Lipman.

Four years older than Lynn, Robert Lipman was born in 1931, the second and last child of Abraham Lipman, who had made millions investing in New York City real estate. His considerable holdings included Fifth Avenue's famous Flatiron Building and the Essex House hotel on Central Park South.

Robert and his sister, Norma, who was older by four years, lived with their parents at 101 Central Park West, one of Manhattan's most elegant prewar buildings. "They had a large, fashionable apartment facing Central Park," remembers novelist Judith Green, whose family lived on the same floor as the Lipmans, "so on Thanksgiving Day we'd all go there to watch the Macy's parade." Judith, who was about six years younger than Lipman, recalls, "Bobby was the best-looking boy in our building and he was also terribly sweet."

After graduating from Edgewood Preparatory School in Greenwich, Connecticut, Bobby attended the University of Southern California. Judith Green says that because Lipman was so much older, she lost touch with him when she went away to college. The next she heard of him, "Somebody said that he had married a very rich department store heiress."

While Lynn was being described in New York as a retail heiress, Lipman was described in Texas as the heir to a great real estate fortune. But Lynn's first cousin Toby Sackton says the family was not pleased with Lynn's choice. "I had the impression that Lynn went out and married someone that nobody in the family thought was good for her. And I remember it was a hurry-up wedding. It happened pretty fast."

Lynn married Robert Lipman on Saturday, September 18, 1954, at Houston's Temple Beth Israel. The small, candlelight wedding at 7:30 in the evening was, with the exception of sprays of green magnolia leaves, almost all white. Lynn wore a magnificent gown of tulle and handmade lace that was designed especially for her by French couturier Gaston Mallet. The dress, inspired by an English court gown from the time of Queen Victoria, had a voluminous skirt of lace and tulle over silk taffeta which accentuated her tiny waist. She carried her grandmother's prayerbook and a spray of white orchids. She looked almost saintly, a picture of virginal bliss. But whether this look pleased the groom is arguable. It was not long before Lipman let it be known that he liked women who looked like prostitutes.

Following a reception in a tent outside the MacGregor home, which included a lavish roast beef buffet, the bride and groom left for their honeymoon trip to California and Hawaii.

When they returned to Houston, Robert immediately went to work at the store. His title and responsibilities were not altogether clear to the other employees, but almost from the start, he conducted himself as the store's heir apparent. His tallness, if little else, gave him an automatic air of authority.

Despite his impressive air, several employees remember Lipman as unsmiling and unhappy almost from the day he began at the store. But many also recall thinking that it simply took time adjusting to his new job and new family. Things would get better, they said.

Every morning when Tobe, now in his seventies, arrived at the downtown store, he walked through each department and asked a clerk, "How's business?" Whatever the truth, the response was rarely negative.

Still, Tobe feared that the location of the grand downtown store, completed just five years earlier, would soon be obsolete. While downtown was still the center of activity in Houston, Tobe and Bernard could see that the city was expanding at a rapid rate in all directions. In the decade between 1940 and 1950, Houston's population had jumped by more than 50 percent, from 384,000 to 596,000. Houston had the largest growth rate of any city in America, and projections were that well before another decade had passed, Houston's population would reach one million — a milestone much anticipated by citizens and hyped as "M-Day" by leaders of a city where size is everything.

Tobias and Bernard thought that the future of retailing was in the suburbs. But suburban stores were a new concept in the early fifties, not only in Houston but throughout America. Sakowitz could not look for many examples from stores in other cities, as it so often had before making an important retail decision. Tobias and Bernard would have to chart these waters alone, and because Tobias was getting old, the decision rested largely with Bernard. Whether or not to go suburban would be the most critical decision of Bernard's business career.

The land at the corner of Westheimer and Post Oak roads five miles west of downtown Houston was mostly open pasture in

1955, but it was surrounded by rich neighborhoods — River Oaks, Tanglewood, Memorial — which were home to wealthy Sakowitz customers. Bernard thought the site was an ideal location for a suburban store. But instead of ordering fancy demographic studies, Bernard and Tobias did something that will live forever in Houston mythology. They sat down on folding chairs on the scrubby land at that intersection and counted the cars that went by. At the end of a long day in the hot sun, they tallied their numbers and made their decision. They would build a store here, in this vast field where no store had existed before.

"There were a number of people who said, 'Oh, those poor Sakowitz boys are going to lose their shirts,'" recalls Robert, who was then in high school. Few retailers today remember Bernard as a great merchant or a great leader, but he receives enormous credit for his help in the family's decision to build the store at Post Oak, ahead of the retail curve. Years later, when the Galleria shopping mall went up across the street, the corner of Westheimer and Post Oak became the apex of Houston's densest commercial corridor. The corner came to rank with the choicest retail land in the United States.

The Post Oak store, completed in 1959 at a cost of $5 million, looked nothing like the glitzy downtown Sakowitz. Surrounded by a parking lot for a thousand cars, and open green field beyond that, the Post Oak store was a two-story white colonial structure with white columns reaching up to an oxblood red, clay tile roof. Obvious was the owners' desire that it resemble a country club rather than a commercial building. A Confederate flag flew at the entrance.

While Bernard, who had finally been made president at age fifty-two, was busy expanding the company, the founders continued to pay attention to details at the downtown store. By walking the floors, Simon saw to it that employees were always on their toes.

The pattern was the same in stores all over America. The owners often came to work early in the morning, left late in the evening, came to the store on Saturday and even on Sunday. They addressed themselves endlessly to details. They did not do this out of fear. They stayed at the store because they loved it. The store was their world, made and operated precisely to their taste. Here they were absolute monarchs with absolute power and with subjects who obeyed them absolutely. It was not always so at home or in the rest of the world, but here they commanded a world of their own making.

While business was booming at Sakowitz in the late fifties, Robert was studying history at Harvard, where he had enrolled in 1956. That same year, the son of another Texas retailer entered Harvard. His name was Richard Marcus, the only son of the by then legendary merchant Stanley Marcus of Dallas's fabulous Neiman-Marcus. Chance had it that both Robert and Richard were assigned to live in Eliot House.

It also happened that Neiman-Marcus had just opened a store in downtown Houston. Because of this, Richard assumed that Robert was well aware of Neiman-Marcus while he, just eighteen, knew far less about Sakowitz. "We're the guys who sort of landed on his doorstep," says Richard, who had recalled hearing his father say that Neiman-Marcus did not receive a welcome by the Sakowitz family in Houston. But when Richard met Robert at a freshman mixer, the meeting was friendly and the two Texans soon found themselves sharing many mutual friends at Harvard.

"At that time, everyone at Harvard had heard of Neiman-Marcus," says Peter Miller, who was from New York and whose roommate was Richard Marcus. "Neiman-Marcus had a magical name. It was internationally known, but very few people, if anyone, at Harvard had ever heard of a store called Sakowitz."

Richard agrees and says he suspects that that fact "was vexing to Bob."

Still, retailing seemed far from Robert's mind at Harvard. He was accepted into one of the school's exclusive undergraduate clubs, The Fly, which counted among its earlier members Franklin Delano Roosevelt.

"Bob was a very purposeful kind of guy," recalls classmate Peter Miller, who was in a different final club, The Spee. "He was a charming guy but also a very strong-willed, intense fellow. He would target something and go for it."

Serious and bright though Robert was, he could also be a figure of fun. "I remember very well the way he shook hands," says Miller. "He gave you a good look in the eye and a strong handshake and he'd wink at you. His friendly approach was very strong and directed and occasionally people would smile about it."

Also remarkable was Robert's hairstyle, which he wore in a

pompadour and which Miller believes was an attempt to look taller. It was no secret that Robert was very bothered by his height. Although Robert says he is five feet ten, he appears to be closer to five feet seven; but he invariably augments his height with high-heeled cowboy boots and a cowboy hat — or, at Harvard, with a pompadour.

Once, when Richard Marcus was walking across Harvard Yard with Robert, Richard mentioned someone "who is about as short as you are," and with that, Robert swung his fist into Richard's stomach. Richard did not mean the comment critically, but he quickly realized that Robert was sensitive about his height and he was careful not to mention it again.

By his sophomore year, Robert had made friends with and shared a suite with a group of history majors who would influence his life: Michael Rockefeller, Nelson's son, and Wat Tyler, a descendant of United States President John Tyler. He also became friends with Robin Tavistock, who was next in line, after his father, to become the Duke of Bedford.

Years later, one of Robert's secretaries recalls, "Robert told me that at Harvard he and Michael Rockefeller and Robin Tavistock sat around and talked about the burden of having a famous name. I couldn't believe he was comparing himself to these people. That tells you a lot about what Robert thinks of Robert."

Rockefeller, especially, had an impact on Robert. He "helped pique my curiosity and interest in the arts," Robert told a reporter years later. "Boston, Cambridge, Harvard gave one an overwhelming sense of respect for the intellect."

Robert's hero was Leonardo da Vinci, the ultimate Renaissance man, the man who, in Robert's words, "did everything — art, architecture, military, engineering," a persona that Robert would try to take on himself after college.

Bernard eagerly anticipated his son's return to Texas. He had impatiently awaited the day he could bring him into the store and give him the kind of free rein that he had not been given by Tobias.

Although Bernard could also have been grooming his son-in-law, Robert Lipman, he was not. As Lynn explained to a reporter, "He was drinking when we got married, but then he really started drinking. . . . He was very immature."

According to Robert Sakowitz, "Lipman's father was a very hard taskmaster who made his first million dollars before he was twenty-one and never let Bob forget it. I think one of the things that ate him up was that he never proved himself to his father or to himself."

Not only did Lipman have problems with his own father, but also he increasingly grew to believe that Bernard did not want him to have any power at Sakowitz. Rather than fight the battle at the store, he decided to try the real estate business — and far from Houston. So he and Lynn and their new baby, Steven Bradford Lipman, moved to Palm Beach, Florida.

But in Palm Beach, instead of feeling happier, Lipman seemed to grow even more unhappy. His drinking increased, and he began to have extramarital affairs. The Racquet Club on Miami Beach was where the action was in the 1950s, and that is where Bobby Lipman began hanging out. Bobby was a better-than-average tennis player, but tennis was not the sport that drew many of the rich men to the Racquet Club from across the country.

"I never saw him there with Lynn," says a London business-man who knew Lipman. "The Racquet Club was an action place. You didn't get too many married couples. The club had four tennis courts, a swimming pool, and a lot of apartments. The great thing about it was that each apartment had four exits so you could make a quick getaway."

The club, variously described by some of its former members as a "body swap" and "the greatest puss place in the world," drew many of America's richest men — Augie Busch (of the beer dynasty), Huntington Hartford III, the Kennedys. Lipman was nei-ther the richest nor the most personable man at the club, but he was one of the most successful with women. His reputation grew when one woman whispered to another about him.

News of Lipman's philandering filtered back to the store. "I think Lynn was really in love with him," says Sakowitz hairdresser Bill Flemming, "but it was said that Lipman had slept with every girl from Texas to Florida."

According to friends and acquaintances of Lipman, his prefer-ence was for prostitutes — or, at least, women who looked like prostitutes. When Lynn came into the store one day, after she and Lipman had been living in Florida, employees were shocked at her appearance. "Lipman had gotten her to bleach her hair platinum blond, and she was wearing very red lipstick," says Flemming. "She looked like a hooker. People at the store couldn't believe it."

In 1957, Lynn gave birth again and named this child Douglas Bryan Lipman, but despite the growing family and the move to Florida, Lynn's marriage grew worse. "[Lipman] was physically abusive," says Lynn's first cousin Margaret Sackton Rosan. "I think Bernard actually went to Florida and physically rescued her and the children one day when [Lipman] was at work."

Bernard brought them back to Houston, installed them in his home on MacGregor Way, and a divorce followed. Although Robert Sakowitz says he does not know if Lipman physically abused Lynn, he says, "Bobby Lipman was really treating her badly, so my parents supported their divorce."

But a store employee says that Bernard and Ann "weren't very happy to have her back. I think they always pushed her aside because Robert was always the star. Basically and deep down, this is why Lynn is the way she is today."

Although friends say that Lipman had not wanted a divorce from Lynn, he wasted no time crying over his loss. He took an apartment on Miami Beach, bought a 1959 Cadillac convertible, and had a nose job.

Donald Waugh, who met Lipman in 1959 and became one of his best friends, remembers the first nose: "It was the hugest goddamn nose you ever saw. When he had it fixed, he came out with this little WASP nose, which made him very happy, but I liked the earlier nose. When I saw photographs of Steve Wyatt with Fergie, I said, 'Hey, that nose! That's gotta be Lipman's boy.'"

After the divorce, Lipman went to Houston a few times to see his sons, but Bernard put a stop to his visits because, according to Robert Sakowitz, Lipman was trying to play Steve and Douglas against Lynn.

With Lipman banned from the house on MacGregor, Robert Sakowitz, who had just graduated from Harvard and taken his own apartment in Houston, moved back in with the family to act as a surrogate father to the boys.

While Lynn began dating madly to make up for lost time, her brother spent time with his nephews, teaching them how to throw a football, taking them horseback riding at the family's ranch. Robert's concern for his nephews was loving and unselfish, especially so since he was a handsome young man who had just entered his twenties. He could have been dating furiously, as his sister was. "They were good kids," Robert says, "they needed a father."

Away from Lipman, Lynn returned her hair to its natural blond color and had plenty of dates. And although months passed without a serious suitor, that too was about to change.

Raymond Howard, a salesman in Sakowitz's gift and china department, remembers being astounded by a conversation he overheard at the downtown store. "I was in the basement stockroom when Robert and his father came down. They were talking, and I heard Bernard say, 'Bob, if only I can get you married everything will be all right.'

"Then Bernard left and Lynn came down and she and Robert started talking. Robert was very concerned about something. Then Lynn said, 'Oh, forget about it. I'll get married and get enough money for both of us.'"

5

I N 1901, twenty-three years before Oscar Sherman Wyatt, Jr., was born in Beaumont, Texas, a dusty, flat town located on the Gulf of Mexico at the Louisiana border, men were drilling for oil there, on a marshy hillock called Spindletop. Some local speculators believed that there was oil under the hillock, but they were having great difficulty bringing it to the surface. For more than two years, several different crews of men had tried to tap what they believed was a large pool of oil, but each crew gave up, either exhausted from trying or out of money, or both.

The first commercially productive oil well in America had been drilled almost half a century earlier, in 1859, at Titusville, Pennsylvania. But the Pennsylvania well, drilled a mere 69 feet into the ground, produced only about 400 gallons a day. During most of the nineteenth century, oil was used chiefly for lighting and lubrication, its limited supply making its use as fuel too costly.

As the new century began, few people knew or cared if there was oil in Texas. But that changed on the cold, clear morning of January 10, 1901, a few miles south of downtown Beaumont. As the crew on Spindletop pushed the oil drill bit 1,160 feet into the earth, mud suddenly bubbled and then gushed out of the well, followed by a geyser of blackish green oil. With violent force, the geyser blew off the top of the derrick, and oil shot more than a hundred feet into the air. Farmers and townspeople miles away witnessed the spectacular towering plume of oil, and those who did not see it felt it. Particles were carried in a north breeze, before dissipating and showering the town in oil. The powerful well spouted uncontrolled for nine days before its owners were able to cap it.

News of the phenomenon spread quickly from Beaumont by

telephone and telegraph, and by evening the world knew of the events taking place in the little town on the Gulf of Mexico. Speculators and promoters rushed to Beaumont to make their fortunes, jamming the daily trains and pouring into the city by horse and buggy. In a few weeks, Beaumont's population jumped from 9,000 to more than 50,000.

For more than a year, each time a well was sunk into the Spindletop field, it brought forth a gusher. By 1902, a year after the discovery, 130 wells were producing at Beaumont. Their combined production was more than that of the entire rest of the world.

With the success at Spindletop, the port of Beaumont was among the ten leading ports in tonnage in the United States, and the local economy diversified and grew. But the town whose population had swelled so quickly on a crest of oil had also endured its share of growing pains.

The 1920s began inauspiciously when the city was threatened with an epidemic of bubonic plague brought in by one of the ships docked at Beaumont's port. The city hired a professional rat trapper, and citizens were paid bounties for the rats they caught. Within sixty days, citzens caught 17,482 rats and averted a catastrophe.

An even darker threat had developed at the same time — the rise to power of the Ku Klux Klan. While purporting to stand for traditional Christian values and law and order, the Klan's system of vigilante justice represented lawlessness in its ugliest form. Blacks were the chief victims of the Klan, but tarrings and featherings, lashings, and pistol whippings were also directed against bootleggers, abortionists, and other violators of the Klan's so-called moral code.

In this brutal climate, on July 11, 1924, Eva Coday Wyatt gave birth to her first and only child, a son. The local newspaper got the child's middle initial, as well as his father's, wrong in its birth announcement: "Mr. and Mrs. O. F. Wyatt, 1625 Avenue E. are rejoicing over the arrival of a son, given the name of O. F. Jr."

Oscar S. Wyatt, Sr., was a drunk who worked as a mechanic for the local Gulf States Utilities Company. When the Great Depression hit, young Oscar saw men fighting one another for a place in the breadline in Beaumont, but his mother, he recalled years later, "scrimped and saved" so that there was always enough food on the Wyatt table.

When Oscar Jr. was still a very young boy, the elder Wyatt

moved his family to the small town of Navasota — located sixty miles northwest of Houston in Grimes County — where he continued to work for Gulf States.

Unlike Beaumont, which was flat, dusty, and industrial, the land around Navasota was green, hilly, and among the prettiest in Texas. In addition to its abundant wildflowers, the gently sloping land was endowed with live oaks and tall pines. Founded in 1854, Navasota was named for the river a few miles away, which got its name from a tribe of Indians who had roamed its banks.

As late as the 1930s, cotton was still the chief crop in Navasota, but without slaves, in this part of Texas as in the Deep South, great fortunes were no longer made by growing cotton. Despite its natural beauty, Navasota, with a population of only 4,000, was like any other small, struggling farm community with penny-pinching merchants and citizens. The Wyatts moved into a one-story white frame house, which, even for Navasota, was exceedingly modest.

In the Wyatts' neighborhood were two large families, but as soon as Oscar, an only child, moved in, he showed all the other kids who was in charge. "He was a tough, aggressive kid, a street fighter," says a friend who lived across the street when Oscar was five years old. "We'd have sandlot football games, and he was always the organizer. If an argument started, he was always in the middle of it.

"Mrs. Wyatt was a very nice lady," recalls the boyhood friend, "but Mr. Wyatt was big and boisterous and a heavy drinker."

While the elder Wyatt liked to imbibe, his wife, Eva, remained a strict and pious Southern Baptist. "About the only time Eva would get out of that house, except for church, was for her bridge games," recalls a longtime Navasotan.

In the early 1930s, the Wyatts moved into another one-story white frame house, across town on Victoria Street. When Oscar was about nine or ten, he started leaving home in the middle of the night to escape abuse by his alcoholic father. Carrying a blanket, he would walk three miles to a hill outside town, where he would spend the night by a tree. The next morning, when the fighting had stopped at home, he would return, dress, and leave for school.

The Wyatt home was just two blocks from Washington Avenue, the main street through town where Navasota's most prosperous families lived. From Oscar's tiny front yard, he could see the white brick colonial mansion on Washington where Navasota's most prominent citizen, Dr. Solon Douglas Coleman, lived.

One day, when O.S., as Oscar was nicknamed, was about eleven, he knocked on the Colemans' door and asked if the family needed any work done in the yard. Dr. Coleman, whose own children were too pampered for yardwork, gave Oscar a sickle to cut down tall weeds behind the house. Dr. Coleman noticed that the boy did not stop work until the job was done. Seeing what a hard worker O.S. was, Coleman gave him other work, for which O.S. was paid about a dollar a day. Dr. Coleman liked talking to O.S. while he worked, and an immediate friendship was formed.

In the small town of Navasota, there was barely a soul who did not know or who had not heard that Oscar's father was a terrible alcoholic who abused his wife. Most Navasotans knew that the boy had a very turbulent and unhappy home life, and many felt sorry for him, but no one was quite sure how to help.

But when Dr. Coleman's wife, Mabel, a woman who, according to a longtime Navasotan, "could quote the Bible from beginning to end," learned that O.S. often left his house in the middle of the night to escape the fights at home, she told him her house was open to him at any hour. The Colemans left the door unlocked for O.S., and in the middle of the night, about two or three times a month, they would hear O.S. let himself in. He shared a bedroom with the Colemans' son, Leonard, who was five years younger than Oscar.

Oscar and the Coleman family, which also included a daughter, Lillian Ruth, became very close. While Dr. Coleman gave him work, Mrs. Coleman gave him love. "My mother was so kind and loving to him," says Leonard. "She always tried to convert him to becoming a Baptist, which he would never do."

O.S. became so close with the Colemans that he began spending hours each day at their home, and he often stayed for meals. Oscar was a big eater and very fat, and, says Leonard, "When we were playing, O.S. would run into the bedroom and jump on the bed in our house and when he did, it was not uncommon for the bed to break."

Oscar could be very rough and often picked Leonard up by the hair, but that did not bother Leonard. "I liked tagging along with him because he was a leader. He seemed to know what he was talking about, no matter what the subject was."

But it was Dr. Coleman with whom O.S. became the closest.

"I think my father saw a lot of himself in O.S.," says Leonard. "My dad had come from sort of a similar situation. His father was a doctor, but a poor doctor, so he grew up having to do without a lot of things. Everything he had accomplished he had done on his own through hard work. Also, like Oscar's parents, my father's parents didn't get along. I think my father could sympathize with Oscar because of that."

But what Dr. Coleman seemed to admire most in O.S. was how hard he worked. In the summer, when O.S. laid pipe for irrigation in the cotton bottoms on a farm outside town, tough work at any time but especially in the hot Texas sun, he did the work without complaining and without stopping.

In the evenings, when Dr. Coleman, a general physician, made house calls, he liked to pick up O.S. in his Chevrolet and take the boy with him. On those visits Oscar learned about more than just medicine from Dr. Coleman. He began to imitate S.D.'s feisty and uneven temperament and egotistical manner.

"I think a lot of Oscar's bluster and brashness comes from Dr. Coleman," says Dr. W. S. Conklin, S. D. Coleman's son-in-law. "My father-in-law acted the same way Oscar does today."

When O.S. displayed this blustery temper and egotistical personality at high school, it did not win him friends. "He was always flying off at the mouth," says a classmate. "I think he was acting like such a loudmouth and big shot because he had an unhappy home life."

In addition to his abrasive personality, O.S. had the obvious social disadvantage of being fat. "Everyone called him 'Chink' in high school because he looked like a Chinaman," recalls another classmate. "He was black-haired with a round face and slanted eyes, and he was short, squatty, and fat."

Although O.S. came across to other students as very smart, friends say he rarely studied and was often in trouble. In the words of one classmate, "He would not be uncomfortable breaking the rules. He was very independent."

Nowhere was he more independent, more determined, or more likely to break the rules than on the Navasota High football team. He played left tackle and, at two hundred pounds, was the heaviest player on the team. High school football was king in Navasota in the forties, and stories about the Navasota "Rattlers" were often given as much play in the local *Daily Examiner* as war stories breaking in Europe. Game lineups were listed in the paper, where it was noted, "The line is lightweight but Wyatt does bring up the average."

O.S. was a star player but was frequently called for holding. "I couldn't get him to stop holding," says C. W. Lucas, his coach. "He sometimes thought he knew better than the coach. He was determined to get through that line no matter what."

The incident that many classmates and teachers remember most about Oscar was a star play he made in the famous game against Brenham, a bigger town and Navasota's chief rival. "It was in the beginning of the game, but Brenham was behind, so they started passing," says Coach Lucas. "I told Oscar to get through that line and tackle the passer. Brenham lined up, and Oscar, instead of going through the line like I told him to, backed up, sensing they were going to pass. Their quarterback threw, and O.S. intercepted the pass. Then all of our team members started blocking for O.S. as he ran the ball down the field. He was such a slow runner that some people had to block their players twice. Finally, after running about fifty yards, he took it in for the touchdown."

No one can remember which team won the game, but everyone remembers Oscar's hard-won touchdown.

The majority of students graduating from Navasota High School in the days when Oscar was in school did not go on to college, and in many ways, O.S. seemed an unlikely candidate for college. His parents were poor, and he cared little about learning — or so it seemed. But one day, when O.S. was a junior in high school, he walked up to one of his teachers and told her pointedly, "I'm going to college and I'm going to get an education and make good. And I'm going to give my mother everything she wants."

The teacher had no idea what prompted the comment, but she did not doubt O.S.'s determination. More than fifty years later, when Oscar returned to Navasota for his high school reunion, the teacher revealed this conversation to a gathering of his former classmates. After she told this story at the reunion, Oscar stood up and said simply, "I meant it."

Much of Oscar's relentless determination and many of his strong opinions were formed early in his youth. Throughout his life he deplored nepotism of any kind, a feeling acquired in his early years in Navasota. One summer he worked at the Gulf gas station, a father-and-son operation. The father went away and put his son in charge, but before he left he specifically told Oscar not to work on a particular automobile. Once the father was gone, the son told Oscar to work on the automobile. Oscar did, and when the father returned he fired Oscar for ignoring his instructions. This experience of nepotism was one he never forgot, and it led to results far more important than a teenager losing a job at a gas station.

During the fall of 1941, Oscar enrolled at Texas A&M. Navasota was only thirty miles from the A&M campus at College Station, and Oscar frequently came home on weekends. He was fond of Lillian Ruth Coleman, who was still in high school, and once or twice when he came home he took her on a date. According to Leonard Coleman, the boys at Navasota High did not like it that Oscar was dating one of their girls. Because he was older and on A&M's freshman football team, he presented too much competition for the high school boys.

"They threatened to beat up Chink if he came to Navasota and took her out one weekend," says Leonard. But Oscar showed the high school kids who was tougher. "He came to town anyway, but he brought with him two All-American A&M football players and no one gave him any trouble."

The early forties were a very patriotic time in America, and no family in Navasota was more patriotic than the Colemans. Oscar had tried to enlist in the United States Air Force but was turned down because of his weight. The weight limit was 180 pounds, and by now Oscar weighed 240.

The Colemans did not take lightly the fact that O.S. was not serving his country. They started calling him a "draft-dodger" and a "coward," because he would not lose the weight it took to get into the service.

"We finally teased him into losing weight," says Leonard. "We had a farm outside of town and he went out there and spent six weeks getting into shape. He'd work all day on someone else's farm, but every morning and every evening he would run six miles. He also put himself on a strict diet. My father would drive out there to the farm when he was running, to see how he was doing. Within six weeks, he lost the mandatory sixty pounds."

Oscar remained close with S. D. Coleman, and decades later when S.D. had a leg amputated, Oscar designed an elevator for S.D.'s house from memory and had the elevator built by the time S.D. returned from the hospital. When S.D. died, Oscar returned to Navasota for the funeral and told Leonard Coleman about the blustery S.D., whose manner he copied: "If he can get into heaven, so can I."

Oscar's weight loss in 1942 coincided with his growing desire to fight for his country. From early in his youth, Oscar had been fascinated with flying. At fourteen, he and some friends built a glider, which they towed behind a car. At sixteen, he got his pilot's license and worked summers as a crop duster for local cotton farmers.

There was an element of glamour to the war, and Oscar was now more determined than ever to be a part of it. In 1942, as soon as spring football practice was over, the young man who loved to fly joined the Army Air Corps.

Oscar flew scores of missions successfully, but his luck gave out in 1945. While he was delivering supplies to an air base in the Pacific, his plane crashed. Both his legs were crushed, his jaw was broken, and he had seven fractures to his head. Many years later, he told a reporter about the crash:

"In Okinawa, I had been ordered to move some munitions. . . . Shortly after I took off I felt a god-awful impact. . . . The next thing I knew I was on fire. I had five people with me, and I couldn't make it back to the strip, so I put the plane down, and the whole side of the plane caved in on me. I thought I was dead. . . . When I got out of the airplane, I couldn't see. I didn't know if my leg was gone. I felt the leaning edge of the wing and I got oriented, so I crawled and started counting the bodies until I got my crew out. And they all came out alive. . . . I had to go to the hospital in an ambulance, in and out of consciousness. . . . I could stick my tongue out the side of my face."

After World War II, even with the aid of the GI Bill, Oscar did not have enough money to return to A&M. Instead, he attended classes at Lamar College in Beaumont and leased a 640-acre rice farm near the campus.

A year earlier, on September 22, 1947, he had married Yvonne Humphrey, an attractive blonde with no more money than he had. They were married by a justice of the peace in Kountz, Texas, a tiny town north of Houston where couples frequently came only to marry. Yvonne and Oscar did not stay in Beaumont long. He used his proceeds from a bumper rice crop to transfer to A&M in 1948.

Yvonne and Oscar lived near the campus, and he supported his family by student teaching at A&M and by selling used cars. After graduating from A&M in 1949 with a degree in mechanical engi-neering, Oscar went to work as a drill bit salesman for the Reed Roller Bit Co. With his quick mind and almost photographic mem-ory, Oscar learned the history of virtually every gas field in South Texas and soon became the company's top salesman in the Gulf Coast area.

By 1952, when Yvonne gave birth to a boy, Carl Douglas Wyatt, Oscar was well on his way to becoming very successful.

In the early 1950s, the "law of capture," which had been estab-lished by an 1889 Pennsylvania Supreme Court decision, still applied. Under common law, the owner of the land is owner of the minerals under it. This law raised no problems for minerals that were solids. But since oil moves underground and goes to the near-est borehole or puncture mark in the earth, oil that is located under one person's lease may be pulled into another person's well. Oil migrates from areas of high pressure to areas of low pressure. When a well is drilled in an oil-bearing formation, a low pressure is cre-ated at the bottom of the well. Gas pressure brings oil from the surrounding area, often extending under a neighbor's land. In its decision, the Pennsylvania Supreme Court followed the basic rule governing the capture of wild game. Regardless of where the deer comes from, it belongs to the hunter who captures it on his own land. In the case of oil, the court ruled that it belonged to the well that brought it to the surface.

With the rule of capture, a single well appropriately placed and a little luck were often enough to bring in a gusher. Anxious to sink his first well, Oscar found a six-acre lease in Sinton, Texas. Because he had no money, he mortgaged his 1949 Ford to a Corpus Christi banker for $800 to pay for the cost of his first well. Years later, Henry Ford II gave Oscar a miniature gold-plated Ford. "We paid you $800 for it, and you made a billion," Ford wrote. "We got cheated."

While Oscar was hustling drill bits for Reed, he had met a Corpus Christi independent oil operator named A. A. Moore. Together, they formed a partnership under the name of the Hardly Able Oil Co. That name was soon dropped, and in 1952 they incor-porated under the name Wymore Drilling Co. They began securing leases here and there, many of which other oilmen felt were of questionable value at best. These were leases overlooked by the big oil companies — swampy areas or river bottoms, or simply small slips of land between other big leases.

Hole after hole that they sank was dry, and Wyatt had to bring in investors to keep the company afloat. Then their luck turned. In early 1953, Wymore drilled in the St. Joseph Field in Webb County, a field where a dozen dry holes had been drilled by other companies. Wymore's first hole, the thirteenth in the field, produced nothing, but the second was a significant discovery. For years, the field reportedly paid its investors $1.5 million a year.

The company's practice of picking a lease here and a lease there, forming a patchwork quilt of oil properties, began paying off. But the young company was not without its problems. In 1953, Wymore was sued twice — once for $75,000 and a second time for $85,000 — for allegedly drilling "slant hole" wells in violation of state regulations. Wells are supposed to be drilled straight down and not slanted to reach someone else's property. Both suits were eventually settled out of court, but Oscar has fought his reputation as a "slant driller" ever since.

For all his early success in the oil business, it was gas, not oil, that would make Oscar really rich. One night in the early 1950s, as Oscar flew his plane over the desolate South Texas landscape and came upon the Orange Grove Oil Field, he had an idea. Looking down at the flares of gas burning in the night, he realized he could make a lot of money if he found a way to use the gas that was flared as waste. The gas was flared because none of the big pipeline companies thought it worthwhile to build a line into the Orange Grove Field. Oscar decided to collect this waste gas and offer it to one of the big gas companies. After dissolving his partnership with Moore, in 1955 he founded Coastal States Oil and Gas Company (soon renamed Coastal States Gas Producing Company). He based his company in the South Texas town of Corpus Christi, a city of slightly more than 100,000 on a bay in the Gulf of Mexico. Surrounding Corpus Christi on the other three sides were some of the state's largest gas fields.

Although gas was plentiful, it was not easy for a newcomer to break into the gas business in 1955. The gas industry was very tightly controlled by a few large companies. Unlike the oil business, where money can be made in production, refining, and marketing, in the gas business of 1955 there was only one way to become wealthy: transportation. The big pipeline companies had immense power over producers because without a connecting pipeline a gas well was useless.

The major pipeline companies would hook up with a field only if the field had considerable proven reserves. These companies paid royalties to all the owners in a field — whether or not they had wells on their property — in proportion to each owner's share of the underground oil and gas reservoir. The companies decided among themselves to allow one million cubic feet of gas a day for each eight billion cubic feet of reserves, a formula designed to promote the field's longevity. The companies respected each other's territory, which avoided duplication of expensive pipelines as well as competition.

By 1955, the big Texas gas companies already had built pipelines into all the big known Texas gas deposits. But there were thousands of small farms and homesteads that nobody had bothered to exploit. These small landowners were eager to sell their gas, but they couldn't afford to build the pipelines needed to move the gas. So Oscar did it for them. Starting with sixty-eight miles of pipe, he built pipelines into the small fields that the majors had disdained.

Coastal signed contracts with small landowners who were known in the industry as "town lot operators" because their tracts were often ten acres or less. They had been paid a pittance under the big companies' practice of paying landowners in the proportion of their acreage to that of the whole field, whether or not a well had been drilled on their little piece of land. Coastal paid less per thousand cubic feet for the gas than did the big companies, but the town lot operator was still much better off selling gas from his own well to Oscar than he was under the proportional ownership formula imposed by the big companies.

Not surprisingly, Oscar's tactics enraged both the larger producers and the established pipeline companies because he threatened their monopoly. The town lot operators began producing far more gas than lay underneath their own small tracts — much of the gas came from beneath the plots of neighboring landowners in the field. Although this was legal under the rule of capture, the major companies complained that Wyatt's method for gathering gas was, in effect, stealing.

There were also complaints that Coastal stole gas in the way the company measured it. Because gas is neither solid nor liquid, measuring it is an inexact science. The best measuring tool is a complicated instrument known as an orifice meter, but even with this, meter readings are subject to interpretation. Producers frequently complained about Coastal's calculations.

"Charges of meter-tampering were buttressed considerably by the fact that Coastal occasionally reported 'negative line losses' to the Railroad Commission — in other words, more gas came out of Coastal's pipelines than went into them," wrote Paul Burka in *Texas Monthly*. When small producers complained of not being paid for all the gas they fed into Oscar's pipelines, his frequent response was "Meet me at the courthouse."

Once Oscar had achieved success with the town lot operators, Coastal became a gas gatherer. The company acted as a broker, buying and packaging gas for resale to the big companies.

Oscar was having no trouble finding markets that wanted gas. In fact, he was always in need of more gas. Labeled the energy source of the future, gas was clean, efficient, easy to use, and, best of all, cheap. Because he was already getting all the gas he could from small fields, he began bidding against the major pipeline companies in the big fields. This created a serious problem for the big companies because they pegged all their payments to the highest prices they were paying in a field; if they started paying more for gas to one producer, they had to raise all their payments.

So the large pipelines let Coastal outbid them and then purchased their gas from their newest competitor, Coastal. Not only did the big pipeline companies suddenly find themselves needing Coastal, they were making Coastal rich by paying the upstart company a brokerage fee.

In the five years since its founding, Coastal had increased its assets from $3 million to $48 million. Despite its dubious reputation for honesty and fairness, no one could deny that Oscar Wyatt was a man on the move.

At thirty-six, the company's chairman exuded such a strong optimism that the atmosphere at Coastal was pervaded with a sense of destiny. The staff was small, young, dedicated, and overworked, and no one worked harder than the boss. He arrived at his Corpus Christi office early in the morning, before anyone else, and he was always the last to leave.

"It was fast and furious," recalls one of the company's attorneys. "Mr. Wyatt was a go-getter. He was a glutton for work."

While Oscar had established a name for himself as an up-and-comer in gas industry circles throughout the state, in Corpus Christi he was not widely admired.

"Oscar came in here with lots of big ideas for his company to grow and for the city to grow," says a longtime resident. "A handful of men had controlled politics for decades in this town, then all of a sudden here comes this upstart outsider trying to tell them how to change what they thought they were doing perfectly. No matter how hard he tried, Oscar never could change their minds."

Corpus Christi (Latin for Body of Christ) was discovered on Corpus Christi Day, 1519, and was visited infrequently by Spanish mariners and buccaneers. The town on Corpus Christi Bay, at the entrance of Nueces Bay, was incorporated in 1852 and was briefly captured during the Civil War. Although the town grew very slowly in the nineteenth century, that changed in 1924, when gas was found in abundance in the area.

An even bigger boom occurred during World War II when a huge naval air-training station was built. In the decade that followed, the city's population nearly doubled, to 108,000. But by the early 1960s, it seemed to Oscar that the city's leaders stood in the way of real growth for Corpus Christi.

Oscar learned just how much the city's leaders wanted to buck him when he attempted to win a zoning permit to build a $500,000, forty-eight-lane bowling alley in an existing shopping center. Business owners at the shopping center supported Oscar's plans, but Mayor Ellroy King sharply questioned the plans and forced Oscar to spend months proving why he should be allowed the permit. Oscar won in the end, but whether all his efforts were worth it only Oscar knows.

In 1956, after nine years of marriage, Oscar divorced Yvonne, who reportedly told a friend, "Oscar's the only man I know who has a mattress strapped to his back for convenience."

Twelve days after his divorce became final, he married an airline stewardess from Milwaukee. Mary Margaret Schuster, a pretty, petite brunette, was soft-spoken and demure. On the surface the marriage seemed like a mismatch. She appeared as weak as he was strong.

Not long after Oscar and Mary Margaret married, they built a house a few miles south of downtown and just a few blocks from the bay in a subdivision called Hewit Estates. No ordinary house, the large square structure made of glass and pale yellow and black brick looked like a two-story commercial building. So out of place was it — even protected by a high wall in the same yellow and black brick — that it seemed Oscar was trying to shock his conservative, establishment neighbors.

In fact, no sooner did the bricks start going on than a rumor began to circulate. According to a Corpus Christi resident whose family lives in the Hewit Estates today, the reason for building such an unusual home was Oscar's thrift. The house was built with materials left over from a pale yellow and black brick building downtown — Oscar's Petroleum Tower.

6

WITH THE POSSIBLE exception of General Antonio López de Santa Anna, whose soldiers killed every last Texan at the Alamo in 1836, no one is more hated in San Antonio than Oscar S. Wyatt, Jr. But it did not start out that way.

When Oscar first came to San Antonio in 1960, it was as a suitor. He wanted to win the gas supply contract that for thirty-eight years had been held by Louisiana's giant United Gas. By its monopolistic arrogance, United had paved the way for Oscar.

In 1960, as its last contract was about to expire, United raised its price from 17 cents per thousand cubic feet to 30 cents. In addition, United refused to give a firm price for the full term of the contract, insisting instead on a cost-plus price, and it also refused to dedicate specific gas reserves to fulfill the San Antonio contract.

San Antonio's five-member City Public Service (CPS) Board, which operated the city-owned electric and gas utilities, was no ordinary municipal utility. It was made up of a group of the city's rich and powerful businessmen, who were answerable not to the City Council but to themselves. Angry at years of United's high-handed manner, CPS refused its proferred contract and advertised for competitive bids for a twenty-year contract for up to two trillion cubic feet of gas. In addition to United, Houston Pipeline bid and so did Coastal.

The lowest bid came from two independent San Antonio businessmen, Glen Martin and R. F. Schoolfield, who had no company, no gas, and no pipeline, only a name — the Alamo Gas Supply Company. Just how badly CPS wanted cheap gas for the city was obvious when it awarded the contract to the upstart Alamo Company. Alamo's bid, at 16 cents per thousand cubic feet, was a penny less than United's soon-to-expire contract.

In the months that followed, Alamo had numerous difficulties. Because there were few small companies in the gas transportation business, Alamo did not have a wide selection of companies to turn to for help. But Coastal was one. If the company needed pipe, Oscar was there to provide it. Each time Oscar helped Alamo, he took in exchange shares of Alamo stock.

The CPS Board watched nervously as Coastal, which had already gained a dubious reputation in South Texas, began to own more and more of Alamo.

"We weren't enthusiastic about Coastal becoming involved," says then board member and attorney for the King Ranch, Leroy Denman. "Coastal had treated people fairly roughly at times in South Texas, and I'd had some experiences with Coastal and their pipelines. I was involved in some controversies where Oscar would offer a rancher a pittance for a pipeline right-of-way across his land. Then, if he couldn't get it, he'd go for condemnation, and he forced counties to give him rights-of-way when they didn't want to."

Denman, admiringly known today as "the silver fox," for his thick, white hair, his polished ways, and his business acumen, was the aristocratic antithesis of the parvenu Oscar. "He was a rough-and-tumble guy from a rough-and-tumble business in a rough-and-tumble era," Denman says about Oscar.

But that did not stop Oscar from trying to fit into San Antonio society, especially as he began to own more of Alamo. At the same time that he was taking Glen Martin's company right out from under him, Oscar was using the socially prominent Glen to make his way into San Antonio society.

"For some time, Oscar made quite a splash here," says Denman. "Coastal made grants to the San Antonio Symphony, and I think Oscar truly wanted to be a feature here. He wanted to be loved."

"By the time Alamo delivered its first cubic foot of gas in April 1962, the company was little more than a subsidiary of Coastal," wrote *Texas Monthly*. Within another year, Coastal acquired all that remained of Alamo's stock and dissolved Alamo entirely. Oscar named this subsidiary Lo-Vaca Gas Gathering Company.

At the same time that Oscar was working to acquire San Antonio's contract, he was fighting a similar battle at the state capital. It was simply Oscar's good luck that the contracts to supply gas to

Austin, Corpus Christi, and San Antonio all came up for renewal between 1960 and 1962.

Just as in San Antonio, Austin's gas contract had been held for thirty-seven years by United Gas of Louisiana. In Austin, Oscar presented an attractive proposal. He promised that, in return for the business, Coastal would never ask the Railroad Commission for higher rates, no matter how high the field price of gas climbed during the life of the contract.

Coastal had gone out of its way to appear cooperative. Oscar's eagerness to answer questions of the city council made him a striking contrast to the stuffy and aloof representatives from United Gas. What seemed most telling about Oscar Wyatt's willingness to work with the council was Coastal's bid itself — submitted in the form of a signed contract complying with all the city's specifications. There were two other bidders, United and Humble, but Coastal got the contract.

Despite the increasingly combative atmosphere between himself and the city fathers of his hometown, Oscar next went after Corpus Christi's gas contract. By early 1960, Corpus Christi had already agreed to a new twenty-year contract with Houston Natural Gas, which had served the city for the last eight years.

When, six weeks before the election, Corpus had not taken competitive bids for a new contract, Oscar publicly questioned whether Houston Natural's contract was the best one available. When his request was ignored, he began a fight. He trailed Mayor Ellroy King — who had earlier resisted Oscar's efforts to build a bowling alley — and spoke against Houston Natural's plan. Finally, King agreed to a televised debate.

King opened the debate by describing Oscar as a would-be bidder who had aimed a loaded shotgun at the council's head and threatened "to pull the trigger if we don't accept his rules."

Oscar, however, wisely remained cool and reasonable and made a good case for the city to take bids. The city fathers agreed with King, but Oscar developed a larger block of voters. He had spent weeks gathering support from blacks, Hispanics, and liberals who were willing to back him in his fight against the entrenched establishment.

When Oscar finally forced a referendum, Houston Natural was rejected by a margin of two to one. This did not give Coastal the contract, but it at least allowed Coastal to make a bid.

Houston Natural made a new, five-year bid that the city said was more attractive than Oscar's twenty-year bid, and the fight got nastier. According to the *Wall Street Journal*, during the contract fight, Oscar "packed a gun and once escaped with his life when a car tried to run him off the road in downtown Corpus Christi."

After several more months of bickering, Corpus Christi finally awarded its contract to a small and relatively unknown company, Lumar Gas. But Lumar, like Alamo Gas in San Antonio, made promises it was unable to fulfill, which allowed Coastal to step in and buy out Lumar's contract. Coastal then raised its bid from Lumar's 18 cents per thousand cubic feet to a hefty 23.5 cents, with regular price escalations.

Oscar had gambled in San Antonio and Austin and Corpus Christi that he could buy gas cheaply enough to meet his fixed-price contracts for years ahead. But all three cities would be in for a shock, and they would be partly to blame for that shock. So eager were they to make short-term savings that they failed to look at the risks in Oscar's irresistible contracts.

When Oscar was not busy putting together gas properties, he became an avid sailor, and in this sport, as in the brutal sport of business, he was a fierce competitor. When he joined the Corpus Christi Yacht Club, it quickly became evident that he viewed sailing as he did everything else and would play to win at all costs. A story has long circulated about the time he attended his first planning meeting for the Yacht Club's annual sailboat competition. "Now tell me," he reportedly asked his shocked fellow members, "how would anyone know if one of these guys started their motor during the race?"

Oscar was friends with another Corpus Christi oilman, Jack Manley, who had a very sexy wife named Bonnie. After a stint as a Hollywood starlet, Bonnie had married Jack and moved to Corpus Christi. Even away from Hollywood, she exercised her chief talent. "Bonnie was a flirt in a class by herself," says a Dallas society matron. "She was very cute, and when she walked into a room, all eyes focused on her." Oscar invited Jack and Bonnie to join him and Mary Margaret on a flying trip to several islands in the Caribbean. Oscar flew his own plane from Tampico to Merida to Jamaica to Haiti, often landing on tiny airstrips carved out between mountains, and never exhibited the slightest concern about his ability.

Jack was impressed that Oscar was so adept at piloting, but he was even more impressed with Oscar's general savvy about life.

"Before we were cleared for takeoff in Merida," Jack recalls, "a Mexican guy in a uniform who spoke English came on the plane and said he wanted an additional one hundred dollars for some cockamamie charge. Without batting an eye, Oscar said, 'Certainly, if you'll just sign here. We're guests of the Mexican Oil Company and they're paying all our expenses, so we're sending all these bills to them.'

"This wasn't true, but you could see the wheels turning in this guy's mind. He looked at this piece of paper and wondered if it was worth it for one hundred dollars to get in real trouble. The Mexican guy tore it up and was gone.

"Oscar was very fast on his feet. He is so strong and so smart that he just exudes this feeling of both mental and physical power."

Jack was not the only passenger on the trip who admired Oscar's power. According to Jack, at some point, either right before, during, or right after the Caribbean trip, Oscar began an affair with Jack's wife Bonnie, a big-breasted, blue-eyed blonde who, prior to going to Hollywood, had been a two-time runner-up in the Miss Alabama beauty pageant.

"Bonnie had a maid who used to call us and tip us where Manley was going to be," Oscar told *Vanity Fair* in 1991.

Although Bonnie and Jack had had a stormy and unhappy marriage and were headed toward divorce, Bonnie waited for Oscar to make the first move. She let him file for his own divorce first. No less careful in selecting an attorney to bring her divorce suit, she hired Tracy DuBose, Oscar's chief litigator.

Jack, who had had two wives before Bonnie, and has had two more after her, "just could never say no to a woman," says a friend of his. There is a widely circulated story, probably apocryphal, that Bonnie once left the house to run errands and returned unexpectedly to find Jack in bed with another woman. Seeing his wife standing in the bedroom doorway, Jack laughed and asked, "Now Bonnie, who are you going to believe, me or your own eyes?"

"Jack was rich, as we all were," says a fellow Texas oilman, "but Oscar was different. He had the killer instinct. He was smarter and tougher and more determined, and he worked eighteen times harder than any of the rest of us."

Jack did not wonder what it was about Oscar that so appealed to Bonnie: "I just assumed it was because he was on his way to being very rich."

And what Oscar saw in Bonnie was obvious to those around

her. "She's not beautiful, but she has the most vivacious, vibrant personality. I don't think she's ever had an introspective moment in her life," says Dallas oilman Bill Hudson, who saw Bonnie and Jack often when they were married. "Mary Margaret was a nice girl, but that's what she was, a girl. A little mousey brunette. Then suddenly along comes this blond time bomb Bonnie. I think Oscar had outgrown Mary Margaret."

Born Bonnie Bolding, one of seven children in the family of a Church of Christ minister in Birmingham, Alabama, Bonnie could curse as well as Oscar, and even in a room with Oscar she was the center of attention. No other woman or man could keep the spotlight in the presence of Oscar except Bonnie.

If Oscar was looking for a trophy wife, Bonnie seemed to be it — and more. What seemed most remarkable about her was that she had almost as much energy as the absolutely frenetic Oscar. This fact was not undermined by her revelation years later that for extra pep she liked to take "a dollop of honey" before making love.

Jack Manley had no intention of contesting Bonnie's divorce petition, but it soon appeared that Bonnie and Oscar thought he might.

"When Bonnie and I were separated, I got a call from a friend who said he was having a party in L. A., so a girl from Dallas and I flew out for it," says Manley. "I didn't know we were going until a few hours before we left, but when I got there, there was a bug in the television set in my room at the Bel Air Hotel."

Jack says he learned from one of Oscar's lawyers that it was Oscar who had bugged his room. "Can you imagine Oscar doing that in a matter of a couple of hours? I didn't even know I was going until right before I left. He was going to all this trouble."

Jack decided to get a message to Oscar's attorney: "I told him, 'If Oscar will give me half of the money that he's spending on detectives for Bonnie, I'll write up that I was found in bed with three male albino midgets.'"

Oscar, meanwhile, had little trouble getting his divorce from Mary Margaret, to whom he had been married for five years. They separated in July 1961 and were granted a divorce three months later, in October.

On December 9, Jack and Bonnie got their divorce, and she moved into Oscar's house on Hewit Place. She and Oscar made plans to marry almost immediately. "They wanted to marry before the end of the year to get the tax deduction," says Manley.

The day after Christmas, in an afternoon ceremony in Birmingham, Alabama, Bonnie became the third Mrs. Oscar S. Wyatt, Jr. After a large wedding at Birmingham's Church of Christ, the bride and groom left on a trip to the Orient. But the honeymoon atmosphere was short-lived. They fought bitterly, beginning almost immediately after their return to Corpus Christi. The underlying source of their problems seemed to be the volatile combination of Bonnie's flagrant flirting and Oscar's intense jealousy.

"Bonnie flirted with every man that passed her on the street — and not just rich oilmen and society types, but the chauffeur and the gardener too," says a male friend of Bonnie's.

Bonnie and Oscar had barely unpacked their bags from the Orient trip when, in January 1962, Oscar filed a divorce document. They soon took another trip, she later claimed, without her knowing about the divorce filing.

But in February, less than two months into their marriage, the document — alleging that immediately after their marriage, Bonnie began a course of "harsh and tyrannical treatment" toward him — became public. The suit was quickly dismissed, however, by District Judge Cullen Briggs, a family friend who had attended their wedding in Birmingham.

They continued to live together, but any hope that they would reconcile ended in early March when they flew to Abilene, Texas, for a black-tie ball. They were invited as the guests of Scott Taliaferro and his wife, Patty, who was chairman of Abilene's social event of the year, the Philharmonic Ball.

Abilene, a dusty West Texas town 140 miles west of Fort Worth with a population of 90,000 in 1962, was known locally as "the buckle of the Bible belt." On March 3, the *Abilene Reporter-News* ran a large photograph of Patty Taliaferro, chairman of the second annual Philharmonic Ball, and her husband, Scott, greeting their weekend houseguests from Corpus Christi — Mr. Taliaferro's sister, Mary Wallace, and her husband, Bill, and Bonnie and Oscar Wyatt. The accompanying story explained that the Wallaces and the Wyatts had flown up to Abilene Friday afternoon on one of Oscar's planes and would return to Corpus Christi Sunday afternoon, following a brunch for two hundred guests in the foursome's honor.

"Oscar and Bonnie were mad at each other before they came up here," Patty Taliaferro still insists today. But for the first day and a half of their visit, Patty's house party went smoothly. The trouble began very early Sunday morning, after the ball at the Abilene Country Club, when Patty invited a small group of friends to continue the party back at her home. Bonnie got into a bridge game with Scott Taliaferro and two other guests, while Oscar played host and fixed drinks for the guests.

At around four o'clock, Patty finally went to bed. When she left the room, Scott and Bonnie and two others were still playing bridge, but by now Oscar was sound asleep on the couch, snoring.

Around five o'clock in the morning, Oscar got up and told Bonnie it was time to go back to the hotel. But she was not ready to leave. As he charged toward her, she jumped up and held onto a door. "We're leaving," he shouted. "No we're not," she shouted back.

Oscar then grabbed her and pulled out a large clump of her hair. Still in her floor-length evening gown, she then took off running around the couch. Oscar ran after her. In the melee, either Bonnie or Oscar knocked over a lamp, which crashed to the slate floor and broke into tiny pieces. She then ran barefoot over the glass, and her foot started bleeding.

Scott Taliaferro shouted at Oscar to stop and tried to restrain him, but without success. Scott was no match for the 220-pound A&M tackle. The only thing Scott could hold onto was Oscar's tuxedo shirt, which immediately ripped off in Scott's hands. Oscar then easily shoved Scott aside and took off after Bonnie.

Patty, in another wing of the large house, awoke to Bonnie's screams and rushed into the living room in her nightgown. Patty recalls, "I went out there and yelled at Oscar, 'Get a hold of yourself!' But he didn't pay any attention. He just acted like you weren't even there."

As Scott Taliaferro called the police, Bonnie and Patty ran through the house. They ran into the master bedroom and locked the door, but Oscar, charging furiously after them, broke right through the door and kept chasing Bonnie.

Meanwhile, Mary Wallace, Scott's sister, who had been in the card game, ran into the dressing room, shoved Oscar, and screamed, "How dare you hit my brother." In the scuffle, Mary's beaded, floor-length gown ripped apart and the beads spilled onto the floor.

When the police arrived minutes later, they found bare-chested Oscar still in his tuxedo pants, Bonnie with a bloody foot and a large clump of hair missing, Mary Wallace trying to hold together her ripped dress, a disheveled Scott Taliaferro, and the Philharmonic Ball chairman in her nightgown.

The police immediately arrested Oscar and led him out of the house and into a police car. As he was climbing into the car, Oscar had a parting shot for the Taliaferros. "You're going to be sorry that you ever did this to me," he shouted.

As her husband pulled away in the police car, Bonnie did something that must have finally outraged Oscar beyond reconciliation. She went to the phone and called Oscar's pilot, who was staying at the same hotel where Bonnie and Oscar were registered. She told the pilot that her mother in Birmingham had suddenly become ill and that she needed to fly there immediately. She said she would meet the pilot very shortly at the airport and that Oscar would not be going with them. The pilot, knowing nothing about the events of the last few hours, obliged his boss's wife and met her at the airport about an hour later, around six o'clock in the morning.

"They kept Oscar locked up until morning when he could get a lawyer on the phone to come get him out," says a woman who was working for the *Abilene Reporter-News.* "I think the police wanted to keep him there until he sobered up."

He reportedly pleaded guilty to being drunk, causing a disturbance, and using abusive language and was fined $65.

Around ten o'clock, at about the same time the airplane carrying Bonnie touched down in Birmingham, the police were releasing Oscar from jail.

"If you know Oscar," says Jack Manley, "you can imagine how mad he was when he walked out of that jail and his airplane was gone."

When Oscar got out of jail, he called Patty and apologized and told her to send him the bills for the damages he had caused. He paid for the damages, but she did not invite him back.

Years after the incident, when Oscar ran into Scott Taliaferro, he joked to someone else in front of Scott, "Here's a man whose house I tore up one night."

Bonnie stayed in Birmingham for nine days and later testified at a divorce hearing that she spent three of those days in a hospital recovering from the Abilene fight.

Oscar had earlier put a bug in the television set of Jack Manley's hotel room when he wanted to marry Bonnie. Now he put a surveillance bug in Bonnie's station wagon.

Oscar filed a second divorce suit, but again the judge dismissed it. In the late summer of 1962, they again reconciled, but for the last time. On September 28, Oscar filed yet another divorce petition. This suit contained his toughest charges yet against his wife, some of which, Bonnie later charged, must have come from his surveillance.

The suit charged that "in the early part of the month of April, 1962, the Defendant, while on a trip to Palm Springs, California, carried on for a week or more a constant series of flirtations with numerous other men, and on at least one occasion late at night had illicit sexual relations in an automobile with some man whom this Plaintiff does not personally know, but whose name, this Plaintiff assumes, was known by the Defendant."

Oscar charged that, immediately upon returning from their honeymoon, "the Defendant commenced and has since then carried on almost without interruption, improper, flirtatious and, on occasions, illicit relationships with other men, both in public and in private."

Oscar also accused her of cursing him with "vile language," of drinking habitually, and of having married him for his money. He said she constantly pressured him to buy her expensive gifts and deposited money that he gave her for household expenses into her numerous personal bank accounts, while she "consistently failed to provide enough food" for the household. The suit also stated that "prior to the filing of this suit, he discussed with Defendant the obvious necessity of his obtaining from her a divorce, and that Defendant's reply was for him to get his checkbook out."

This time, Bonnie filed a cross-action, and at last the case was not thrown out by the judge. A trial date was set, and South Texas anticipated a nasty courtroom battle. But on December 9, 1962, the eve of the scheduled trial, the case was settled. The settlement records were sealed, but a male friend of Bonnie's, who had kept an eye on the case through her lawyer, says Bonnie got a flat cash settlement of $1 million.

In 1962, the $1 million surely seemed a better bet than another request she made. "For a divorce settlement," she reportedly told Oscar, "just give me the rights to your life story."

Oscar got to keep the house, and Bonnie moved to New York, where she took a job as a stockbroker and rode a bicycle to work. An intimate friend who saw her often in New York says she enjoyed her independence as a single woman in New York.

But she did appear to want more when, in 1969, at age thirty-six, she tried marriage yet again. While working in New York, she met and married Chicago businessman John E. Swearingen, then chairman of Standard Oil of Indiana, the then $4 billion corporation that ranked fifteenth on *Fortune*'s annual list.

Swearingen, who was fifty-one when they married, was as refined as Oscar was rough, and some of Bonnie's friends from Texas wondered how she would fit into Chicago's upper-class society. "She reinvented herself," says Bill Hudson. "It was like you never knew her in her past life."

But while her old friends might not have recognized her, some new ones did. As a Chicago reporter wrote, "Mrs. Swearingen's arrival here in 1969 was greeted by an almost deafening sound of cat-like screeching, derisive laughter, and astonished gasps."

If Bonnie did not slip quietly and unnoticed into Chicago society, it was in part because of her candor, which is so blatant it almost seems innocent. "I just love oil and oilmen," she was quoted saying at the time of her wedding to Swearingen. "All my husbands have been oilmen who have been heads of their companies."

7

I N MARCH 3, 1963, a photograph of the thrice-married and divorced Oscar ran in the society section of the *Houston Post.* Pictured with him at a black-tie art auction at the Houston Club was an attractive twenty-eight-year-old divorcée, Lynn Sakowitz Lipman. Like Bonnie, Lynn had a cute, youthful, cheerleader look. She wore her blond hair in a short flip, and she had a bright, perky smile.

Although it was among the first photographs to appear in the press of Oscar and Lynn, this was reportedly not their first meeting. Val Renken, a longtime family retainer, says, "Ann said that when Oscar was still married to Bonnie, he would come to the Sakowitzes' house and sit in their kitchen and have coffee with Ann and Bernard and Lynn. They all three found Oscar very charming."

But when word got around Houston that Lynn was seeing Oscar, the Sakowitzes' friends started issuing warnings about the oilman from Corpus Christi. "People would come up and volunteer to my father, 'I understand Lynn's going with Oscar. You'd better be careful,'" says Robert.

Bernard listened to the warnings. According to one story, Bernard went to his good friend Robert Mosbacher and asked about Oscar. The story goes that Mosbacher, who also was making millions in the oil business at the time and later served as Secretary of Commerce in the Bush administration, gave Oscar a high approval rating.

Lynn and Oscar's courtship was fast and wild, as typified by the marriage proposal. "Once, Oscar was flying me somewhere in his plane, and we were talking about getting married," Lynn told a reporter. "I said, 'Oscar, you've never proposed to me!' And he said, 'That's because you're going to propose to me. Now do it.' And I said, 'I won't.' And he said, 'Oh, yes, you will,' and then he put the plane in a dive and I thought we were going to crash. So I threw myself on him and said, 'Marry me!' and he said, 'O.K.,' and then he brought the plane out of the dive."

Bernard wanted to be certain that if Oscar walked out on Lynn, as he had on three earlier wives, she would, at least, be well off financially. Before the marriage took place, Bernard demanded that Oscar give her $1 million worth of stock in his Coastal States Gas Producing Co. By 1963 standards, this was a considerable sum, but parting with it was perhaps not too painful to Oscar. In the fiscal year that ended in June 1963, Oscar's young company made a $9 million profit.

This reverse dowry enabled the marriage to go forward, and on July 29, 1963, Oscar and Lynn married in a small, private ceremony at Ann and Bernard's home on MacGregor Way. Then, just as Oscar had with Bonnie, he took his new bride to the Orient, but this time the honeymoon also included a trip to Alaska to hunt polar bear.

When they returned, they moved into the house at Hewit Estates. Lynn's sons, eight-year-old Steven and six-year-old Douglas, meanwhile, continued to live with Ann and Bernard in Houston, where they were enrolled at St. John's private school. But Corpus Christi, to no one's surprise, would never become home to the former Lynn Sakowitz. She and Oscar began looking for a house in Houston, and just a few months after they married, they found one.

The house, at 1620 River Oaks Boulevard, was Houston's grandest mansion. Although it had stood vacant for almost a decade, the magnificent two-story art deco stone mansion, set on 3.8 lush acres next to the River Oaks Country Club, was the ultimate symbol of wealth in a city spouting oil riches. Not only was the home famous for its beauty, but also it was fabled because its previous owner was Hugh Roy Cullen, the king of Texas oilmen and one of the richest men in the world.

Cullen, a descendant of Texas patriots and grandson of the author of the law creating the Texas public school system, was a third-grade dropout. But he was daring and hardworking, and he had a nose for oil. A wildcatter who used "creekology" in hunting for oil — a combination of geology and witchcraft — Cullen was barely in his twenties before his Quintana oil company made him millions. He seemed just as relentless at giving away his money as he had been making it. He almost single-handedly endowed the University of Houston and many other of the city's nonprofit institutions. His charitable foundation is still today one of the most important benefactors in Houston.

In 1929, Cullen said that since he was a boy he had dreamed of one day building a great "white house," and that now — during the Great Depression, with so many people out of work — the time had come to begin it. He told his wife, Lillie, "Let's build a house and give some of them jobs." He insisted that the home's contractors pay top wages.

He hired a Houston architect, John Staub, who had built other great mansions, but this was the architect's finest. Staub situated the house on the lot so that it faced the country club and snubbed the boulevard. Of course, Staub had no way of knowing that the next couple after the Cullens to inhabit the grand home would be snubbed by the country club. The driveway entrance is to the east of the house; to the south is a long, sweeping lawn bordered by tall magnolia and oak trees; and to the west is a giant reflecting pool with an art deco fountain at each corner.

Inside, the home is like a nineteenth-century French château, with twenty-foot elaborately carved ceilings, tall windows, and tenfoot arched doorways. White and slate gray Italian marble, shot with veins of *rouge royale,* lines the foyer and gallery. One of the home's most magnificent features is its marble stairway, built in a graceful reverse-S curve and distinguished with a banister of pewter foliage and Steuben glass fleurs-de-lis. The domed ceiling over the stairwell is embossed with a bas-relief Greek key and palm design.

By the time it was completed in 1933, three years after construction began, Cullen had given work to hundreds of men and, in all, had spent $1.8 million on his dream home. This did not include the tens of thousands of dollars spent on landscaping the property, after sending a horticultural expert roaming through South Carolina, Alabama, and Louisiana to find azaleas, camellias, and rare shrubs.

In 1955, two years before Cullen's death, the family moved out of the house and into a smaller home.

The "white house" had an asking price of $650,000. Oscar snapped it up in November 1963, reportedly for $400,000, which was considered a steal even in 1963 dollars.

The ink on the new deed was barely dry before the *Houston Chronicle,* on December 15, 1963, ran a spread of photographs of the young Mrs. Wyatt in her new River Oaks home. Titled "Princess in a Palace," the *Chronicle* article provided one of the first glimpses into a life that would become among the most photographed in the world. There was Lynn, dressed elegantly in some of her ensembles from her second trousseau, leaning against a marble column in the empty, cavernous living room.

The fact that the *Chronicle*'s fashion editor spelled her name "Lynne" went unnoticed by most readers. It would be some years before she was known simply as "Lynn" and no one had to ask "Lynn who?"

The house at 1620 River Oaks Boulevard would have as much to do with defining Lynn Wyatt as anything else in her life. It was a long way from MacGregor Drive, where she grew up, and even farther from Oscar's boyhood home on Victoria Street in Navasota. Mr. and Mrs. Oscar Sherman Wyatt, Jr., had arrived.

The Wyatts did not explain why in due course they rather grandly began referring to their house as Allington, but history reveals that Allington Castle in Kent, a building of the late thirteenth century with Tudor additions, was the home of the poet Sir Thomas Wyatt (1503–1542).

Lynn wasted no time decorating the home. Soon after the article appeared in the *Chronicle,* she flew to Dallas to talk with society decorator John Astin Perkins. She took with her the photographs that had appeared in the paper. Perkins remembers that "she said Oscar had given her the house for a wedding gift, and when she said this, I said to her, 'Oh, how nice.'"

Perkins was ecstatic. "Doing this house was the ultimate job," he explains, "because it was a great house and it was empty. It had not a single stick of furniture in it."

Lynn was also the ultimate client. "She was very decisive," says Perkins. "She wanted me to work out three or four color schemes and three or four styles of furniture, and she would choose from that."

Perkins flew to New York and spent two weeks picking out everything from furniture and fabrics to works of art and ashtrays, from which Lynn would choose. Lynn took her mother with her to New York, and they checked into the Plaza Hotel. Every day, they would tour the showrooms of New York's best antiques dealers.

There were even private showings in private homes, and one wealthy New Yorker threw a cocktail party in her honor, in the hope of selling a major work. Lynn enjoyed the party, but the host did not make a sale.

Each evening Lynn and Ann Sakowitz turned in early at the Plaza, ordered their dinners sent to their suite, and reviewed the price lists of items they had seen that day.

To Perkins's amazement, Lynn "came to New York on a Monday and left on Friday and in those five days made all the selections for the house. This included the entire downstairs and the master bedroom."

Soon after that, enormous moving vans of furniture began arriving at the house in Houston. They contained ten mammoth chandeliers, all of them Steuben or Waterford glass, beautiful rugs made in Portugal, an enormous dining room suite with eighteen chairs, as well as various other chairs, desks, tables, and sofas.

The home's soaring marble columns and formal French furniture — Louis XV and Louis XVI signed pieces — combined with traditional draperies made it look more like a grand Parisian *hôtel de ville* or the lobby of Paris's Hôtel de Crillon than a new-rich oilman's home in Houston, Texas.

Basking in Lynn's new reflected glory, Ann Sakowitz was given to bragging, "Oh, what Lynn has done for Oscar." But whenever she said this within Bernard's earshot, he snapped, "It's Oscar's money that's done for Lynn."

Allington fit Lynn like a beautiful Chanel suit. In the grand, new home, she seemed for the first time entirely comfortable, at ease with herself — as the French say, *bien dans sa peau.* She was indeed like a princess in her palace. And if Lynn was a princess, her two sons, Steven and Douglas, were little princes. Soft-spoken, well-mannered, and perfectly groomed, they were almost too polite and grown-up to be real. Margaret Sackton Rosan, Lynn's first cousin, recalls playing with Steve and Douglas when they were children. "They were like little movie star kids," says Margaret, who was six years older than Steve. "They were very, very well behaved and very controlled. They knew how to act when they were about six and seven years old. And they were always dressed handsomely, in little sport coats and ties."

Oscar, friends say, adored the two boys, and not long after Lynn and Oscar married, he adopted them. They had not seen or heard from their real father in years.

But the image of elegance and refinement that Lynn and her sons projected may have been masking something dark and sinister. Barely had the Wyatts moved into the house before a terrible rumor began to make the rounds in Houston society. Among the rumor's varying versions was that Oscar, having fathered a child with Lynn in 1964, Oscar S. Wyatt III, had a vasectomy, after which Lynn became pregnant. According to the story, when Lynn told Oscar she was pregnant again, he knocked her down the winding marble staircase at Allington. Not long after that, the story goes, Oscar went to his doctor and learned that the vasectomy had not been successful. Their second child, Bradford, born in 1965, was given the middle name Allington.

Whether any or all of the rumor is true is unknown, but Oscar, in an April 1991 *Texas Monthly* cover story, said it is his favorite rumor about himself. "Years ago, there was a story making the rounds that I threw Lynn down the stairs when she was seven months pregnant," he told *Texas Monthly*. "Can you imagine anything more ridiculous? For one thing, just think how expensive that would have been."

What Oscar meant when he made this cruel joke is unknown. Was the expense he was referring to the medical cost? Did he mean it might have led to a divorce action which, in Texas, meant giving up half his fortune to his wife? Or did it mean, as was then rumored, that it might cost him his life because his father-in-law had allegedly told him, "If you ever touch Lynn again I'll kill you"? The story about Oscar pushing Lynn down the stairs began on the Bluebird Floor at Houston's Methodist Hospital. The Bluebird organization is a prestigious group of five hundred Houston society women who volunteer their time to various charitable organizations. A Bluebird member says she remembers being at the hospital when Lynn was on the floor.

"She was in the hospital under an assumed name," says the Bluebird worker. "All the Bluebirds were talking about the fact that she was very badly bruised and she was in there healing. One day, Bernard came to see her. I didn't see him there with my own eyes, but I was volunteering on the floor and everyone was talking about it."

Robert Sakowitz says that if this event did happen, he has no knowledge of it. "From what I understand, he had hit his previous wives, and I thought that there was maybe one situation [with Lynn], but I don't want to pass it on since I have no fact."

Enough people have witnessed Oscar's treatment of his wives to keep the rumors alive. Dallas oilman Tom Marsh recalls an incident during a party at Tom's mother's house in Amarillo in the mid-1960s when it seemed that Oscar might hurt Lynn physically.

"When Sakowitz opened a store in Amarillo, my mother had a party for the family to welcome them to Amarillo," says Marsh. "During the party, Oscar started really cutting down Lynn, and finally he said to her, 'Come on out to the guest house and let's finish this.'"

Marsh says everyone standing around at the party assumed Oscar ordered her outside to do more than abuse her verbally. "She went with him," says Marsh. "But after they were out there a few minutes my mother went out there and said, 'Now Oscar, in our home, men do not treat their wives cruelly. Now you just go on right back inside and join the rest of the party.' He did, and that was that."

The various tales of Oscar's abuse of his wives allow amateur psychologists to make what connection they will with Oscar's father's abuse of his mother that regularly drove the boy to leave home in the middle of the night.

Robert Lipman had disappeared from Lynn's field of vision, but his reputation from coast to coast and in Europe was notorious. After Miami, Lipman moved to Beverly Hills, where he took a large apartment and hung out at the Polo Lounge in the Beverly Hills Hotel. "Lipman made Errol Flynn [the late Priapian movie star] look like a priest," says Lipman's friend Donald Waugh. "There wasn't a wilder guy anywhere than Bob."

What shocked friends and strangers most about Lipman, then a virile thirty-year-old, was not that he graphically propositioned married women moments after meeting them at parties, or even that he liked to have sex with Palm Beach's old grandes dames — very rich, prominent widows in their sixties and seventies. What most shocked was his enthusiastic exhibitionism.

"He had an abnormally large private and he would unzip his pants at a party and stick it in a girl's martini," says Waugh. "He whipped it out in the Polo Lounge in California and at Annabel's in London. We'd be at a party and I would turn around and see him, and they'd scream, holler, and yell, 'He's doin' it again.'"

Writer Philip Van Rensselaer, who met Robert a decade later, also recalls, "He loved to mention his penis, which he said was the biggest in the world."

Robert may have been bragging, but he was hardly exaggerating, a fact Van Rensselaer discovered when Lipman unzipped his pants and exposed himself at a dinner party. "It was this huge sculpted thing. It was like an elephant's trunk. It was unbelievable," marvels Van Rensselaer.

By 1964, Lipman's partying canvas had expanded to include Europe. "He'd be in Stockholm, then Hamburg, then London," says Waugh. "He was a star in Copenhagen. They were very free-thinking and they adored him."

Lipman was a frequent houseguest at homes Waugh rented around the world, including a house at Marbella. One afternoon, as friends gathered for drinks on the terrace of the Marbella house which overlooked a swimming pool, Lipman and the "three-hundred-pound daughter of an ambassador" got in the swimming pool. While the house party shouted and applauded from the terrace, Lipman and the woman had intercourse. "It was like two killer whales going at it in the shallow end of the pool," remembers Waugh.

By the mid-1960s, however, his antics were becoming less amusing even to his hard-core partying buddies. In Europe, he began experimenting with marijuana and harder drugs, which he abused just as he had alcohol. "He was one partying fool. If he wasn't drunk or stoned," says Waugh, "he was asleep."

He rarely spoke of Lynn and his sons, but friends say he missed them. Wherever he was, he had with him photographs of Lynn and the boys, and he usually put them on the nightstand by his bed.

During the summer of 1967, Waugh had taken a house in Málaga, and Lipman came to stay with him. One night in a bar in Málaga, when Lipman was very stoned, he stumbled over to Waugh and hit him for no reason. "He was wild, crazy, out of his mind," says Waugh. "I picked up a chair and knocked him out. Then a couple guys helped me carry him home."

Waugh says he took care of Lipman for a couple of days, then told him to leave. "You gotta get help," Waugh said. Robert agreed and packed his bags. But he did not get help. When Waugh took him to the airport in Málaga, he caught a plane for Rome, looking for the next party. In Rome, he bought Jean Paul Getty, Jr.'s white Rolls-Royce, partied there for two or three weeks, and then headed for London.

8

T HE EARLY 1960s were a wild, flamboyant time in Houston. The city's population was growing at a rate of 50,000 to 70,000 a year and had long since outdistanced its two Texas rivals, Dallas and San Antonio. When "M-Day," the day Houston's population reached one million, finally arrived on July 3, 1954, citizens sported bumper stickers announcing "I'm One in a Million — Houston" and celebrated so wildly that the *Houston Press* declared with typical Texas hyperbole, "This is a bigger story than D-Day."

The early sixties were one of America's optimistic periods, when the horrors of World War II were in the past and the hopefulness inherent in youth magically infected the whole population. Life with Father Eisenhower, peaceful and pleasant as it had been, was over, and young Jack and Jacqueline Kennedy were leading the new dance. They were rich and stylish, and the future would be Camelot, which in Texas translated into megarich and lots of jewelry. Texans were buying big cars, building big houses, hiring bigtime decorators, and they were convinced that profits could only get bigger.

Amid this local and national boom, Bernard wanted to expand his company to include a number of new stores beyond Houston, and he wanted to do so rapidly. He began to imagine Sakowitz as a regional, perhaps even national, chain. But he also wanted the company to remain privately held and family-owned. To that end, Sakowitz had for years not paid stock dividends and had been accumulating profits.

According to Robert, talk of a buy-out began when Simon Sakowitz's side asked that the company start paying dividends on its stock. Because Simon's son-in-law, Gaylord Johnson, Sr., had earlier left the store, Simon and his grandson, Gaylord "Gee" Johnson, Jr., were the only members of his side of the family drawing income from the company.

Robert recalls, "Our side said we needed to keep every cent of the company in the company, so they said, 'Buy us out.'"

After nearly two years of negotiations, Tobias and Bernard agreed to pay close to $4 million for the stock of Simon and his heirs. The sum was to be paid over a twenty-year period at 4.5 percent interest. The name Sakowitz Bros. was changed to Sakowitz.

Bernard had for years contemplated the day when he would be fully in charge. But it was a bitter finale for Simon and his children and grandchildren. The buy-out occurred on New Year's Eve, 1964, in the downtown office of the accountant who represented the store.

"The buy-out was eerie. I had a kinda sickening feeling in my gut," recalls "Gee" Johnson, Simon's only grandson. "I'd been involved in the store since I was born. I'd spent my time working summers and Christmases. I had been through Bloomingdale's training program, and I had been told all those years that Robert and I were going to run the store."

At the time of the buy-out, Gee was working in the boys' department, and although he was allowed to stay on, Simon tried to warn his grandson that he had no future at Sakowitz. Gee also recalls that Simon was convinced that the store would not survive under Bernard and Robert. "When we sold out with the twenty-year payout plan," says Gee, "Simon said to me, 'I think you're going to be lucky if you get your money. I don't think they'll make it that long.' Those were his exact words."

The payout was to end in 1984. Simon's heirs did get their money — but just barely. Sakowitz filed for bankruptcy in 1985, just one year after the last payment was made.

Simon stayed on after the buy-out, but he was deeply hurt and humiliated in the last years of his life. "After Simon's side sold out," says Bernard's brother, Alex Sackton, "Bernard insisted that Simon not be paid a salary, so he worked with no salary at all, no pay whatsoever, for the last five or six years of his life. It was a terrible thing for my Uncle Simon."

After the buy-out, Simon was also excluded from any part of the decision-making process. "He was like a fish out of water," recalls Gee Johnson. "He was really hurt by that."

Simon died on December 30, 1967, just two days shy of

his adopted eighty-fourth birthday. An editorial in the *Houston Chronicle* lauded him as a "generous, selfless man whose long life was one of spectacular achievement." Lest anyone confuse which Sakowitz he was, the editorial said, "Simon was the tallish, slender, reflective brother who talked slowly." Ah, yes, readers could say, the one who stood at the door and greeted customers.

Tobias, at the time of his brother's death, was in poor health and bedridden. With Simon's death and Simon's heirs out of the way, the only person blocking Bernard's way of absolute ownership was his brother, Alex. Like Simon, Alex had begun urging Bernard to pay shareholder dividends. Now that it was his own son making the requests, Tobias told Bernard that the store could afford to pay dividends and should. Tobias thought it unfair that Alex and his family received none of the fruits of the company. But Bernard again insisted that all monies derived from Sakowitz be plowed into the future expansion program.

When Robert joined the store full-time in May 1962, it was not without having considered other careers. During college, he had spent a summer in Hollywood, working at Paramount Studios. For a while, it looked as though Texas might lose him to Hollywood. He even became a blond that summer, but he decided against an acting career.

After graduating cum laude from Harvard in 1960, he had gone to Paris, lived on the Left Bank, and considered a career in banking, but he ended up at the great Paris department store Galeries Lafayette, where he made the decision that retailing was the best career for a Renaissance man.

"Retail," he says, "was the only business that covered every field I was interested in — finance and economics, art and architecture, advertising, promotion, theater, administration, personnel, psychology, philosophy."

After serving the mandatory retail terms in Bloomingdale's and Macy's training programs in New York, Robert got a call from his father. The store's Young Houstonian Shop was in trouble. It was time for Robert to come home.

At the store, he immediately earned his reputation as a maverick. Instead of the usual conservative styles, Robert bought radically fashion-forward clothes, and Houston responded favorably. In his first year, by his own report, he increased the department's sales 57 percent.

But Robert was not content simply to buy for the Young

Houstonian — he already had much bigger plans. Neiman-Marcus's Fortnight celebrations had become famous around the world. These were important storewide promotions of merchandise which each year featured the fashions, arts, and foods of a different country. They became a showcase for Stanley Marcus's taste and his brilliant flair for publicity. Robert and Bernard saw no reason why Sakowitz could not stage its own version of a Fortnight, which Sakowitz would call a Festival. One of the most memorable was the British Festival in 1964. Robert and his parents traveled to London to collect merchandise for the Festival, and while they were there, the press followed everywhere they went — from Claridge's, where they lunched with Richard Burbridge, the head of Harrods, to a visit to Woburn Abbey, the ancestral home of Robert's Harvard friend Robin Tavistock, the Duke of Bedford's son.

To entertain at the Festival's opening-night party, Robert decided to bring in a British rock group recommended by an associate; the band was unknown in America. But after figuring the cost of paying the band's fee and booking a hall — $25,000 — Robert instead opted to invest the money in more inventory. Five months later, the group appeared on the *Ed Sullivan Show*. The band Robert had decided not to introduce to America was the Beatles.

The Fab Four aside, he brought to Houston much that was hip among the young, and his own lifestyle set an example. The walls of his apartment were covered with contemporary art, a collection he described as "early polyglot." While his friends from St. John's continued to dress as they had in school — uniform khakis and white cotton shirts — Robert dressed as the evolving rock generation did on London's Carnaby Street, in mod bell-bottoms and flowered silk shirts. Suddenly, what Robert wore became the standard for what was "in" in Houston.

In 1967, the *Houston Chronicle* named him one of the city's most eligible bachelors. In an article titled "Variety — That's What Bob Likes" the *Chronicle* described him as a man of varied interests and discriminating tastes. "Girls who know their Beaujolais from their Chateauneuf du Pape," the article explained, "are likely to find a meeting of the minds with Bachelor Sakowitz."

Some readers who read that green was his favorite color "because it's so soothing" also noticed that it was not long before Sakowitz's gift boxes changed from gray-and-white pinstripe with a red border to what became known in Houston as "Sakowitz green."

In 1968, Boaz Mazor was a twenty-six-year-old Israeli who had just arrived in New York from Paris to sell high-fashion merchandise for a new and virtually unknown Spanish designer named Oscar de la Renta. During Boaz's first year at Oscar de la Renta, he met the young merchant prince from Houston, who had come to the showroom to buy.

"Bobby was so attractive. God, he was the sexiest thing in the world," gasps Mazor. "He had those teeth and that smile that made you melt. He was so dashing. Bobby was the ideal of everything the American male from Texas looked like."

Mazor remembered that Robert wore an elegant pin-striped suit with cowboy boots. But it was not just the cowboy boots that gave Robert a Texas aura. "He acted so cool. He had an aura that said, 'Here we are from Texas. Texas is a big state, the richest state in the nation and we're coming and buying your line.'"

When Robert worked for Galeries Lafayette in Paris, he decided that the big French designers were the giants of the future, but to date they were not exporting their prêt-à-porter clothes to America. The French designers showed handmade ("couture") models of their clothes, and American stores sent buyers to Europe to buy the models they then had copied in America. Sakowitz wanted to be the first store in America to import French prêt-à-porter.

In 1968, Robert pulled what may have been the biggest coup of his retail career. It happened when he was only twenty-nine, and it defined his career in a way that nothing else would again. When Robert learned that André Courrèges, the iconoclastic French designer famous for introducing the miniskirt, was going to make ready-to-wear clothes, he flew to France and convinced Courrèges to introduce the clothes in Houston.

When Bonwit Teller's president, Mildred Custin, learned about Sakowitz's deal with Courrèges, she hopped a plane herself to meet with the French designer. According to Robert, she promised Courrèges an order five times the size of Sakowitz's if he would debut his collection at Bonwit's.

"He didn't want me to know about it," Robert told a reporter. "I got back on an airplane, and I said, 'André, wait just a minute. We've got a handshake deal. No contract, that's true, but we've got a deal that we'd launch it in Sakowitz Houston, Space City USA, because it ties in with the couture of the future. You agreed to that, you're a Basque! You're the closest thing to Texan in Europe, your word is your bond! Just give us ten days to three weeks to launch it first. New York won't even know it, nothing happens outside of New York according to a New Yorker. I won't even make a blip!'"

The delivery arrived as promised, but contrary to his word, Sakowitz made more than a blip. Robert ran a half-page ad in the *New York Times* announcing the arrival of Courrèges fashions in Houston. Orders came in from around the country, and the Courrèges coup turned into a major story. It landed Sakowitz, for the first time, on the international fashion map. Robert had the keen insight to go after Courrèges, but also he had shown an extraordinary gift for persuasion. He was able to hold onto Courrèges when a larger and more famous store than Sakowitz tried to snatch him away. He then had the shrewdness to put large dollars behind his accomplishment and make it known to the world. There was probably not a retailer in America who did not learn then and there about the young merchant from Houston who had landed one of the hottest young designers in the world. Robert's reputation soared along with Courrèges's.

And Robert was just getting started. When Yves Saint Laurent, the biggest name in fashion, announced that he planned to introduce his prêt-à-porter in the United States later that same year, Robert again got on a plane for Europe, offering to help Saint Laurent with logistics. He wound up with the exclusive rights to YSL in Texas. This meant that not only did he have YSL exclusively in Houston, he also owned YSL in Dallas (where he then built a free-standing YSL boutique), which, from Robert's perspective, may have meant more even than the Courrèges coup. To beat Neiman-Marcus on its own turf, well, there was no sweeter success for Robert Sakowitz.

"Saint Laurent was really *the* top French couturier the year that Sakowitz locked him up," says Richard Marcus, who was soon to become president of Neiman-Marcus. "We were chagrined that we couldn't get Saint Laurent — for whatever reasons, whether we wanted it or we just didn't want him to have it."

At that time, Neiman-Marcus was unwilling to build separate boutiques for designers in its stores, which is what Saint Laurent demanded. In contrast, Robert demonstrated just how willing he was to bow to the designer by building a very high-tech, very expensive glass-enclosed Saint Laurent boutique in the downtown store. Although many retailers at first scoffed at such promotion of designers — even Sakowitz itself had long refused to use designers' names in promotional ways in the store — Robert's innovation with Saint Laurent was soon widely copied at the best stores across America.

Even at its most competitive, the retail world was still a fairly small and friendly fraternity in the 1960s. It was almost unthinkable for the dominant retail family in a town not to welcome a newcomer. But when the Marcus family from Dallas opened a store right across the street from Sakowitz's Post Oak store in 1965, no welcome was forthcoming.

"They very, very deeply resented the fact we moved to Houston," says Stanley's brother Lawrence Marcus, who was put in charge of the Houston store. "They felt we were horning in on their territory."

Every year, the three most prestigious awards in the American fashion industry were those presented by the fashion consultant Tobé, by the cosmetics firm Coty, and by Neiman-Marcus. In 1969, Neiman's decided to present its awards in Houston, at a show-stopping, black-tie event at the Contemporary Arts Museum. Jean Muir and Missoni were among the designers honored that year. As was always the case, the national fashion media boarded planes for Texas and turned out in full force to cover the event. In a classic example of retailing one-upmanship, the day of the Neiman's award, Sakowitz filled its windows with designs by none other than Jean Muir and Missoni.

Bernard and Robert and Ann had long since become obsessed with the competition posed by Neiman-Marcus. "They talked about Neiman's constantly," says family retainer Val Renken. "I remember Ann saying all the time, 'If Neiman's had Bob running their store, they'd steamroll us.'"

Sakowitz Bros. was five years old in 1907, when Al Neiman and his business partner, Herbert Marcus, Sr., opened a store in the dusty town of Dallas. Like Sakowitz, Neiman's sold expensive merchandise from the start, but while Sakowitz was a men's store, Neiman-Marcus was a high-fashion women's store. Soon after Herbert Marcus's eldest son, Stanley, joined the business in the 1930s, it gained a national — and then international — reputation as one of the leading purveyors of high-fashion merchandise and impeccable service in the world. No American merchant before or since has had Stanley's publicity and merchandising genius.

But like so many merchant families in the 1950s and 1960s,

the Marcuses became fearful that with a death in the family, the government would step in and make an arbitrary valuation of the common stock for inheritance tax purposes. To guard against this possibility, Neiman-Marcus took some of its stock public in 1954. Although the Marcus family retained majority ownership, says Richard Marcus, "there was still the ever-increasing possibility that someone would acquire not a controlling interest but a significant interest to make a difference in how the business was run."

After watching Saks Fifth Avenue expand nationally during the 1960s, Neiman's wanted to do the same. But to do so, Neiman's needed a major infusion of capital. The only way to accomplish this was by selling out to a major company. So in 1969, Neiman-Marcus sold to Carter Hawley Hale, a large chain of stores. This was not an unusual scenario but one that was played out at family-owned stores across America.

In addition to the need for a public market for shares (to pay inheritance taxes), in many cases there were not enough prestigious jobs for the growing number of heirs, or enough profits for many heirs who wanted careers and lives away from the store but wanted income from their shares in the store. As a result, in the two decades following World War II, virtually every important store in America was sold to a chain.

That the Sakowitzes thought they could do what Stanley Marcus in Dallas, the Riches in Atlanta, and the Goldwaters in Phoenix could not do said much about the Sakowitzes. But as fewer and fewer stores remained family owned, instead of worrying why all these store owners were out of step with him, Robert became more and more proud that his store differed from all the others.

When bachelor Bob turned thirty in 1968, he had already made his mark in Houston social circles and, as a result of his Courrèges coup, he had made more than a blip in retail circles. But in terms of recognition for himself, nothing he had done at Harvard or at the store could even begin to garner the amount of publicity he was about to receive.

The fact that Houston's society writers were scooped on the news by *New York Daily News* gossip columnist "Suzy" was an indication of just how big a story this was. On November 27, 1968, in "Suzy's" column appeared the news that wealthy New York debutante Pamela Zauderer was engaged to marry Texan Robert Sakowitz.

Just as Oscar would be instrumental in Lynn's becoming an international celebrity, Pam transformed Robert from a prominent actor on the local stage to a national star.

Pam was the younger daughter of George Zauderer, a very wealthy New York real estate investor, and his wife, Audrey, a fixture on New York's society pages. Pamela's only sibling, Cheray (pronounced "Cherry"), was four years older and had recently married pianist and socialite Peter Duchin.

The Zauderers lived in a lavishly decorated apartment at 911 Park Avenue and spent weekends at a sprawling country estate, Apple Blossom Farm, at Mt. Kisco, New York.

Pam's childhood was even more privileged than Robert Sakowitz's. She was surrounded by servants at home. At school, Brearley, she was surrounded by the daughters of other rich New Yorkers. When Audrey and George Zauderer traveled to Europe and Africa, they often took their daughters.

The family was Jewish, but "not very religous," says Pam. "We didn't know a rabbi."

One of the rites of passage for Pam's set came in 1962 when she was presented at New York's International Debutante Society. With thick, dark hair, large brown eyes, soft, pale skin, and a rosebud smile, Pam was the prettiest debutante in *Town & Country*'s June debutante issue.

News of her coming-out ball under a big tent at Mt. Kisco filled New York's society pages: "Some 700 guests savored a connoisseur's dream of a dinner. Salmon in aspic, capon in raisin sauce and all the trimmings. Lester Lanin and his Merrymen played, down by the lighted pool, where letters five feet high spelled Pamela," wrote the *New York World Telegram & Sun*. "Gorgeous, dark-eyed Pam was having just about the biggest coming out party we had ever seen."

The fact that Audrey Zauderer had cultivated the leading society columnists of New York — including Eugenia Sheppard, who was a frequent guest at Apple Blossom Farm — contributed to the amount of ink devoted to young Pamela. At the time of her debut, Pam was already part of Cholly Knickerbocker's "Smart Set."

"Mr. Zauderer had made a great deal of money, and Mrs. Zauderer tried very hard to get those two girls into society," says a friend who knew the family well. "Mrs. Zauderer tried to get her point across that they are not going to be just another Jewish family but that they are going to be a major society family."

After graduating from Briarcliff College, Pam enrolled at New York's Institute of Fine Arts and the National Academy of Art, hoping to become an artist. Instead, she found her niche in fashion and public relations, both of which seemed suited for the beautiful young lady with a model's figure and a natural flair in front of the camera.

The Zauderers' good friend Charles Revson offered Pam a job in Revlon's publicity department, but she turned it down to take a job with a new and avant-garde fashion shop, Paraphernalia. As PR director for Paraphernalia, Pam worked with the fashion editors of *Vogue, Mademoiselle, Glamour*, and *Harper's Bazaar*.

Pam shared an apartment with Houston heiress Coco Blaffer, of the Standard Oil millions, who recalls, "Pam had four double closets filled with ball gowns. She was definitely the prettiest girl around, with all her clothes."

In 1967, *Women's Wear Daily* ran on its cover large photographs of Pam, Charlotte Ford, Mrs. William Hutton, and Natalie Cushing, under a bold heading: "These are some of the prettiest girls in New York. They started the Pucci Gucci syndrome."

By the time Robert was introduced to Pam on the dance floor at Manhattan's fashionable Le Club, she had become one of the most photographed young women in America. "I think Bobby was attracted to the publicity, the fact that I had gotten so much press," says Pam.

Soon after the introduction at Le Club, Coco Blaffer invited Pam to Houston for a weekend, and while they were there, they went to a party at Allington. Lynn was in her thirties and had four children; Pam was only twenty-one and barely out of college; but the two women immediately hit it off. Lynn was very impressed with the rich New York debutante whom she was reading so much about in the press. Pam was impressed too, standing in the Wyatts' kitchen: "I opened this gigantic refrigerator door and there was a solid wall of champagne bottles."

At the party, Lynn asked Pam, "Would you mind if I had my brother call you? He's in New York on business."

Pam smiled and said she would be delighted to have him call, but when she told Coco Blaffer what Lynn had said, Coco discouraged the idea of a date with Bobby Sakowitz, whom Coco had grown up with. "I said, 'I don't think you're going to like him,'" Coco recalls. "He was spoiled, and he thought he was fabulous because he went to Harvard."

Pam went anyway, and by the end of the date, she was sorry she had. "We argued through dinner and at the end of the evening, when I was closing the door, I said, 'You're the most opinionated son-of-a-bitch I've ever met.'"

They did not see each other for nearly a year, but somehow he convinced her to see him again, and in early 1968 they began dating seriously. In October of that year, Pam received the ultimate publicity when *Time* ran a full-page color photograph of her with the cutline "Dashing as no squaw ever was, Pam Zauderer dances at one of Manhattan's newest discotheques, Nepentha, in a costume inspired by American Indian styles."

A month after the *Time* photograph appeared, Robert took Pam to a Harvard-Yale football game. While they were sitting up high in the stadium, Robert handed Pam a box of Cracker Jack. A Cracker Jack addict, she began eating happily, and soon she came across the surprise, a ring. But she noticed that it was not a plastic code ring; it was a seven-carat emerald-cut diamond engagement ring. Robert proved that he too had a knack for publicity. Together, they were a publicist's dream. Long after their divorce, Robert Sakowitz said Pam "was the girl I was *supposed* to marry," meaning the right sort.

According to family retainer Val Renken, Robert's ambitious mother wanted the marriage. "At an anniversary party for Ann and Bernard," says Renken, "Pam was there, and Ann whispered to me about her, 'Oh, my God, she's a madonna, she's a saint.'"

After their engagement was announced, Robert went to the store and picked out their china and silver patterns. One of the china patterns he selected was Rothschild Birds by Herend. Pam then joined him in the department, saw what he had chosen, and said, "Bobby, if you think I'm going to eat off those fucking birds you've got another thing coming."

As the Christmas holidays approached, Robert and Pam rushed around New York making wedding plans and attending parties in their honor. One of their first stops to announce their engagement was the showroom of Oscar de la Renta. When Robert and Pam broke the news, de la Renta was thrilled. Mrs. Zauderer and her two daughters were among the designer's most important clients. Instead of buying through stores, they placed orders for thousands of dollars' worth of suits and dresses directly with him at wholesale prices. In addition, de la Renta was a major supplier to Sakowitz. In Oscar's eyes it must have seemed a marriage made on Seventh Avenue.

For a wedding gift, de la Renta gave Pam the original sample of a pair of black gauze harem pants embroidered with gold stones and pearls. The pants, which cost $6,000, were part of the collection that had won him the 1968 Coty Award. Top model Lauren Hutton had been photographed in the pants in *Vogue*, and now Pam would be too. Not long after de la Renta made the gift, the Italian designer Valentino gave a party at New York's Pierre Hotel and turned the ballroom into a tent. Robert and Pam attended the party, and she wore the pants. Naturally, she was photographed, and her picture appeared in several of the next day's society columns.

Pam and Robert's upcoming nuptials were all the talk in New York. "I won't be going in person," one invited guest joked. "I'm going to stay home and watch it on television." But the wedding was becoming an ordeal for both the Sakowitzes and the Zauderers. First, there was the problem of the rabbi. The Sakowitzes offered to send their own from Houston, but there was no suggestion that they would ship him with the 10,000 yellow roses they were having flown in from Texas at a cost of $8,000.

Robert flew to New York and accidently left his cutaway in Houston. Bernard said he would bring it with him when he and Ann came the next day, but amid all the excitement, Bernard boarded a plane leaving his own tuxedo in Houston. A few hours before the rehearsal dinner, the president of Sakowitz, who owned all those suits in all those stores, had to rent a tux.

If the Sakowitzes were flustered by the wedding ordeal and ill at ease among their son's more social and much wealthier in-laws, they hid their feelings well. The rehearsal dinner was held in the elegant Crystal Room of the Delmonico Hotel on a cold, rainy, January night, but inside the room glowed with warmth. Strolling musicians opened the festivities with "The Eyes of Texas," and Peter Duchin, Robert's soon-to-be brother-in-law, began his toast to Robert, "Oh, serene cowboy . . ." which brought down the house.

Lynn stood up and tearfully toasted Robert and Pam, declaring, in her perfect Texas accent, "I just love my little brother."

The wedding was receiving so much publicity that friends were competing to give big gifts that would be reported in the press. Charles Revson gave the bride and groom a cruise through the

Mediterranean on the twenty-one-crew-member Revson yacht, the *Ultima II.*

On Thursday, January 30, 1969, after a ceremony at the Zauderers' Park Avenue apartment, where a string quartet from the New York Philharmonic played the wedding music, the party scurried down to the roof of the St. Regis Hotel on Fifth Avenue to a reception for seven hundred guests that included a six-tier wedding cake with a cowboy and cowgirl on top.

The party was covered extensively in a half-page story in the *New York Times:* "Miss Pamela Georgea Zauderer, one of the more glamorous rich girls about town, was married yesterday to Robert T. Sakowitz of Houston in what was probably one of the most spectacular nuptial events in Manhattan in some time."

In the many news stories about the wedding, Lynn was given just a passing mention. In those days in New York, she was only "the groom's sister." But Pam's high profile did not escape Lynn's or Oscar's notice any more than it did Robert's. "We're not like you people," Oscar said bluntly to Audrey Zauderer, the mother of the bride. "We don't get our picture in the paper."

With Pam and Robert the darlings of the fashion world, Lynn may have felt unimportant by comparison. But on one of Robert and Pam's first Christmases together, Lynn had her own excitement, and all of Bobby and Pam's press could not diminish it. It happened during Christmas lunch at Allington.

Tobias and Ruth, Bernard and Ann, and Robert and Pam had gone to the house on Christmas Day to open gifts. The four young Wyatt boys had already opened their gifts and were running around the house playing with them. But Lynn had received nothing from Oscar.

She explained later, "Everyone had opened their gifts, and we were ready to go in for our big Christmas brunch, so I thought, well, maybe I was a bad girl and wasn't going to get anything from my husband. All of a sudden, Oscar said, 'Well, aren't you going to open your present?' And I said, 'What present?' He pointed way up to the top of the tree, which went all the way to the ceiling, to an envelope that was perched there. I couldn't imagine what it could be. I said, 'I can't even reach it.' We had to send for a ladder, and it got to be a big thing, with all the family standing around. I opened up the envelope, and there was the deed to this beautiful house, with a divine love note attached and a P.S. that said, 'and the taxes have been paid.'"

Some years earlier, Lynn had told her Dallas decorator that the house was a wedding gift from Oscar, and some years later, in a lawsuit over ad valorem taxes, both Lynn's and Oscar's names appear as its owners. But by then both of them had become far too expert at getting publicity to let the truth stand in the way of a good story.

Tobias Sakowitz had been in failing health since 1965, and by the end of the decade, he had stopped going to work. He rarely even left his apartment.

Bernard and Ann dutifully visited Tobias, but the visits were often stilted, says Alex Sackton. "Ruth used to say, 'When Bernard comes he doesn't have that much to say to his dad, but when Bobby comes they just talk endlessly and with a great deal of interest.'

"My father thought the world of Bobby," continues Alex. "Bobby was very personable and articulate, and he impressed my father with his knowledge. He was much quicker in picking up on things than my brother, Bernard. I think my father was very comfortable with the idea of the store someday in Bobby's hands."

One hot July day in 1970, an ambulance pulled up to the side entrance of the Post Oak store. Two nurses and two orderlies climbed out and wheeled a hospital bed into the store. Lying very still in the bed with his head propped up on pillows and a sheet pulled up to his neck was tiny, frail Tobias Sakowitz. As one orderly pushed and another pulled, a nurse walked along on either side of the bed pulling an IV, from which a tube went into each of Tobias's arms.

In this manner, the eighty-eight-year-old surviving founder of Sakowitz toured his store one last time. He was very weak, but he managed to utter hello to the longtime salespeople who rushed over to greet him. Occasionally, he asked, "How's business?" or, pointing to a piece of merchandise, "Is dat selling?"

After an hour or so, his bed was lifted back into the ambulance, and the ambulance pulled away. Tobias died six weeks later, on September 24, 1970.

His death occurred the day before the first Saturday of Sakowitz's annual Dividend Days sale, always the store's second-biggest volume day of the year; only the day after Thanksgiving was bigger. On that Saturday, the family ran an advertisement in Houston's newspapers stating that in tribute to Tobias the store would be closed that day. It was a move that might not have pleased the deceased.

"Mr. Tobias would have been moved by the gesture to close the store, but he was a merchant who was all business," an employee said wistfully. "He probably would have died a second time had he known we closed the store on the second-biggest volume day of the year."

9

NO MURDER could have appeared more commonplace and insignificant. On Tuesday, September 19, 1967, the dead body of an unknown teenage girl was discovered by her landlord in her tiny, third-floor, eight-pound-a-week studio apartment at 17 Walpole Street in Chelsea, London.

But by the next day, London's newspapers had begun building up excitement about the murder. The victim was "a French girl, aged 18, blonde, slim and attractive . . . believed to have been sexually assaulted," hypothesized the *Daily Telegraph.*

"Bundles of love letters were discovered near her half-naked body . . . sprawled across a divan wearing only a pyjama top," the *Daily Mirror* screamed.

The most complete story that day, with a sexy picture to feed its readers' appetites, appeared in the *Evening Standard.* It identified the victim as Claudie Danielle Delbarre, who made her living as a bar hostess but "is also believed to have worked as a model."

In London, as in New York, Los Angeles, and Texas, the line between "model" or "starlet" and prostitute has never been immutably etched in stone. No matter how her friends described her, police detectives believed Claudie's main profession was prostitution, a conclusion indicated in part by the two brown diaries filled with names of male friends.

The next edition of the *Evening Standard* brayed, DIARIES MAY NAME GIRL'S KILLER.

The public's interest in the life of a girl like Claudie Delbarre is often minimal compared to the public's hope in these cases that famous names will be "outed." The ideal such outing had occurred only four years earlier, in 1963, when a London prostitute,

Christine Keeler, had revealed that she was sleeping with both John Profumo, the Secretary for War in Prime Minister Harold Macmillan's government, and with a Soviet Embassy naval attaché. The front-page, worldwide scandal, so erotically prolonged in the press, finally precipitated the fall of the Tory government.

Now again in London, readers wondered what names and telephone numbers of high government officials, members of the nobility, royalty, and the church, movie stars, and millionaires might be revealed by Claudie's two brown diaries.

The suspense reached its height when the *Evening Standard* revealed, "The names of nine London businessmen — some of them wealthy and all in high salaried jobs are among the scores of names in the two brown books."

But while some 70 police officers would interview more than 250 men and women in two days, no serious leads were revealed to the press.

How she was murdered was no less chilling than the why or the who. A postmortem examination determined that she had a cerebral hemorrhage as a result of blows to the head but that the cause of death was suffocation. A blue bedsheet had been rammed down her throat.

It was the kind of titillating murder that Fleet Street loved. But stories in the press virtually ceased on September 24, when London's Press Association sent a private, confidential, and not-for-publication memorandum to editors at the request of Scotland Yard: "The commissioner understands that the press has the name, nationality and description of a man whom the police wish to interview in connection with their inquiries into the death of Miss Claudie Danielle Delbarre. The commissioner would be grateful if editors would refrain from publishing these particulars as publication would seriously interfere with the investigation."

The following day, a second secret memorandum asked editors to refrain from revealing that "the man whom we wish to interview is out of the country."

But, of course, there were leaks. On Friday, the thirteenth of October, the *Daily Express* revealed that the man sought by Scotland Yard for the murder had been traced by the FBI to a psychiatric hospital in the United States, but no name was given. A month later, on November 11, the *Daily Telegraph* revealed that the man was undergoing psychiatric treatment in a private psychiatric hospital outside New York and that he was the son of a wealthy New York businessman. But still no name was given.

Finally, on March 8, 1968, almost six months after the murder, the accused man was arrested in Hartford, Connecticut, at the Institute of Living, a $1,200-a-day psychiatric retreat where many Hollywood and Broadway personalities sought treatment. The murder suspect, it was finally revealed, was thirty-seven-year-old Robert Steven Lipman.

For centuries the church had been the chief refuge or sanctuary for criminals, because it was beyond the reach of the political arm of the police. By the middle of the twentieth century, a madhouse, or psychiatric institute, had become the closest refuge to a church because theoretically anyone who is mad is not legally responsible for his or her actions. But when the British government filed papers to extradite Robert Lipman to face a murder trial in London, neither his doctors nor his attorneys made any effort to keep him confined to the facility. He was never described as a threat to society. His chief problem seemed to be a seven-year history of alcohol and drug abuse.

Hartford attorney Paul Orth and his partner Peter Sullivan were named to represent Lipman in England's extradition attempt. When Orth went to the Institute and showed Lipman a pile of news clippings about the murder and police photographs of Claudie's dead body, Lipman acted both curious and interested. "He was responsive and trying to be helpful," says Orth. "His basic story was that he didn't recollect anything about the murder."

Although it was impossible to tell it from the London morgue photographs, Claudie looked not entirely unlike Lynn or, at least, like Lynn Wyatt looked for that short period of time when her hair was bleached platinum blond and she wore thick red lipstick. Claudie wore the kinds of whorish clothes that Lipman had begged Lynn to buy. Obviously, Scotland Yard had more evidence than merely that the dead girl had the look that turned on an American by the name of Robert Lipman. Just what evidence Scotland Yard had was revealed at an extradition hearing before U.S. District Judge M. Blumenfeld in Hartford.

Lipman, dressed in a modish suit, white turtleneck sweater, and shiny, ankle-high boots, sat impassively at the hearing, his six-foot-six-inch frame slouched in a chair as he learned the details of his capture.

After the murder, an eyewitness reported seeing a very tall man fleeing down Walpole Street. It just so happened that a Scotland Yard detective remembered that, not too long before the murder, a very tall man had been prosecuted for possessing cannabis. The detective searched his files and found that the man's name was Robert Lipman. When he compared Lipman's left forefinger print taken during the drug prosecution with the print on a broken glass — that detectives found under Claudie's bed and believed was used to bludgeon her — the prints tallied. So just a few days after the murder, police were sure they had their man, but it had taken six months to track him down and bring him to justice.

On March 28, 1968, Judge Blumenfeld ruled that Lipman be extradited, an action that was legal under a reciprocal 1931 treaty between Great Britain and the United States permitting extradition for capital offense. Lipman was reportedly the first American under the treaty to be extradited on a charge of murder.

By April 22, the judge's order was endorsed by Secretary of State Dean Rusk, and on May 1, Lipman landed at Heathrow Airport escorted by two London detectives who had been sent to bring him back for trial. The London press swarmed around him, trying to see the face of the man responsible for such a bizarre and horrific murder, but Lipman made this impossible by covering his head with a blanket.

Lipman's murder trial was held in London's Central Criminal Court. Better known as the Old Bailey, the court occupies the site of Newgate Prison, whose prisoners have included Daniel Defoe, William Penn, and many of the people on whom Charles Dickens based fictional characters. Lipman's trial proceeded with the same choreography, the same long white wigs and black robes, and with much of the same rhetoric and forms, as when Milton's writings justifying the execution of Charles I were burned by the common hangman there in 1660 or when Jonathan Wild, the notorious thief-catcher, was hanged there in 1725.

When the Old Bailey trial commenced on October 7, 1968, there were plenty of spectators, but none of Lipman's family nor even any friends came to support him. There he sat, all alone, sad and weak. In fact he looked so frail and thin that his defender, Queen's Counsel Michael Eastham, brought earlier photographs of him for the jury to see. Eastham wanted the jurors to know just how handsome Lipman had been before the tragedy of the murder.

Eastham opened by telling the jury that Claudie Delbarre was killed by a man on a fantastic "trip to hell on the drug STP." He carefully took the jury through Saturday, September 16, 1967, the day when Lipman met Claudie. He explained that during the morning Robert smoked opium and cannabis and in the afternoon went to a photographer's studio in King's Road where he sniffed amphetamine. Then he went to a friend's flat and smoked "hash." There Lipman paid his friend between eight and ten pounds for a blue pill and a white pill. He was told that the blue pill was "great acid from the States."

"We do not know what that was," Eastham explained, "but some doctors think it was more likely that the blue pill was STP, a drug with which Lipman had had no former experience and which had more drastic consequences than LSD."

At about 9 P.M. Lipman went to a party at the flat of another friend and smoked some cannabis. Two hours later, the party went to the Baghdad Restaurant, where they met Claudie. They then proceeded to a club called The Speakeasy, where they danced a while, and then Claudie asked Robert if he had any LSD. When he said that he did, they left and went to her flat. It was about 4:15 A.M.

Lipman, on the stand, explained the events that followed, as well as he could remember.

"Did you intend to have intercourse with her?" Eastham asked his client.

"Yes, sir," said Robert, adding that he had taken off his shoes and socks and gotten into bed with her.

"Did you, in fact, have intercourse with her?"

"No."

When Eastham asked why he had not, Robert replied, "The trip started. The LSD turned me on and I went on a trip. I became part of a series of electrical impulses going along parallel and horizontal lines. A feeling came over my body starting from my head and going right through and as it went through my body, I lost all feelings. It was a very weird sensation. I could not control anything.

"I felt myself shooting out into space and I felt the earth opening and I plummeted right down into it, into the centre of the earth, and found myself in a den of monster snakes which I was fighting off and battling with and they were huge, prehistoric types, scaly with fire shooting from their mouths. I felt the fire coming from their mouths and I was trying to fight them off. I felt I was fighting for my life. I hit out at them, I kept hitting and hitting with my fists until I had killed them all."

When Lipman came out of the "trip" at about 6:30 A.M. on Sunday, September 17, Eastham explained, Claudie was lying motionless on the bed.

"When I came to I was fighting to keep conscious," Robert testified. "I shook her and tried to move her. I did not get any response and I knew something amiss had occurred. I remember being entangled in a sort of web which restricted my movements. I absolutely panicked with the shock."

Robert testified that he then covered her body and left the flat.

But John Mathew, the Crown's prosecutor, painted a different picture of the events of September 17. He explained that a very tall man who looked like Lipman was seen half running and half walking down Walpole Street toward the King's Road, away from Claudie's flat, on Sunday morning, after the murder. Within fifteen minutes, said Mathew, Lipman had arrived disheveled, unshaven, and wearing no tie at the Knightsbridge Green Hotel. Only five days earlier Lipman had booked a room for a fourteen-day stay, said Mathew, but on this morning he demanded his bill immediately.

He went to his room, but within a minute or two he was back downstairs, Mathew told the jury. According to the hotel clerk, Lipman was "agitated, hopping up and down saying, 'Quick, quick, where's my bill.'"

He paid his bill and then went to a travel agency on Curzon Street and said he wanted to fly to Lisbon "at once." Told that there was no flight until 2:30 P.M., he bought a ticket on a 12:30 flight for Copenhagen and then on to Lisbon.

The prosecutor explained to the jury that Lipman's defense might well be that, for the jury to return a verdict of murder, there must be an intent to kill, but that he was so under the influence of drugs at the time that he had no ability to intend anything. If it were found that Lipman was under the influence of drugs and incapable of intent to do anything, Mathew explained, the Crown would still say that it was an unlawful assault and, therefore, manslaughter.

On October 10, 1968, after three and a half hours of deliberation and by a majority of 10 to 2, the jury found Lipman not guilty of murder but guilty of manslaughter on two grounds: first, that he knew, when in his normal state of mind, that the acts he later committed while on a "trip" were dangerous, and, second, that he was grossly negligent and reckless in taking drugs and he must have realized it would be unsafe to others if he did so.

The judge sentenced Lipman to six years in prison and said that he would recommend Lipman for deportation at the completion of his sentence.

Robert Lipman was a name that the Sakowitzes were anxious to forget. When Robert's mother telephoned her former daughter-in-law when the murder was revealed, Lynn was unwilling to talk about it. "When he killed that girl his mother was just devastated," Lynn told a reporter twenty-four years later. "She would call me and cry, but by then I was so removed from Bobby Lipman it was as if she was talking about someone I hardly knew."

It has often been rumored in Texas, as well as in some circles in New York, that Lipman died in jail. But this is impossible since, in 1974, after his release from jail, he was seen by half of New York society at a party at the El Morocco nightclub.

The El Morocco party was hosted by Philip Van Rensselaer, a sixteenth-generation member of New York's manorial family whom Truman Capote once labeled an "upper bohemian" because he moved in both extremes of the social world. Van Rensselaer says he invited Lipman to his party without knowing about the murder, but he was quickly informed at the party that Lipman was persona non grata in New York society.

But Van Rensselaer says that he "sensed a fellow member of the lost generation" and continued to see Lipman. "He was in the bohemian world too. He just traveled around Europe, living from one day to the next. He was spontaneous and enthusiastic, like most of us vagabond nomads and our manic personalities."

Van Rensselaer and Robert first met in Athens, in 1974, after Lipman got out of prison. "He was with a very young blond girl of about eighteen," says Van Rensselaer, "and I found them both very attractive so I invited them to my house on the island of Hydra, and they stayed with me about two weeks."

Van Rensselaer says that when Robert was in Hydra he talked about Lynn and his sons. "When I told him that I'd gone around the world with Barbara Hutton, he said, 'Oh, did you ever meet my wife, Lynn Wyatt, in Monaco?' And I said, 'Oh yes. And she is lovely.' He was very pleased to hear this.

"He adored Lynn. He said he loved Lynn and that she was very,

very sweet to him, an angel. When I asked why they divorced, he said, 'Oh, I was stupid. I began to drink and ruined everything for myself.'"

While Robert and his girlfriend were staying with Van Rensselaer, they saw a French newspaper that pictured Steve and Douglas Wyatt, who were then both in their late teens. Van Rensselaer says Robert beamed with pride over the pictures. "He thought they were so handsome, and he said, 'I'm sure they're going out with all the prettiest girls.'"

Philip, seeing how proud Robert was of his sons, finally asked, "Are you going to go see them?"

"Yes," Robert replied, "maybe I will."

But he never did.

Although Lynn told her sons that their father was hit and killed by a streetcar in Vienna, there has long been speculation by the press, as well as by some friends of Lipman's, that he did not die this way. There are even stories that he did not die at all.

Nigel Dempster, gossip columnist for the *London Daily Mail*, says the Sakowitz family has told conflicting stories through the years about Lipman's death. "The streetcar in Vienna is the story we've been publishing, given the fact that's what the Wyatt family says happened."

Dempster adds, however, "He didn't die in prison, which is what the Sakowitz family said a long time ago."

In October 1992, Dempster said that, according to a source, "Oscar said, as recently as a year and a half ago, to his sons, 'If you ever speak to your father again, you're cut off.'

"Now, you can't speak to dead men," says Dempster. "Obviously, it suits Oscar and Lynn to say that Lipman is dead."

In a book published in 1993, a lover of Steve Wyatt's reveals a conversation she had with Steve in which he told her, "I never really knew my real father. My mother separated when I was six, and I have no idea where he is now."

Steve's use of the present tense seems to indicate clearly that he believes his father could be alive.

But Robert Sakowitz says he believes the story that Lipman was killed by a streetcar. Robert says, "[Lipman's] sister saw the body."

Even those who believe he may still be alive and living under an alias admit that, at six feet six, his would not be an easy body to disguise.

10

B Y 1965, it seemed that the only direction Coastal's stock could go was up. Oscar's long-term contracts to supply gas to San Antonio, Austin, and Corpus Christi had given him tremendous borrowing power. In one transaction, he obtained a $75 million line of credit from Houston's Bank of the Southwest without having to pledge any physical property as collateral. The contracts alone were enough to satisfy the bank.

With plenty of borrowed money, Oscar then bought up even more gas pipelines. His extensive acquisitions gave Coastal a monopoly throughout a major part of Texas.

Year after year, Coastal's earnings showed huge annual gains. Net income doubled between 1962 and 1964. It doubled again by 1969. In just five years, between 1960 and 1965, Coastal's revenues increased from $17.6 million to an astounding $69.5 million. In the next half decade, between 1965 and 1970, revenues would almost quintuple, to $322.9 million.

"Every year a record year" became the company's slogan. But beneath this optimism were signs of trouble.

As early as 1966, Coastal warned publicly that the gas reserves of Alamo — the start-up company that Coastal took over to supply San Antonio's gas — were only half the original estimates. On learning this, San Antonio's Public Service Board displayed little concern. The board simply expected Coastal to make up the shortage by buying new reserves. Although the price of gas had risen slightly in the four years since Alamo won the contract, gas was still cheap in 1966, and it was up to Coastal to make up its deficiencies — or so San Antonio's board assumed.

Its members could not have been more shocked when Oscar bluntly told them he had no legal obligation to replace the reserves at contract prices. Those prices, he said, applied only to the reserves the company had when it signed the 1962 contract. Replacement gas would cost them more.

The board responded by asking Coastal to prove the size of the reserves dedicated to their city. Again, the board was shocked when Coastal refused. Its reserve figures were private information, Coastal said. The board could rely on data contained in Coastal's annual reports to stockholders and published statements made by Oscar at annual shareholders' meetings.

Despite the board's frustration with Coastal, at least for some months there was little cause for alarm. But that changed in 1968, when Coastal curtailed delivery to San Antonio's power plants. Coastal claimed that the curtailments were caused by technical problems in the pipeline, but some members of the board, leery of Oscar, suspected otherwise. During the next three years, the board repeatedly asked for information about Coastal's reserves, and Coastal repeatedly responded by mailing copies of its most recent annual report.

The board might have been willing to work with Oscar had he told the truth early on about his lower-than-anticipated reserves. But Oscar chose another course. "He's a master at bluff," says then CPS board member Leroy Denman. "There's no question about that. That's been the way he's gotten along all his life."

Oscar's bluffing took various forms. According to Coastal's 1971 annual report, the company had 11.3 trillion cubic feet of gas. Later, Coastal would be accused of counting as reserves "every cubic foot of gas that went into its pipeline, including gas it was hauling for others — gas that Coastal did not own, would never own, and could not make available to long-term customers."

By the early 1970s, the price of gas at the wellhead had risen to 35 cents per thousand cubic feet — more than twice what it had been at the time Oscar won the three city contracts. Because Oscar's fixed-price contract with San Antonio was for 23 cents, this price escalation at the wellhead meant a substantial loss to Oscar on every thousand cubic feet of new gas he bought.

While continuing to deny that he was short of gas, in 1972 Oscar complained that gas was becoming increasingly scarce at the same time that the price was rising, and he finally announced that he wanted out of his fixed-price contract. Renegotiation of his contract was necessary if Lo-Vaca was to remain healthy, he said. All the while he was pleading with San Antonio to negotiate with him, there were more curtailments, forcing brownouts and business closings.

The board was in no mood to bargain with the gasman who had repeatedly refused to reveal the size of his reserves. It held tough.

Oscar tried other means of getting around his commitments. A Coastal lobbyist got a bill introduced in the Texas Legislature that would authorize the Railroad Commission to set rates without regard to contract prices. The bill became known as the "S.O.S." bill, short for "Save Oscar's Shirt," but it never got through committee.

Coastal's customers were beginning to suspect that Oscar was using the gas that should have been dedicated to his fixed contracts to make spot sales to interstate pipeline companies. Their suspicions proved to be correct. By 1972, Coastal was selling 200 million cubic feet of gas daily to interstate pipeline companies, which were paying between 30 and 35 cents per thousand cubic feet, compared to the 23 cents specified by the San Antonio contract. Not only was Coastal reaping tremendous profits by making spot sales, but it was also making lucrative brokerage deals. There were times when Coastal would learn that a package of gas was available, but rather than increase Lo-Vaca's reserves, Coastal would locate a buyer and get a brokerage fee, as well as a fee for transporting the gas.

In addition to the direct economic benefit of these spot sales, there was an even greater indirect benefit. Because Oscar's profit on the Lo-Vaca contracts shrank with the rising price of gas, he had to find other means to continue Coastal stock's phenomenal growth pattern established during the 1960s. Spot sales were one way to assure the continuous profit increases — and their attendant boasting privileges — that had made Coastal the darling of Wall Street.

The harsh reality for Oscar was that if he continued to fulfill his contract with San Antonio at 23 cents, while having to buy new gas at 35 cents, he would lose money. The harsh reality for San Antonio, and now for Austin and Corpus Christi, who also suffered curtailments, was that the cities were stuck with Lo-Vaca. Building pipelines (the only way to move gas) and shoring up reserves took months, sometimes years. The board shuddered to imagine the prices a United or a Houston Natural would charge if San Antonio went back on its knees asking for gas.

In the midst of its Lo-Vaca troubles, in January 1973, Coastal purchased the giant Colorado Interstate Gas Corporation, a 6,000-

mile system supplying gas utilities in the Texas Panhandle, Oklahoma, Colorado, Utah, and Wyoming. The purchase was Coastal's first major move away from its Texas roots and became the base for subsequent acquisitions and expansion projects. But the purchase would not help Lo-Vaca, whose troubles were growing.

The winter of 1972–73 was one of the coldest in Austin history. When the temperature dipped below zero, the University of Texas, with one of the largest enrollments in the country, had to shut down for nearly a week because its gas supply fell critically low. Coastal insisted that it had not anticipated such cold temperatures and was unprepared to deal with the problem. A popular 1970s anti-Northeast bumper sticker in Texas read, FREEZE A YANKEE. Oscar, some noted, was now generously expanding this to include his fellow Texans.

Austin and Corpus Christi had already joined San Antonio's demands for answers about Lo-Vaca's ability to meet its fixed contracts. But the cold winter pushed reasonable concern into outrage. Now, all across Texas, the Lo-Vaca story was front-page news.

Lowell Lebermann, then an Austin City councilman, still remembers what happened when gas prices soared: "Oscar made the economic decision simply not to supply the people with whom he had contracts. He said, 'I don't have the gas. I didn't contemplate these uses — the cold weather and the growth of the area.'

"That was an absolute lie," says Lebermann. "He was selling his gas into the spot market for four and five and six times what he could sell it to the people with whom he had contracts."

Part of the problem was beyond Coastal's control. The Arab oil embargo had thrown the nation into an energy crisis, causing natural gas prices to soar. At the same time, new discoveries of gas fields were dwindling and proven fields were playing out.

Finally, in March 1973, Oscar did what he promised Austin he would never do: he went before the Texas Railroad Commission to ask for a rate increase.

In Texas, as throughout America, the regulation of various businesses has historically been necessary, not for any reason as frivolous as the protection of the citizens but in order to protect the businesses from their own brutal greed. Texas governor James Stephen Hogg no sooner took office in 1891 than he established a state railroad commission. Hogg had no sentimental concern for the consumer. On the contrary, he was worried about cutthroat competition among the railroads. He created the agency to fix uniform rates and "to give security to the carriers."

In 1917 the Texas Railroad Commission was given the supervision of oil and gas activities and in 1929 the authority to limit, or prorate, production in the oil fields. With the discovery of the great East Texas field, it became obvious that the seemingly unlimited supply of oil would drive down the price. The Railroad Commission's proration efforts were intended not only to keep prices up, but also to address another problem. When oil was pumped out too fast, the underground pressure was too quickly dissipated and much oil was left underground that more careful practices could have recovered.

What soon became clear to the Railroad Commission was that, for several years prior to 1973, Oscar had engaged in selling large quantities of gas from his dedicated reserves to large interstate pipeline companies.

Based on rumors that Coastal's supplies were not even remotely adequate to fulfill its contracts, on June 5, 1973, the company's stock plummeted to 7, down from a 1972 high of 55. As the owner of two million Coastal shares, Oscar suffered a paper loss of almost $100 million in that period.

A day after the stock fell to 7, the Securities and Exchange Commission stepped in and ordered a ten-day suspension of trading in Coastal stock. The SEC — citing rumors about the accuracy of Lo-Vaca's reserves — acted at the request of United States Representative from San Antonio Henry B. Gonzales, who called Oscar a "twentieth-century version of the robber barons" and "a plunderer of the people."

Later, on the floor of the U.S. House of Representatives, Gonzalez asserted that Oscar's burning wish was to become "king over Texas energy," and he added about the energy czar: "A more corrupt nor least [sic] trustworthy person could hardly be imagined."

In reply, Oscar told the *Wall Street Journal* in 1984: "Gonzalez is a mental incompetent and has been for years."

The Lo-Vaca hemorrhaging was finally slowed in July 1973, when the Railroad Commission filed a petition in District Court in Austin that resulted in the court appointing a new five-member Lo-Vaca board and a supervisor to act as a liaison among the Lo-Vaca board, the District Court, and the Railroad Commission.

Finally, it seemed to the cities, Oscar would be made to honor his contracts. Again, they were wrong.

In September 1973, after three months of hearings, the Railroad Commission ruled that Coastal would be temporarily released from its fixed contracts and that it could begin charging its customers 5 cents per thousand cubic feet over its cost. If the Railroad Commission's temporary ruling left Lo-Vaca with much uncertainty about the future, it was even worse for the more than four million Texans who lived in the cities and towns served by Lo-Vaca. They suddenly saw their electricity and gas bills triple and quadruple.

Oscar's greed did more than just skyrocket utility bills. The Lo-Vaca scandal was killing efforts to bring new businesses and industry to the cities Lo-Vaca served. "He made Corpus Christi and San Antonio and his other customers look like Banana Republics," says former Austin councilman Lowell Lebermann. "Companies were saying, 'We don't know if we can move there because we don't know if we can get electrical or gas power through the local distribution company.'

"Oscar is a genius in gas marketing, and he's absolutely ruthless. As I said in front of the city council one time in an absolute burst of anger and candor, 'There are people in prison who have offended society less than Oscar Wyatt.'"

Lebermann's feelings were echoed across the state. In San Antonio, where the Lo-Vaca scandal had pushed stories about Nixon and Watergate off the front pages, one city official likened Oscar to Joseph Goebbels, Hitler's propaganda minister. That South Texans put Oscar on a level with one of the world's most evil men showed the degree of their contempt. *Texas Monthly* summarized it best: "Once Wyatt was hailed as an entrepreneurial genius; now he is vilified by critics who seem to blame him for most of the world's evils since the Defenestration of Prague."

When Oscar and Lynn married in 1963 and bought the Cullen mansion in Houston, Oscar continued to call Corpus Christi his home. Many thought this was also a promise to keep Coastal's headquarters there. For a decade Oscar divided his work week between Houston and Corpus Christi and kept offices in both cities. But in the summer of 1973, with the Lo-Vaca scandal getting worse every day, Oscar packed up his company and moved Coastal's corporate headquarters to Houston. He moved the company's offices into the new, gleaming, glass Conoco Tower, in suburban southwest Houston, just a mile from River Oaks.

The relocation seemed logical for a number of reasons. Houston, a booming metropolis of 1,250,000, was the largest city in Texas and the center of the oil business in America. By the mid-1970s, Coastal States Gas Corporation, with its complex of forty-one corporations and subsidiaries, formed the eleventh largest corporation in Texas. It ranked among the top two hundred on America's Fortune 500 list of the nation's top corporations.

In June 1974, Oscar agreed to appear at a public hearing in San Antonio, but he wisely had a bodyguard meet him at the San Antonio airport and escort him to City Hall. Approximately one thousand protestors, some carrying skull-and-crossbones flags, were on hand to greet him. Inside City Hall, as he explained that he was unable to meet his contract with the city, a furor broke out in the audience. There were catcalls, boos, and angry questions shouted at him. At one point he responded bravely, "Calling Oscar Wyatt a robber baron won't get San Antonio any more gas."

Oscar got out of San Antonio alive, but the city kept his attention when, in July 1974, it filed suit against Coastal. The original lawsuit was for $50 million, but that figure was soon increased to $200 million and ultimately to $436 million.

Other utilities and cities throughout Texas were closely following what happened in San Antonio. CITIES WANT LO-VACA BLOOD, cried the *Corpus Christi Caller-Times*. So it came as no surprise when San Antonio's suit was quickly followed by a $625 million suit by Corpus Christi's Central Power and Light Co. Lawsuits by the the Lower Colorado River Authority and the City of Austin soon followed. By 1975, the half-billion-dollar company that Oscar had built from scratch, that had become the darling of Wall Street, faced more than a billion dollars in lawsuits.

Responding to the suits, Oscar tried to place the blame elsewhere by saying that Coastal did not create the gas shortage, while emphasizing only half the problem — skyrocketing costs at the wellhead.

"There is no way you can deliver gas at 24 cents [per thousand cubic feet], when the wellhead price is $1.60," he blustered to a House Energy Crisis Committee in Austin in September 1974, while failing to account for the spot sales he made at enormous profit to himself and to the detriment of Lo-Vaca.

Although Oscar kept up a tough front, by early 1975 Lo-Vaca was facing bankruptcy and Oscar's lifelong nightmare of again being poor seemed justified. Despite his public pugnacity, Lynn Wyatt later described to a reporter what a difficult time this was for her husband. He "would just wander through the house all night long," she said. "He was absolutely obsessed."

Oscar had made it a practice to support judges and politicians in their political campaigns, and he had contributed heavily to opponents of judges who ruled against him. According to the *Corpus Christi Caller-Times*, when a former Duval County judge went to prison, Oscar visited him there. The paper reported that Coastal States Corporation kept the judge "on a retainer fee as a lawyer when he was county judge."

But even Oscar's vast political connections in South Texas seemed insufficient to rescue Lo-Vaca.

When Bernard Sakowitz became president of the store in 1957, Simon's side stood in the way of his absolute power. A decade and a half later, with Simon's side about to be bought out, Bernard turned his attention to getting the stock owned by his brother, Alex.

Alex, who owned 25 percent of the company, had mixed feelings about selling his stock. "My father always said, 'This stock is your best investment, always hold onto it,'" says Alex. "The only reason I was ever persuaded to sell was that no dividends were paid for thirty or forty years. The stock was worthless to me."

Alex had also heard that the store was having financial difficulty. What upset him even more was his belief that Bernard and Robert benefited personally from the store at the expense of the store's other stockholders. "There was never a distinction between Bernard and Robert's personal roles and that of the store," says Alex's son Toby Sackton, "no distinction between corporate money and their own money.

"My grandfather lived his life for the store. The idea of doing something for himself that wouldn't be supportive of the store would have been unthinkable," says Toby. "Bernard and Robert were more interested in what the store could do for them than in what they could do for the store."

Alex saw the abuses grow worse with Robert's rise in the company and finally told Bernard he wanted to be bought out. But Bernard told him he could not afford to buy him out at that time because he was currently purchasing Simon's shares.

But mirabile dictu, Alex soon learned that Oscar was interested in buying Alex's shares for Lynn for about $2.5 million. "Oscar said something to me to the effect of he always gives his wives a million dollars," recalls Alex.

What Alex did not know was that Bernard and Robert had made a sub-rosa agreement with Oscar that they would make payments to him for Alex's stock, and then Oscar would write his own checks to Alex. In 1992, looking back, Robert said, "We were always convinced that Al knew that we were going to buy his stock and that Oscar was just a facilitator for the purposes of the law."

Another part of this agreement was worked out in Oscar's library at Allington, where Bernard had gone to ask Oscar to give his personal guarantee to the stock purchase note. Oscar had not become rich by making deals in which there was no profit for him, in which he merely acted as a conduit.

"Dad, I'll sign the note," Oscar later testified under oath he told Bernard, "on the condition that you divide the property of your estate up equal between Lynn and Robert with Robert holding one share more of voting stock of Sakowitz, Inc., and my wife having share and share alike in the estate."

Robert would later dispute Oscar's allegations about this deal Oscar said he had with Bernard. "Oscar is correct to the degree that my father said the estate would be split fifty-fifty in its totality," says Robert, "[but] not asset by asset. He was never going to put me in a position that somebody else would run the company except for one share. He would never put me in the position whereby I couldn't run a company that I'd devoted my life to."

But Oscar testified that the men had a handshake deal and that when Bernard left the mansion, Oscar was satisfied that Bernard would keep his word "because I think he was an honorable man."

The document to purchase Alex's stock was signed on March 26, 1974, and the payout was to continue for fifteen years, through 1989.

"All the paper work and legal work was with Oscar Wyatt Trustee — so as far as I knew he was buying my stock for Lynn," says Alex. "Each year, I was getting money from Oscar Wyatt."

Alex Sackton's suspicion that the store was in trouble in 1974 was justified. In fact, the company was in desperate straits. In the words of Simon Sakowitz's grandson, Gaylord Johnson, Jr., "The store in 1974 damn near took the tubes."

Part of the problem resulted from vigorous competition when

a number of nationally known stores opened branches in Houston. By the early seventies, Sakowitz had to contend not only with Neiman-Marcus, but also with Saks Fifth Avenue, Marshall Field, and Frost Bros.

"When I opened Saks Fifth Avenue in Houston in 1974, Bob was absolutely bound and determined that he was going to blow Saks off the face of the earth, that there was not going to be one single thing that Saks could offer a customer in town that Sakowitz couldn't," says Harry Berkowitz, who became Sakowitz's general merchandise manager in 1976. "When I joined Sakowitz, there were still hundreds of thousands of dollars in merchandise that had been bought to compete in 1974 and that had never been marked down, never liquidated, and the company was in a very serious financial bind. I spent my first year ameliorating buyers, merchandise managers, and vendors because there was no money to pay bills. The store was so overextended."

Still, the competition presented by Saks Fifth Avenue and others was minor in Robert's mind compared with the competition created by Neiman-Marcus. As early as the 1960s, one fact about Robert Sakowitz had become obvious. His goal was to become the next Stanley Marcus, and if he put Neiman-Marcus out of business along the way, so much the better.

Robert did not know Stanley well, but he had heard and read enough about the merchandising legend to know that Stanley represented everything Robert wanted to become. Stanley never made a great deal of money at the store or profit for the store, but he gained an international reputation as the ultimate merchant prince. When national and European dignitaries visited Texas, they did not want to meet cattle barons or oil tycoons or governors or senators. They wanted to meet Stanley Marcus. He was the arbiter elegantiarum, an international star in a way that no other Texan had ever been.

It seemed not so much that young Robert Sakowitz wanted his store to become as great as Neiman-Marcus, but rather that Robert wanted to become as famous as Stanley.

Among the most obvious attempts to imitate Neiman-Marcus was Sakowitz's "Ultimate Gifts." Neiman's had its "His and Her" Christmas gifts, which were often extravagant but always witty — his and her camels, his and her airplanes. These were publicized in newspapers and on television around the world the moment they were revealed.

Sakowitz on occasion exceeded even Neiman's extravagance, one year offering a "bathtub and the diamonds in said bathtub that it would take to cover an average female adult up to the neck. $118,335,000.00."

A customer could have built in his own backyard a replica of Italy's famous Trevi Fountain. Also for the backyard, Sakowitz offered a swimming pool built in the shape of the state of Texas with a 30,687-gallon capacity. "The National Swimming Pool Institute will secure the builder of the pool," the catalogue explained, "and upon completion we will deliver the equivalent amount of Perrier to fill your pool. $127,174.32."

Sakowitz's Christmas catalogue was right there with Neiman-Marcus's, held up for the world to admire on the *Today Show* and the *Tonight Show with Johnny Carson.* The revelation each fall of Neiman's "His and Her" and Sakowitz's "Ultimate" gifts was an exciting national story for everyone wanting to know what those filthy rich Texans were up to now.

In his drive to outdo Neiman's, Robert took the gift idea a step further. Rather than limit the "Ultimate Gifts" to tangible things, Robert introduced idea gifts. Among the more imaginative was the "Gift of Knowledge," by which customers could purchase lessons from experts in various fields: lessons in conversation from Truman Capote, piano from Peter Duchin, skiing from Jean Claude Killy. Who better than Robert, the self-confessed, ultimate Renaissance man, to offer the Gift of Knowledge?

Then there was the celebrity dinner party, featured as the "Ultimate Gift" in the 1978 catalogue. For $94,125.00, a customer could have dinner with "twenty-one of your worldly friends like Walter Cronkite, Neil Armstrong, Gloria Steinem, Arthur Ashe, F. Lee Bailey, Tom Wolfe and Bruce Jenner."

Not all the resulting publicity, however, was exactly what Robert had sought.

The celebrity-dinner gift backfired. Just as soon as the catalogue arrived in mailboxes throughout the world, the store started receiving angry phone calls from some of the celebrities listed who claimed that they had not been contacted about having their names used. Gloria Steinem called to complain; Walter Cronkite was so angry he sued the store. Criminal defense attorney F. Lee Bailey was no less angry than the others. A few months after the furor, Bailey visited Robert at his office at the downtown store. He began by telling Robert how upset he was over Sakowitz's use of his name, but then quickly changed the subject. "You know, I've written a book," Bailey said, pulling the book out of his briefcase. "Do you have a book department?"

Robert did not miss a beat. "We do now."

Sakowitz created a one-book book department for F. Lee Bailey's book and threw a lavish book-signing party.

Because of the outrageousness of many Ultimate Gifts, there was the problem of believability. Some gifts were so extravagant that the press began to question whether the store could make good on its offerings. One catalogue offered a two-passenger "flying saucer, Discojet, still in its experimental stage until FAA certification is complete." The cost of the Discojet: $1,125,000." The item made exciting reading in the catalogue, but would this space-age vehicle ever actually be developed?

Some customers wondered what had happened to the days when Sakowitz just sold pants and neckties and ladies lingerie?

By 1974, the store had changed dramatically, and the most obvious indication of this was the man who was running it. While Bernard, even as he talked of expansion, seemed content to do so methodically, Robert seemed overly impatient to exceed his father's and even his grandfather's success.

Robert arrived at the store earlier and left later than most employees. At two o'clock one morning, the downtown store manager got word that the store's security alarm had gone off. She drove downtown in the middle of the night, met two police officers at the store's entrance, and together they combed the store. As she walked through a second-floor department, the store manager noticed a man standing against a wall. When he turned toward her, she saw that it was Robert. Startled, she demanded of the boss, "What in the world are you doing here?"

"Oh, I just had an idea for a new display," he replied nonchalantly, "and I decided to come down here and see if it would work."

After becoming president, Robert often said that he had been determined to prove that he had earned the title. "The toughest thing in the world was to overcome those who were the constant detractors, those who would say, 'He's the boss's son, what do you expect?' You have to do 150 percent before they think you've done 100 percent," he said.

When Robert was still in his thirties he appeared to be growing impatient to assume the store's presidency. The last thing Bernard wanted was to repeat his own father's mistake, to keep the title from his son after he was prepared for it. Bernard, as a result, may have overcompensated, or he may simply have realized that his health made it too difficult to continue as president.

After suffering a heart attack in 1965 and undergoing heart bypass surgery in 1972, Bernard then suffered a stroke. Although he was still mentally alert, by the mid-seventies he had started leaving the store at about two o'clock each afternoon. Bernard and Ann spent about four months of the year at their house in Scottsdale, Arizona.

Because the company also had a store there, Bernard's decision to hold the annual shareholders meeting in Scottsdale in 1975 did not raise suspicions or questions. But it did come as a surprise when Bernard stopped everything during the board meeting to pass a small box to his son. When Robert opened it, he found a gavel.

"Son, I know it's placed in very, very capable hands," Bernard said emotionally.

"It was a crying day for all concerned because it was a momentous occasion," says Ann Sakowitz. The passing of the gavel meant that the thirty-seven-year-old Robert was the new president of the company.

But not everyone was pleased with the transition. Around the store, he was viewed as a maverick with a great deal of energy but with very little direction and self-editing. Bernard had not assumed the presidency until he was fifty-seven. Robert was taking the helm a full two decades before his father had.

"In 1968, we went to a meeting during which Robert spoke at length," recalls a longtime employee, "and when we left the meeting I said, 'If he gets his hands on the company, he'll destroy it.'"

The same employee sadly recalls another incident that occurred a few years later at the Festival of Fantasies, soon after Tobias Sakowitz's death. "It was a Sunday night before the opening of the Festival. Robert showed me an exhibit which was a large gold rock surrounded by elves who were panning for gold. He turned to me and said, 'See that rock? That's real gold plate. You gotta lay it on big for these suckers.' You know how I felt? I said to myself, 'How many pairs of pants did Mr. Tobe have to sell for him to do that?'"

But most employees seemed to agree that Robert had a great charisma and a gift for phrasemaking. "He could sell you dog food and make you think it was steak," said one employee. "He could charm the pants off a nun," said another.

11

OUSTON'S BACHELOR BOB had overnight become one half of Houston's most "In Couple." Nothing more typified the perfect match than their twin cheerleader sweaters, his with BOBBY in big letters, hers with PAM. One read about them constantly and saw them portrayed enjoying marital bliss. There they were in a spread in *People*, on bicycles in front of their home, conversing on the escalator at the downtown store, and lounging under a fur blanket in bed, reading the Sunday papers. But their marriage was less idyllic when reporters were not following them at the store and when cameras were not in their bedroom.

By the mid-1970s, Pam had become very unhappy, in part the result of a tragedy in May 1969, just four months into the marriage. Pam and Robert had spent their honeymoon camping in a tent at the Sakowitz family's Thunderbird Ranch in East Texas. It rained continuously during the four days they were at the ranch, and, as a result, they spent most of their time inside the tent making love. "Because of the rain I did not get out of the tent and repair to the bathroom as I should have," says Pam.

A few weeks later, when Pam and Robert were in London on a buying trip for the store, Pam began feeling terribly nauseous. She called her mother in New York, told her her symptoms, and cried, "Mom, you don't suppose?"

Audrey Zauderer immediately arranged for her daughter to visit a London gynecologist whose clients included a number of British royals. "He examined me for about two seconds and said, 'Well, Mrs. Sakowitz, you're pregnant,'" recalls Pam. "I looked around his office, which was filled with portraits of Queen Victoria and Queen Elizabeth, and said, 'Oh, shit.'"

But when she broke the news of her pregnancy to Robert, he was ecstatic. At first, Pam was not happy about the idea of a baby, but her apprehension soon turned to excitement as she returned to Houston and began to set up a nursery.

But then, just a few months into the pregnancy, Pam began experiencing terrible pain. In May, she went to her doctor, who immediately sent her to the hospital so that he could examine her under an anesthetic. Before administering the anesthetic, the doctor had explained that her pregnancy was a life-threatening situation and had her sign a disclaimer form. The examination revealed that Pam had an ectopic pregnancy, in which the fetus expands in the wall of the uterus. On that day, the doctor aborted the fetus and performed a hysterectomy.

When Pam came out of the operation and learned that she would not be able to have children, she was devastated. Only twenty-three and a newlywed of four months in a strange town without her own family or close friends, she felt alone and frightened. But at this most traumatic time of her life, Pam says, her husband did two things for which she would never forgive him. Both related to the pregnancy.

"After I signed the release form before the operation, Bobby left the hospital for a meeting. When I was wheeled in to be examined under an anesthetic, Bobby was gone."

Then something even worse, in Pam's view, happened. "I didn't want anyone to know that I had had a hysterectomy, but he went all over Houston telling people. We had a big fight over this. This was *the* major fight of our marriage."

Pam and Robert had moved into a large white colonial home set among tall pines on a fashionable street in River Oaks. Mrs. Zauderer had made the down payment on the house and paid the monthly mortgage.

With no children to care for and a maid to take care of the house, Pam began devoting much of her time to the store. She helped with decorating, and she accompanied Robert on buying trips. But her greatest contribution came from the expert use she made of her model's looks and her press connections. The latter brought constant publicity to the store, and the former received the ultimate compliment when a mannequin manufacturer modeled its form — which it sold to several major department stores in America — after her beautiful face and size 6 body. One needed only to read *W* — not just the society and fashion columns, but also the advertisements — to get an idea of Pam's value to Sakowitz.

In large print, an ad in *W* asked, WHERE DID PAM SAKOWITZ SLEEP LAST NIGHT? Below the large print was a photograph of the Sakowitzes' home in Houston, and below that, smaller print read, "At home is the answer. On Wamsutta sheets. Mrs. Sakowitz chooses Wamsutta, so can you."

Pam's sister-in-law, Lynn, watched closely but rarely commented to Pam about all the publicity she received. "She never said anything," says Pam, "but I knew she was watching me and taking it all in."

According to Pam, Lynn underwent an important change beginning in 1970, when Robert and Pam were named to the International Best-Dressed List. "In the sixties, Lynn and Oscar led a very quiet life. Oscar was not well liked, so they weren't invited out to parties," says Pam. "But when we made the Best-Dressed list, she was wildly jealous of Bobby and myself and she was determined to get on the list too."

The International Best-Dressed list — made from results of a poll of two thousand international fashion observers — was run by New York publicist Eleanor Lambert. When the list was started in Paris in 1922, it was run by the top couturiers as a bow to their best customers. World War II exiled the list to New York in 1940, and its criteria changed to include anyone with good looks, good clothes, and the good fortune to show them in public.

When Robert invited Eleanor Lambert to a store Festival in the early 1970s, Pam's mother, Audrey Zauderer, accompanied Eleanor on the trip to Houston. Robert barely knew Eleanor, but Audrey knew her well and showed her around when they arrived.

Pam says that after that, "Lynn hired Eleanor, and that was the beginning of her social ascent."

Ann Sakowitz, meanwhile, was so thrilled with all the publicity her son and daughter-in-law were receiving that she displayed the articles about them on a table in the foyer of her home. Lynn was too perceptive not to have noticed how important Bobby's publicity was to Ann Sakowitz. Wanting to please her mother, says Pam, Lynn decided to get the same for herself.

At this same time, not more than a year into Pam and Robert's marriage, a tension arose between the Wyatts and the Sakowitzes.

"Oscar's crudeness really bothered Bobby," says Pam. "He

would just bristle at things Oscar would say. In the middle of Christmas lunch, with the children there, Oscar would talk about tits and asses. I'll never forget, Oscar said, 'You get a guy by the balls and his heart and head will follow.' This was his favorite line.

"I decided, early on, this man is just trying to shock — it's a power thing. So I wasn't going to let him affect me, but it was very difficult for Bobby. Here's Bobby trying to be accepted into Houston society and having this roustabout as his brother-in-law. No one cared that Oscar had made his money overnight. The problem was he had a reputation for being crude and also that he drilled slantways.

"Oscar must have felt that Bobby was embarrassed by him," says Pam. "And Oscar didn't think much of Bobby. Oscar was always saying to Bobby, 'Oh, you were born with a silver spoon in your mouth. I made my money.' Bobby, then, would try to laugh it off or have a good comeback for Oscar. Bobby was very clever that way."

Oscar did not often come into the store, but gift and china buyer Val Renken remembers one time when he did. "Lynn had picked out some things for Oscar to look at and then have sent as wedding gifts to a few of his friends. When he came into the gift department to look at these things, which included a sterling silver frame and sterling tray, he said, 'God damn, she's got taste for shit.'"

Pam was not eager to become a mother, but because her friends hinted constantly that it was time she adopt a child, she and Robert applied at the Edna Gladney Home in Fort Worth, considered one of the top adoption agencies in the United States. When exactly nine months later, in October 1973, a blond, blue-eyed baby boy arrived, their friends wondered, How perfect can a perfect marriage be?

They named their new baby Robert Tobias Sakowitz, Jr., and called him Roby (pronounced Robbie). "He was the sweetest, darlingest baby," says Pam. "He was everybody's dream baby. Bobby and I were both very excited to have him."

In Texas, there is a mandatory six-month waiting period before adoptions are final. Each month, as required, the Sakowitz family's longtime pediatrician examined Roby and filed a report with the Edna Gladney Home. Near the end of the six-month period, Pam received a startling telephone call from the Gladney Home. An agent called to say she was flying to Houston the next day to meet with the Sakowitz pediatrician and take the baby to a neurologist at Houston's Methodist Hospital.

Pam hung up the phone, overcome with emotion. She felt shock, hurt, and sadness. She had assumed Roby was in excellent health. Her hurt turned to anger, and she telephoned the pediatrician and demanded an explanation.

"Well, we're concerned he hasn't met some developmental milestones," the doctor replied. He said little more and then hung up.

The following day, after Roby was examined, Robert and Pam and the agent from the Edna Gladney Home joined the neurologist in his office. Holding little Roby in his lap, the doctor turned to Pam and Robert and said, "I'm very sorry to tell you that Roby has cystic fibrosis and severe mental problems. He probably won't live past his teenage years."

As the doctor described the child's mental condition, Pam and Robert sat stunned. Then the woman from the Edna Gladney home spoke: "I'll be taking Roby back with me after lunch. You are no longer the right parents for him."

Pam started crying and pleading with the agent from Edna Gladney. "My God, we can afford care for him," Pam cried. "Please let us keep him."

"You are no longer the right parents for him," the agent repeated. "He needs to be with a grandparent-like couple where he'll be the only child. You'll adopt other children and you'll go on skiing vacations and he'll have to be left home. You're no longer right for him."

That was the last time they saw the baby they had cared for and loved for nearly six months. "It was worse than your child dying," says Pam. "It was like she just took him away. He was just gone. We had a business meeting in Minneapolis the next day, and I'll never forget, we just got on that plane and we were crying so hard people were looking at us. Just tears and tears."

Pam was still deep in mourning when she and Robert learned, just four months after Roby was returned to Edna Gladney, that they were the parents of another baby boy. This child, eight days old, arrived on August 28, 1974. Like the earlier baby, he was blond and blue-eyed, and to Pam's horror, Robert insisted on naming the child Robert T. Sakowitz, Jr., and calling him Robbie.

"To Bobby, there had not been two individuals. Robert T. Sakowitz, Jr., was what the first son was going to be named, period," says Pam.

Hurt as she was, Pam tried not to make the naming of the baby another issue in their fragile relationship, but she simply could not bring herself to call the boy Robbie. So she nicknamed him for his blond hair and called him Sandy.

"I never made a strong bonding with the second baby that arrived. I don't even have any pictures of those first six months. I didn't even really go into the room much. I was still mourning the first baby."

The return of the first baby caused a number of cruel and catty remarks that are still made today, usually by those with no knowledge of what really happened. The most common of these: "They returned the child the way you would exchange a dress or a pair of pants at Sakowitz."

Robert's insensitivity in not keeping Pam's hysterectomy confidential, the loss of their first adopted child, and the arrival of the second four months later proved too much for Pam.

"When we got Sandy in 1974, the marriage started going bad," Pam says.

But not all the trauma was related to her problems with children. Pam had begun to lose respect for Robert because of the way he acted in business.

"What love I had faded real fast when I saw the way he was with people," says Pam. "He would never give anybody a raise. He would say to me, 'Jimmy Shanken is the best woman's merchandiser in the country. We are so lucky to have him.' But he'd never give him a raise. He'd say, 'Let's see how long we can go without [it].' And that's why talented people left. He drove them to the embarrassment of having to say that they started looking elsewhere. He would give somebody a raise only if Neiman's was trying to hire them.

"What was a major problem for me was things like his promising to buy $10,000 worth of merchandise from a certain designer or manufacturer and when the time came to put in the order, writing it for $9,500.

"One time he borrowed several fourteenth-century polychrome wood Madonna sculptures from a friend of my mother's for a store Festival, and one of them got damaged. The store had insurance, but he wouldn't claim on the store insurance because he was afraid they wouldn't cover things in the future. My mother's friend had to claim it on his insurance."

In a similar situation, airline executive Tom Slick loaned Robert a Picasso painting for a show at the store. The painting, according to Slick, was damaged while in Sakowitz's possession. Slick demanded payment for the damage, but when payment was not forthcoming he filed suit. The lawsuit dragged on for four years before the parties settled.

It seemed to be more than just stinginess that drove Robert to welsh on deals or cut corners at the expense of others. At times, his determination to get something for nothing, or to get more for less, seemed not so much a matter of money as a matter of proving his manhood, of always winning and never losing.

"The problem was that he did things that were unethical, and all of a sudden I realized, my name's on this too," says Pam. "I think when you lose respect you lose love."

Pam would often make business suggestions to Robert, but they were usually carefully offered just as suggestions. "We didn't fight," says Pam. She did, however, tell him if something embarrassed her. "He was forever saying, when we met new people, 'My name is Bob-Sakowitz-my-family-has-the-last-independently-owned-chain-of-specialty-stores-left-in-America.'

"It was like it was all part of his name. I finally said, 'Quit saying that. Let people discover it.'"

But Robert was not likely to stop boasting. He was determined to spread his name. The reason for this, according to Pam, was that he wanted a political career and the store was simply a means to that end.

"Robert wanted to be a senator and he wanted to use the store to get there. He talked about expanding the business all around the state to get a constituency base."

Robert's interest in politics had begun years earlier. He wrote his Harvard thesis about the 1948 race of Lyndon Johnson for the United States Senate, one of the most crooked in Texas history, in which Johnson defeated Coke Stevenson by ninety-seven votes, all of them dead men from South Texas's Duval County.

If he did run for political office, however, it seemed increasingly that Pam would not be there by his side. In 1976, while Robert was on a buying trip, Pam went skiing with some friends in Vail, Colorado. On the trip, she got together with other Houston-

Tobias and Simon Sakowitz's first store, The Globe, in 1902, the year it opened in Galveston. Tobias is at left, behind counter. (*Toby Sackton*)

Left to right, Tobias, Simon, and Bernard Sakowitz, in front of their just-opened suburban Post Oak store in Houston in 1959. (*Houston Public Library*)

Lynn Sakowitz as a
cheerleader, pictured in
her 1953 San Jacinto
High School yearbook.

Robert Sakowitz, a guard
on his high school foot-
ball team, pictured in the
1956 St. John's yearbook.

Oscar Wyatt's third wife,
former Hollywood star-
let Bonnie Bolding, in a
studio publicity still.
(*Birmingham Public
Library*)

Lynn in the living room at Allington. (*Houston Chronicle*)

Lynn, the new (fourth) Mrs. Oscar S. Wyatt, Jr., in 1963, at Allington, her mansion in Houston's River Oaks. (*Houston Chronicle*)

Christmas 1968 lunch at Allington. Clockwise from Lynn's left are: Brad Wyatt, Ann Sakowitz, Steve Wyatt, Robert and wife Pam Sakowitz, Oscar Wyatt, Trey Wyatt, Tobias and wife Ruth Sakowitz, Douglas Wyatt, Bernard Sakowitz. (*Pamela Z. Bryan*)

The exterior of Allington, viewed from the estate's entrance. (*F. Carter Smith/Sygma*)

Twenty-six-year-old Robert Sakowitz at his parents' Thunderbird Ranch in East Texas. (*Val Renken*)

Hunting at Oscar's South Texas ranch in 1968 are, from left, Douglas and Steve Wyatt, Lynn, Oscar, and Robert. (*Pamela Z. Bryan*)

In happier days, Robert visited Lynn on the French Riviera. With them are, left to right, Douglas, Trey, and Brad Wyatt. (*Pamela Z. Bryan*)

Robert and his bride, the former Pamela Zauderer, at their wedding reception at New York's St. Regis Hotel. With them is Pam's brother-in-law, pianist Peter Duchin. (*Pamela Z. Bryan*)

Pam Sakowitz with the nationally distributed store mannequin that was modeled after her. (*Bob Bailey Studios, Inc.*)

Pam and the James Dean look-alike on Charles Revson's yacht, *ULTIMA II.* (*Pamela Z. Bryan*)

Robert Sakowitz rejoicing over his and
Pam's second adopted son, Robbie.
(*Pamela Z. Bryan*)

Robert with his second wife, the former
Laura Howell Harris, in 1990 in New
York. (*Robin Platzer*)

The maverick merchant prince in his
ubiquitous cowboy hat at the Louvre in
Paris. (*Houston Chronicle*)

Lynn and her elder sons,
Douglas (left) and Steve,
at a Sakowitz gala in
1984. Both men resemble
their natural father, Robert Lipman. (*Houston
Chronicle*)

The chairman, trying to
speak to his employees
following the store's 1985
bankruptcy. (*Wide World
Photos*)

ians, including businessman Tony Bryan and his wife, Josephine Abercrombie, an eccentric oil heiress with twin passions for prize-fighters and thoroughbred horses. Pam did not care much about meeting Tony, but she had long wanted to meet the celebrity Josephine. Tony, however, wanted to get to know Pam, and after their first meeting, he offered her a ride back to Houston on his company's jet. She accepted, and, once on board, noticed Josephine was not accompanying them. When they arrived in Houston, Tony asked Pam if she would like to see his and Josephine's house, a magnificent white antebellum mansion on River Oaks Boulevard. She agreed, and as he showed her around the house, he completely surprised her by making a pass at her.

She was not displeased. "I thought Tony was very attractive," Pam recalls. "He said their marriage wasn't very good and that Josephine had wanted a divorce for some years. Mine wasn't very good either."

Pam began to see Tony on the sly. "From very early on, Tony said, 'Don't be afraid because if anything gets exposed, I'll take care of you.' A few months into the relationship he asked me to marry."

Pam said yes. "I fell in love with Tony, but I didn't tell Bobby for a few months. Then I just couldn't stand it anymore, so I asked Bobby for a divorce."

When Pam told Robert she wanted a divorce, in September 1976, Pam says, he was shocked.

"Is there anybody else?" Robert asked.

Pam did not want to lie. "Yes, there is. But I don't want to say who it is."

Robert stamped out of the room. But later that night, he came into the bedroom and slept in the same bed that they had always shared.

"This went on for months, his sleeping in the same bed with me," says Pam. "We didn't have relations, but he didn't move out of the bedroom, either."

Although Pam thought it peculiar that he stayed at the house, she felt so guilty about having fallen in love with someone else that she did not ask him to leave. And *she* certainly was not going to move out of the house. As far as she was concerned, it was her house. It had been a wedding gift from her mother.

But Pam misjudged what a tough opponent she had in Robert.

Oscar knew a private detective in Los Angeles, and Robert called Oscar and asked how to reach the detective. Immediately, the detective called Robert. "I asked him if he had any equipment for tapping a telephone because I wanted to tap my own telephone," Robert later testified under oath.

Two days later, the detective arrived at the house with a tapping device. Robert showed the man into the garage, where they found the phone wires. While the man stood behind him and instructed him, Robert secretly planted the bug. Because the tapping unit was battery operated, all Robert had to do was periodically, when Pam was not around, replace the used cartridge tapes with blank ones. The used tapes Robert secretly locked away in the downtown store's vault.

Even after Pam filed divorce papers, Robert continued to live at the house. Pam still felt too guilty to push him out, and she still was not sure why he stayed. Nor was anyone else, but Houston and New York society speculated about it endlessly.

"Suzy," in her November 8, 1976, column in the *New York Post*, wrote, "Pam and Bob Sakowitz of the string of specialty stores in Texas and Arizona are still living together, even if Pam has filed for divorce. Does that clear the air or muddy the waters?" When a rumor that Pam and Tony were spotted coming out of a motel on the edge of downtown circulated, friends joked about that large-print advertisement for Wamsutta Sheets. WHERE DID PAM SAKOWITZ SLEEP LAST NIGHT?

While the press, friends, and store employees wondered about the peculiar living situation at Inwood Road, Pam, while Robert was at work, talked on the phone with Tony. She also got on the phone with her friends and gossiped about "how fabulous Tony was." She talked of the places they had sneaked off to together. As her girlfriends listened to every word, she described in titillating detail his talents in bed and even in the back seat of a car. Pam says Tony made love so much better than Robert, who, in her words, was "plain vanilla" in bed.

Not all her friends were the model and measure of fidelity; they giggled and gossiped and revealed their own confidences, as well.

Then one day the servicemen for the home's burglar alarm system came out to the house to check the alarm. Something was causing the alarm to trigger on its own, without prompting. Robert was at his office, but Pam was expecting him to arrive at the house any minute to pack and then leave that afternoon for a European buying trip. Pam was in the master bedroom when her maid, Ella Mae, came running up the stairs. "Mrs. Sakowitz, come here, come quick," Ella Mae shouted.

Pam followed her down the stairs and into the garage, where the maid pointed to the phone box. The cover on the box was open, exposing the phone wires to which a recording tape was attached. Terror-stricken, Pam looked up at the burglar alarm repairmen. One of them, backing away, frantically stammered, "Ma'am, we don't have anything to do with this."

Pam, of course, knew that they were not responsible for tapping the line, nor did she have to wonder who was. "It suddenly dawned on me why Bobby hadn't moved out of the house. He had stayed so he could tape my conversations."

For a moment, Pam considered "having it out" with him when he came home to pack, but then decided not to let him off so easily. As the repair truck pulled away, Pam ran back into the house and upstairs, where she got two pairs of white dress gloves out of her dresser. She gave one pair to Ella Mae and put the other pair on herself. Wearing the gloves and working fast before Robert arrived home, together they removed the tape from the phone box, then closed the box. Having decided to act as though nothing was up, Pam went back upstairs and worked at her desk, and the maid began vacuuming downstairs.

Soon, Robert arrived at the house, walked upstairs, and packed his suitcases. Pam did not speak to him, and he did not say a word to her, which was now routine. Pam and Ella Mae, acting as though nothing had happened, listened carefully to his footsteps. After packing, he walked downstairs and into the garage. Once he was in the garage, Ella Mae moved into the kitchen. When he came back into the kitchen, she looked up from her work. His face was stark white.

"I wanted him to go on that trip worried to death about who removed that tape," Pam says. "I never said a word and he left the house."

Having accomplished that, she then threw piles of his clothes, books, records, and, in Pam's words, "everything else he owned" into her car and drove the six blocks to Allington. She sped up the drive and pulled her car under the porte cochere and up to the large glass front door. She then opened her car door and threw her husband's things at the mansion's front door.

"The maid came running out screaming, 'Miss Pam, why you doin' this?'" Pam recalls. "I was crazed I was so angry. As I pulled away, Lynn's maid was taking everything in."

The Wyatts' maid notified the store, and a Sakowitz truck sped to the house to collect his things on the ground.

When Robert returned from Europe, Lynn and Oscar invited him to move into Allington with them. Robert says Oscar was already thinking ahead about a divorce trial. "If you live in an apartment and you look like you're penurious, they're going to hold that against you," Robert says Oscar told him. "If you go out and take a big apartment or a house, then they're going to say that you have all this money. So come live with us."

Oscar was a useful brother-in-law to have around. He knew where to turn when Robert needed a wiretapper, and now he was offering shrewd advice on preparing for what promised to be a difficult divorce case. Oscar had been through three divorces himself.

Oscar and Lynn's apparent concern for Robert was not one-sided. A year earlier, when Robert heard that *Texas Monthly* was researching an article on the Lo-Vaca scandal, Robert called the magazine's publisher, Michael Levy. Every month since *Texas Monthly*'s first issue in 1973, Sakowitz had run a full-page ad on the first right-hand page in the magazine. When Levy verified that such an article was being written, Robert told Levy he was pulling Sakowitz's ads. With the exception of a few small ads years later, Sakowitz never advertised in *Texas Monthly* again.

By the time Robert moved into a guest room at Allington, reports of his taping Pam's phone calls had spread quickly through Houston's cocktail circuit, turning what had been just juicy gossip about their marital troubles into terrifying news. Who could say for sure what was on the tapes? Who knew which marital or extramarital relationship might come under close scrutiny in a public courtroom? Suddenly, more than just Robert and Pam's relationship was at stake.

"A lot of my girlfriends were very upset about his wiretapping," says Pam. "He made a lot of people in Houston very nervous and very mad."

The Sakowitz divorce — with allegations of extramarital affairs and wiretapping, and with such a flamboyant cast of characters — had the makings of a great tabloid story. But not a word about what happened inside the courtroom in *Sakowitz v. Sakowitz* appeared in the local newspapers. Such was the power of one of the city's biggest advertisers.

At the opening of the trial, on May 23, 1977, Pam got more than an inkling of just how tough her husband of eight years was going to be.

"Robert wanted a jury trial," says Pam, "and he wanted divorce for reasons of adultery, which means he had to prove that I had committed adultery."

The tapes, it seemed, would provide all the evidence he needed. "Every incident about Tony on those tapes he wanted entered [into the trial]," says Pam.

But once the trial began, it seemed to Pam that Robert had taped her conversations not for evidence about her affair with Tony. "What Bobby really wanted on those tapes was who I felt my mother had given the house to," says Pam. "It wasn't about the 'other man,' it was about money."

Audrey Zauderer, when she made the gift of the house to Pam, had wanted to put the deed in Pam's name alone. But Pam, not wanting to hurt Robert's feelings, insisted the house be put in both her and Robert's names.

On the eighth day of the trial, Pam was on the stand when Robert's lawyer asked if she had had any affairs with anyone other than Tony. Pam's attorney thought the question so prejudiced the jury against her that he called for a mistrial and the judge granted it.

Nine months later, the case went back to court, but this time it was heard by a judge instead of a jury. The judge ruled that the house had been a wedding gift to both Robert and Pam, and therefore it was community property. On February 24, 1978, after nine years of marriage, a divorce was granted.

But Robert's legal battle was not over. His tapes were subpoenaed as part of a grand jury investigation into the legalities of his wiretapping. The case was dropped, however, and Pam insists that the reason it was dropped was because of pressure from Leon Jaworski, the powerful head of Houston's Fulbright & Jaworski, who had a few years earlier served as Watergate's Special Prosecutor and who, before that, had been a member of Coastal's board of directors.

Pam got custody of three-year-old Robbie, and four months

later she married Tony Bryan, who had gotten his divorce months earlier and become chairman of the Pittsburgh-based Fortune 500 company Copperweld Corporation. In the fall of 1978, Pam and Robbie joined Tony in Pittsburgh, where she was soon as high-profile as she had been in Houston.

In the 1980s, when Pam divorced Tony, as with Robert, she had tremendous difficulty getting him to leave their house — a Georgian brick mansion once owned by cereal heiress Marjorie Merriweather Post — and finally had to resort to a court order. No one who has ever looked at Pam has the slightest difficulty understanding her husbands' reluctance to leave her house.

12

IN THE LATE SEVENTIES, the Texas economy was booming, and Robert Sakowitz had both the authority and the money to try to prove, through the medium of his store, that he was indeed a latter-day Leonardo. He used the store to express the varied aspects of his self-confessed genius.

Robert wanted a phrase that would appear regularly in ads and in the catalogues that customers could associate with Sakowitz. He came up with "the quality of being special."

"He got a lot of quizzical looks for this because it didn't make sense," says a store executive. "Does it mean that if it's special, it's quality? Or is it that if it's a quality thing, it's very special? The fact that people asked, 'What are you talking about?' is what he liked about it. It was an attention-getter."

Since his introduction of Saint Laurent and Courrèges, Robert had brought many other new, hot designers to the store. While these chic, expensive styles excited younger customers, they were less than enthralling to Sakowitz's longtime customers, a conservative carriage trade that preferred linen to metallic.

But this fact did not lessen Robert's obsession with European designs. "The store had a study done in the late seventies that said the Sakowitz customer was very conservative and would never go for the French and Italian designers," says a former secretary of Robert's. "But he threw the study in the wastebasket, because he personally enjoyed going to the Paris shows."

Press coverage was essential if he was to put his store on the world fashion map, and Robert knew that hot designers were what made headlines.

Robert was constantly thinking of new ideas for merchandise, innovations that would set Sakowitz apart from other stores. He must have been thinking more of himself than the store when he came up with the phrase "Damn I'm Good!" and then rushed to have it put on ties, towels, bathmats, and money clips. When he announced this idea to his staff and the response was less than enthusiastic, he was undaunted. His merchandisers could snicker all they wanted, said Robert, convinced that the item would be a big seller, and he was right. The "Damn I'm Good!" concept was a hit that lasted two years — a very long shelf life in the fashion business.

Robert increasingly referred to himself as an image maker. He used the word "I" more times in a sentence than most people did in a day, and he talked in flourishes. He exceeded even his own penchant for self-aggrandizement when he told a reporter, "When you are innovative with a great deal of taste, you provide an experience for people that's part of the higher human experience."

It was obvious why one wag dubbed him the "prince of prolix."

Curiously, his pretentious, self-serving speech was not a turn-off for the press. On the contrary, reporters loved the things he said, the image he projected. In the words of one employee, "The press worshipped the water Robert walked on."

Robert's ability to charm the press in America was minor compared to his success with the press in Europe. At the designer showrooms of Paris and Milan, Robert was the merchant that reporters seemed to love most.

"In Paris, at the shows, Robert would come out with beautiful speeches, very flowery things to say about the designer's collection," says an American store owner. "The reporters from *W* and *Women's Wear Daily* would race over to him because he talked at length about the collection and he was very good at it. He made a lot of noise."

Robert had become a star in Europe. He and his buyers were always seated front and center at Paris's couture and prêt-à-porter shows. The fact that Sakowitz appeared year after year, regardless of whether the collection was a good one, scored points with the designers. Some big stores skipped an occasional collection, but Robert was always there, sitting at the edge of his seat. In fact, by the end of the seventies, he seemed more than simply an observer at the shows; he was an eager participant, going behind stage and making suggestions before and after; talking the show's every detail into a pocket tape recorder that had become an appendage not unlike the trademark cowboy hat that was so beloved by the Europeans and laughed at by Americans.

To buyers from New York and Chicago and Los Angeles, the hat and the man personified the Texas they knew — big, rich, and vulgar. Bobby Sakowitz was the ultimate showoff, and the hat said it all. When reporters for *W* or *Vogue* or *Harper's Bazaar* asked him sarcastically about the hat, he always replied seriously, "I wear that hat so my buyers can spot me in a crowd," to which one Sakowitz employee, noting Robert's less-than-average height, replied sarcastically, "If he wants to be seen in a crowd, he'd better get up on a box."

Just as he kept himself at a frenetic pace, he also demanded of his buyers much longer hours than most store executives required. "We were on a buying trip in China," says a Sakowitz buyer, "and we had worked a marathon week, nonstop. It was Sunday afternoon and I had wanted to see the Great Wall all my life, but he wouldn't let me take the time off. He made me work."

Robert bought large quantities from Yves Saint Laurent, Valentino, and the men's designer Ermenegildo Zegna. These, and other European and American designers, were eager to sell to Sakowitz exclusively in Houston because they knew their collections would be well represented. Saks Fifth Avenue or Neiman-Marcus might place a much larger order with a designer, but the merchandise was then divided among a dozen or more stores throughout the country. Sakowitz typically placed a smaller order, but the bulk of that merchandise went into one or, at most, two stores in Houston.

Despite Robert's success at getting exclusives from top-name designers, he complained about what he called "the big pencil," the ability of the chains to win exclusives simply because they placed larger orders. Robert believed that without additional volume he would lose many of his exclusives.

In the 1970s, the guaranteed minimum wage, 20 percent interest rates, and skyrocketing inflation threatened to destroy the store, he says today, unless he increased volume. "You cannot run a business with those increases in operating costs unless you expand your volume," he says. "The only way you grow your business is by additional merchandise and additional stores."

So he began the stepped-up expansion that would ultimately

bankrupt the company. It had taken more than two decades, from 1951 until 1974, for Sakowitz to grow from one to six stores. In addition to the four stores in Houston, in 1969 the company had bought an established store in Amarillo, Texas. And in 1974, Sakowitz built the Scottsdale store, its first outside Texas.

Whether for his own political career, for economic reasons, or vanity, Robert wanted his name spread throughout the Southwest, and he was not going to take two decades to do it. When he talked about "opening a store a year," he butted heads with longtime General Manager Blake Speer, whose job had been opening new stores and who insisted that such a rapid expansion would make it impossible for Sakowitz to maintain the service orientation that made it successful. When Robert was named president in 1975, Speer was among the first to go.

In Speer's place came Harry Berkowitz, who had successfully opened a Saks Fifth Avenue store in Houston in 1974 and who had come from the great Frost Bros. retailing family of San Antonio. Perhaps best of all in Robert's mind, Berkowitz had worked at Neiman-Marcus. He knew Dallas. There were few things that were certain about Robert's future as a retailer, but one was that he was going to open a major store in Dallas, a store so grand that the world, including Stanley Marcus, would notice, and Robert Sakowitz would win the recognition he deserved.

Robert's broader plan was to capitalize on the oil boom by opening stores not only in Dallas but in a number of the fastest-growing towns of the Southwest — San Antonio, Austin, Midland (Texas), and Tulsa (Oklahoma). But he also talked of opening stores as far north as Denver or Kansas City and as far east as Memphis or New Orleans.

To spread the Sakowitz name still farther, there would be, in additon to the full-size stores, smaller, free-standing "Sakowitz IIs" (under 100,000 square feet with a more limited selection of merchandise). He also would build boutiques in hotels, office buildings, and suburban shopping centers.

These stores were so astonishingly disparate in size and therefore selection that customers no longer knew what to expect from the name Sakowitz. Worst of all, almost without exception, Robert's new stores were built in the wrong location. Robert's grandfather had been known for his genius in choosing the right locations for his stores. How could Tobias's grandson be so inept at choosing *his* store locations?

The problem was that Robert's decisions often seemed predicated on where he got the best real estate deals, and, in many cases, he personally had a stake in those deals. The site he chose for a store in San Antonio was in a proposed mixed-use development that was out in the country where virtually no retail traffic had existed before. Robert was part owner of the land on which the store was to be built.

Even though Harry Berkowitz was the third-highest-ranking executive in the company, Robert never told Berkowitz that he had a personal stake in any of the store's real estate deals. So when Berkowitz, a native of San Antonio, told Robert that the San Antonio site was a terrible place to put a store and Robert refused to heed Berkowitz's advice, Berkowitz was baffled. Robert had, however, received the approval of Sakowitz's board of directors to have a personal stake in the San Antonio store's real estate.

But the fact that Robert personally made a $1 million profit when the store backed out of the San Antonio project and he sold the land did not sit well with the Wyatts. Douglas Wyatt would later use this as an example of Robert's manipulation of the company to benefit his personal real estate holdings.

With time, Berkowitz also began to object to the smaller Sakowitz IIs and the hotel boutiques, which, partly because they were badly located, received little traffic and became a drain on the company. One Sakowitz boutique, located in the basement of the Plaza of the Americas Hotel in Dallas, faced a concrete wall and access to it required a special elevator.

At first, Harry Berkowitz liked to joke, "Every time I go to the bathroom, Robert opens a new store." As time passed, however, the maverick expansion became impossible to laugh about.

One of the problems of opening so many new stores so quickly was the boss's insistence on having his say about so much of what went into them — from architecture and decoration to merchandise. With so many new stores to fill, Robert logged about 200,000 flight miles a year (sometimes on the Concorde), covering Europe and the Far East in pursuit of things for the stores.

But the biggest problem in opening so many stores so quickly was that it dangerously leveraged the company. When Neiman-Marcus, a much bigger and better store than Sakowitz, decided to expand nationally, the Marcuses knew they had to sell to a company with the resources to finance such an expansion.

At the same time that Robert was trying to spread his name

on stores across the Southwest, he was presented with another vehicle for personal exposure. In 1977, the young publisher of the start-up *Houston City Magazine* called Robert to solicit a Sakowitz advertisement.

"I don't want to just take an ad, I want to be an investor in your magazine," Robert told the publisher, Gary Easterly. Surprised, Easterly told him to call the person in charge of raising capital for the magazine.

But Robert persisted with Easterly. "You need mailing lists, right?"

In no time, Robert had become a 10 percent owner of *Houston City*. "He paid about $6,000 or $8,000 [for $25,000 worth of stock], but the primary way he got the stock was [by] giving us the store's [customer] list," says Easterly. Robert also agreed that the store would be a constant major advertiser in the magazine.

Robert was looking for a way to get into the media, a chance to have a voice, says Gary. He had had great success wooing the press; now he had the even greater power of controlling the press.

Robert seemed to reach new heights of pretention when, with Gary's help, he started *The Magazine*, an upscale fashion sheet copied after Neiman-Marcus's *N-M Edits*, which went to the store's biggest-spending customers. According to Gary, *The Magazine's* purpose was not to make money but rather "to promote image."

That it did. It displayed Robertspeak at its most pretentious. The magazine opened with "the message" from executive editor Robert: "All photographs have a singular quality of seizing both space and time of a split second. Good photography will convey a sense of the surroundings and feelings of the event with its goals and detailed facts — from where it was seized, from what emotions it was wrenched, from what mood and spirit it was and, more importantly, does it truly depict what was meant to be portrayed?"

Instead of clear and concise nouns, verbs, and adjectives, Robert went for the more grandiose. He spoke not of "demographics" but of "physiographics"; he did not "try" to show, he "endeavored" to show. He did not use the word "indication" if "manifestation" would almost work in its place.

Perhaps the best example of his love of "conceptualizing" was his fascination with I.D.A., a merchandising concept he dreamed up and then spent more than $1.5 million developing.

I.D.A. stood for three types of Sakowitz customers: the "I" represented the Innovational customer, the cutting-edge customer, whom Robert described as "the person who wanted to be first no matter what," which represented 5 percent of Sakowitz's clients; the "D" stood for the Directional customer, the person who followed the latest trends, comprising 35 percent of the customers; and the "A" was for the Acceptational client, the client who bought only after a style was accepted, which made up 60 percent of the store's clients.

Robert considered the genius of his idea, then reconstituted the entire buying staff and made buying assignments based on the segment of the market that related to I.D.A. Some sportswear buyers were told to buy I, while others were told to buy D.

The rationale for buying and displaying according to the I.D.A. concept was one thing; selling this way was quite another. Salespeople were expected to size up a customer as she walked through the door, make a quick determination about which category she fell into, then subtly lead her to that section. Because customers often do not wear into a store the type of clothes they are there to buy, accurate categorizing was usually impossible.

"[I.D.A.] was a bit contrived," says Richard Marcus, who was chairman and CEO of Neiman-Marcus when Sakowitz opened a store in Dallas. "You can label a customer innovational when she walks in the store and she may totally surprise you."

Berkowitz thought I.D.A. symbolized Robert's approach not only to merchandising but also to life: "Robert wanted to be the next Renaissance man. Whether it was boxing or philosophy or wines, everything he did he approached in a very psychological, intellectual way. He had developed this I.D.A. theory, and every facet of his life was going to be built on the theory that he developed. He wasn't interested in living on anybody else's theory."

If Robert appeared arrogant and headstrong, it may have been because he was given so much power at such an early age. What happened when Robert took over reminded Stanley Marcus of "a ball that's held under water, and when let go, it flies out of the water without restraint."

In fact, Bernard and Ann were absolutely adolatrous of their son. The affection between father and son was mutual and expressed openly. Bernard and Robert almost never greeted each other without a kiss.

Ann Sakowitz thought her son a genius, and she could see that Robert had a level of expertise and sophistication that surpassed Bernard. "I love my husband dearly but I knew his failings," she said. "If it hadn't been for Bob, on my hand to God, we would never, never have gotten internationally known."

Handsome, popular in Houston society, and beloved by the press, Robert, by the late 1970s, seemed to have only one dark area in his life — the continuing trauma of his breakup with Pam.

A friend of Robert's who sat next to him on an overseas flight in 1979 was surprised that a year after the divorce, he still seemed very upset over it. "We were sitting on the upper deck of a 747, and for some time Bob was just pouring out his soul about what a devastating experience the divorce had been, what a mess it had all been."

Pam also felt terrible repercussions from the divorce. What bothered her the most now was her feeling that Robert was undermining her relationship with their son, Robbie. She had custody, but when Robbie returned from visits to Houston, he acted petulant and spoiled. Pam grew so tired of "fighting this Bobby influence that I finally said to Robbie, 'Look darling, where do you want to live? You can live anywhere you want.'"

Seven-year-old Robbie chose to live with his father. Robert learned the news when Pam telephoned him after Robbie had returned to Pittsburgh following a Christmas visit with Robert in Houston.

"His mother called and said, 'I'm sending him,'" recalls Robert.

"I said, 'It's the middle of the year. You're just springing this on me.'

"She said, 'He'll be on the plane.'

"I said, 'You tell me when. But don't you *ever* expect me to send him back, other than the same visitation rights I had, because he's staying here now.'"

A Sakowitz vice president still remembers the day in 1981 that Robert announced in a storewide meeting that Robbie would be coming to live with him: "In the dozen years that I had known and worked closely with Robert Sakowitz I never saw him happier than that day."

Robert had great dynastic feelings, say friends and employees. Little Robbie would carry the Sakowitz name into the next generation; he was the future merchant prince — or so Robert hoped. To that end, Robert made sure little Robbie got an early start. The cherubic, blue-eyed, towheaded boy was barely out of diapers when Robert started bringing him to the store, holding him on his lap during store meetings, and having employees take him around and teach him different facets of the store's operations.

Oscar's troubles with Lo-Vaca grew dramatically in January 1978 when the Texas Railroad Commission ruled that Lo-Vaca was not entitled to the rate relief that the commission had earlier approved. After nearly five years of regulatory proceedings and litigation, the Railroad Commission ordered Lo-Vaca to revert to its original fixed prices on its gas supply contracts.

Since September 1973 the price of gas at the wellhead had increased from 55 cents per thousand cubic feet to more than $2.00. And now Coastal was forced to stop passing on to its customers the increased gas costs. Even worse for Coastal, the Railroad Commission ordered Lo-Vaca to refund to its customers the differences between the interim rate set by the commission and Lo-Vaca's original contract prices. At the time of the order, Lo-Vaca said those refunds would total $1.6 billion. Lo-Vaca insisted that its total equity capital was only $576 million and that the order, if it stood, would bankrupt the company. Most significant of all, the commission's order named Coastal jointly liable with Lo-Vaca for the obligation.

Coastal and Lo-Vaca charged that the commission had "dropped an atomic bomb" on them and referred to the decision publicly as the "Nagasaki Order."

Coastal and Lo-Vaca filed motions for rehearings, claiming that the order was punitive and confiscatory and would result in the bankruptcy of the companies. Prior to this, Coastal suffered a $27.5 million judgment in a suit it lost to the Lower Colorado River Authority. And this loss was as nothing compared to the $436 million fraud and breach-of-contract suit Coastal faced in San Antonio, the largest civil damage suit ever to be tried in Texas.

Preliminary hearings in the trial began in September 1976, but because of the size, visibility, and complexity of the case, attorneys estimated that the hearings would last three to four months before jury selection would begin. One attorney speculated that the trial itself, which was scheduled to be heard four days out of each week, could easily last a year.

Meanwhile, settlement discussions involving the board, the

city, and Coastal were being vigorously pursued. Although some in the press believed there were people in San Antonio who would rather see "a bankrupt Oscar Wyatt than have a warm home this winter," the board and the city recognized the disadvantages of bankrupting its gas supplier. Therefore, settlement discussions revolved around how to maintain the Coastal pipeline system in a reorganized corporation as a viable transporter of gas to its four hundred customers, while extracting the maximum amount of money from Oscar Wyatt and his companies.

In January 1977, the hearings in San Antonio were recessed so that attorneys could participate full-time in settlement discussions that appeared to be making progress. For the next twelve months, attorneys representing not just San Antonio but several of Lo-Vaca's other customers worked to hammer out a settlement. Discussions focused on finding a way for Coastal to spin off Lo-Vaca as a separate company to be owned by Lo-Vaca's current customers.

The settlement that was finally worked out and approved by the District Court in Austin, which had supervised Lo-Vaca for the last five years, resulted in the largest spin-off in American corporate history. It called for Coastal to divest Lo-Vaca, renamed Valero. Lo-Vaca's four hundred customers would get $115 million in Valero preferred stock. They also would get 14 percent of the common stock, giving them about half of the total $240 million equity. The other half of the equity would go to Coastal's shareholders — with the exception of Oscar Wyatt. Although Oscar owned 7 percent of Coastal, he was specifically prohibited from getting any Valero shares, a loss he estimated at $40 million.

As an additional penalty, Coastal was obligated to spend $180 million on exploration over the next fifteen years and sell any new gas it found to Valero at 15 percent under the then going market price.

The court appointed representatives from Austin, San Antonio, and Corpus Christi to represent the cities' interests on Valero's new board. One of the board's first decisions was to move Valero out of Houston, where Coastal was based, and relocate the company in San Antonio.

Valero board members' efforts to bring credibility to the new company were helped by Valero's immediate growth. In its first few years, Valero's stock tripled. Today, Valero is an $850 million company.

News of the settlement prompted *Fortune* magazine to shout, TAKE THAT OSCAR WYATT, but beneath this headline was a more telling subheadline that read, "Or How to Win by Losing."

While Oscar was certainly punished for his sins, the Valero settlement left him far from broke. Oscar retained his $262,000-a-year chairmanship in a very alive Coastal Corporation. The company emerged from the Lo-Vaca scandal with assets of $2.5 billion, in part because Oscar had expanded into different areas during the 1970s.

In the mid-1970s, Coastal became a major player in crude oil trading. Rising prices and contradictory government efforts created opportunities for huge profits. In 1979, Coastal collected a $60 million profit from crude oil trading.

Coastal had been operating a refinery in Corpus Christi since 1962. In the late 1970s, when it purchased refineries in California and Belgium, it increased its capacity to 400,000 barrels per day. Also during the seventies, Coastal bought eight ocean tankers to transport crude and a chain of gasoline stations in the Midwest.

Coastal made a major push in international oil exploration with ventures in Indonesia, Syria, the Congo, New Guinea, and Libya. In 1979, Coastal became the first American company to import oil from China. The company also expanded from the oil and gas business with ventures in uranium mining in Texas and Liberia and coal mining in Kentucky and Utah.

Oscar's Coastal Corporation would continue to grow, and he would have many other great business successes. More than a few times in the future, he would create a scandal, either by breaking the law or appearing to, but never again would he be so vilified as in the 1970s. Nor would he — no matter how hard he tried — be able to shake his reputation as greedy and deceitful and the most hated oilman in Texas.

As the 1970s drew to a close, Oscar and Robert had made themselves constant subjects of press coverage. Now Lynn was on the verge of making her name as well known as her brother's and her husband's.

She had made one of her first steps in that direction in 1974, when — with the help of publicist Eleanor Lambert, with whom, Robert Sakowitz says, "she had become extremely close" — Lynn made it onto the International Best-Dressed List. Four years later, in 1978, she had already been retired to the Best-Dressed Hall of Fame, bestowed on those who made the list three years in a row. When Oscar learned of Lynn's Hall of Fame honor, he asked her, "Does this mean you don't have to buy any more clothes?"

In addition to her looks, Lynn had great charm and wit and a strong sense of herself. She played up her Texas background wherever she went (outside the Lone Star State). Her brother never doubted her ability to succeed at whatever she wanted: "Never underestimate Lynn Sakowitz," says Robert. "She's determined, and she is a very, very strong person."

New York costume jeweler Kenneth J. Lane remembers how he first learned about Lynn in the 1970s. "Truman Capote called me and said, 'I'm having a luncheon for the most marvelous girl from Texas. Her name is Lynn Wyatt.'"

Anyone back in Houston who had any doubts about the sensation Lynn was becoming in New York had only to look at the photograph on an October 1978 cover of *W* of Truman with both arms wrapped lovingly around Lynn's shoulders.

Lynn was becoming a regular in New York society columns. "Suzy" gushed over her floor-length sable coat and speculated about whether she wore it to the grand divertissement at Versailles. She was the glamorous department store heir married to the rich oilman.

It appeared to some that Robert was now watching his sister in much the same way that Lynn had earlier watched Pam. "I always felt that the person Robert really wanted to be was Lynn," says one of Robert's secretaries. "Lynn was very much a part of the international jet set, but Robert was only on the fringes."

Lynn's popularity was rising in the United States, but it was in Europe where she was making the biggest name for herself. What had helped her most in her ascent in Europe was her friendship with Princess Grace.

Lynn got to know Grace through one of Grace's best friends, Kelly Van Remoortel, an American divorcée who had moved to Monaco with three young children in the 1960s when she married the conductor of Monte Carlo's Symphony. In the 1970s, when Kelly Van Remoortel moved to Houston, Lynn pursued a friendship with her. Kelly had remained close with Grace, and this helped pave the way for Lynn's friendship with Grace.

When Lynn began renting a house on the French Riviera each

summer, she not only got to know Princess Grace, she also saw that Steve got to know Prince Albert, who was close with Kelly Van Remoortel's son, Mike Powers.

A friend of Grace's recalls that Lynn had little difficulty working her way into Princess Grace's fold. "She just charms her way around, and Grace fell for it," says the friend, implying that Lynn was using Grace. "Princess Grace, like so many people in that position, was so naive."

But if Lynn did use Grace to make a name for herself, Grace did little to avoid it. On the contrary, she appeared to revel in Lynn's attention. Just how willing Grace was to be part of Lynn's publicity orbit became obvious in June 1978, when Lynn and Oscar threw a black-tie dinner dance at Maxim's in Paris in honor of Grace's elder daughter, Princess Caroline, and her fiancé, Philippe Junot.

The party was the culmination of everything Lynn had worked for: there she was standing with Princess Grace, both beautifully dressed and smiling happily, as Europe's paparazzi captured the moment for the world to see.

It seemed typical that Texans would host the party that caused Maxim's maître d' to walk around the room exclaiming, "I've been here forty years and I've never seen anything like this."

To ensure that the party was not too staid in this restaurant famous for waltzes and other stately dances, the Wyatts imported three bands for the evening. During the first course of poached lobster in court bouillon, guests were entertained by the Magic Violins, fixtures at the Villa Fontana in Mexico City. Performing during the main course of duck with peaches were the Richy family, three sisters popular in the record world and in New York. And after dinner, the cream of European royalty got out on the dance floor and bobbed up and down in the European version of disco dancing to the music of By-Pass, a band from Colorado.

"If the Wyatt party is something everybody is talking about and will go on talking about for a long time, it's not only because of the lavishness but the guest list too," wrote New York columnist Eugenia Sheppard. "Out of the 130 that filled Maxim's main dining room, the guests included almost every well-known European celebrity you've read about."

There was Prince Fouad, son of the late King Farouk of Egypt; Princess Feirial, sister of the king of Jordan; the Duke and Duchess of Bedford; Prince Alexander of Yugoslavia with his wife, Barbara;

Helene Rochas; Baron and Baroness Guy de Rothschild; Baron David de Rothschild with his wife, Olympia; the Duke and Duchess de la Rochefoucauld; Marc Bohan; Princess Ghislaine de Polignac; Baron Alexis de Rede; the Duke d'Orleans; Carolina and Reinaldo Herrera; Stavros Niarchos; Estée Lauder; Mrs. Gerald van der Kemp; Maryll and Bernard Lanvin; and Betty and François Catroux.

Less than a decade earlier, at Robert and Pam's extravagant, celebrity-studded wedding reception at the St. Regis, Lynn was barely noticed. But since then, Lynn had keenly observed how her sister-in-law, Pam, captivated the press, and she had listened to her mentor, Eleanor Lambert. Just how far she had come since that night in New York in January 1969 was obvious at her party at Maxim's. Never again would anyone not remember seeing Lynn.

The most obvious change in Lynn was her constant smile. She has an unusually wide mouth, so wide that, when she smiles, it is almost as though her entire face becomes a smile. Because of the very wide mouth and wide-set, almond-shaped green eyes, she looks like a prettier Lauren Bacall.

This was the same smile she had worn in her high school cheerleading photograph, but it had disappeared early in her adult-hood. In photographs during her early years with Oscar, she often wore a very subtle, almost blank smile, and in some photographs she is not smiling at all; she appears unsure of herself, almost frightened.

But now, with the confidence of her friendship with Grace and her rising popularity in the press, it would have been difficult not to smile. She was the happy, carefree party gal whose only title was Texan, but who was obviously having a ball at her own affair. She wore a very slinky halter-top gown, and her lion's mane of hair, which was quickly becoming her trademark, swirled around large diamond earrings. She displayed a rare combination of sex appeal and refinement. To many guests that night, the Texas blonde seemed not unlike their friend Princess Grace.

13

LYNN WYATT'S move to St.-Jean-Cap-Ferrat in 1980 could not have been more brilliant. Precisely as the choice of Allington had immediately made the Wyatts stars in Houston, so their selection of Villa Mauresque, the former Riviera home of Somerset Maugham, as their summer home made Lynn a major player in international society.

There are larger and grander villas on the Riviera but none with more mystique than that of the best-selling British novelist and playwright who had held court there from the mid-1930s until he died in 1965. No one thought that Lynn had selected Mauresque as a place to retire from the world. Rather she had selected it as the battlefield for her final and victorious attack on the world, that is, as she defined the world.

During the 1930s and 1940s, Mauresque had been a point of pilgrimage for writers and artists, for world leaders, and for royalty. Winston Churchill, the Aga Khan, the Duke and Duchess of Windsor, Rudyard Kipling, H. G. Wells, and Noel Coward were among the villa's regular guests. Maugham's hospitality had put the tiny jewel of St.-Jean-Cap-Ferrat on the social map.

The Cap's 580 acres had once been the exclusive and very private preserve of Belgian King Leopold II, who so loved the site that he built himself a palace, as well as separate houses for each of his three mistresses, one just sixteen years old. He also gave a plot of land to his confessor, a retired bishop. At almost the farthest point where the Cap juts out into the Mediterranean, the bishop had built a Moorish-style villa with horseshoe windows and columns, colonnades and a cupola — hence the name Mauresque.

Maugham purchased the villa in 1928 and removed its Moorish facade, so that what remained was a square white villa built around an arched courtyard. At one end of the seven-bedroom house, a broad terrace overlooked the sea. Maugham also built a long rectangular marble swimming pool, a tennis court, and an orangerie where he grew oleanders, camellias, tuberoses, sweet peas, and avocado trees imported from California. Inside, the house was filled with great modern art, some of it gifts from Maugham's neighbors. Matisse designed a bathmat for the house; Jean Cocteau's inscribed books were in Maugham's library.

But it was not simply the setting that gave the villa its great glamour; it was the owner. Guests were asked to be quiet in the morning so that he could write without interruption; lunch was simple, but dinner was lavish. No less memorable than the conversation to most of the guests was the endless variety of dishes served. Maugham took special care never to repeat a meal. "I stayed there for three weeks, and he served eggs different every morning," says New Yorker Jerry Zipkin. "When I said I had to leave, he said, 'Good, because I thought I was going to have to repeat an egg dish.'"

Dinner table conversation ranged from Whistlerian and Wildeian wit to brutally bitchy badinage. His guest lists were designed to maximize wordplay at his table, where each competitive participant inspired the others. It was an elegant, intellectual world that could forgive cruelty but not banality.

Long before Maugham, writers had been drawn to the Riviera, that narrow belt of coast between the Alps and the Mediterranean that stretches from Spezia on Italy's Gulf of Genoa westward to Hyères on France's Côte d'Azur. Open to the south and protected by mountains from the north and east winds, it has so remarkably mild a climate that much of the vegetation is subtropical, including noble date palms and pomegranates. The roses, violets, and hyacinths for years supplied the French perfume industry. The natural beauty of the coast with its steep crags plunging into the deep blue water has attracted artists as well as ordinary millionaires since before the early 1800s when Byron and Shelley lived and wrote on the shores near Spezia.

Even after Maugham's death in 1965, Mauresque would continue to be known as his villa. Some would be afraid to buy a house formerly owned by a famous person, afraid of unfavorable comparisons. But Lynn knew that buying Maugham's villa would give her instant recognition and that she could at least match its earlier guest lists.

After Lynn installed herself at Mauresque, which sits on the highest point of the peninsula, *Town & Country* featured her in an article on the Riviera. Stretched out on a divan in her living room, with the courtyard and a marble Moorish fountain behind her, she was the Madame Récamier of the 1980s and serenely happy in that role.

She had come a long way since she first recognized that she was unwelcome as a member of Houston's best country clubs, and she had become as surefooted as a chamois in her climb. If she could not make it to the top in Houston, she would go to Europe and make her name, then return home a star.

"A social device that goes back quite far in American history is to leave your hometown and establish yourself in New York, then go back to where you came from," says New York social historian Jerry Patterson. "People who were striving to become a part of their local society in the nineteenth century used to move to New York and try to make it with the Vanderbilts and Astors. When they returned home, people would say, 'She really must be great because I read in the New York papers that she sees the Vanderbilts.'"

Lynn's friendship with Princess Grace played a major role in her success not only at home in Houston — when her friends read in the papers that Grace had been to a party at Mauresque or that Lynn had spent a leisurely summer afternoon at Monaco's pink palace — but also in Europe. Grace was one of the most beautiful, elegant women in the world, and she had one of the world's most-written-about titles. The fact she was so often seen with Lynn greatly advanced Lynn's social career.

Lynn had also made a name for herself in Europe by being seen and photographed in the company of the most important couturiers — Valentino, Yves Saint Laurent, Givenchy, Christian Dior's Marc Bohan, and Chanel's Karl Lagerfeld.

The mutual back scratching of socialites and designers reached its peak in the 1980s when more American women than ever before could afford to pay thousands of dollars for haute couture. Only in recent years, since the late 1960s, had couture become big business. A profusion of new perfumes and prêt-à-porter lines in the 1980s largely depended on the success of each season's new haute couture. As the size of these fashion businesses grew, so did their international advertising and so did the international publicity of the designers, who now became widely recognized stars.

Formerly, with the exception of Coco Chanel and a very few others, designers were merely tradespeople, the social equivalent of the butcher or the hairdresser. This changed after World War II and accelerated during the late 1960s and early 1970s when European couturiers exported their ready-to-wear to America and stores such as Sakowitz began building them boutiques. Increasingly, rich hostesses were eager to have designers at their parties, just as earlier hostesses had star pianists or writers to decorate their dinner tables. The society woman/famous designer relationship became so big in the 1970s that New York publisher John Fairchild created an entire newspaper, *W*, to chronicle the phenomenon and profit from its advertising.

Today, when Oscar de la Renta or Saint Laurent or Bill Blass is photographed at a party with Ann Getty or Chessy Raynor or Anne Bass, it brings both the designer and the rich society woman prestige by association. This prestige translates to dollars for the designers. If Lynn Wyatt is pictured in a Saint Laurent dress in *W* or *Harper's Bazaar* or *Paris Vogue*, the advertising value to Saint Laurent is immeasurable. Conversely, when Lynn wants a Givenchy gown, she goes to the Paris showroom where Hubert de Givenchy himself helps her. What price accommodation the designer makes is a carefully kept secret.

At the same time that designers had become stars, the term "walker" came into fashion. With so many designers unmarried, they became sought after as escorts of rich society women who were either single or whose husbands did not share their passion for parties. Today, many men, including Oscar Wyatt and former president Ronald Reagan, often find it not only acceptable but preferable to have their wives escorted to a party by a fashion designer, so the arrangement is comfortable and profitable for all concerned.

Lynn's associations with Princess Grace and the world's top designers were only partially responsible for her success in Europe. The chief reason Lynn made it, when so many other rich, beautiful women in America with the same goal have not, is simply who she is and that she is always herself.

What immediately beguiled the Europeans was that she acted and sounded so Texan. As evidenced by the huge success of the TV series *Dallas* abroad, Europeans have long been fascinated with Texans, a fact that did not go unnoticed by Lynn any more than it had by her brother, Robert, who always wore a cowboy hat and cowboy boots at the Paris couture shows.

The international jet-set is a very small clique of perhaps only four or five hundred people, not much larger than the four hundred maximum who could fit into Mrs. Astor's ballroom. But in Lynn Wyatt's time the partying locus had expanded to the circumference of the globe. Whether it was a couture showing in Paris or a horse race at Ascot — where she stood in the Royal Enclosure with Bootsie Galbraith, wife of the American ambassador to Great Britain — Lynn made it a point to be at the right place at the right season, and she appeared to do so as effortlessly as a PTA mother in Omaha attending her son's Little League game. Some friends suggest that the reason Lynn has so few, if any, enemies is she is not in one place long enough to make them.

Only a small fraction of her hundreds of fellow jet setters, however, were invited to her Villa Mauresque, to her Safari party, her Gypsy party, her Flower Power party.

Although Europe was where Lynn focused most of her attention at the start of the 1980s, she was conducting the same sort of campaign in America. She was seen and photographed more and more often at the chicest parties in New York — a party at Park Avenue's Seventh Regiment Armory hosted by Cartier; a small birthday bash on the St. Regis roof, where she was seated next to fashion empress Diana Vreeland.

When she was not flying to New York for a small dinner or big charity ball, she was decorating Allington with the most important new names and making it easy for members of the international press to meet their recurring deadlines with just the sort of stories they need on a relentlessly regular basis.

On June 4, 1980, she had a dinner party for fifty guests honoring her friends Diane Von Furstenberg and Barry Diller. Among those at the dinner was Andy Warhol, the snow owl, who had flown in to see the installation of the twin portraits of Lynn he had just completed. Installed over the living room mantel, like a diptych above an altar, the portraits were not only beautiful but, because of the artist's fame, the ultimate in chic. In the world of publicity, Lynn and Warhol were perfect mates, their relationship consummated not in bed but on the sheets of newsprint.

Warhol aside, Lynn had not felt it important to fill her homes with great works of art, an expensive necessity for many at her economic and social level. Instead, she demonstrated her originality and self-confidence by hanging paintings she had done herself — oils in the Impressionist style.

The night following her Warhol vernissage, Lynn hosted the world premiere of the soon-to-be hit movie *Urban Cowboy*. In addition to the movie premiere at a Houston theater, Lynn threw a huge after-party at the mammoth Houston honkey-tonk Gilley's, where the movie had been filmed. *Urban Cowboy*'s stars, John Travolta and Debra Winger, of course flew in for the party.

Andy Warhol discussed the movie premiere in his diary: "There were thousands of paparazzi and fans because they'd never had a world premiere in Houston before. Jerry Hall and Lynn were standing in front of the theater with the TV crew and Lynn was becoming like Barbara Walters: 'And now we have the famous artist, Andy Warhol, and Jerry and Cyndy Hall who're stars in the movie, and say, Jerry, where'd you get that costume?'"

Part of Andy's fascination with Lynn was that she shared his genius for publicity. He mentioned her frequently in his diaries, often commenting on her prominent seating at parties and her looks. About one of her parties at Villa Mauresque, he wrote, "Lynn was wearing a dress that was split up the sides and you could see all her breasts and she just had a little bikini on and she looked beautiful. She has a great body."

A year later, when Andy wanted to do Ivana Trump's portrait, he showed Ivana and Donald Trump one of the multiple portraits he had done of Lynn, "so maybe they'll get the idea."

It is doubtful whether a century from now Andy Warhol's work will be remembered, but in this century it was important to know him and be painted by him. It was important because celebrities like Lynn Wyatt showed that it was important. What was becoming obvious to many who knew Lynn was that Jerry Hall and Andy Warhol and Liza Minnelli were just as happy to be in Lynn's spotlight as she was to be in theirs.

Visitors to her home could not help being impressed by Lynn's extraordinarily catholic taste in celebrity friends. She threw prodigal parties for Luciano Pavarotti, Placido Domingo, and Beverly Sills, but at least as lavish were her parties for Liza, Mick Jagger, and Sammy Davis, Jr. When England's Windsor Castle loaned an art exhibit to Houston's Museum of Fine Arts, Princess Margaret came to town for the opening and stayed with Lynn. It was no wonder that, by the early 1980s, Houston society had renamed Allington "the Wyatt Regency."

Just as the Lo-Vaca fight was about to be settled, more negative stories about Oscar's business tactics were revealed in the press. *Texas Monthly* broke the news in February 1978: "Later this month, the Justice Department is expected to ask for criminal indictments against four major energy companies — Exxon, Mobil, Texaco and Coastal States — and one large independent, Summit Gas Company of Houston."

The magazine explained that the charge against the companies was "conspiracy to defraud consumers of millions of dollars by illegally selling 'old' oil . . . as 'new' oil."

Oscar, as well as Coastal and one of its subsidiaries, along with others, was being investigated "for alleged criminal oil price violations involving the sale of low-priced domestic crude oil as high-priced foreign oil" in the wake of the Arab oil embargo.

In an effort to prevent unscrupulous price gouging in the oil industry, the government had passed an Emergency Petroleum Allocation Act, and in 1978 the FBI began an investigation of possible offenders.

Typically, Oscar attacked his attackers. He filed suit against the FBI and the Justice Department to stop them from harassing him and his company with threats of indictment. He later told the *Wall Street Journal* that he filed suit against the government "just to show the bastards they weren't scaring me."

To fight the government's charge of price fixing, Oscar hired Fulbright & Jaworski's much admired Thomas R. McDade. Oscar uses McDade as his head gunslinger when a fight is serious enough, and this fight was very serious. The maximum sentence was a year in jail.

The United States Attorney for the Southern District of Texas charged in a Criminal Information: "That on or about December 31, 1975, . . . Oscar S. Wyatt, Jr., individually and in his capacity as Chairman of the Board and Chief Executive Officer of The Coastal Corporation . . . [and others] . . . [engaged] in a practice which constituted a means to obtain a price for crude oil higher than permitted by regulation . . . By concealing the true price of 331,458.98 barrels of domestic crude oil . . ."

For all Oscar's furious denials and blustering, he was quick to have his attorneys start negotiations for a plea bargain beginning on January 4, 1980. A week later Oscar appeared in federal court, pleaded guilty, and was fined the maximum, $40,000, which he paid by check three days later.

In the Guilty Plea that Oscar signed, he swore, in paragraph III: "I understand the elements of the offense, and I am entering this plea of guilty freely, voluntarily, in the exercise of my own good judgment, and because I am guilty."

It seems likely that what brought Oscar to his quick confession of guilt was in paragraph VII, which read: "I am aware that the maximum sentence provided by statute for this offense is imprisonment not to exceed one year or a fine not to exceed $40,000 for each violation; and . . . may be imposed in the sole discretion of the Presiding Judge."

But the words "imprisonment not to exceed one year or" had been scratched out by the United States Attorney, J. A. Canales, who had initiated the charge.

In addition to Oscar's fine, Coastal pleaded no contest and paid the government a refund of $9 million to the Department of Energy. Holborn Oil Company, a Coastal subsidiary, pleaded guilty and was ordered to pay $1 million in civil penalties, and Coral States Crude also pleaded guilty and was also directed to pay $9 million to the Department of Energy.

Once safely out of the shadow of the jailhouse, Oscar for almost two years fought various reengagements in court.

On September 25, 1981, after months of McDade's maneuverings, Judge George E. Cire vacated Oscar's earlier guilty plea and fine on grounds of a faulty government plea bargain, and Oscar pleaded guilty to an amended criminal information. He admitted to a misdemeanor oil pricing violation and again was sentenced to pay the maximum fine of $40,000, which he had already paid in 1980.

Oscar is, of course, not the only oilman who has broken the law. Several of the successful oilmen of the generation before Wyatt, such as Clint Murchison, Sr., and H. L. Hunt, built their fortunes on "hot oil," illegally pumped and sold in excess of the legal "allowable."

But what seems to differentiate Oscar Wyatt is his lack of hypocrisy about "doing good." Mobil and Exxon publish their purported virtue, for example, by supporting public television, but any such gestures by Coastal or by Oscar personally are rare and remarkably modest financially.

Instead of advertising how virtuous he is, Oscar has relentlessly insisted how bad he is, and this, as it does with a naughty, lonely child, has brought him much more attention than he would have garnered in the much more crowded and competitive field of do-gooders.

Nothing has helped Oscar more to prove his "badness" than his deep and abiding love of litigation. When it comes to filing lawsuits and meeting his enemies (and friends) at the courthouse, Oscar is like an addict. He is a plaintiffaholic, whose thirst for confrontation in the courtroom is unslakable.

Most large companies and successful businessmen know that lawsuits, either those that they file or those filed against them, are a necessary part of doing business, and Coastal and its chairman are entitled to their fair share. But Oscar's lawsuits are different in both number and kind. They run the gamut from high-profile fights over ten of millions of dollars to petty disputes where as little as $700 is at stake. Oscar also is notorious for suing the government over matters large and small.

In one case, Oscar reportedly thought he had an ironclad $19 million contract to sell the U.S. military 182 million gallons of aviation fuel, but the military ended up buying less than half the fuel specified in the contract. Oscar sued the federal government, and the case went all the way to the U.S. Supreme Court, which ruled that Wyatt was not owed damages.

In another suit, he spent $3,000 suing the government to recover $700 worth of whiskey that he claimed United States Customs agents had improperly confiscated from his plane in New York.

In May 1981, the board of Coastal passed a resolution that authorized management to begin studying the desirability of a "possible redeployment and restructuring of the operations and assets of the company." This was to include advice from investment banks and "consideration of possible disposition or spinoff of significant portions of Coastal's assets and operations."

Aware of the enormous latitude this gave Oscar and of his usual shrewdness and creativity, investors went wild and the influx of buy orders for Coastal on the New York Stock Exchange the morning after the board meeting resulted in a halt in trading.

On May 14 and 24, 1981, the *Houston Chronicle* ran articles about the spin-off, respectively titled, "Wyatt is likely to be winner whatever happens at Coastal" and "Officials questioning close ties between Coastal and spinoff."

The articles led the fifty-five-year-old Oscar to sue for libel. His suit declared that, prior to the articles, "Wyatt enjoyed the respect, confidence and esteem of his friends, neighbors and business colleagues in Texas as well as . . . of other parts of the world." He charged that the *Chronicle* had wickedly and maliciously intended to "injure, disgrace and defame Wyatt" causing him "great injury and damage."

This is reminiscent of a story about Willus Britt, a customer in a Klondike saloon who kept company with a hooker named Nellie. One night Willus ran out of the saloon and emptied his revolver at a stranger, who escaped. When another barfly asked what the man had done, Willus replied, "He insulted Nellie," to which the questioner marveled, "For god's sake, *how?*"

The *Chronicle*, in its reply to Oscar's suit, said that its statements were true, fair, and reasonable criticism of matters of public concern and that if Wyatt's reputation was injured, it had been injured by articles previously published in other newspapers and periodicals.

The paper, in order to prove the accuracy of its articles, demanded a mass of documents that might embarrass Oscar, including those relating to the spin-off or sale of any Coastal subsidiary; those relating to Coastal's being investigated by the Commerce Department, SEC, Justice Department, and the Canadian or any other government; those relating to guilty pleas by Oscar, and those concerning any Coastal business with any Arab nation that participated in the boycott of firms doing business with Israel.

Oscar had again blustered and threatened, but faced by an opponent with deep enough pockets and a strong enough resolve not to be bullied, Oscar hesitated and backed down. The matter never came to trial and was settled on August 23, 1985, when the court entered a "take nothing judgment in favor of the defendants . . . and against plaintiff Oscar S. Wyatt, Jr."

In most civilizations, men have found it useful, perhaps even essential, to invent sports, in addition to the blood sports. These competitive games, requiring strength and skill and sometimes shrewd thought, apparently assuage inborn feelings of competitiveness and even brutality. As a boy, Oscar played football with an often uncontrollable ferocity. Later, he was an excellent and instinctive sailor and hunter. It seems possible that Oscar's litigiousness may best be explained as a form of sport — a complicated and ferocious game in which he has two important advantages — a rich supply of anger and a rich supply of money.

14

___

ON APRIL 24, 1981, Bernard Sakowitz woke at his home in Paradise Valley, Arizona, and said he wanted to visit the Scottsdale store. So the store's gift and china buyer, Val Renken, a frequent houseguest of Bernard and Ann in Arizona, drove him to the store, put him in his wheelchair, and pushed him through it. The seventy-four-year-old chairman, weak and in ill health, greeted salespeople and toured the store one last time, in much the same way that his father, Tobias, had on a hospital bed at the Post Oak store. Not long after Val and Bernard returned home, Bernard suffered a heart attack and died.

In Bernard's will, Robert was left shares of stock in the store, while Lynn received what her father deemed to be the cash equivalent, $700,000. This, Oscar would say later, was contrary to the agreement he had made with Bernard on that day in 1974 when Bernard and Robert had asked him to guarantee personally the Alex Sackton note. Oscar said later, under oath, that he had agreed to sign the note only on Bernard's assurance that Lynn and Robert would receive "share and share alike" in Bernard's estate. Oscar noticed that the will was dated October 5, 1980, just six months before Bernard died.

Oscar was not a man to forget a deal or forgive the person who welshed on it. But, in this case, he did not blame Bernard; all his anger seemed to be directed toward Robert.

Almost from the time Oscar came into the family, there was no love lost between him and Robert. Each was a constant reminder to the other of his own shortcomings. Oscar disdained the easy, privileged upbringing Robert had received; Robert saw in Oscar a man who reminded him that, because of that privileged upbringing, he had to do better and accomplish more to win respect. As long as Bernard was alive, Oscar and Robert were civil to one another, but Bernard's death and his will changed that. It marked the beginning of the public split in the family.

After ten years of trying to open a store in Dallas, Sakowitz finally did it in July 1981. National newspapers and local cocktail parties were filled with catchy phrases signaling the arrival. "An invader in the land of the enemy," reported the New York Times News Service. In the words of another observer, "Bobby saw himself as the new Achilles who had come to Dallas to vanquish his Hector, Stanley Marcus, and drag his body three times around the downtown store."

From the outside, the three-story, 127,000-square-foot store looked like a giant, square, pink marble bunker. It loomed large in the harsh Texas sun, all by itself in a newly named "Sakowitz Village on the Parkway," surrounded by an enormous parking lot and a string of small boutiques under construction.

Inside, the store was a showcase of pink marble — handpicked by Robert himself at President Marcos's Philippine quarries — high ceilings, and beautiful burled woods. The store was more grand than any other in Dallas, including the flagship Neiman-Marcus downtown.

The opening of the store had come none too soon for Sakowitz. After years of failed negotiations to build a store on an open parcel of land adjacent to Neiman-Marcus's Northpark store, Robert finally negotiated a real estate deal — in which he had a personal stake — to build across from the Neiman's at Prestonwood Mall in far north Dallas.

"We thought we'd return the favor," Robert said, referring to Neiman-Marcus's landing on Sakowitz's doorstep in the early 1960s in Houston.

But unlike the Sakowitzes, who snubbed the Marcuses when they came to Houston, the Marcus family cordially welcomed the Houston retailer. Richard Marcus toured the new store with Robert and complimented him on its beauty. Even though prior to Sakowitz's opening Richard viewed Sakowitz as serious competition, he always gave the impression that it was friendly competition. Richard had a scaled-down model of a billboard made from a photograph he had taken of Robert with a boa constrictor around his neck. The billboard's headline read, "Neiman-Marcus Welcomes Bumptious Bob and His Boa to Dallas."

While most Dallas retailers were impressed with the elegance of the store, many also breathed a sigh of relief. The merchandise presented less of a threat than anticipated. It seemed that Robert had been carried away with the sophistication of the Dallas woman. There were large quantities of "Innovational" clothes and too little of those less extreme fashions that make the money in retailing.

Nor was the store well stocked with merchandise. "I walked through the first floor and said to myself, 'How nice, Sakowitz has gone into the furniture business,'" says the then president of Dallas's Federated-owned Sanger-Harris department store. "There were beautiful armoires and gorgeous fixtures and a collection of African masks in beautiful display cases. It was magnificent, but there was very little merchandise."

Yet, according to general merchandise manager Harry Berkowitz, "the store did forty percent over plan" in its first year. "It was such a tremendous success we had to go back and revise all our budgets."

Within sixty days of the Dallas store opening, Robert presented Berkowitz with a leased Mercedes 450 SL. "This is just a way of saying thanks for Dallas," Robert told him. (Robert himself drove a Sakowitz-green Lamborghini.)

"I think Robert thought that with the Dallas store, and with our successes, that we'd be on our way to a lot of other cities," says Berkowitz. "We were having such incredible increases and things were coming so easy for us that it was hard to realize that there might be a tomorrow. The sky was the limit."

As long as times were good, the store thrived. Dallasites were spending money so wildly in 1981 that even if Sakowitz did only a fraction of the business done there by Neiman-Marcus or Lord & Taylor or Marshall Field or Saks Fifth Avenue, it still did a good business. But when times turned bad, Sakowitz was the first to fall.

A large part of the store's eventual problems was its freestanding location. Customers who were shopping at Prestonwood Mall had to cross a very busy four-lane street to get to Sakowitz. In the view of too many potential customers, the store was not enough to make the trip worthwhile.

And even as late as 1981, many women remained loyal to the hometown store. A Dallas socialite whose closets were filled with

Valentino and Saint Laurent and who has a flair for the unusual says, "I went out there occasionally, but I continued to do most of my shopping at downtown Neiman's. That's where I've always gone. The saleslady who waits on me at Neiman's had also waited on my grandmother."

Other potential customers stayed away because of a deep rivalry — not just between Neiman-Marcus and Sakowitz, but also between Dallas and Houston, the two largest cities in the most boastful state in the union. Despite its early success, within eighteen months of the store's opening it was obvious that this time Robert had gone too far. He was out of his depth in the big pond of Big D.

Just when it seemed that Lynn could not possibly be more in favor with Prince Rainier and Princess Grace and, therefore, more in the spotlight, Grace asked Lynn to chair the fiftieth anniversary of Monaco's Bal de la Rose.

Founded in 1931 to benefit the American Hospital in Paris, the Bal de la Rose was the social highlight of the season, and the selection of Lynn Wyatt as chairman was a first. No American had ever chaired the ball. To many society men and women, it seemed extraordinary that a Texan should receive this honor. But not to Grace. Part of what Grace liked so much about Lynn, aside from Lynn's charm and interest in Grace, was the publicity that Lynn brought to Monaco. One of Grace's goals was to bring more attention to the tiny principality that depended on the tourist trade. If Grace succeeded in increasing tourism, and if the tourists brought more rich Texans to gamble at the Casino, so much the better.

Always aware of the international appeal of Texas, Lynn decided that instead of the Ball of the Rose, the event would be called the Yellow Rose of Texas Ball. It would have Texas flourishes, and on the eve of the ball she would host an informal party that would be pure Texas — with barbecue beef, Lone Star longneck beer, and a country-and-western band.

As plans got under way and she told her Texas friends about them, the guest list grew. When the chartered 707 lifted off the runway at Houston's Intercontinental Airport on Thursday, April 2, 1981, it contained fifty-four of Lynn and Oscar's friends. When night fell and large quantities of liquor and champagne had been consumed, Oscar changed into red flannel pajamas and charged up and down the aisle, making sure each guest had an air mattress and an entire row of seats to sleep on. But once Oscar and Lynn had gone to sleep and the cabin lights were turned off, not every mattress supported only one person.

The next morning, the luggage console in the Nice airport turned with an interesting assemblage: piles of Louis Vuitton luggage, fifteen cases of Lone Star longnecks, hundreds of pounds of barbecued beef and sausage, and a paper sack marked "Straw hat, Nellie Connally."

Lynn's Western soiree may have been an even bigger hit than the ball itself. Both the Americans and the Europeans, wearing yellow bandannas supplied by Lynn, danced to the Western music and devoured mounds of imported barbecue. One Houstonian spoke for many Texans when she said, "This is the first decent meal we've had since we've been in Europe."

The following night, the ballroom in Monte Carlo's Sporting Club was magnificently decorated with four thousand yellow roses, an idea Lynn may have gotten from former sister-in-law Pam's St. Regis reception, and the ceiling sparkled with thousands of tiny white lights. The eight hundred guests entered the ballroom to the strains of one hundred violins.

With Lynn and Oscar and the Grimaldis at the head table were Lynn's close friend Dior designer Marc Bohan, designer Emilio Pucci, ballet's George Balanchine, journalist Arnaud de Borchgrave, and Robert Sakowitz. Lynn wore an off-the-shoulder yellow-gold Valentino gown with a large ruffle that swept around her shoulder and down the back of the gown. When she took to the dance floor with Prince Rainier, she looked good enough to fit the role of princess.

As the reigning monarchs of the principality of Monaco, the Grimaldis usually left the Bal de la Rose right after dinner. That is protocol, so that the other guests may feel free to depart. But on this night, Princess Grace, in her diamond tiara and blue chiffon Dior ball gown, stayed long after the program ended, dancing the "Cotton-eyed Joe" to the music of Houstonian Chubby Lee's Western Electrik Band.

Grace was correct in thinking that the party, chaired by Lynn, would be covered extensively in the world's society pages. In society, from Los Angeles to Palm Beach to Madrid, the most commonly asked question was "How can Lynn top this?"

Just three months after the Bal de la Rose, Lynn threw another extravagant party in the south of France — this time at her own

Villa Mauresque. Guests who came to her parties from neighboring villas often arrived by sea — as they had in Maugham's time — motoring over to Mauresque at sunset and anchoring their yachts in the bay. A cool sea breeze played among the tall pines surrounding the house, providing the perfect climate for the Black-and-White Ball that she gave in July 1981. The guests looked dashing in their black and white. No guest was more elegant than the hostess — in a slinky white Saint Laurent gown with black straps over her open back — except, perhaps, Princess Grace, who was dressed all in white.

"It looked like a thirties movie," Lynn said later. "I was just waiting for Fred Astaire and Ginger Rogers to waltz through."

As had become the custom at Lynn's parties, the guest list of sixty-four included a large group of movie stars and titled Europeans: the Duke and Duchess of Bedford, actor David Niven, model Marisa Berenson, nightclub owner Regine, longtime director of Versailles Gerald van der Kemp, Mick Jagger's then wife, Bianca, and, of course, the Grimaldis.

In early September 1982, as Lynn had just returned from the south of France, she learned the terrible news that Princess Grace had been hurt in an automobile accident. Grace had been planning to come and stay with Lynn at Allington in just a few weeks, but now, it appeared, the visit would have to be postponed. Then the news got worse. Bulletins out of Monaco said that Grace had died from internal injuries suffered in the accident.

After giving the press a quote — "She was such a good friend; she was so loyal. I am devastated." — Lynn flew to Monaco to attend Grace's funeral. Lynn was, however, able to pull herself together sufficiently to have Joanna (Mrs. Johnny) Carson to dinner at Allington on the eve of her departure.

As long as Grace was alive, reporters treated her and her family with respect, in part because she was so gracious and treated the press with respect. Prince Rainier, however, did not have Grace's facility for dealing with reporters, and when publicity-seeking Lynn was thrown into the equation, it was destined to turn brutal — and it did.

The week in February 1983 that ended in front-page headlines in the New York tabloids — RAINIER IN ROYAL RAGE and PRINCE OF FURY — began innocently enough when Lynn decided to fly to New York and spend three days with the recently widowed Prince of Monaco.

Rainier and his younger daughter, Stephanie, had made the trip to New York — the first since Grace's death — during the weekend of February 20, to visit Prince Albert, who was enrolled in a finance course at New York's Morgan Guaranty Trust Co.

Lynn's reason for joining the Grimaldis in New York was ostensibly to attend a board meeting of the Princess Grace Foundation. Established after Grace's death, the foundation had been an idea of the Princess's during her lifetime: to support the careers of young artists in drama and ballet.

But Lynn did not merely fly to New York for the meeting and then fly home — though the Grimaldis doubtless later wished she had.

The press would have hounded the now very eligible Rainier even had Lynn not been along. But because Lynn was beautiful and because her identity was unknown to the mass of general city-desk reporters and photographers — she caused a storm of media attention. From the moment she first appeared on Rainier's arm, reporters pushed and shoved to get close to the woman with him, who was variously described as "the blond mystery woman," and the "Grace Kelly look-alike."

On their first night together, they had a quiet dinner at the small, chic, Upper East Side restaurant Le Cirque, accompanied by Monaco's consul general and his wife and Prince Albert and a date. The real trouble began later, when they left the Regency Hotel, where the Grimaldis were staying. Lynn climbed into the limousine first, without incident, but when Rainier stepped up to the car, several photographers pushed their cameras into his face. Angry, he shouted obscenities and slugged sixty-one-year-old photographer Hy Simon in the eye.

Instead of slipping out of town and defusing the growing scandal, Lynn joined Rainier again the following night for theater and dinner. When they arrived on Broadway for a performance of the musical *Nine*, there was an even larger mass of photographers, including an unfortunate Vinnie Zuffante, who was standing in the way of the theater door. "Rainier came up and said, 'You little bitch bastard,' and slugged me in the face," recalled Zuffante.

It was the second time in twenty-four hours that the Prince had punched a photographer; it was also the second night in a row that Rainier was with the same woman. The photographers pushed past Rainier and held their cameras over his head — she was the one they wanted.

While the princely family was devastated by the throng, Lynn was in her element. Moving in and out of public places, the Grimaldis always tried to hide their faces from the cameras. But Lynn did the opposite. She inevitably turned toward the cameras and flashed her killer smile.

Even more unthinkable in the eyes of Monaco's first family, Lynn spoke with the press. Trying to defend Rainier, Lynn told a reporter about the first slugging incident: "When all the photographers rushed in, I ran to the car — but I was watching and I'm sure he did not hit him with his fist."

After the show, Rainier took Lynn and his children to "21" for a late supper, after which the entourage tried to sneak out of "21"'s service entrance to avoid the cameras at the front door. But as their limousine pulled away from the curb, the media arrived in time to catch Albert with the middle finger of one hand upraised in an unprincely fit of temper. The front of the next day's *New York Post* captured Albert's finger and screamed: "Albert gives N.Y. the bird — & daddy slugs second fotog."

Finally, "Suzy," the *New York Daily News* columnist who had covered the Wyatts and the Sakowitzes for years, stepped in to set the record straight about the "so-called 'mystery woman' accompanying Rainier." The woman was Houston socialite Mrs. Oscar Wyatt, a married mother of four, "Suzy" explained.

"Suzy" insisted that all the talk was much ado about very little, but then scolded Lynn and Rainier for their behavior. "If you make a public appearance like that together — granted a long friendship, granted Lynn Wyatt is married — you take your lumps. Everyone concerned is far from a wide-eyed innocent. All must have known they'd be photographed big and hit the papers big. Perhaps Lynn should have saved herself the trouble and stayed in Houston."

"Suzy" then said, doubtless a little too sharply for Lynn's taste, "We've also had to listen to a lot of bull about how Grace and Lynn are such startling look-alikes. Other than their both being blonde and glamorous, there is not even a resemblance."

With Lynn's face splashed all over the New York newspapers, Oscar's phone was overloaded with incoming calls, and he had a typically wry remark for the press. "When my wife is in New York," said he, "I can't think of anyone I'd rather have her go out with than my friend Prince Rainier. If the opposite were true and the tables were reversed, I'd do the same for him."

A few days after her trip to New York, Lynn and Oscar flew to Los Angeles to attend a party that First Lady Nancy Reagan hosted for Queen Elizabeth and Prince Philip at 20th Century Fox. But in California, with Oscar in tow and Queen Elizabeth very much alive, Lynn was only a bit player.

"Suzy's" revelation that Lynn was married to her own Texas oil prince did little to quell the gossip about Lynn and Rainier. The headlines continued for weeks after the Grimaldis had departed New York. In mid-March, the tabloid *Star* jumped on the story when it screamed: THE INSIDE STORY OF MYSTERY BLONDE WHO FULFILLED PRINCESS GRACE'S FINAL WISH.

"Glamorous Texas multi-millionaire Lynn Wyatt, the late princess' most intimate friend, was answering a desperate plea from Grace's daughter Stephanie to keep a vow that she would always look after the royal family after Grace confided to Lynn she had a dreadful fear she was going to die," burbled *Star*.

The paper also implied, quoting a "royal friend," that there had been a longtime liaison between Lynn and Rainier. "They have been meeting in Monte Carlo for a while. The only reason they went out in public last week was due to Rainier's desperate need for her help. They have been talking on the telephone and meeting in private for months. She has already saved Rainier from collapse on many occasions."

Other less bold types might have gone into hiding, but Lynn was not about to cool it publicly with the Grimaldis. On March 27, just a month after the scandal she had caused in New York, she had Rainier's eldest daughter, Princess Caroline, as her houseguest at Allington. Caroline was on a tour of American cities to drum up support for a campaign to rebuild Shakespeare's Globe Theater on its original London site.

Lynn, however, did set some ground rules for the press this time, probably because Caroline's bodyguards insisted on it. Reporters were almost a fixture at Allington, but on this occasion they were kept outside the house except for one fifteen-minute interval when they were allowed inside. Once inside, they were under strict instructions not to speak to the evening's honoree even though she would be only inches away from them.

Oscar's nine killer German shepherd guard dogs were well known around Houston. Whether the dogs were a deterrent or the Houston press was simply not as vicious as the New York press, the media was on its best behavior.

During the spring and summer, Lynn was busy working on plans for the Princess Grace Foundation gala to be held the following February. New York would have been the natural place for the gala, and Lynn said, "We probably could make more money in New York, but we chose Washington because it's more elegant."

Some social observers wondered whether, in fact, Rainier had refused to return to New York.

Washington was the venue, but the ticket price was pure Texan: an astounding $10,000 per couple for the weekend, which began with a Friday-night reception at the White House with President and Nancy Reagan and ended with a Sunday brunch hosted by Secretary of the Navy John Lehman at the State Department.

The Saturday dinner dance was one of Lynn's finest moments. Seated on President Reagan's left during dinner (Princess Caroline was on his right), she wore an appropriately somber expression as Prince Rainier made a brief and loving speech to the evening's six hundred guests about his deceased wife. Lynn had wowed the rich of Texas and the titled of Europe. Now she had wowed Washington, too.

It was just a year later that President Reagan appointed Lynn to the board of visitors at the U.S. Naval Academy.

Following the weekend, Washington columnist Betty Beale, calling Lynn the capital's "hostess with the mostest," began her column:

> WANTED: Lynn Wyatt, wife of Houston oilman Oscar Wyatt, for a Washington hostess. It was her experienced know-how and connections that put over the whole Princess Grace Foundation weekend in the Capitol City.
> Washington is ready for a hostess like that.

Lynn had become a celebrity, someone who is famous for being famous, and what had helped her more than anything else was something that contained no mystique at all. It was simply self-discipline — the discipline to focus on each goal and achieve it.

Nowhere is this more obvious than in the time and effort she devotes to her physical self. Her hair, her makeup, her body receive endless attention. She had her own personal trainer before most people had heard the term. Wherever she is in the world, she puts herself through a vigorous daily exercise routine, usually indoors and usually to the accompaniment of cassette tapes recorded just for her. In Houston and in the south of France, she swims daily, and at Vail and Gstaad, she is an energetic and adept skier.

Five feet six, with tiny hips and small breasts, she is a small size 4, but she has a great appetite and maintaining her weight takes discipline. In the early eighties, for the figure-conscious, she advocated cold cereal for dinner followed by ice water through the evening. Instead of alcohol at parties, she takes a glass of water with a slice of lemon.

She has been quoted extensively in *W* with tips on how to avoid wear and tear in the peripatetic jet-set world, explaining that she never eats airline food but always drinks plenty of flat mineral water during flights. She tells how during flights she makes frequent trips to the restroom, where she splashes Evian water on her face and exercises as much as possible. "I lift each leg up very high or I'll stretch," she says.

A self-confessed perfectionist, she can be among her own most ardent detractors: "I look at myself in the mirror and I see more flaws than the average person sees." She says that sunglasses are her favorite fashion accessory because "they hide a multitude of flaws."

Lynn even worries about her spectacular hair. Bill Flemming, who began as a hairdresser at Sakowitz's downtown salon in the 1950s, had done Lynn's hair since she was in high school, and was still doing it in the early 1980s, says, "Lynn's hair is fabulous because it's thick and the perfect texture. You can do anything in the world with it."

Because Lynn's once blond hair had turned naturally brown by the time she married, Flemming says, getting it just the right color of blond takes a three-step process. "We'd bleach it, then color it with ash blond color, then we'd do highlights."

This was a much more precise definition than that given by a later hairdresser, Clay Ellison, who once described the look as "fried, dyed and shoved to the side."

Some observers find Lynn too perfect or plastic to be attractive. "I wonder how she'd do if she was hosed down," says a Washington socialite.

"I don't know what she'd look like without all her armor," says an acquaintance, adding, "There are jokes about Lynn in London, like, 'Make sure Lynn doesn't fall down and break her hair.'"

But her close friend top designer Bill Blass says Lynn looks just as good on a Saturday afternoon, romping in the woods at Bill's Connecticut estate, as she does at the fanciest society ball. "She wears whatever she wears with great authority," says Blass. "You can't imagine anybody looking better in jeans and boots and a T-shirt than she does."

Years ago, when Blass saw Lynn at a party in a dress of his, he walked over to her and whispered, "You have the dress on back-ward." Then, after pausing a moment, he smiled and added, "And it looks better that way."

Blass says the reason Lynn has outshone so many other rich society women around the world is her "innate honesty." He says, "She is what she is. She doesn't try to be anything else. She not only looks very attractive, she's got that great booming Texas laugh and she has a sense of fun."

Lynn has used the same obsession with detail to achieve success as a hostess as she has in devoting time to her physical self. Houston's top bandleader, who has played the city's society parties for forty years, says, "Lynn gives specific, written instructions about the music and the schedule, right down to the minute she wants the band to begin playing.

"During dinner, she will look over at the band and direct with her eyes and with the slightest nod of her head. She's motioning for the music to be louder or softer, or for the band to pick up the tempo or slow it down. She knows exactly what she wants, and you'd better be on your toes every minute."

Lynn's best talent as a party-giver is that she is able to oversee every detail of her parties without appearing to. The band may feel under intense pressure, but her guests are unaware of the behind-the-scenes maneuverings. "What's so exceptional about Lynn's parties is that they are completely unaffected," says New York cabaret pianist Bobby Short, who does not perform at Lynn's parties but is a guest at her table. "Her parties are totally simple and relaxed and warm, as she is. I think she strives to give her guests exceptionally good food and comfort and music and a good time."

When in Houston, Lynn has three favorite kinds of parties: dinner for fifty guests with dancing; dinner for twenty-two with piano music; or Oscar's favorite, dinner for eight in the wine cellar.

Lynn also opens her home for parties benefiting numerous charities and organizations, but, like most top society women, she has always focused her time and money on just two — the Houston Grand Opera and the Alley Theater.

The Opera's governing board early recognized what an asset she could be and made her a vice president. She quickly proved they were right. In June 1980, as chairman of the Opera's Silver Anniversary Cash Reserve Campaign, she wrote on her "Mrs. Oscar S. Wyatt, Jr." letterhead to each member of the Opera's governing board asking for their donations to the $1.2 million campaign: "With the last $167,000 left to raise I now turn to you and ask your serious consideration of a one-time 25th Anniversary gift or pledge to help put us over the top and qualify for additional matching funds."

Next to her signature she wrote in longhand, *"Please* help!" The result was an outpouring of funds that netted the Opera $60,000 more than its goal.

In 1984, the skin-care company La Prairie used Lynn's face in its national advertising, for which she exacted a fee of $50,000 that she insisted be paid to the Houston Grand Opera.

By the mid-eighties, Lynn had become known in American society, as well as European, and the ultimate expression came in June 1985, when she was the cover of *Town & Country*. It was not only her beauty that landed Lynn on the cover.

"What makes Lynn stand out from the crowd is her extraordinary affability and accessibility," says longtime *Town & Country* editor-in-chief Frank Zachary. "I find her without any pretension whatsoever."

It is impossible to exaggerate just how unusual Lynn is in this respect. Whereas many of Lynn's fellow climbers piously pretend that they care nothing about being pictured and written about in the press, indeed that they allow publicity for themselves only out of duty for the causes they work for, Lynn has no such affectation.

Once an editor or writer expresses interest in writing about her, Lynn takes charge of her press coverage. "When I called and told her I wanted to include her in an article about Texas," says an international journalist, "she said, 'But of course, dahlin'. How marvelous! Who is the editor of the story? Who is the photographer? When will it be published? How much coverage will be devoted to me?' All of this comes out of her like a computer."

A *Town & Country* writer recalls the time he telephoned Lynn in Europe to get a quick quote for an article titled "Stinginess

Among the Rich." "When I asked her about her favorite stinginess, she first told me how thrilled she was to hear from me and that she would call me the next day," says the writer. "She did call the next day with a witty quote; and called again the following day and again the following day, each time from Europe and each time with the tiniest changes that marginally improved the already very acceptable quote."

Her quote finally ran as: "I simply cannot throw away all that silky smooth tissue paper that comes in the boxes with new clothes. I smooth it out and keep a big stash of it in my closets, both in Houston and in France. The only reason that I'm not buried in it is that I travel so much: I use the tissue paper in packing, to keep my clothes from wrinkling."

Just as with her quotes, she is compulsive about her photographs. Robert Clark, a former special projects editor of *Town & Country*, says, "Because she's been photographed by so many of the great masters — Helmut Newton, Norman Parkinson, Francesco Scavullo, Andy Warhol — she knows exactly what her best angles are. She knows how to do the twinkle, how to give the smile, give the little bit of laughter that doesn't show too much teeth."

Bill Blass says it is obvious why, when Lynn appears at a party, photographers immediately gather around. "New York photographers, whether it's the *New York Times* or *Women's Wear*, are pretty blasé but not where Lynn's concerned. They know they'll get an attractive picture, so they always photograph her."

15

OSCAR'S MONEY had helped Lynn get to a certain point, but the question now was whether his reputation would prevent her from going farther. "In London, they whisper," says a peripatetic jet-setter, "that Lynn's second husband is worse than her first, and her first was a murderer." Nowhere were the whispers louder than in Houston. Lynn was charming and beautiful, but Oscar was too tough and too crude, society said. His millions may have bought him the Cullen mansion at the head of River Oaks Boulevard, but they would never get him in the country club next door. A rumor about Oscar and River Oaks Country Club has circulated so long that it is part of his myth. One day when the club's board of directors met at the club, Oscar allegedly stormed into the meeting and growled, "The only reason I'm not a member of this club is my wife's a Jew," to which one of the board members reportedly replied coolly, "No, Oscar. We *like Lynn.*"

"We have at least a dozen Jewish members, maybe two dozen — I don't think anyone keeps count," says a River Oaks member. "I promise you, Lynn is very desirable, and there are many people who would love to have her as a member. Oscar is just too damn mean. Sure, there are tough oilmen and people rough around the edges in the club, but no one in a league with Oscar."

Oscar seems to understand what it is that makes him, in Dr. Johnson's phrase, "a very unclubable man."

"Why do you think the Alfalfa Club has never asked me to be a member?" Oscar asked a reporter about the prestigious Washington club. "They don't let me in because they know they can't control me, and I might say anything I goddamn want."

A leader in Texas's oil and gas business recalls, "Exxon every year used to have a party in Houston at which the New York executives came down and met the Houston oil fraternity. One year, the president of Exxon called me and he said, 'Now, we really have to invite the whole Houston oil fraternity. Oscar Wyatt will probably be there, but you know *why* we have to invite him, don't you? We have to invite everybody.' It's like he was saying, 'We have to invite the garbage man too.'"

Yet, not everyone agrees that Oscar would be a detriment to a prestigious club in Texas or elsewhere. George Parker, a director of Texaco and a member of some of the nation's most exclusive clubs, says, "Oscar would add a lot to any club because he's done something with his life. He's not living on five generations of inherited wealth like a lot of the guys in my clubs."

Several men who are part of what passes for Old Money in Texas privately admit that they find Oscar very appealing. They admire his brilliant mind and they find his candor refreshing.

"He's the meanest, crudest, foulmouthed son-of-a-bitch in the world, and I *like* the guy," says a Dallas oilman, "because you know exactly what he thinks."

Former secretary of commerce in the Bush administration Robert Mosbacher once summarized the feeling of many Texas business leaders: "Oscar does and says overtly what everyone else does and says covertly."

George Parker recalls when Texaco's directors had Oscar and General Motors' then president Roger Smith, as well as ten or twelve other top Fortune 500 executives, to Texaco's Wyoming ranch one weekend. The men had gathered in the ranch house when Roger Smith began a conversation about coal as the auto fuel of the future.

"This set off Oscar," George recalls, "and he said point-blank to Roger, 'You guys at GM don't know how to make cars. Your cars aren't worth a damn.'"

There was nervous laughter among the group. Oscar's contempt for Smith was withering. "This was supposed to be a friendly, relaxed setting," says George. "We weren't there to discuss the future of GM, for gosh sakes."

As the others listened, Oscar continued ranting at Smith. "I've got three people in the hospital right now from accidents caused by your machinery," he said.

Although everyone in the room other than Oscar felt very

uncomfortable, no one was about to ask Oscar to let up on Smith. When Texaco was bankrupt a few years earlier, following a $10.53 billion legal judgment in favor of Pennzoil, Oscar had personally written a check to Texaco for $125 million.

A former vice president of Coastal recalls the time he was taking a customer, a U.S. Steel executive, to lunch and Oscar got on the elevator. "I said, 'Mr. Wyatt, I'd like you to meet Mr. Bradigan with U.S. Steel,' and Oscar turns to the guy and says, 'U.S. Steel is the most immoral fucking company that ever fucked another company in business. When business is good they fuck you. When business is bad they fuck you even more.' The door opens and he gets off. The man was so embarrassed. I was speechless. I didn't know what to say, so I said, 'Well, that was our chairman of the board.'"

By the eighties, Oscar had become famous for being equally crude and foulmouthed to women, even in the most elegant social settings.

Christina Zilker recalls her first exposure to Oscar at a dinner party for fifty guests that she and her husband gave at their antebellum mansion on River Oaks Boulevard.

"We had moved to Houston and I had become friends with Lynn, but I had never met Oscar, so I seated him on my right at my table," says Christina, a very attractive blonde. "When we sat down to dinner, he turned to me and the first words out of his mouth were 'I know some Greek guy you fucked.'"

Christina could hardly believe her ears. Oscar's words were not whispered. They were spoken loud and pointedly and they demanded a response.

"Obviously, he was trying to shock me," says Christina, "but I wasn't going to let him do this. So I turned to him and said, 'Oh, do you really? Well, you see, I only know one Greek . . .'"

Oscar interrupted, "Oh, but I can't remember his name."

"Well, let's see," Christina said matter-of-factly, "I only know one Greek and his name is Taki Theodocropolis and I've never slept with him but do let me know if you remember the name."

"Oscar didn't respond," says Christina, "and I went back to eating my appetizer."

Christina was able to laugh off Oscar, but others have not been so lucky.

"I was seated next to him at a dinner at Allington," recalls a Houston socialite. "And during dinner, he reached over and put his hand up my skirt. I tried to fight him off, but he kept doing it. I was furious. I was so humiliated. But he was laughing and having a good time. I told my husband I would never go to another party there again. But regretfully I did, and again I was seated next to Oscar. So before dinner I went to the table and changed the seating. Lynn wasn't pleased at all about my doing this, but I wasn't about to sit next to him again."

Often his jokes are at a junior-high-school level. When rumors circulated years ago that Oscar had once had cancer, a reporter asked him, "Have you had cancer?"

"Cancer? Hmmm. Maybe I have," he responded. "What was her last name?"

A female guest at a party asked Oscar, "How are you?"

"Better than anyone *you've* ever had," he replied.

Oscar's obvious lack of manners is not the result of ignorance or stupidity. On the contrary, his efforts to shock polite society with his rude and crude comments seem as carefully studied and crafted as Lynn's quotes for the fashion and society press.

"He does this as a power thing," says an international socialite and female friend of Lynn and Oscar's. "He's marking his territory, like a dog urinating on a hydrant. He's saying, whether he's a guest or the host, 'This is my table. This is my party. I'm the one calling the shots here.'"

Not every woman is offended by his crudeness.

"Oscar's not terribly attractive physically, but he has a powerful sexual magnetism," says the beautiful novelist Nancy Holmes. "Onassis had it and Paul Mellon has it. I've seen it being around these two men and I see the same thing in Oscar. It's very exciting to be around a powerful man, and, say what you want, a lot of women, myself included, think there's a certain appeal to the rudeness and the roughness."

But often Oscar's comments are designed not only to shock, but also to hurt. He seems especially to enjoy telling women that they need to lose weight, an insult that he must have decided long ago demonstrates how tough he is, and which is perhaps related to his struggles with his own weight.

He has been known to put down even Lynn to others. An acquaintance of Lynn's recalls a party where she said to Oscar, "Lynn looks so beautiful," to which Oscar snapped, "With what I spend on plastic surgery she ought to."

But Lynn was quick to defend Oscar — even if it seemed she was damning with faint praise — when profiles of Oscar appeared in *Vanity Fair* and *Texas Monthly* in 1991. "All that stuff about Oscar's profanity . . . that's ridiculous. Sure Oscar's vocabulary is dotted with profanities . . . but not in *every* sentence," Lynn exclaimed.

A former Coastal vice president, Jeff Dorrell, says Oscar uses insult as a weapon at the company. "Sometimes I'd say something in a meeting and he'd say, 'You've got to be the dumbest mother-fucker I ever met.'

"A long barrage of insults would inevitably follow," says Dorrell, "including the following: 'Didn't we fire the guy that hired you? Wasn't he stupid too?

"'You're just another one of the fourteen thousand idiots that I employ here. Get out of here. You're too stupid to have a meeting with.'

"At first when he did this," says Dorrell, "I was struck speechless. I was really humiliated. I expected to be fired. I didn't discover until later that he made this sort of attack on everybody, and I think he loses respect for a person if they're shaken or physically cowed. I think he likes you to fight back."

But insult is only one of his weapons in business. His charm is at least equally dangerous. When Oscar turns on the full force of his charm he is absolutely irresistible. A Dallas attorney recalls a meeting with a client of his and Oscar in the 1960s when he warned his client not to sign a contract Oscar was offering. "Buried deep in the contract was a sentence that essentially said, 'Despite all else, you do what I want.'"

Oscar, the attorney recalls, "grinned, put his arm on the client's shoulder, and said, 'Now, are you going to let this Harvard lawyer bust our deal?'"

"My client was completely taken in, signed the contract, and, of course, not long after Oscar screwed him to the wall."

By the mid-eighties, friends and critics began calling the Wyatt match simply a marriage of convenience because Lynn and Oscar lived separate lives. While Lynn was jetting to New York and Los Angeles and Europe, Oscar was off on business in the Middle East.

Not only were they apart almost as much as they were together, but also Oscar protested so loudly about Lynn's lifestyle and her parties that some who did not know him well assumed he really hated his wife's social career.

"I do all that jet-setting horseshit because it gives my wife pleasure," he told a reporter in 1991. "I don't want to know who's sleeping with whom or what jewels Mr. So-and-So gave his wife for her birthday. I just don't give a damn."

While Oscar does do the jet-setting number because it gives his wife pleasure, that is only part of the story. More important, the money he spends underwriting Lynn's clothes and jewelry, her travels and parties, and homes in the south of France and Houston significantly benefits his business. It was Lynn's friendship with Princess Margaret that gave him a public visibility with England's royal family that increased his stature in the business world.

When Dallasite Nancy Hamon spent $400,000 to take one hundred friends on a Mediterranean cruise on the *Sea Goddess*, Lynn and Oscar were on board. According to a New York socialite also on the cruise, Oscar insisted that he and Lynn go on the cruise because it included a visit with Saudi Arabian oilman Adnan Khashoggi. The woman says that at a lunch Khashoggi gave at his Moroccan palace for Nancy Hamon's guests Oscar jockeyed for position to get close to Adnan. "Oscar stayed very close to me because he knows how well I know Adnan," she recalls.

Oscar did get his talk with Adnan, and the morning following the lunch, Oscar and Lynn politely departed the *Sea Goddess* when one of Oscar's planes came and picked them up.

If international financiers like Henry Kravis, politicians like François Mitterrand, automobile manufacturers, and major publishers are part of the glitterati, it is not primarily because they want their pictures or names in the columns but because this is where the power wielders discuss deals, or at least lay the groundwork.

Lynn's reputation in international society has made her into a trophy wife for Oscar. When he married her, she was beautiful and from a good Houston family, but now she was much more. She had become a well-known figure around the world. She had climbed to the top of her field just as he had in his.

"Oscar sees feminine perfection in Lynn," says Nancy Holmes. "She's a good business deal for him, and good businesses make good marriages."

While observers had begun to ask why Oscar stayed with Lynn if he supposedly hated her jet-setting career, a more commonly asked question was why she stayed with such a crude man when she could divorce him and still be very rich.

But those close to Lynn say that she stays with him because she loves him and what she loves most about him is his strength.

In 1984, Lynn described Oscar to the *Wall Street Journal* as "the type of person who would have been thrilled to live in the wild wild West." She explained that her husband delighted in riding horses, tending cattle, hunting big game, and reading the romantic western novels of Louis L'Amour.

"If Oscar were marooned in Alaska," Lynn also said in the *Wall Street Journal*, "he'd survive somehow and by the next week he'd probably be doing business with the Eskimos." And, at another time, she said, "Oscar is alive and always thinking. That's what keeps me interested. I would be bored to death married to a man who likes to go to all of the parties I go to."

But while she was off doing her own thing, and he doing his, what exactly each was doing became a source of speculation. Oscar made no secret about the fact that he saw other women. He took women to dinner in Houston, where he made very little attempt to hide his affairs. He even took his son Douglas with him on at least one such occasion, as Ann Sakowitz testified in her deposition in *Wyatt vs. Sakowitz.*

When word of Oscar's being spotted on visits to a particular woman's apartment reached a Houston gossip columnist, she privately referred to these as "Big O Sightings," but she was far too discreet to report them in her column.

Unlike her husband, if Lynn was having extramarital affairs she was a model of discretion. Despite the speculation in the press that she had had a fling with Rainier and the age-old gossip that she has had affairs both with French president Valerie Giscard d'Estaing and former Texas governor John Connally, there was no evidence.

But a lack of evidence did not stop the whispers, giggles, and raised eyebrows of Lynn's friends when they imagined how Lynn occupied her time on those nights apart from Oscar. A very rich and attractive Houston woman whose family has long been close to the Wyatts and Sakowitzes remembers Lynn's reaction when she mentioned to Lynn that they had a friend in common.

"I had an affair with Warren [Beatty] and he mentioned Lynn to me. He told me that he had met Lynn at the Carlyle [hotel in New York] and that he thought she was a very sexy woman. He kinda had a sparkle in his eye when he said this.

"I'll never forget Lynn's reaction when I told her this. I said, 'We have a friend in common.'

"And she said, 'Who's that?'

"And I said, 'Warren Beatty.'

"And she turned very dark red and said, 'Oh, do you know Warren?'

"And I said, 'Yes. And Warren thinks you're a very, very sexy lady.'

"She just laughed."

What makes Lynn sexy is not just her beauty, but also that she is a world-class flirt. Lynn explained to *W* that to be a great temptress one should be "people-oriented, enjoy stimulating conversation, build confidences and give a lot of yourself, but in an innocent and harmless way."

Whether it is Warren Beatty or Prince Albert seated next to her at a party, she flutters her eyes, lowers her chin, laughs at all the right moments, and appears consumed with interest in what her dinner partner has to say. When one of Lynn's sons was preparing for his first date, Lynn told him to notice the color of the eyes of the girl walking into the room, while at the same time making the girl he was with feel she was the only girl in the world.

Houston's top bandleader says, "In four decades, I have never seen anyone on the dance floor glue their eyes to their dance partner the way Mrs. Wyatt does."

By the 1980s, two of the most smitten of Lynn's male admirers were her eldest sons, Steve and Douglas, who were then in their twenties. When she boasted that she was spoiled being the only female in a household with six men (including her stepson, Carl), those who knew her knew she was telling the truth. Steve and Douglas were handsome, virile men, and they could not have helped notice the way their friends looked at their mother and wanted to know her age (something Lynn had admonished them in high school never to reveal).

In 1986, Douglas escorted Lynn to a black-tie party of the Princess Grace Foundation in Dallas. Seated next to him at dinner was a *Dallas Morning News* columnist, who looked around the party at actor Cary Grant's beautiful wife, Barbara, and actresses Jill St. John and Stefanie Powers, and then whispered to Douglas, "Even in this stellar group, your mother is outstanding."

Douglas, who at twenty-nine had his father Robert Lipman's height and mesmerizing violet-blue eyes, nodded and listened intently, then blushed and said, "My mother is the sexiest, most attractive woman I know." After going on at some length about how Lynn appealed to men of all ages, he confessed, "If I could trade places with any man in the world it would be Oscar Wyatt."

The columnist, who attended an average of ten parties a week and heard endless cocktail talk, after a time found very little of it shocking. But Douglas's words were jarring. He appeared to mean precisely what he said. But it was Steve with whom Lynn seemed more enamored, and he with her.

Even when Steve was a little boy, she doted on him. Now that he was grown, her affection for him had increased.

Lynn herself once coquettishly described Steve as her "love object."

A young Houston heiress who dated Steve in the mid-1980s says she found Lynn's relationship with Steve so unnatural that behind his back she called him "Oedipus Wreck." Says the girlfriend, "Lynn treated Steve much more like a gentleman caller than a son."

In fact, not long after they started dating, the girlfriend grew very troubled by Lynn's interest in the relationship and by the influence she had over Steve.

"One night, a beautiful night with a full moon, Steve and I decided to go up on the roof at my apartment tower. We took some blankets and pillows and we had to sneak up the fire escape. We also took a bottle of champagne and when we got up there, it was this great night. We ended up making love.

"The next day Steve said, 'My mom thought that sounded like so much fun last night.'

"I said, 'Steve, did you feel compelled to tell her *everything?*'

"He said, 'Oh, yes, I tell her *everything.*'

"And then I thought, you know, there's something kind of sick about this."

"Steve talked a lot about how fabulous his mother was and that she had such a great figure," says the girlfriend. "Lynn was the standard for Steve, and I knew that it wouldn't work out for us because I couldn't be more unlike Lynn in every way."

Because Steve and Lynn were so obviously admiring of each other, both Steve's and Lynn's friends wondered how Steve would ever find a woman strong enough to compete with Lynn. The world was about to find out.

16

I S THAT ALL we make?" Lynn Wyatt would gasp at Sakowitz board meetings when the company's profits were revealed.

"Yes, Lynn," Robert would have to admit. "It's a penny business." Lynn just did not understand the retail business, Robert would say to himself. She was used to hearing Oscar talk in billions of dollars. How could he ever compete against Oscar's success?

Robert likes to prove his point that his "is a business where pennies count" with a story of oilman Clint Murchison's asking Stanley Marcus what his profit percentage was on all those "marked-up" dresses at Neiman-Marcus. Stanley, after explaining that there were also such things as "markdowns," revealed his profit percentage, to which Clint replied, "Hell, we spill more than that."

The big money in retailing has never been made on high-end merchandise, and Sakowitz had never made a killing. What was surprising, however, was that even at the height of the Texas oil boom, during the most flamboyant and most lucrative time in Houston's history, when oil prices were at $48 and $49 a barrel, Sakowitz made only a meager profit. In 1982, the company's best year, on sales of $120 million, Sakowitz made only a 4 percent pretax profit, or about $4.8 million. By contrast, Federated Stores (Bloomingdale's, I. Magnin, Filene's) during the same period had a goal of 10 percent annual net profit, after taxes, and often achieved it. Not only was 4 percent a small pretax profit, it was a miserable profit for supporting Robert's ambitious expansion plan — and that was when times were good.

Because the expansion was mostly in cities with oil-related economies, when oil prices fell into the $30 range in 1982, Sakowitz's customers disappeared. Oil-rich women, who had thought nothing of paying $4,000 for a Galanos gown during the boom, suddenly stopped buying.

"It was like a wall came down," recalls a saleslady. "One day they were buying like mad and the next, they were gone. It was almost eerie."

Just as stores and other businesses unrelated to oil had profited enormously from the oil boom of the seventies and early eighties, they came crashing down with the bust. In 1983 alone, 951 businesses with assets totaling $3.7 billion filed a record number of Houston bankruptcies.

At the same time that oil prices fell and the customers stopped coming, Sakowitz had — in addition to its increased operating expenses — the added burden of interest and principal payments on money borrowed for the expansion.

There were other problems, not the least of which was the chairman himself. The self-proclaimed Renaissance man was increasingly intent on controlling everything that happened at the store.

"He was very much a one-man band," says then Neiman-Marcus chairman Richard Marcus. In his view, that spelled disaster.

"I recognized early on," says Marcus, "that there was no way in hell a person sitting in one store could be what my father was and his father had once been to one store. You had to put an organization in place that can embrace the vision you have, buy into it, and support it."

Robert had not assembled a capable management team and given it real power. "Our biggest problem at Sakowitz was that we rewrote the script every day," says a company vice president. "Robert is the most unpredictable person I've ever known. The rules on everything changed constantly."

Robert played executives against each other. They would meet individually with the boss and propose a project. Many times they would leave his office believing their proposal had been accepted, only to learn later that he had then discussed the proposal with someone else who wanted it changed or dropped.

"The final version was whoever got to Robert last, at the end of the day, before he went home," says the same vice president. "To get in last, we stood outside his door, jockeying to see who could get the last word with him. He was constantly on his way to the airport, and we fought like crazy to be the one who got to drive him, to have the final word that day."

Because Robert did not permit decisions to be made on lower levels, every plan and idea had to be brought to him for approval. "I'm sure there were talented people in the organization, but he had no bench strength," says Richard Marcus. "No one ever rose to senior-level management positions that could have possibly succeeded him. I don't think he wanted that kind of strength."

In order for Robert to have a say in the minute details of the store, news of almost everything that was happening in each of the company's eighteen stores had to be brought to his attention. This resulted in too many meetings, in which Robert gave careful consideration to tiny matters: wall coverings, the lighting in dressing rooms, the typeface and type size in advertisements.

A small sign on his desk read NO SURPRISES. An executive says the sign meant "'Don't tell me later about something that's already in the works. I want to know *everything* from conception on.' He drilled that into our heads."

At a time when Robert was committing millions of dollars to inventory and expenses for new stores, when he had bankers and real estate developers and important vendors to deal with, he took time to attend the regular Tuesday advertising meetings and involve himself with every detail of every ad.

When a vice president of the store complained to Robert about the time wasted in endless meetings and the layers of bureaucracy he had created, Robert replied, "Okay, we'll appoint a committee to figure out a way to get information to me better."

In 1983, as profits continued downward, instead of reducing the number of meetings, Robert began scheduling two or more at the same time in conference rooms near each other. This enabled him to run back and forth between meetings and pretend to himself that he was conducting them simultaneously. In fact, this only wasted more of his staff's time. Because no decisions of any substance could be made without him, employees sat waiting for the sound of his running feet. Only after he skidded into the room, and blessed or threw out their decision, could they move to the next item of business.

Because nothing angered Robert more than being told he was wrong, few employees were willing to risk their jobs, as Charles Eastman, the store's creative director, had. Robert was unhappy with the cover of a catalogue and wanted it changed even though Carol Waldrop, head of the catalogue division, explained that to alter the cover at that stage of the process would cost $85,000. Carol decided to bring in Eastman to explain how technically difficult it was to make the change.

After listening at length to what Robert wanted, Charles Eastman finally began to explain, "Robert, this is absolutely ridiculous . . ."

Robert's face turned beet red, and he slammed his fist on the table. "My name is on the outside of this store. Do you understand that?" he yelled. "This is my store. I own it. This is how it's going to be. Don't you ever, *ever* tell me how to run my store."

"He kept slamming and slamming his hand on the table," recalls Carol. "He was exploding. The only thing the guy did was tell him the truth."

Robert's insecurities ran deep. If he hated to hear the truth, it also appeared that he hated his sycophants. In Robert's 1956 St. John's annual he had quoted Oscar Wilde: "Ah, don't say that you agree with me. When people agree with me, I always feel that I must be wrong."

It was curious that a man well educated and well trained to take over the business, who worked so hard and had such important early successes with Courrèges and Saint Laurent, could be so insecure.

The clearest expression of this insecurity was the anger he displayed when people called him "Bobby," the name he had had as a boy around the store. "Bobby" must have seemed like a term of derision to him because it was the name of a little boy, the boss's grandson who had not yet accomplished anything.

But despite the criticism by Sakowitz employees about Robert's insecurities and poor business judgment, many admit that it was difficult not to become caught up in his buoyant enthusiasm.

"Mr. Robert is a visionary and a genius," says a former executive, recalling store meetings in which Robert would fire off an endless succession of "imaginative ideas" for everything from private-label merchandise to new catalogues and new stores. "He made the decisions on everything because he was the smartest."

By the end of 1983, oil prices had dropped into the low 30s, and Sakowitz now operated stores in eighteen locations. With the expansion and its concomitant debt burden greatly reducing

Sakowitz's chances for survival, Robert did the unthinkable. He announced plans to open yet another new store — this one in Tulsa.

By then, the oil town of Tulsa, Oklahoma, had one thing in common with Sakowitz Inc. — both were on a downslide. Given Tulsa's economic climate, a wiser merchant would have scrapped his plans to open a store there. But Robert had been negotiating with the Tulsa mall's developers — in his own as well as the store's behalf — since 1978. To pull out now meant throwing away half a dozen years of hard negotiations.

"I was with Robert when he went to Tulsa to look at the property," recalls Val Renken. "The bankers and advisors told him not to open in Tulsa because the economy was so bad. But he personally had a piece of the deal and he was determined to go forward with it."

Only those who knew Robert well knew why he did not throw out those plans or, at least, curb them. For so long had he been called a Merchant Prince that he had begun to believe it, to believe that he had some divine right, that he was not subject to the rules and limits of ordinary men.

Perhaps the worst expression of this was his decision in June 1983 to take a million dollars out of the company for his own use, when the store was leveraged to the hilt, when oil prices had plummeted, and when many of his customers had disappeared. He first moved the million dollars out of Sakowitz and into a company he owned called Shamrock Shops. He then invested $750,000 of that million dollars in an oil deal that ultimately earned him personally six million dollars.

Robert would later testify in court that two years prior to taking this million dollars out of Sakowitz he had deposited a million dollars of his own money in the company and that he was simply taking his money back. An intercompany account between the store and Shamrock Shops, which he owned, let him move money back and forth freely, prompting one reporter to write, "Robert, as they say in Texas, knew how to cut a fat hog."

The Wyatts were outraged when they learned what he had done with the million dollars. They were also angry when he told a magazine writer in 1981 that because Sakowitz was privately held, "We don't have to worry about, say, quarterly reports to shareholders or their disapproval. With this type of operation you can be a maverick, a very daring maverick, and get away with it."

This quote would haunt Robert when it appeared years later in another major magazine article and ultimately a decade later in court.

When Lynn heard at board meetings about actions Robert had taken or proposed to take that seemed wrong, she would sometimes ask Oscar about them at night. Knowing that if she mentioned Bobby, Oscar would say that what he had done was wrong, she instead would say, "If you had the following happen at Coastal . . ."

It seems almost inconceivable that anyone as smart as Oscar did not know exactly what she was doing.

But occasionally Lynn still came right out and asked Oscar's opinion of Robert's deals. One day in 1983 Robert drove out to Allington and, sitting in Lynn's living room, explained to Lynn that he personally had an opportunity to make $100,000 as a consultant to another specialty store. Lynn at first gave her approval, but then, after discussing it with Oscar and deciding it was a conflict of interest, she voted against it. Not until years later would Lynn come to see just how important her vote was to Robert's personal deals involving the store. In a 1991 deposition, after being repeatedly forced to admit to Robert's attorney that she had voted for deals that she now questioned, Lynn exploded, "So if we all vote for him to murder somebody that means it's okay for him to murder somebody?"

In early 1983, Robert began a courtship of a twenty-four-year-old divorcée, Laura Howell Harris. He was attracted to her from the moment he first saw her, at a charity ball on a date with his nephew Steve Wyatt. Blond, blue-eyed, and taller than Robert, she looked like a high-priced fashion model.

The next day, Robert called Steve and asked whether he was dating Laura seriously. Steve said no, they were just good friends. When Robert asked Steve if he minded if he asked Laura out, Steve again said no. From that moment, Robert began a hot pursuit of Laura, who was nineteen years his junior.

Business associate Gary Easterly recalls one day in Robert's office when Robert pulled out some photographs of Laura: "I said, 'Who's that?' and he said, 'It's a girl I'm dating. She's taller than I am.'"

Easterly says he recalls the conversation because "Robert's been freaked out about his height all his life."

Today Robert says that he is five feet ten and Laura is, in his words, "five feet nine and a quarter." But Robert appears to be five feet seven and Laura almost six feet.

Robert and Laura were a generation apart in age and a world apart in background. Laura Howell was born in 1959 in Galveston. Her father was a petroleum engineer and her mother a school-teacher. When Laura was still a youngster, the family moved to the tiny town of Liberty, Texas. By the time Laura entered high school, they had moved again, this time to the blue-collar Houston suburb Deer Park. After graduating from Deer Park High School, Laura went to work as a secretary for an oil company.

It was not long before Laura met her first husband, Mark Harris, whom she married in 1981. Mark had recently graduated from the University of Texas and gone to work for a Houston oil company. Laura told Mark's mother that she had attended the University of Texas. A friend of Mark's parents, however, said that he had checked and that she had not attended the university.

Later, in a large newspaper spread on Laura and Robert, she was described as having a degree in marketing from UT. But another check in 1992 also failed to turn up any records of Laura having attended UT.

Laura and Mark's marriage lasted just over a year and produced no children. She quickly reentered the dating market, where she met Steve Wyatt. He had not known her long when Robert came on the scene.

The romance, with its whirlwind buying trips and a complete outfitting at Sakowitz, was, as Laura told a reporter, "Like a fairy tale for a girl from Deer Park."

In February 1984, a year after they met, Robert proposed when he and Laura were dining at a Houston steak house. Robert had secretly slipped a large diamond ring around a cigar. After dinner, he asked the owner to bring a humidor and then asked Laura to pick out a cigar for him. She chose the one with the diamond. It was almost as clever as hiding a ring in a box of Cracker Jack.

Elaborate plans were already under way for a June wedding when Laura told Robert that she was pregnant. So the wedding was moved up to April. On April 23, 1984, *Houston Chronicle* gossip columnist Maxine Messinger explained, "Bob Sakowitz and Laura Harris had been planning to wed June 9, but decided they didn't want to wait." Maxine said that they hurried up and tied the knot over the weekend with a wedding at Robert's home with only the immediate families on hand. Even though Maxine did not report why it was that Robert and Laura "didn't want to wait," Houston society was immediately curious.

Store executives were not curious — they were furious when they learned that Robert planned to take a three-week honeymoon in Africa. Three weeks was a long time to be gone, especially at this critical time, and the nature of the trip — a hunting safari — meant he would be virtually unreachable while he was away.

After the honeymoon, during one of the store's advertising meetings, Sakowitz executives got their first look at the woman who was occupying so much of their boss's time. After the usual Tuesday ad meeting, Robert took the stage in the downtown store's large meeting room and announced, "And now what I'm sure you've all been waiting for." He turned to the wings where Laura was waiting.

"She walked onto the stage in a drop-dead black-white-and-gray suit," recalls an executive. "The suit was couture and obviously made for her. But she looked scared to death. She smiled and didn't say anything. She just stood there onstage."

The introduction was not unlike unveiling a new line of sportswear. To the employees — and probably to Laura — it was awkward, uncomfortable, insulting. After a minute or so had passed, Robert took her hand and led her offstage.

But the store's employees and Houston society both agree that Laura has proved to be one of Robert's best choices. Not only is she beautiful, she is kind, down-to-earth, and a devoted mother. What perhaps is also important to her success as a wife is that she is not, in her own right, a social competitor to Robert, as Pam was.

By summer, things at the store were not as blissful as they were at home. Many employees were losing their jobs or having their salaries cut. "I had been at Sakowitz seventeen years, and I was running the Town & Country gift department when Robert made me a salesperson rather than a manager," recalls Mary Ellen Carey, then in her sixties. "Suddenly I was on commission. He really talked down to his employees. He said to me, 'It'll be better for you if you're on commission. You'll be in business for yourself with all your expenses paid.' I said to him, 'Mr. Sakowitz, I look at the figures. It's better for me to be on salary.'

"He moved a lot of people out of management jobs and either fired them or made them salespeople, and they were forced to take salary cuts. He then filled their former jobs with new, inexperienced people at much lower salaries."

By fall, many vendors began to insist on cash before they delivered their goods. The more rumors circulated about trouble, the more wary manufacturers became about delivering prior to payment. Sakowitz's cash-flow problem worsened, and less merchandise arrived. Many employees felt helpless to do anything but watch the store's slow death. They began to fear that they would lose the jobs they had held loyally for years, many for decades.

In 1984, the worst year in the history of Sakowitz, the company reportedly had losses of $3 million on sales of $120 million. But while the store was starved for funds, Robert continued to put substantial sums of money into other projects unrelated to the store. At this very moment, Robert did something for which many of his employees would never forgive him. He bought a mansion on River Oaks Boulevard.

The purchase was made in the name of one of Robert's attorneys because, according to one of his secretaries, Robert wanted to keep it "hush-hush as long as he could." He and Laura planned to do extensive remodeling of the house before they moved in, anyway.

Robert says he used a third party to avoid the risk of having the price go up when the seller learned the buyer was a Sakowitz. This does not explain, however, why he worked to keep it a secret after the purchase was made.

Unbelievably, suicidally, at this same time, Robert began what would become a half-million-dollar investment in another magazine venture. In 1984, he accepted an offer to buy 90 percent of the stock in a start-up magazine called *Texas Sports World*. The magazine, based in Houston and patterned after *Sports Illustrated*, was the idea of Gary Easterly, who had earlier helped Robert acquire stock in *Houston City Magazine* and who had worked on Sakowitz's *The Magazine*.

"Robert agreed to finance the direct mail test to find out our market," says Easterly. "The store paid for some of it, and Robert paid for some of it."

On at least two separate occasions, says Easterly, the checks for Robert's personal purchase of stock in *Texas Sports World* were drawn on the account of Sakowitz Inc. "I picked up these checks at John Panto's office at the store downtown," recalls Easterly. John

Panto paid the family's bills. Although this indicates that the store paid for some of Robert's stock in *Texas Sports*, it is possible that this money — as Robert says was the case with the million dollars he withdrew from Sakowitz in 1983 — was, in fact, his own money that he had put in the Sakowitz account.

Meanwhile, buyers in every department were pleading with vendors who refused to ship goods without receiving cash payment in advance. The catalogue division had to return $600,000 in customers' orders from one catalogue alone because vendors would not ship items to fill the orders unless they were paid in advance. The $500,000 Robert put into the magazine would have much more than paid the cost price of this already sold merchandise.

Just as he had kept his house purchase a secret, Robert managed to keep his investment in *Texas Sports World* under wraps, but the magazine was a growing problem. It continued to drain off cash. To counter this, he and Easterly agreed that they needed to raise cash from outside investors. They hired an investment banking firm, but the firm had difficulty from the start — and one of its biggest difficulties was Robert's name.

"We'd call people and they'd say they were interested, but when we'd mention Robert's name," says one of the investment bankers, "they'd say, 'No, thank you.' He had a reputation around town of being hard to get along with and not a good businessman."

Laura knew about Robert's investment in the magazine and was not pleased. Although she did not appear to object to his initial stock purchase in the magazine, as the months passed and he continued to sink $30,000 or $40,000 at a time into the venture, she became increasingly unhappy about it.

One Saturday, Gary Easterly rang the doorbell at the Sakowitz home in River Oaks. Laura opened the door and, without taking a breath, said, "Gary, the silver's in the dining room. Come get it."

After that, Robert continued to put money into the magazine, but he did it behind Laura's back. He made Easterly and the investment bankers promise they would not tell Laura about it.

An even bigger problem with the magazine arose when the investment bankers finally found people interested in purchasing stock. "He didn't want to give up his majority share of the stock," says one of the investment bankers. "In his mind, it was better to own a majority share, even though he knew that without a cash infusion the magazine would not survive."

The magazine ultimately did fold and Gary Easterly sued Robert over it. They fought the suit for four years before settling in 1992.

Just as when his business was atrophying for want of its lifeblood — money — and he took money from it for unrelated speculations, similarly, when the business needed every waking hour of his effort, he wasted a substantial part of his time recording each day for posterity. Nothing better illustrates his fatal confusion between image and substance than his insistence on talking virtually every detail of every day into a small tape recorder. One of his three secretaries did nothing but transcribe the tapes all day, every day. According to another secretary, he was obsessive about the recorder because he believed that his life was so important that there should be a clear record of it, from him.

"The way he talked everything into that recorder symbolized him," says the secretary. "There was no editing. Every little detail was important to him, but he never stood back and got the big picture."

The year 1984 ended with the store in desperate trouble, so it was another shock when Robert began 1985 with plans to open yet another store — in Austin — marking the company's twentieth location. He also announced the possibility of opening a store in San Antonio.

As usual, he tried to put a happy face on ugly rumors. "Remarks about a sale, merger or the viability of our company pop up from time to time," he told a reporter, "but we always seem to be expanding or creating something new just about the moment they occur." What he said was true; that was the problem.

While Robert appeared to be a weak and ineffectual leader, Oscar continued to prove just how tough and strong he could be. Coastal, which had opened the eighties with a string of giant corporate raids, in March 1985 became embroiled in a bid to acquire American Natural Resources, a Detroit-based oil and gas company. It was Coastal's third attempt in as many years, but although the first two attempts failed, no one was counting Oscar out.

The *New York Times*, in a March 1985 article titled COAST-AL'S CHIEF PLAYS TO WIN, quoted Oscar: "Whether I lose at tennis, gin rummy or marbles, I don't like it. Whenever we tender, we want to buy the company. If it gets nasty, so be it."

Earlier, in 1983, a Coastal subsidiary had started a takeover of the Texas Gas Resources Corporation, a Kentucky-based interstate natural gas pipeline company. When Texas Gas's chairman began evading Oscar, the latter reportedly dispatched two corporate detectives to trail him. Despite Coastal's tough tactics, the takeover failed when Texas Gas found a "white knight" in CSX Corporation. But Oscar's efforts were far from fruitless. Coastal came away with $26 million when CSX gave Coastal an $18 million "peace offering" and bought out Coastal's stake in Texas Gas for $8.4 million more than Oscar paid for it.

Less than a year later, in February 1984, Oscar began a $2.4 billion bid for control of the Houston Natural Gas Corporation, one of the nation's oldest, biggest, and most profitable intrastate pipeline operators. Houston Natural was the company from which Oscar had wrested the contract to supply gas to Corpus Christi in the early 1960s.

Houston Natural, which was also based in Houston, retaliated with its own bid to buy Coastal, spawning a flurry of lawsuits in what quickly became one of Texas's most fervid takeover battles.

HNG was in the business of transporting and selling gas within Texas, a line of business that Coastal had been ordered out of after the 1970s Lo-Vaca debacle in which the company failed to fulfill its contracts to supply gas to Texas cities. Memories of Lo-Vaca caused the state attorney general's office to jump into the HNG fight. Alleging "irresponsible and gross disregard for the public interest in Coastal's mismanagement" of Lo-Vaca, the attorney general, Jim Mattox, got a court order temporarily restraining Coastal from further action in attempting to acquire HNG. Mattox's suit contended that Coastal's attempt to acquire control of HNG violated the terms of a court order and a decision by the Texas Railroad Commission that were part of the 1979 Lo-Vaca settlement.

Two days before a scheduled hearing, Coastal and HNG agreed to end their mutual takeover battle. But again Coastal came out a winner — with a $42.1 million "peace payment" from Houston Natural.

"We made money. And we made a few enemies," Oscar said about his attempts to take over Texas Gas and HNG. "But we don't worry about that because we're working for profits, not popularity."

OSCAR WYATT IS READY TO RAID THE OIL PATCH AGAIN, said *Business Week* in July 1984. But this time, "Wyatt will be under more pressure to consummate a deal, rather than merely bullying another company into buying back his shares at a 'greenmail' premium."

The following spring, Coastal set its sights on American Natural Resources Corporation in Detroit, a giant gas distribution network, which also owned interests in oil and gas wells and Appalachian coal mines. At first, ANR resisted the takeover bid in which Coastal offered $60 a share. Coastal then increased its offering price to $65 per share.

The two-week takeover battle, which culminated in a "friendly" $2.5 billion transaction, made Coastal the owner of one of the largest gas distribution networks in the country, with more than 21,000 miles of pipelines ranging from Texas and Louisiana to the Middle West and the Rocky Mountain states. Coastal's annual report called the merger the largest single event in its thirty-year history. The company's 1985 revenues also were the highest in its history, $7.3 billion — and all of this at a time when Texas energy companies were filing record numbers of bankruptcies.

Despite his enormous success in the 1980s, Oscar showed no signs of slowing down to savor his victories. He continued to be the first at the office and the last to leave; he pushed ahead with the same mix of ferocious tenacity and overpowering charm he had exhibited in the early 1960s when he convinced a large portion of the state to purchase his gas at irresistible, if wildly optimistic, terms.

For years, perhaps for most of his life, he had been a complicated, complex man, capable of stopping a dinner party or business meeting with a cruel remark. But at the same time, he exhibited a concern for and loyalty to his close friends and employees that seemed as passionate and genuine as his desire to make money.

There are countless stories about Oscar's personally paying for legal or medical help for Coastal employees, of sending his plane for a sick employee or writing a check to bail an employee out of jail.

This generosity extends even beyond employees to mere acquaintances. A woman attorney who did some work for Douglas Wyatt says, "When my dad was sick, I saw Oscar and he said, 'I have a plane and we can take him (meaning my dad) anywhere.'

That's the kind of thing he does. He's loyal. Oscar may do the craziest things in the world but I'd kill for him."

Leonard Coleman, son of the Dr. S. D. Coleman of Navasota who took in Oscar on those nights when Oscar left home as a boy, says Oscar has never stopped being grateful to the Colemans. "Around 1980, O.S. gave about $150,000 for the new addition at the hospital [here in Navasota]," says Coleman. "I'd say he's given about $50,000 since then."

Usually Oscar's gifts are more meaningful than they are expensive. Coleman says that when his father, S.D., had heart problems in the 1960s, and the Navasota hospital could not afford a machine to monitor the heart, Oscar gave one to the hospital.

His kindnesses also extend to his neighbors in the villages surrounding his ranch in South Texas, where each year Oscar distributes baskets of turkeys to the needy.

A South Texas woman who lives in Hebronville, a neighboring town to Oscar's Tasajillo ranch, carefully points out, "I think he does nice things for people. On the other hand, I don't think he wants anybody to use him."

Oscar has many dedicated, longtime friends, but, naturally, these friends do not make headlines the way his enemies do. "Oscar can be cruel. He enjoys being cruel, but not to his friends," says a Houston oilman who has been Oscar's friend for three decades.

That he can feel compassion for others is obvious to many, including Luke Fullen, a Sakowitz men's clothing salesman for forty years. When Oscar needed suits, he called Luke, who drove out to Oscar's office and showed Oscar a selection. "One day I showed up with eight or ten suits and I laid them out on a big long table," recalls Fullen. "Mr. Wyatt came in and said to a business associate, 'Luke here is going to try to sell me these suits.' Then I spoke up and said, 'No, Mr. Wyatt, I'm not trying to push these off on you. I don't get a commission on the family house accounts.'"

Fullen says he had the impression that Oscar felt bad about the comment he made. "I think he felt guilty," says Fullen, "because after that he gave me some free tickets for some clients of mine to the Super Bowl."

At the very moment that Robert was fighting to save his company, Lynn threw her most lavish birthday party ever at Cap Ferrat. It took place just a few weeks before the store filed for bankruptcy, and it received the usual extensive press coverage, including a long and flattering column by New York's "Suzy" on "the party of the season."

Wrote "Suzy": "About 74 of the best the international set has to offer came to help Lynn Wyatt, a smashing blond from Houston with all the money in the world, celebrate in style."

The words *a smashing blond from Houston with all the money in the world* did not go down easily either at home in Texas, where the column was syndicated and where Lynn was considered synonymous with the store, or in New York, where manufacturers' and bankers' requests for payment from the store had repeatedly gone unanswered.

But the potential reverberations in Houston and New York were far from the minds of the revelers at Lynn's birthday party, whose theme was India. Chanel's Karl Lagerfeld dressed Lynn in the costume of an eighteenth-century Indian prince — a white turban decorated with pearls and feathers and an emerald clip, a long white embroidered jacket with jeweled sleeves over tight pants, and tiny shoes that curled up at the toes. Strands of pearls and rubies hung from her neck, and a pearl-encrusted sword was tucked in the five-inch-wide Lagerfeld belt cinched around her tiny waist.

As "Suzy" explained, "Hardly anyone mistook Lynn for Mother Teresa."

Oscar too wore a turban — his was gold with a ruby and diamond pin — and, like his wife, he wore an Indian dagger stuck in a gold lamé sash.

On this night, a warm but breezy evening in July, the guests, who looked like they had just arrived on the Bombay Limited, included the usual assortment of titled Europeans and couturiers, as well as artists and industrialists. There was Henry Ford II in a Nehru jacket, the Dowager Begum Aga Khan in a sari, and Prince and Princess Alexander of Yugoslavia and Prince Albert of Monaco in striking jeweled turbans.

Several hours of champagne and cocktails were followed by a midnight spread of fancy Mediterranean delicacies interspersed with Texas-style food (barbecue, tamale pie, fried chicken) laid out on tables on the terrace under the stars. Three orchestras entertained guests throughout the villa.

Even Oscar, not one to stay late at parties, seemed to have a good time. He did not say goodnight to the guests until three o'clock in the morning. But the last orchestra did not stop playing until 4:10 A.M., after which Lynn too went to bed.

If Robert's troubles with the store and Oscar's growing anger at Robert bothered Lynn, it was not apparent to her guests on the Riviera. She had tried to stop Oscar's berating of her brother, but without success. Lynn had learned long ago to accept what she could not change; it was part of what had made her so successful.

17

I CAN'T BELIEVE IT. I can't believe it," Robert Sakowitz said again and again as he stared at the registered letter and felt a giant knot form in his stomach. The date was July 26, 1985, and the letter meant the end of the line for the store his grandfather and great-uncle had founded eighty-three years earlier.

The letter came from Sakowitz's main creditors — a five-member banking group, led by New York's Chase Manhattan, which held the store's $27 million note. The banks declared Sakowitz in default of its loan and demanded immediate payment.

"I had never truly believed they would do that," Robert said later. "I never, ever thought that they would call the note."

It was a damning confession.

Few were the employees and customers who did not see the end coming. Robert should have been the first to understand just how severe the situation had become. For months, he had struggled unsuccessfully to convince suppliers to extend more credit and banks to lend him more money. In fact, his predicament had become so desperate that a month earlier, on June 1, the banks demanded that Sakowitz put all its charge account receivables in a Houston bank.

After pulling himself together, Robert called an emergency meeting of the board of directors for the next day. The board's decision was swift and predictable. The store would file for protection from its creditors under Chapter 11 of the federal bankruptcy law.

On the morning of August 1, as Sakowitz Inc. filed bankruptcy papers at the courthouse, nine blocks away at the downtown store, employees were called one by one into the store manager's office. Some employees were simply told that the store was reorganizing under Chapter 11 and that they should continue to assume business as usual; others were told that they were no longer needed. This same scenario was repeated at all the other Sakowitz stores. Many men and women who had been with the store the longest and made the biggest salaries were among the first to go.

"Everyone was crying," recalls a longtime employee at the downtown Houston store, "either for themselves and their own plight or for their associates with whom they'd worked so closely for so many years."

Raymond Howard, a gift department salesman who joined the store at age eighteen in 1957 and stayed for twenty-eight years, was heartbroken the day he left. "I was let go at the bankruptcy, and as I was leaving the store through the employees entrance, I came face to face with Ann Sakowitz," Raymond recalls. "I said to her, 'I'm really so sorry to see this.' She looked me in the eye and replied, 'What do you expect with all the employees stealing us blind?'"

Even at this moment, Howard remained loyal to the family that, he believed, had given him so much. "In her defense," Howard says, "Mrs. Sakowitz had lost a great deal. She was cornered."

A day later, Robert took out a full-page ad in both Houston papers: "Rather than sell . . . we have sought to continue to operate through a legal proceeding called Chapter 11. It expresses our strong commitment to 'Return to our Roots.' Our vendors are working with us as we reconcentrate our company and all its efforts in Houston . . . We will focus on our home territory."

Typically, he put a happy face on the devastating news. "I don't consider this a negative story," he said. "We're refounding the company under a whole new structure."

According to petitions filed with the U.S. Bankruptcy Court in Houston, the company's assets totaled $73,606,835 and its liabilities, $63,987,314. Although the banking group's $27 million note was largely secured, there were hundreds of unsecured creditors, mostly vendors who had not been paid. Hickey-Freeman of New York, the maker of expensive men's suits on which Simon and Tobias had built their success, was listed as an unsecured creditor. Having done business with Sakowitz since the turn of the century, Hickey-Freeman had been one of the last vendors to continue to extend credit to the store. At bankruptcy, Hickey-Freeman was owed $107,408.

Employees were told that outstanding expenses would not be

paid, nor would vacations and overtime. But these were relatively minor hardships compared to the fears employees harbored. And as if they had not paid dearly enough already, the employees were told that they should do something publicly to show their support for the chairman. After the bankruptcy, the women and men — those lucky ones who had not yet lost their jobs, but many of whom had already taken dramatic cuts in pay — reached into their own pockets and came up with several thousand dollars to buy full-page newspaper advertisements in both Houston papers.

"The employee family of Sakowitz wishes to demonstrate our deep-rooted support of Robert T. Sakowitz, the Sakowitz family, and our company," said the ad. "We realize Chapter 11 was not the only choice, merely the most unselfish one."

On the same morning that the ads ran, Robert arrived at the Post Oak store to find hundreds of employees gathered around a large stage with a podium in the middle of the parking lot. The sun was already high, the temperature was well into the nineties, and the Houston humidity was wilting the impeccably dressed salespeople. Several employees carried balloons, and others held a sign that read, "Mr. Robert, We Are 100% Behind You." A large crane lowered a big oak tree into a hole in front of the store. Like the newspaper ads, the tree was paid for personally by the employees.

Once the tree was safely in the ground, Robert jumped onto the stage. As always, he looked dashing in one of the Zegna suits he favored. He wore a flower in his lapel, but today it looked more like the sad symbol of a pallbearer than the elegant boutonniere of an international fashion arbiter. He stepped up to the microphone, but before he could say anything, he was overcome with emotion. He dropped his head into his hands and stepped back from the microphone. Newspaper photographers clicked their cameras furiously, and television cameramen caught the dramatic moment on film. The audience was silent, waiting for him to begin. When Robert continued to hold his head in his hands, Ann Sakowitz finally rushed onto the stage to help her son. She thanked the employees for their kindness, and, after loud applause, mother and son wrapped arms and helped each other down from the stage.

Perhaps he had at last been humbled. Now it was time to play down his own image and concentrate on the survival of the store — or so employees thought.

The floods of newspaper and magazine articles that appeared in the coming weeks were far from kind. Almost all the articles said Sakowitz's problems were threefold: the drop in oil prices, the highly leveraged expansion program, and Robert's lack of management skills. But it was the last of these that caused the most comment.

Business Week gave the most succinct and most accurate explanation: "He committed the oldest sin of a family business. He wanted to do everything."

But what stood out most in the articles about the store was that Robert blamed everybody and everything for the mess except himself. He said the press was "negative," the banks "intransigent," the market gossipy, and suppliers skittish. He blamed his downfall on Houston's overcrowded and ferociously competitive retail scene and the unforeseen plummet in oil prices.

"In a few scattered comments," suggested *Texas Monthly,* "in a few scattered interviews — and, one suspects, in the middle of the night — he has even blamed himself."

But it was not only the collapse of the oil industry, the ambitious expansion program, and Robert's mismanagement that brought down Sakowitz. Stores across the country, many of which were even older and better known than Sakowitz, were in trouble, and other great names had already disappeared: Bonwit Teller, Gimbels, B. Altman.

Stores that had previously been owned by a family that insisted on superb service were now in the hands of chains whose bookkeepers did not know or care about fashion or quality or good service — they were paid to budget for greater profits. So the bigger stores soon had fewer salespeople and less merchandise to show.

The discount store and the 1980s leveraged buyout frenzy also injured the once seemingly impregnable position of the great American department stores. Americans who were complaining that department store service was not as good as it used to be were simultaneously buying more and more at discount stores, which proudly advertised that they had lower prices because they offered less service. Although the 1980s cannibalism of American business by Wall Street was not limited to retail store chains, the pattern of buyout — an intolerable debt burden of junk bonds, selling off good assets and junking the rest — has scourged almost every chain: Federated Dry Goods (Filene's, Bloomingdale's, Burdine's, Bullock's) bankrupt; Allied Stores (Jordan Marsh) bankrupt; Carter Hawley Hale (Neiman-Marcus, Bergdorf Goodman) dismembered.

A common question was why Sakowitz had not sold out to one of the retail chains in the fifties or sixties, as had almost all the top specialty and department stores in America. Defending the family-owned status, Robert said, "We never had anybody come up and give us a hard-and-fast bid." But he also admitted that even had there been a bid, "I think the price would have been below what we thought the potential was early on. We were really trying to get [the store] to the point where we could get something for it."

But his terrible troubles at the store were not Robert's greatest problem. By far, the greatest was his brother-in-law. Robert did not yet realize it, but the fight of his life was about to begin.

It started with a phone call right after the Chapter 11 announcement, and it concerned the payment of the Alex Sackton note.

"Okay, cowboy, who's gonna pay it?" Oscar reportedly said.

"Oscar, as you know," Robert says he replied, "I have been trying to negotiate a deal so that everybody gets protected, but at this point if I were, as CEO of Sakowitz, to pay you, that would be a preference payment and it's against the law. It really is the proverbial brother-in-law deal. I can't do that."

"Like hell, you won't," Oscar reportedly replied, "'cause I'm gonna come after you personally."

According to Robert, he then explained to Oscar that the Sackton note was not his personal debt and that "that incensed [Oscar]."

Robert had been fearing and anticipating Oscar's ire. Just a few weeks before the bankruptcy, Robert had called his uncle Alex Sackton in Austin and told Alex that Sakowitz Inc., not Oscar Wyatt, had been paying for the buyout of his stock through the years. Robert then asked Alex if he would allow Oscar to remove his name from the guarantee for the stock buyout and instead allow Sakowitz Inc. to guarantee the payment.

"It will be helpful to me, and it will not make any difference at all to you," Alex says Robert told him.

Knowing the store was in trouble, Alex did not hesitate. "No, Bobby," Alex told his nephew, "I will not give up that personal guarantee from Oscar Wyatt."

Alex recalls, "He just kept saying to me, 'It won't hurt you a bit, but it will help me out a lot.' But if I had done what Bobby wanted I would have got only what I'd already received, and I had four more years to run.

"Oscar told me that Lynn had told him, 'Go ahead and pay the [Sackton] notes and lose that amount of money,'" says Alex. "But Oscar wouldn't do that. The first year after the bankruptcy, Oscar demanded and got money from Bobby and Lynn to pay it personally.

"I could not understand why Bobby should not have taken that on as a personal debt. Oscar had personal reasons for giving that guarantee. He did it only because Bernard asked him to."

Robert today says his phone call to Alex was simply an effort to "negotiate" his way out of a precarious situation. "What I was trying to explain to [Alex] is that I'm going to have hell with Oscar if he has to pay this instead of Sakowitz. If [Alex] feels that's a dishonorable thing to do, to try to negotiate, I'm sorry."

For Robert to characterize his request to Alex ("It will not make any difference to you") as negotiation does not alter the definition of negotiation but it defines Robert.

Alex, Bernard, and their families had been estranged for years. So it was not very surprising, when Alex died in 1992, that neither his sister-in-law, Ann Sakowitz, nor his niece, Lynn Wyatt, went to Austin for the funeral. But interestingly, Robert Sakowitz went. What was even more interesting — and upsetting — to Alex's children was their discovery later that the very moment the funeral ended Robert raced to Alex's house and told the housekeeper he wanted his uncle's Sakowitz memorabilia to take back to Houston. Because Alex's children had not returned from the funeral, the maid had to decide whether or not to let him have the memorabilia. And she did not hesitate to refuse his request.

According to one of Alex's daughters, even after the maid told him he could not take anything of Alex's with him, the maid watched him because she "was worried he was going to actually take something." He did not take anything, however, and left before Alex's children arrived at the house.

Oscar appeared to have no bad feelings toward Alex; his anger was directed entirely at Robert.

As early as 1981, when Bernard was still living, Oscar had told both Bernard and Robert that he believed certain parts of the expansion program were ill-advised. And in February 1985, six months prior to the bankruptcy, Oscar had written a letter to Robert asking to see certain of the company's financial statements. Robert responded in a letter that stated all the reasons why Oscar legally was not permitted to look at company records, but then he ended the letter, "As your brother-in-law, I would be more than willing to share the information with you personally."

For whatever reason, Oscar chose not to accept the offer to look at the books. During a deposition in September 1991, Oscar said he did not look at the books because "the financial viability of the corporation was virtually nil . . . banks were getting out of his lines or were out of the lines . . . we were afraid that by auditing or getting involved in Mr. Sakowitz' corporate books, that we would bring the house down and be liable to Robert Sakowitz for any action that we might take . . . So on advice of counsel, we pulled away and we would not look at his books because we knew it was just a matter of time until he ran for cover."

If Oscar had been searching for an excuse to fall out with his brother-in-law, Robert's refusal to pay the Sackton note provided it, especially considering that the quid pro quo — Lynn's getting half of Bernard's stock in his will — never happened.

Friends, business associates, and competitors say that there is nothing Oscar loves more than making and interpreting contracts. He likes to take any possible advantage not only because of the financial profit involved but because it proves how much smarter he is.

"If you make a deal with him, you'd better be sure you understand exactly what the contract says," explains a fellow oilman. "He'll do exactly what he says he'll do, but you'd better have the same understanding he does of what that is."

For Oscar to have gotten the worst end of two deals with Bobby — the Sackton note and Bernard's unkept promise of the Sakowitz stock — was unbearable. The financial loss was nothing, but to have been outsmarted by Bobby infuriated Oscar. In fact, Bernard's betrayal, which Oscar was certain had been engineered by Bobby, had turned out to be a blessing. Lynn had received $700,000, and the stock she did not receive was now worthless. But that did not lessen Oscar's fury.

Following the Chapter 11 filing, Sakowitz brought in a New York–based retail consulting firm, April-Marcus, to help liquidate all but four of the chain's stores. Among the company's eleven major stores and eight smaller ones, only the four most successful of its Houston locations survived. The now ghostly downtown store was not among the survivors.

April-Marcus advanced Sakowitz $4 million and brought in an additional $3 million in merchandise, which provided desperately needed inventory for fall. But the relationship between Sakowitz and April-Marcus was difficult at best.

"[Robert] didn't want to accept the reality of the situation," says April-Marcus's president, Marvin Blumenfeld. "He knew that some stores would have to be liquidated, but he didn't want anything that made it look like Bob Sakowitz was in trouble. He was still trying to keep up his image at a time when, image be damned, survival was the key."

Robert, according to Blumenfeld, gave the impression that it was beneath his dignity to be promotional, to advertise price-slashing, "Everything Must Go" sales. Blumenfeld says that he understood Robert's reluctance to use such heavy promotional advertising, but that the store had no alternative if it was to stay in business.

Many manufacturers who had not been paid turned the outstanding balance due from Sakowitz over to factors, businesses that buy accounts receivable at a discount. "Bob felt it beneath him to go to the factors hat-in-hand and tell them how they would get paid," says Blumenfeld. "These were people who might get paid $25,000 a year. In Bob's estimation, they were little people. But these were people he had to have a rapport with if he was going to work out his problems."

Despite these differences, with the help of April-Marcus, Sakowitz swiftly and dramatically scaled back its operations, cutting its stores from nineteen to four and its work force from 2,200 to 410.

By January 1986, Sakowitz had repaid $14.5 million of the $27 million owed to its five-member banking group. But despite the slashing of its operations and partial repayment of its bank debt, the company still showed serious weakness. Between August 1985 and January 1986, the four ongoing stores had an operating income of only $1 million. And despite income generated by the liquidation sales, during that same period the company posted an operating loss of $2.5 million.

As winter turned to spring and the store's viability remained dubious, Sakowitz's unsecured creditors — seeking a total of about

$20 million — said in court filings that the only way for the troubled retailer to resolve its financial problems was to seek aid from a buyer or investor, or to liquidate. In May, the unsecured creditors committee threatened to intervene with its own reorganization plan if Sakowitz did not speed resolution of its Chapter 11 case.

After months of threats from the unsecured creditors, in August, Robert reached an agreement with them. He promised to submit a plan to them, as well as to Sakowitz's pre-petition bank creditors, by no later than February 1987.

Robert said he had great new plans for the store — a new look, new merchandise strategies, and new fashion lines. With the unsecured creditors committee momentarily off his back, he could concentrate on running the store.

Or could he?

Although Robert and Lynn had partially reimbursed Oscar for the payment he made to Alex Sackton in September 1985, no payment from Robert was forthcoming in September 1986, and Oscar was forced to pay Alex with his own money.

Three months later, Oscar did what many in Houston society considered unthinkable — even for Oscar Wyatt. Six days before Christmas, he sued his brother-in-law.

The lawsuit, filed on December 19, 1986, and seeking more than $1 million in damages, alleged that Robert's "corrupt actions" drove the once prosperous store into bankruptcy and that Robert misled stockholders and board members to cover up "his plunder." The suit said that Robert had "succeeded in milking the assets of Sakowitz, Inc., for his personal advantage and wealth while at the same time converting Sakowitz, Inc., from a previously-prosperous business into an insolvent entity."

Oscar charged that Robert "lived off Sakowitz, Inc.," taking valuable art, food, and wine without reimbursing the company and "without accounting for his theft." Oscar accused Robert of charging the company for personal expenses, including travel and entertainment, maids, and landscaping for his home.

And the suit said, "But for the misconduct of Robert Sakowitz which destroyed the ability of Sakowitz, Inc., to make the note payments to the Sackton Family Group, Wyatt would not have been required to honor his personal guarantee to the Sackton Family Group."

The suit also charged that, in September 1985, Robert had

orally agreed to reimburse Oscar for his future payments to the Sackton Family Group but that he had not done so.

Oscar told reporters that he deeply regretted filing the suit and called the suit "strictly business," which did little to appease Robert.

"Oscar is very litigious, and peace seems to torment his soul," Robert said in response to the suit. "It's a spurious lawsuit, totally without merit."

But was it without merit? To some employees the charges of taking items from the store rang true. Around the time of the bankruptcy, furniture and fixtures began disappearing from the downtown store. Gift and china buyer Val Renken recalls that a few weeks before the bankruptcy, "I had to inventory everything and then Robert took all these things home."

A store executive recalls, "I had a lot of stuff sent out to his house on Brentwood in the middle of the night, which is something I did at his instruction. I know that the giant chandelier that was in the downtown store went out to his house because I personally was in charge of having it sent out there."

Through the years, store managers and department heads had become accustomed to seeing unexplained expenses of Robert's show up on their budgets. According to a Sakowitz vice president, even Robbie Sakowitz's private school tuition was billed to the store.

One of Robert's cousins, in 1993, tried to defend how Robert used the store, explaining, "Robert never did anything different than what he had seen his father do. All families do that. Why shouldn't they? It's their company."

This was indeed a practice Robert had learned from his father. In one example, when Bernard and Ann bought new furniture for their home in Paradise Valley, Arizona, they billed the cost to the Scottsdale store, wiping out that store's entire profits for the year.

Texas society scorned Oscar for bringing the suit and causing such a terrible public spectacle. "This should have been settled at home in one of their living rooms," said a Houston society maven.

But while many thought it inexcusable to sue a brother-in-law, some did not think it a baseless suit. A Houston woman recalls, "The question was 'If the store is bankrupt, where did he get the money to buy that house on River Oaks Boulevard?'"

Oscar had opened a Pandora's box of questions about Robert's business judgment, his integrity, and his compassion for the thousands of Sakowitz employees and hundreds of unsecured creditors. And Oscar was only getting started.

The unsecured creditors committee (which had intervened in Oscar's lawsuit against Robert) also increased its pressure on Robert, who was now desperately searching for someone to buy the store. A number of potential buyers did appear, only to lose interest when it came time to put up money. Houston in 1987 was still in dire financial straits.

In 1986, the price of oil had plummeted again, this time to a shockingly low $10 a barrel (the inflation-adjusted equivalent of $3 a barrel in the 1970s). Foreclosures began to dot the Texas landscape, and newspapers across the state devoted several pages each day to stories of failed businesses and failed dreams.

Within two years, in 1988, 113 banks would fail in Texas alone, accounting for more than half of the nation's 200 bank failures.

The trauma of falling oil and real estate prices marked the most pernicious economic downturn in Texas since the Great Depression. Many of the state's most famous men and women were destroyed by debt they could not repay, including Clint Murchison, Jr., and Herbert and Bunker Hunt.

Three of Oscar's closest friends suffered huge losses. Former Texas governor John Connally bet heavily on Texas real estate and lost the bulk of his fortune in Chapter 11. World-famous heart surgeon Denton Cooley, who reported more than $9 million in income from his medical practice in 1987, listed his debts at $99 million when he filed for Chapter 11 in 1988. Like so many others, Cooley had borrowed heavily and invested most of his millions in real estate.

When Oscar's good friend John Mecom, an independent oilman, faced bankruptcy, Oscar devised a plan to pay off Mecom's debts. According to *Texas Monthly*, when Oscar presented his idea, explaining, "I think this will get you out of debt and give you about $2 million a year to live on," Mecom shook his head and replied, "If all I had to live on was $2 million a year, I'd rather go broke."

But no one even remotely interested in purchasing Sakowitz doubted that the economy would eventually improve. The bigger problem Robert had in finding a buyer was that Sakowitz was considered a dinosaur in the retail business. Its physical plants were outdated, its inventory was sketchy, and its direction for the future was uncertain. The store was badly managed at a time when the best-run stores in America were in trouble.

In late spring, the unsecured creditors committee gave Robert a "drop-dead date" by which he must have a commitment by a major investor or buyer for the store, or the creditors would file to convert the Chapter 11 reorganization proceedings into Chapter 7 liquidation.

"We had to have the ability to stop the hemorrhaging," says Pat Hughes, attorney for the unsecured creditors. "We were seeing our monies falling even lower, and we had to try to salvage something."

The drop-dead date was Tuesday, September 16, at eight o'clock in the morning.

On September 8, just eight days before the dreaded date, Robert received a call from Paul Carter, the president of the American retail arm of the Australian real estate conglomerate L. J. Hooker Corp. Carter seemed like the white knight the store had been waiting for. Hooker was run by George Herscu, a Rumanian expatriate who built a fortune as a commercial real estate developer in Australia in the 1960s and 1970s. After succeeding on a smaller scale, Herscu was often quoted as saying that he looked at the United States and decided "only a fool can fail."

Herscu had already begun a billion-dollar buying spree in America in 1986 and 1987, snapping up famous retailers, including Bonwit Teller and B. Altman, when he heard Sakowitz was looking for a buyer.

Just hours before the drop-dead date, Robert received a letter from Hooker confirming a merger. Douglas Wyatt, having received Lynn's stock assignment, was trying to block the merger, in which Robert had made a deal for himself to receive 20 percent of the new company, while Hooker got 80 percent, and Lynn, Ann, and the Bernard Sakowitz trusts got nothing.

Robert still viewed the store as his entitlement. He acted as though he had the inalienable right to do with it whatever he wanted. He spoke of the store as something "I devoted my life to," as though his years at the store came at great expense to him, as though he had done the family a favor by taking on the leadership and ownership of what was then one of the best retail institutions in America.

Robert was at the helm when Sakowitz was bankrupted and the family's shares were wiped out. Another man might have felt an obligation to compensate his family for the devastation that had taken place under his presidency, and to share with them this 20 percent. But he did not give one share of what he was to receive to his family.

Douglas eventually stopped fighting his uncle in bankruptcy court and sued him in probate court, in a case that would become famous as *Wyatt v. Sakowitz*.

Just three days after Robert was served with Douglas's suit, Robert was hit with yet another family-related suit. Post Oak Center Inc. (POCI), the company that owns the valuable land on which the Post Oak store is located and whose stock is held mostly by Robert's cousins, filed suit claiming that Robert in 1983 illegally obtained a sewer permit to the land. The suit said that Robert was president of POCI at the time of the purchase and that he did not tell the other shareholders about the opportunity to obtain the permit.

"Bobby, without any consultation or knowledge of the owners of POCI, went out and bought these sewer rights from the City of Houston and certified that he was the owner of the land when he wasn't," says his cousin Toby Sackton. "As far as calling himself the owner of the land, that was essentially stealing. If he had possession of [the rights] and somebody else wanted a development there, he could block it. That confirmed everything I'd heard about the way Bobby used some of the powers of the store for his own personal aggrandizement."

In reply, Robert said under oath that he had long had a dream to develop a parcel of land surrounding the Post Oak store and that he did not seek his family's participation because he had been turned down on a similar request a few years earlier.

Oscar shared Robert's relentless work ethic. Both men worked as long hours as anyone else in their companies. But they were unlike in the way they used their time. Whereas indecision often immobilized Robert, Oscar prided himself on being quicker than his competitors. Former Coastal vice president Jeff Dorrell remembers when benzene tripled in price in 1987.

Dorrell figured that Coastal could make $187,000 a day as long as the price spike lasted, but Coastal's benzene plant was idle. Dorrell wanted permission from Oscar to start the plant immediately but had to go through his boss to get to Oscar. Dorrell's boss wanted him to do studies and research on the project before meeting with Oscar, but Dorrell thought that was busywork and refused.

"We get in the meeting and my boss says to Oscar, 'We think we ought to start up the hydrodeocculation unit,'" recalls Dorrell. "So I said to Oscar, 'West Texas Intermediate, $17 a barrel. Benzene, $100 a barrel. I rest my case.' That's all I said. I could see this horror-stricken look on my boss's face. He wanted me to rattle on about the shift in supply and demand balances, which is why Texaco takes six months to make a decision on something. So my boss says, 'Well, tell Mr. Wyatt some more about why it's like this and how long this is going to last.'

"I said, 'No good reason. Not very long. And we don't care.'

"Then Wyatt says, 'Start it up,' and he got up and walked out of the room."

18

After Douglas's trip to Cap Ferrat, where he accepted Lynn's stock assignment, and before filing suit against Robert, Douglas made an important trip to Lake Lure, North Carolina. He was in the process of purchasing seventy-five acres of land near the small scenic lake located thirty miles southeast of Asheville. In addition to looking at the property, he wanted to spend the weekend with some new friends who also owned property around the lake.

He proudly showed one of his new friends — a top model with the Eileen Ford agency — around the property he was preparing to buy. During the tour he told her, "This is where the ships are going to come get us."

She listened carefully as Douglas explained that because his house was located up on the hill — as opposed to his friend Frederick Von Mierers's house, which was down in the valley next to the lake — when the great flood came in 1989, his house would be the only one left standing.

In fact, according to Von Mierers, all of Lake Lure and the Blue Ridge Mountains were going to survive the millennium, and therefore it followed that all of the region would survive the 1989 flood.

Perhaps Douglas had not been a member of the Eternal Values cult long enough to have fully grasped the future, which was odd since he was already being touted as the leader of the cult when the world spins off its polar axis in 1999.

But if the beautiful Eileen Ford model with Douglas ever considered setting him straight, she might have known he would not listen to her. Women, according to the cult's leader, Frederick Von Mierers, were not put on earth to lead people.

"All women are selfish cunts," Frederick told his followers, "and the only thing they can do is to use those pussies to help the boys."

Frederick, who was as beautiful and corrupt as Dorian Gray, often followed this opinion with the comment "Women just need to be pounded."

How Douglas became involved with such a bizarre cult, one that advocated hatred for women and Jews and considered homosexual men the highest form of human evolution and Jewish women the lowest, was a mystery — except to those with intimate knowledge of the cult's workings.

"They bring you in with this story about living in harmony and doing the right thing," says a former cult member. "The stuff about hating women and Jews and people who are different comes later, and it's done in a way that makes fun of all the differences people have. It was done to break down barriers, which is very important in cult psychology. This is part of breaking down people's histories so that there's no allegiance to anything but the group. Douglas, I'm sure, bought the house at Lake Lure for peer approval."

Eternal Values recruited men and women who were well-to-do, good-looking, and smart. Because Douglas fit at least the first two of these categories, and because he had impeccable social connections, he was a prime candidate for membership. "Be nice to him," Frederick reportedly told a cult member about Douglas. "He will buy everything for you."

Psychologists suggest that among those most susceptible to cults are people who have felt abandoned in childhood. They are often drawn to the sense of belonging and the sense of family that cults provide.

Douglas's childhood had made him the perfect cult victim. Left alone a great deal when he was young, and always in the shadow of his older brother, Steve, Douglas grew up feeling unloved, say family and friends.

"I always felt sorry for Doug because Lynn and Oscar focused all their attention on Steve," says Robert's first wife, Pam Zauderer Bryan. "I felt so sorry for him that when we got Roby, we asked Douglas to be a godparent to him."

Sakowitz family retainer Val Renken says that the favoritism shown Steve was painful to Douglas. "Douglas has always thought his mother favored Steve, and he still thinks it."

Renken says that he still vividly recalls the phone call he received at his home one night in the early 1960s, when Douglas was a young boy. "Won't you please come see me?" Douglas begged. "It's my birthday and I'm here at the house all alone."

According to Renken, at the time of the *Wyatt v. Sakowitz* trial, the only photograph in Douglas's office was of the family's black cook, Florence, who had recently died.

Trey Wyatt felt the same loneliness caused by his parents' absence. With his parents so often gone, Trey and his younger brother, Brad, had as their mentors the adults who *were* around: policemen, garbage collectors, postmen. These city workers could often be found in the kitchen at Allington, enjoying a piece of pie or cake just baked by the Wyatt cook, Florence. As Trey and Brad grew older, they began riding with the policemen in their patrol cars and learning aspects of law enforcement. One day, while riding in a police car, a patrol officer suggested Trey enter the police academy in Harris County.

When Trey not only enrolled, but also told his parents he was considering law enforcement as a career, there was no objection from Lynn and Oscar. Lynn was, in fact, pleased with the idea because she thought it taught her son street smarts. So Trey dropped out of Texas A&M after his freshman year and became a Harris County patrolman for two years. But when he saw his career going nowhere, he decided to return to college. After graduating from A&M, he went to work for a bank in Corpus Christi.

Brad, who is sixteen months younger than Trey, also became a patrolman, and is making law enforcement a career.

Oscar has made it clear to his sons that they are on their own financially, just as he was from a very early age.

It was Douglas, observers say, who suffered the most of all the children. "Not only is Douglas not tough by nature," says a once close friend, "but also he is very sensitive and unbelievably naive."

One of the cult's former leaders, a man who worked as closely with Frederick as anyone else in promoting Eternal Values, was amazed at what easy prey Douglas was for Frederick.

"Douglas believes things without discovering the truth for himself," says a former cult member who insists on anonymity. "He takes things absolutely at face value."

The former leader remembers that when Douglas first became involved in the cult, he and Douglas became fast friends and that soon thereafter, when Frederick turned on him, so did Douglas. "Frederick said to me, 'You're evil,' and when I talked to Douglas after that, all he would say is 'You're evil.' Frederick really twisted Douglas's head around."

Impressionable as he was, even Douglas probably could not have been pulled into Eternal Values had Von Mierers not taken him carefully and gradually through each layering of the cult's beliefs. A master salesman, Von Mierers had found a willing buyer. The ideas were secondary. What Douglas was buying into was a family, a sense of purpose, a definition of himself as important.

Frederick was born Freddie Meyer or Mierer to Jewish parents who ran a dry-cleaning shop in Brooklyn. The exact date of his birth is a mystery, but by the 1960s, as a handsome, blond, blue-eyed model and the lover of fashionable New York interior decorator Billy Baldwin, Von Mierers had made inroads into the fringes of New York society. Eager to mask his real past, he claimed that his parents had died in a car crash and that he was the godson of Mrs. Earle Kress Williams, an heir to the dime store fortune.

During the 1970s in New York, Von Mierers became an astrologer to the rich. At first, when he told the fortunes of his friends, at parties in Oyster Bay or Nantucket or in the elegant salons of Park Avenue apartments, it was a lark. But as word spread about the handsome model with psychic ability, he began charging for his services. Eventually, he became such a hit that he held seminars for hundreds of people in a Park Avenue church. On his own television show on late-night public-access cable TV in New York, he lectured on Eastern philosophy and comparative religion.

The Frederick whom Douglas met in the 1970s was very different from the Frederick whom Douglas came to know well in 1987. The new Frederick had convinced his dozens of rich, well-educated, yuppie followers that he was the reincarnation of the prophet Jeremiah and an alien from the Arcturus star system. Frederick said he had come to earth to prepare a leader for the New Age, after the earth spins off its axis and is destroyed in 1999. He was using very sophisticated programming techniques and a complex mixture of religions from Christianity to Hinduism to attract followers.

The series of steps leading to a person's induction into the cult began with a "life reading," a cassette recording by Frederick, which he described as "your soul's report card." It discussed the way in which the person had "evolved through reincarnations" and in what ways he or she needed to improve. Next came Frederick's "gem prescription," a list of precious stones that the person should buy, usually for tens of thousands of dollars, "to ward off evil things."

What was most astonishing about Douglas's involvement in the cult was the speed with which he was swept into Frederick's inner circle. In 1987, just months after receiving his life reading, for which he paid $300 in advance, he appeared to be hooked. He displayed none of the skepticism of many cult members who had compared life readings and, noticing that they had reincarnated from the same place, questioned Frederick about it.

Frederick the con artist had a quick reply: "Of course, dear, you were all together."

Douglas simply described his life reading as "amazingly accurate and also very personal."

Soon Douglas began traveling to New York from Houston one or two weekends a month to be with Von Mierers. At first, they met over tea at Frederick's apartment at 405 East 54th Street.

The apartment, which Frederick said felt as things did on the planet Arcturus, was shockingly high-tech, with high-spectrum pink and violet colors and acrylic and glass furniture set against mirrored and pale blue lacquered walls. The room was cleansed with air purifiers and negative-ion machines.

Frederick controlled the leases on at least four other apartments in the building, each of which was occupied by two or three fellow cult members. While Douglas sat having tea with Frederick at his apartment, cult members came and went. Many were graduates of Ivy League colleges; many were models; they all appeared to have high-paying jobs. Most were in their twenties or thirties. They did not drink or smoke. Frederick had convinced his followers that a spiritual life was the only life worth living and that this entailed adhering to a strict food-combining diet and refraining from sex.

"You see how terrible your families are?" Frederick often railed. "It's what they eat." Frederick told new members to "think of your body as a Lalique vase" that you would treat with care.

Dealing with sexual desires was more difficult. He admonished his male and female followers, "Don't become a cock worshipper," and reminded them, "Jesus, Rama, Krishna, Buddha did not come to promise you another piece of ass." Still, sex was permitted as long as it was among members within the group. At times, Frederick even encouraged sex — if it meant he got to participate.

"Frederick's favorite kind of thing was to bring in a male prostitute to deflower the men," says a cult member. "Sex was never between just two people. It was done in a group way."

It was reportedly not uncommon for bisexual male prostitutes to be brought in for an evening and paid to have anal and oral sex with the females in the cult, while the males in the cult watched. To make things especially interesting and no doubt to break down racial barriers, the prostitutes were usually black and Frederick referred to them as "chocolate lords."

Frederick demanded strict loyalty to the group, but keeping his beautiful followers happy and loyal required both verbal and physical domination. Those who made it into the cult's inner circle witnessed beatings and oral humiliation directed at individuals.

Frederick scolded any member he thought had been unloyal to the group and he spent a good deal of time accusing cult members of being egotistical. "You need to sit on an eight-foot dildo in the middle of Park Avenue," he told the women models, as if that would help them deal with their giant egos.

"If you're a woman, you're told that you are a temptress and you're conniving and that once in this group you need to leave all that behind," says a female former cult member. "As long as the abuse was directed at me, I could handle it, but when they asked me to direct that same kind of abuse to others, that's when I bucked the system and got out."

Women were placed in subservient roles in the cult. Several female members were ordered to cook and clean for the men, which included getting down on their hands and knees and scrubbing the apartments' floors until they were spotless, yet another attempt by Frederick to help women deal with their egos.

Female members also were useful in escorting male cult members to parties. Douglas was among those for whom Frederick arranged a regular escort. In Douglas's case, she was a strikingly beautiful brunette model, Susan Bearden.

Susan and Douglas hit it off immediately — so much so that when Douglas told Susan he needed $20,000 to pay his taxes she gave him the money. Why he did not have the money himself or did not get it from his parents is a mystery.

Once, when Lynn asked Douglas to take her to Merv Griffin's birthday party in California, Douglas asked if he could bring Susan. Lynn said absolutely not. She wanted Douglas to escort her and her alone. Douglas went — without Susan.

As Douglas became more involved with the cult, he began spending his nights in New York, sleeping on a straw mat on the floor next to Frederick's bed.

No one wondered why it was that Douglas, a relatively new recruit, was being paid such special attention. Douglas's mother had social connections and his father had money, the two things Frederick Von Mierers cared about most. One of the first things members had to do on being accepted in the group was to write letters to their families, especially their mothers, telling them how much harm had been done to them as children. But Douglas was not made to write such a letter. Frederick told Douglas "to keep in good with his mother," says a cult member.

Lynn was interested in Von Mierers and reportedly tried to arrange meetings with him several times. But for some reason, Von Mierers never would meet with her. He did, however, do a life reading for Lynn, and on the tape he reportedly told her not to be sexually inhibited. "Dear," he said, "you don't want to be fucked by an Italian truck driver, you want to be fucked by the truck."

Lynn purchased $70,000 worth of Eternal Values gems, and she would later insist that Von Mierers did not teach hatred but the opposite. She called it "love of mankind."

Lynn clearly had not heard Frederick's "Karma and Destiny" tape, which explained anti-Semitism as something "Jews had coming to them."

"People who persecuted the Jews in the Inquisition perpetrated by the Christian Church," says the tape, "reincarnated as Jews in Nazi Germany."

One of the great mysteries about Douglas's involvement in the cult is how he, the son of Jewish parents, could willingly belong to a virulently anti-Semitic organization. But Frederick seemed to have an explanation for everything. According to a friend of Douglas's, Von Mierers told Douglas: "You incarnated as a Jew, but you are not a Jew."

This was brilliant strategy by Von Mierers, for Douglas had never felt comfortable with his Jewish heritage. When Douglas was twenty, he had converted to Christianity.

*   *   *

Roger Hall first met Douglas Wyatt in early 1988. They both had season tickets to the Rockets, Houston's professional basketball team, and both had seats on the floor of the Summit auditorium where the Rockets played. After getting acquainted during the games, Douglas and Roger had lunch (Douglas's consisting mainly of watercress), after which a package containing an Eternal Values tape arrived in Roger's mail.

Roger listened to the tape and told Douglas he found it intriguing. Soon, more tapes arrived from Douglas, and Roger was further intrigued. Roger had long been fascinated with Hindu philosophy, and it seemed to him that much of what Frederick preached on his tapes contained elements of Hinduism, including belief in reincarnation and in the healing properties of certain precious gems.

Douglas and Roger began to see each other almost daily and, according to Roger, while jogging, having lunch, or watching rented movies at Roger's house in the evenings, they discussed the teachings of Eternal Values to the exclusion of virtually all other subjects. Douglas also told Roger that if he wanted some healing gems, he could get them through Eternal Values at a price considerably below market value. Skeptical about their powers, Roger says he decided that, if purchased at a discount, they were at least a good investment.

Roger gave Douglas three money orders for gems, totaling $44,000, which Douglas delivered to Frederick in New York. Having listened to the tapes and purchased gems, Roger was on the verge of becoming more than just peripherally involved in Eternal Values. But at just this moment, in March 1990, *Vanity Fair* writer Marie Brenner did an explosive exposé of Von Mierers and the cult, titled "East Side Alien."

The article said that the Manhattan district attorney's office was looking into charges that Von Mierers was involved in a multimillion-dollar gem ring. It also portrayed the cult not as a group that studied comparative religion and practiced quasi-Hindu philosophy, but one that taught hate and was sexually aberrant.

Roger says that while the article "shook" his relationship with Eternal Values, it galvanized his relationship with Douglas, who went into hiding when the article appeared on newsstands. "He stayed at my house and [my wife and I] helped him change his phone number, until the whole thing died down," says Roger.

Douglas was quoted in the *Vanity Fair* article: "Frederick has helped so many people. It is all very positive. He saves them from their egos. When you wear your gems you can't be fooled by people and things that are evil. You see everything like it is. It's real bottom-line."

He was also described as having done nothing to stop a brutal physical beating by Frederick of a member who wanted out of the cult.

Lest any reader wonder about Douglas's background, he was identified in the article as "a Houston lawyer whose mother, Lynn, is the famous blonde socialite married to Oscar Wyatt." Roger says Douglas told him that, when the article appeared, Lynn vomited for three days straight and could not get out of bed.

Douglas's New Age guru also did not escape Oscar's notice. Oscar questioned Douglas about his involvement with Frederick, who died not long after the article appeared. Douglas says that Oscar said to him, "I understand that your friend Frederick died of AIDS."

Oscar pointed out that Frederick had received some bad publicity — as if Douglas had not noticed — and he told Douglas he would have to deal with the flap the article created. "Other than that," said Douglas, "Dad respects me to live my own life."

Not long after the article came out, Roger began to feel differently about the cult. "When I got to the inner core of beliefs, I told Douglas I wouldn't have anything more to do with those people," says Roger. "[The cult] completely disrupted my value system. I have a seven-year-old daughter whom I love very much. I can't hate her just because that's one of the teachings — to hate women."

Roger also was angered by Douglas's insistence that he read anti-Semitic propaganda by Henry Ford, about an alleged Jewish plot to take over the world. Roger says he refused to even look at the materials.

What shocked Roger considerably more, he says, was what he took to be a pass at him by Douglas: "My wife and kids were upstairs, and Douglas and I were in my study. I was sitting behind my desk and Douglas walks around and gets down on his knees and puts one hand on either arm of my chair, and makes this moony face. I felt a combination of outrage, fear, and shock. The look on my face must have told him to back off."

In 1991, Roger was asked under oath in a deposition, "Did anybody with Eternal Values ever try to entice you into a homosexual relationship?" to which Roger replied straight-faced, "Douglas Wyatt did once and my response was such that it did not happen again."

Roger would later learn from a former cult member that Frederick professed that "all men are gay but some are just not evolved enough" to realize it.

Although Roger continued to associate with Douglas through 1990, soon after that Roger severed all ties with him.

Roger was livid over the fact that he no longer believed that his Eternal Values gems had any mystical value and had far less real value than he was originally led to believe. At the time of the purchase, Eternal Values' in-house appraisal listed the gems at $79,000. But when Roger later had his own appraisals done, he learned the jewelry was worth only about $11,000, or a quarter of the $44,000 he paid for it.

Feeling ripped off, Roger finally told Douglas he wanted his money back. But Douglas told him the gems were nonrefundable, which may have been one of the biggest errors of judgment of Douglas's life. Roger Hall was not about to go away quietly.

19

A NEW ERA DAWNED at Sakowitz in November 1987, when the injection of funds from the Hooker Corp. brought the store out of bankruptcy. Because Hooker owned 80 percent of the company, Robert no longer called the shots. He reported to the chairman of Hooker's American retail operations, Michael Babcock.

"[Mr. Babcock] made it very clear that he was in charge, not me," says Robert. "He said to me, 'You have a reputation as a maverick. I want you to check *everything* with me.'"

The new structure, with its checks on Robert, seemed to work. Within a year of the merger, customers and vendors had come around, and after a grand "reopening" and remodeling of the Post Oak store, things looked hopeful and Robert was amply rewarded.

"In 1989, after our first full year, Mr. Babcock wrote me a letter which was one of the finest letters I've ever received," says Robert. "He said he was very pleased with 1988 and that my $175,000 salary would be increased to $200,000 plus a $75,000 bonus."

The company even announced plans to open three new stores — including one in Robert's favorite battleground, Dallas. Another opened in Cincinnati, Ohio, where Hooker built a mall; a third was planned for Houston.

But in the turbulent life of Robert Sakowitz, this high was soon followed by a plunge. In August 1989, just twenty-one months after Hooker brought Sakowitz out of bankruptcy, the Australian company itself filed Chapter 11. As bad as this news was, it could have been worse. Sakowitz was not included in Hooker's Chapter 11 filing, even though Bonwit Teller and B. Altman — two bigger and more prestigious chains — were.

While Robert proclaimed that it would be business as usual at

Sakowitz and that the operating assets of Sakowitz were not tied directly to Hooker's problems with its banks, he also admitted that Hooker's troubles had made some suppliers nervous. Both customers and employees remembered what happened the last time Sakowitz's suppliers became skittish.

In addition to worrying about Hooker's troubles and how they affected Sakowitz, Robert also was preoccupied with battling the lawsuits against him. The litigation brought separately by Oscar, Douglas, POCI, and the unsecured creditors committee was "extraordinarily draining," he says, "tough financially as well as emotionally."

Oscar was proving to be a vicious opponent, attacking not only Robert but Ann Sakowitz, as well. A year and a half earlier, in March 1988, Oscar had a role in forcing his mother-in-law, Ann, to return a $100,000 benefit that she received from the store after the bankruptcy. The $100,000 was tied to Bernard's employment contract with the store, to be paid to Ann annually, as stipulated in Bernard's will.

Robert's lawyer David Berg, in a deposition in the *Wyatt v. Sakowitz* case, questioned Ann about a series of events that took place before Oscar demanded Ann repay the $100,000.

ANN: We knew that Oscar had been having affairs here and there and when Doug was over here for dinner one night and we were talking about it, I said, "Do you realize that you and Steve are going out with your father with his girlfriend and you and Steve are going along with him?

"Do you realize what you're doing to your mother? This is your mother, not your father's mistress."

And he says, "Well, I've only done it a couple of times, but I won't do it anymore."

DAVID: You . . . yourself had seen Oscar with a couple of . . .

ANN: Yes, I have.

DAVID: Was he with his wife at the Beef and Bird [restaurant]?

ANN: No, he was not. He was with two women. And
the Beef and Bird people said that he had been coming
there frequently, but after I had come there he no
longer went there anymore.

DAVID: Coming there frequently with whom?

ANN: With this particular woman and her friend.

DAVID: Was it after that and after the filing of the
bankruptcy that Oscar Wyatt and Douglas Wyatt
objected to your being paid under the terms of your
husband's employment contract with Sakowitz?

ANN: Yes.

It was also after that, Ann says, that she learned that Oscar
demanded in a meeting of Sakowitz's creditors committee that Ann
return the $100,000. "The creditors didn't bother me until Oscar
began to make a demand upon them for me to return the money,"
she says.

Douglas, who was present when Oscar brought up the
$100,000 with the creditors committee, insisted later that his con-
cern was for his grandmother's legal safety. Had she not returned
the money, Douglas said, she could have been subjected to a fraud
suit by creditors.

Ann was so upset by the turn of events that she called and told
Lynn what had happened. Her own daughter would surely intervene
with Oscar.

"I called Lynn and told her that . . . I had to pay back that
hundred thousand because Oscar was demanding it of the creditors," says Ann. "Later on that same day she must have questioned
Oscar because she called me back and said, 'Oscar said you won't
have to pay it,' and then later on she called back and said that . . . I
did have to pay it."

Ann was exhibiting the same attitude of regal entitlement so
often displayed by her son. In fact, she had no claim ahead of any
of the other hundreds of unsecured creditors.

Robert's position with the Wyatts was not helped by the fact
that he was now living on River Oaks Boulevard in the house he
had purchased just months before the store's bankruptcy. If the red

brick house was a slap in the face to Robert's creditors and former employees, it was even more insulting to Oscar and Lynn. Robert could pay $40,000 in ad valorem taxes — to say nothing of a large mortgage — for the privilege of living on River Oaks Boulevard, but he could not assume the Alex Sackton note as his personal debt, as Oscar demanded.

Oscar often complained about how much Robert had gotten away with, how he had bilked his creditors while he continued to live high. What seemed especially to infuriate Oscar was that he had given Robert a place to stay, had taken him in at Allington during Robert's divorce from Pam, and this is how Robert was repaying his hospitality.

Robert says he is not surprised if Oscar feels this way today. "Oscar is very much like the Mario Puzo characters to whom, 'If I do anything for you, you are beholden to me.' Oscar is that much into control."

Robert says today that he never would have bought the mansion had he known the store would be bankrupt nine months later. But he adds that the fact the store was "having a bad year" was no reason to deprive his family of the new home.

In 1990, Robert decided to try to resolve all four suits against him. So in March, after four and a half years of litigation, a global settlement was reached. Under the terms of the deal, Robert agreed to give Oscar a personal promissory note for $412,000. In addition, Robert's company Shamrock Shops agreed to give Oscar a promissory note for $500,000. Robert had settled with Oscar for $912,000, which was just a fraction less than the $1.2 million Oscar's suit demanded.

In addition, he reportedly paid his attorney $500,000 for the task of settling the case. Robert might not have been a genius at math, but he was able to add $912,000 and $500,000 and understand that $1,412,000 was $200,000 more than if he had simply paid Oscar's demand.

Robert had lost more money settling with Oscar than he might have had he gone to trial and lost — and that was the worst-case scenario. He might have gone to trial and won, or reached a compromise.

Also as part of the complex global settlement, Robert agreed to give the sewer permits, worth at least $310,000, and another $25,000 in cash to the creditors committee. POCI, in turn, agreed to buy a waste water permit from Robert for $620,000, which would fund the $310,000 settlement with the creditors committee.

But one major player was missing from the global settlement. At the eleventh hour, Douglas withdrew from the negotiations. "I settled the lawsuits, thinking that was going to be all there was," says Robert. "At the last minute, Douglas pulled out so that he could continue the game, needless to say, with Oscar later."

Despite Douglas's still-pending lawsuit, three major suits were off Robert's back, which enabled him to focus much of his attention on the store and its new problems.

Hooker was not working its way out of Chapter 11; its debt was increasing, and Sakowitz was once again trying to operate with a cash shortage. Robert, the former amateur boxer, compared doing business under Hooker's bankruptcy to "getting into the boxing ring with your right arm tied behind your back and a broken left arm."

With Robert fighting for the store's life, Lynn, with her typical courage, instead of lowering her profile, raised it. The Houston Grand Opera planned to host a celebration of three hundred years of British Opera, and Lynn decided to invite as her special guest the former Sarah Ferguson, the Duchess of York, who just happened to be the biggest sensation in Europe at the moment. Fergie, it was revealed to the press with careful insouciance, would stay at Allington.

Lynn had met Fergie in London, but she did not know her well. She was much closer with Fergie's mother-in-law's sister, Princess Margaret. Lynn and Margaret had, in fact, become so close that when Lynn was in London she lunched alone with Margaret at Kensington Palace, and when Oscar was with her, Margaret dined with them at Claridge's. Margaret had twice been a guest at Allington, but neither visit by the Queen's sister had generated remotely as much media attention as Fergie's visit would.

Thirty-four-year-old Steve Wyatt had been working in London since 1985, as an oil broker at Delaney Petroleum, a Coastal subsidiary. Having never met the Duchess of York, Steve was delighted when his mother called and said she wanted him to fly to Houston to escort Fergie during her early November 1989 visit to Houston.

The weekend's festivities began with the opera festival's Friday-night performance of *The Mikado*. As cameras clicked furiously, Oscar, Lynn, and Steve together led Fergie into the

Wortham Center. Fergie, five months pregnant, wore a revealing Bellville Sassoon gown the color of a yellow Texas rose, but Lynn was the real knockout in a metallic space suit, cut almost to her navel, with stiff wings that protruded from either shoulder. The avant-garde outfit would have labeled anyone else a "fashion victim" — *Women's Wear Daily's* description of someone who buys an extreme, show-stopping costume straight off the Paris runway and actually wears it — but on Lynn it looked ultra chic.

The highlight of Fergie's visit came on Saturday night when she flew with Steve, Lynn and Oscar, and Douglas and his Eternal Values date to the Wyatts' ranch in South Texas.

Oscar loved South Texas as much as Lynn loved the south of France, and in the early 1980s, in Duval County, one hundred miles southwest of Corpus Christi, he had built the favorite of his homes, his ranch house.

Oscar named his ranch Tasajillo, the Spanish name for a prickly cactus that explodes if it is touched. That the owner shared these properties is obvious.

The house stands alone in the bleakness of the barren, brutal, South Texas landscape, looking not unlike a French Foreign Legion outpost fortress in the endless reaches of the Sahara desert. This was the heat-blasted country that had inspired General Philip Henry Sheridan, Union Army commander of the 5th Military District (Texas and Louisiana) after the Civil War, to declare, "If I owned Texas and hell, I would rent out Texas and live in hell!"

The plane carrying Fergie and her hosts touched down on Oscar's runway. Flying is the only sane means of travel to the ranch house, which sits amid 18,000 rugged acres spanning nearly two counties. The house, a tan structure of Spanish architecture, which covers nearly an acre, is surrounded by six or seven acres of green grass, palm trees, and other plantings; a tennis court; and an enormous swimming pool — all of which are contained within a concrete wall. It is an astounding oasis in the middle of a plain of sand and dust and sagebrush stretching in all directions.

The group entered the compound by car through electric gates and along a grand, ceremonial, circular drive bordered by tall palm trees. A butler took the car at the porte cochere, and Fergie and her hosts walked down a long, open walkway to the front door. Once inside, they entered a massive living room — thirty feet by sixty feet, with a thirty-foot ceiling supported by enormous cedar logs. The extravagant and showy house must have confirmed everything

Fergie had ever heard about things being bigger in Texas.

Oscar kept two helicopters at Tasajillo, and he sometimes used them to hunt game. While someone else piloted the helicopter, Oscar would sit in a passenger seat, shooting at the wild boar or deer that scampered beneath him. Oscar did not take Fergie hunting, but he reportedly did turn over the controls of the helicopter to her and let her crisscross the spread. After a short tour, they returned to the ranch house for dinner.

Lynn had wisely forbidden reporters at the ranch. Now, away from the mass of people that had accompanied her since she arrived in Texas forty-eight hours earlier, Fergie had time to talk freely with her hosts.

Lynn had wanted both Steve and Douglas to come to the ranch without dates. Douglas, however, insisted that he be allowed to bring Susan Bearden, the Eternal Values member he regularly escorted in New York.

Before dinner, Fergie admired the gems worn by Susan, which gave Douglas an opening to discuss Frederick Von Mierers and Eternal Values. Fergie was reportedly so fascinated that Douglas then described in detail how the prescription gems worked, as well as the benefits of a macrobiotic diet.

But it was on Steve that Fergie directed most of her attention during dinner and afterward. Steve was fun-loving, laughed a great deal, and was very attentive to her. Steve seemed like the playful prince she had married who had turned out to be a lot less fun and a good deal more serious than before their wedding — one of those rare occasions when you kiss a prince and he turns into a frog.

The entourage flew back to Houston on Sunday to attend a polo match in which Fergie's father, Major Ronald Ferguson, played. Arriving at the polo match, Steve helped Fergie from the car and shielded her from a downpour with a large umbrella. For the remainder of the afternoon, Steve was never far from her side.

When she departed Houston on Monday, the Duchess gave her hostess a signed photograph of herself, with the inscription "To my dearest and most special friend, Lynn," and she told Steve she hoped they would meet again.

In December 1989, Hooker announced its plans to sell Sakowitz, but there were no takers. Only Robert showed a strong interest in buying the company, and his ability to do so was dubious.

More bad news came in April 1990, when the minority shareholders group (previously the unsecured creditors) filed a petition asking the bankruptcy court to force Sakowitz into Chapter 7 involuntary bankruptcy proceedings or seek liquidation of the store. The minority shareholders claimed they were not being paid the money owed them in the previous deal that brought Sakowitz out of Chapter 11 in 1987. Under that plan, they were to have received ten cents on the dollar of monies owed them.

Sakowitz went on the auction block amid a sea of other retailers for sale, many with much bigger names and more solid financial footing, such as Marshall Field and Saks Fifth Avenue. Even some of the biggest chains were in trouble. Campeau Corp., which had also overstepped its leverage limits, first said it would not sell Bloomingdale's, relented and put it on the market, failed to find a buyer, and then removed it from the sale rack.

The petition to force Sakowitz into Chapter 7 was put on hold by Bankruptcy Judge R. F. Wheeless, but only temporarily. He set a May 7, 1990, deadline for Sakowitz either to find a buyer or liquidate.

On May 4, with no buyer secured, Hooker took Sakowitz into Chapter 11 proceedings, thereby protecting it from the minority shareholders' petition that threatened Chapter 7. Just hours later, a Chicago-based investment group calling itself Sakowitz Acquisition Partners (SAP), Inc., emerged as a possible buyer, offering to pay $4.5 million for the six-store chain. SAP, Inc., was given until May 10 to arrange financing.

By the end of May, there was more bad news. SAP, Inc., unable to secure a letter of credit to buy the company, withdrew its bid, and the bankruptcy proceedings were moved to New York, where a hearing was set for June 6 to decide the store's future.

Robert had pulled off an eleventh-hour deal after the first bankruptcy. Could he do it again? Call him arrogant, idealistic, foolish — he was not a quitter. He believed as strongly as Lynn and Oscar in Churchill's dictum "Never give up. Never give up. Never. Never. Never."

Anticipation was great as the large crowd packed the courtroom of U.S. Bankruptcy Judge Tina Brozman in New York.

Without much ado, Hooker attorney Sheldon Hirshon asked, "Are there any bids for a stock purchase?"

The question was met with silence.

"Is anyone here today to make a bid for the assets of Sakowitz, Inc.?" Hirshon then asked.

Again, the courtroom was silent.

Sakowitz's proud, eighty-eight-year history ended when Judge Brozman signed a liquidation order for the stores, and the crowd of attorneys, creditors, and potential investors filed out of the courtroom.

Robert issued a statement on the court's order for liquidation: "Although I deeply regret that the liquidation will mean the end of a Houston institution, I would personally prefer to nurture good memories of the past than see a future of ongoing inadequacies and operational difficulties slowly and painfully discoloring the warm and enjoyable history that was."

Marvin Blumenfeld, whose consulting firm had helped Sakowitz close its stores outside Houston after the first bankruptcy, says, "When we left the store, I didn't think they'd survive. I don't think Bob learned anything from the whole experience."

The final nailing of the coffin of Sakowitz would take place slowly as the retail chain endured a painful fifty-three-day liquidation. The going-out-of-business sale began with a private sale just for employees and their families, but Robert and Ann Sakowitz's presence at that first day of the sale was met with mixed feelings.

"Ann Sakowitz had a haughty way of acting toward salespeople," says a longtime salesperson. "She expected people to jump at her every wish. At the liquidation sale, she came into the hosiery department and said to a salesgirl who was passing by, 'I can't find my size.' The salesgirl looked her in the eye and said, 'That's not my department.'"

The story made the rounds through the store and caused giggles. There was no greater sin at Sakowitz, where service came first, than for a salesperson to brush off a customer.

Instead of being on hand to thank longtime employees for their years of dedicated service, Robert took his family on vacation during the public opening. Robert may not have been there, but it seemed that everyone else in Houston was.

At the flagship Post Oak store, shoppers of all ages and budgets pressed through the front doors for the early-morning opening day of liquidation. Shoppers swarmed onto the escalator and combed threadbare racks before waiting an average of forty-five minutes for a dressing room and another two hours at the cash register to buy clothes reduced 20 percent.

The usually very polite Sakowitz customers became the opposite as they fought for bargains. Computerized cash registers stalled as cords were trampled underfoot. At one point the escalator stopped under the weight of a continual thrust of shoppers. By mid-morning, a team from the fire marshal's office had to lock the store's doors to help manage the crowd.

Luke Fullen, a salesman in the men's department for thirty-seven years, recalls that on the first day of the liquidation sale, salesmen sold $532,000 worth of men's clothes. "We wondered," Fullen says, wistfully, "where were these people when we needed them?"

The days ticked by. "Last 9 days," said notices in the papers and in the store's windows. Tomorrow the 9 would become 8, a day after that 7.

"Going Out of Business," said a sign above the entrance. "The end of a tradition."

It was all so promotional, Robert would have said, had he come around to the store. Not the Sakowitz way. Nor was bankruptcy, Tobias and Simon would have added.

By Saturday, August 4, the first floor looked like it had been hit by looters. There were empty showcases, empty shelves, empty countertops, empty racks. Heaped in a pile in a corner were mannequins; a list of delivery charges gathered dust on a counter.

In the couture department, the woman known to Sakowitz customers for forty years as "Beavers" stood behind a counter assisting customers, just as she had done thirty-one years earlier when she had helped open the Post Oak store.

"Excuse me, can you tell me where the men's department is?" one shopper asked a salesclerk.

"Right there on that rack," the employee said, with a wave of her arm. "There also are a few pants on a table over there."

The store's remaining bargains inspired little enthusiasm. Time was running out for this former preserve of the privileged and the well-to-do, whose air-conditioning vents once wafted Chanel No. 5 into the air.

The liquidation sale coincided with President Bush's 1990 Economic Summit in Houston. Bush's advance team, after checking out the route the president was to take from his hotel to the summit meeting, saw Sakowitz's liquidation sign bannered across the front of the store and thought it did not bode well for the message the president wanted to send at the summit. Would Sakowitz's liquidators remove the sign just while the motorcade passed, the advance team asked. The liquidators obliged.

Today, the store at the corner of Post Oak and Westheimer stands empty and shuttered. Paint is chipping off the building, and some of the lights in the Sakowitz sign — which, oddly, still comes on at night — have burned out.

In the years following the store's closing, Robert searched unsuccessfully for a job and was finally forced to put his River Oaks mansion on the market. It was impossible not to notice how far his star had fallen.

One of the ironies today is that Lynn, who had started with little compared to Robert, and Oscar, who had started with little by any comparison, had become spectacularly successful, while Robert, who had been given so much, had failed.

As the twentieth century ends and women are finally beginning to take top leadership positions in American business, it is difficult not to wonder whether the fate of the Sakowitz store might not have been very different had its leadership been taken over by Lynn instead of Robert. Her feeling for fashion is recognized internationally. Perhaps even more important, her most obvious character trait has always been an iron self-discipline.

20

STEVEN BRADFORD WYATT was only six years old when he last saw his father and thirteen when he learned that his father was a murderer. The mere mention of Lipman's name made him very nervous and uncomfortable. A Dallas businessman was skiing in Vail in early 1992 when he met Steve on the slopes. Steve introduced himself as Oscar and Lynn Wyatt's son. The Dallas man, who had known Lipman well, said, "But you're really Bob Lipman's son. I knew your dad."

Steve's face turned ashen and lost all expression. "He freaked out totally," says the Dallas man. "All he wanted to do was get away, and he skied off."

An ex-girlfriend of Steve's remembers that one day after she and Steve had dated seriously for months she brought up the subject of Robert Lipman: "When I asked him to tell me what he remembered about his real dad, he said, 'Oscar is my real dad.' That was it. That's all he said."

Oscar, like Lynn, showed great fondness for Steve, who was as outgoing and high-spirited as Douglas was introverted and quiet. "Everything was so focused on Steve that it was like the other children did not even exist," says a Sakowitz family member.

A men's clothing salesman at Sakowitz, who regularly went to Coastal's offices to fit Oscar's suits, says, "Mr. Wyatt liked to talk about Steve being a great athlete and the fact that Steve was captain of his high-school track team. He told about the time that he and Steve had a disagreement. Steve threw up his fists, got out in the middle of the living room, and said, 'Come on, I'll take you on.' Oscar told me he didn't take the challenge because he knew Steve would whip him."

Steve was everything in high school that Oscar had not been — handsome, popular, rich — and while these were traits that Oscar envied or disdained in Robert Sakowitz, in Steve they made Oscar proud. Neither Oscar's first son by his first wife nor his two younger sons by Lynn were handsome or very popular. The handsome Wyatt boys were Lipman's, the ones Oscar had inherited when he married Lynn.

When Steve decided to attend the University of Arizona in Tucson — widely recognized as *the* party school of the nation — few who knew Steve were surprised. After college, he returned home to Houston to go to work. Although now in his twenties, he seemed hardly to have changed from the carefree teenager he was at St. John's.

"He was unbelievably fun to be with," says a tall, blond, rich Houstonian he dated in the mid-1980s. "We had a great, great time. He had a convertible, and we drove around singing the songs to the radio. It was like going out with somebody in high school."

Steve was lighthearted with women, but he also could become very serious, which he did in 1983, when he became engaged to marry the dark, beautiful daughter of a Peruvian industrialist whom he had dated in college. Her name was Dorice Valle Risso, but Steve's friends referred to her as "the Peruvian Bombshell." Plans were under way for Steve and Dorice to marry on an 18,000-foot-high Andean mountaintop, but at the last minute Dorice's parents canceled the engagement, reportedly without explanation.

There were many other women in Steve's life, including American model Denise Lewis, who sold the story of her two-year affair with Steve to the tabloid *Globe*. "Steve's a fantastic lover — the very best I've ever known," said then-thirty-one-year-old Denise. "And that's not just because he's great in bed. We also had a spiritual bond that touched something much deeper."

But the spiritual aspect of their romance was clearly less compelling than their physical needs, which were "so hot and heavy, they once made love in the bathroom of an airliner — because they couldn't wait to get back on the ground."

It was perhaps this same irresistible urgency that resulted in Miss Lewis's pregnancy.

"Steve always obeyed his mother, and I guess in her eyes I just wasn't good enough," the model reveals. "Steve told me Lynn was horrified when she learned I was expecting. 'You better make sure that she gets rid of it,' she told him.

"I wanted the baby more than anything. I loved Steve more than I've ever loved anyone. But I went ahead with the abortion and it broke my heart.

"He said he would pay for the procedure, but he never did."

Many of the girls Steve dated in the 1980s were not even born when Robert Lipman was building his notorious reputation as an exhibitionist, but the young women in Steve's crowd whispered about Steve the way women in his father's crowd had of Lipman.

"I used to hear that Steve's nose, his hands, his feet, and his equipment were all the same size," confides a female friend. "He just has an unbelievable reputation as a relentless lover. He would stick it in a wall socket if he thought it would give him a charge."

By 1989, Steve had been living in London for four years and had made a name for himself — not in business, but on the club circuit. "Steve's social life revolves around a fairly fast European-tinged gang," reported *Tatler*, "which includes a bevy of extremely attractive girls — mostly unmarried and mostly under 30 — who are referred to by rivals as the 'sell-by date' gang and who do the San Lorenzo-Tramp-Annabel's circuit."

But Steve is different from most rich American playboys. He drinks very little, and, save for the occasional fat cigar, he does not smoke. He works hard to maintain his muscular build, and, like his brother Douglas, he adheres to a macrobiotic diet consisting mainly of grains and kelp.

Also like Douglas, Steve is a strong believer in mind over matter; his passion is t'ai chi, a combination of yoga and martial arts. He has followed the teachings of Dale Carnegie's "Know thyself" philosophy and Werner Erhard's EST training. He meditates regularly and gets up each day at 5:30 A.M. "to be with the rhythms of the day."

Most idiosyncratic of all, in London he slept under a blue plastic pyramid. According to ex-girlfriend Denise Lewis, the purpose of the pyramid, which dangled over his bed, was "to cleanse his soul."

As an adult, Steve, like Douglas, became a Christian and made religion an important part of his life. He was also a perfect student of his mother's charm, frequently repeating the name of the person with whom he is talking, always wearing a sunny smile, and talking evangelically about how fabulous everything is. "God, it's a beautiful day," Steve says.

According to Chris Hutchins and Peter Thompson's book *Fergie Confidential*, just weeks after Steve had returned to London, following Fergie's Texas tour, he began receiving telephone calls from the Duchess. With Prince Andrew away serving in the navy, Fergie had found others in whom to confide. At this moment, she was greatly distressed over her stepfather, Hector Barrantes, who was battling cancer.

It was not long before Fergie's car was seen outside Steve's rented London flat, at No. 34 Cadogan Square. It is possible that, at this point, Steve and Fergie were simply good friends. When she came to a dinner party at his flat, Steve had as his date Pricilla Phillips, an American actress who looks not unlike Jerry Hall and who was currently appearing onstage in a small theater above a pub in Chelsea.

Aware of Fergie's interest in the theater, Steve then took her to a comedy at London's Apollo Theater, where they narrowly escaped being photographed together after the show.

Fergie's honeymoon with the press had been short-lived. Following a fairy-tale wedding on July 23, 1986, in Westminster Abbey, in little more than three years of marriage, she had become the target of endlessly critical articles. She was pilloried for her weight, her waddle, her lack of taste in clothes. Couturier Zandra Rhodes reportedly refused Fergie's request for free clothes, claiming, "I don't need the publicity." At first, she had dutifully reacted by slimming down dramatically, learning to walk more gracefully, and even learning to sing to calm her nerves.

But the press and the public found new things to snipe at. Soon after the 1988 birth of the Yorks' first child, Beatrice, who is fifth in line to the British throne, Fergie came under fire for "abandoning" her eleven-week-old child when she went on a six-week Australian tour with her husband.

She was endlessly chastised for shirking her royal duties in favor of skiing, playing tennis, shopping, and dancing. The irony was that what Andrew and the public so loved about Sarah Ferguson at the time of the wedding was her exuberance and devil-may-care attitude. She seemed determined to blow some badly needed fresh air into the stuffy House of Windsor. To many, she seemed more American than English.

A born boat rocker and frank talker, Fergie had charmed Oscar during her visit to Texas. "She's a straight-up girl, very direct," he told a reporter.

But the straightforward, independent qualities, so admired in her as a fiancée, were unfitting in a duchess, the British public said. She should leave her old ways behind.

Fergie apparently decided that, having tried to change and please without success, she should quit trying. With Andrew away again at sea, she decided to go with Steve on a five-day trip to one of the world's most romantic inns.

On May 2, 1990, six weeks after Fergie gave birth to Princess Eugenie — the Yorks' second child and sixth in line to the British throne — Steve flew Fergie on a private jet to Morocco. Accompanying them were Fergie's two-year-old daughter, Beatrice; the child's nanny; two of Fergie's detectives from the Royal Protection Branch; and Pricilla Phillips.

They flew to Agadir on the Atlantic coast of Morocco and then drove to the inn La Gazelle d'Or, located one hundred miles southwest of Marrakesh, just outside the walled city of Taroudant. Steve and Fergie spent all day, each day, together, riding horses through the olive groves and gardens that border the Sahara desert and lounging comfortably on a swing by the swimming pool. They swam in the heated pool and had lunch beside it, while taking in the beauty of the distant snow-capped Atlas Mountains.

Steve and Fergie seemed very much alike: both were fun-loving free spirits who seemed fascinated by the esoteric and the unknown and comfortable discussing the age-old question of the meaning of life.

After five blissful, relaxed days, Steve paid the bill and flew the entourage back to London. But even before their plane lifted off from the ground in Morocco, someone telephoned one of Britain's tabloid newspapers about their escapade.

A few days later, for the first time in British print, Fergie's name was linked with the playboy from Texas. Prince Andrew, her husband of three and a half years, publicly brushed off the story, saying his wife was entitled to be friends with whomever she chose.

But while Andrew appeared the loving and trusting husband, the press was not so kind. Reporters began a feeding frenzy to find out whatever they could about the dashing thirty-five-year-old Steve, whom one aptly described as "a cross between Bobby Ewing and the Incredible Hulk."

It was immediately revealed that Steve was the eldest son of Lynn Wyatt, who had caused her own royal scandal just six years earlier when it was gossiped that she had had an affair with Prince

Rainier. But for some months the biggest piece of scandal about Steve's past remained a secret. What no reporter picked up on was that his real father was Robert Steven Lipman, who also had created a scandal twenty-two years earlier in London when he murdered model Claudie Delbarre.

Scandal ran in the blood of this rich family.

Instead of allowing the stories of their Moroccan holiday to die down, Fergie and Steve continued to see each other. During the summer, when Lynn was in Cap Ferrat, Steve took Fergie to visit her. The stay was brief, but it was not long before they were together again on a plane, this time headed for the United States. Fergie's stepfather, Hector Barrantes, was near death at a hospital in New York and she wanted to see him one last time.

Some friends of Steve's find it difficult to believe that he had an affair with Fergie, only because she is the opposite of the tall, slim, beautiful models he usually dates. But those who know him best know that, when it comes to women, he has always listened to his mother.

Fergie at times found herself sharing Steve with Lynn. When Lynn was in London, Steve took both Fergie and his mother to dinner. Once, when Lynn learned that Fergie was coming to New York for a fund-raising dinner for Britain's Royal Academy, Lynn checked herself into a suite across the hall from the Duchess's in the Hotel Plaza Athenee. Lynn, as she so often did with friends, brought gifts to New York for Fergie and the princesses Eugenie and Beatrice. Just as she had with Princess Margaret and Princess Grace, Lynn worked hard at cultivating the Duchess's friendship because it brought her prestige by association.

Just how close Steve and Fergie had become was obvious when she had him to dinner at Windsor Castle. The Queen, however, was growing anxious over her daughter-in-law's dalliances with the jet-setting Steve. She let Fergie know that she was not pleased to have Wyatt at the castle and she was even less pleased to be seated next to him. But Fergie's faux pas at this dinner was as nothing compared to the dinner she hosted at Buckingham Palace in early August 1990 for Steve and Dr. Ramzi Salman, the head of Iraqi state oil marketing. Iraq at this moment was involved in a border dispute with Kuwait that was growing fiercer by the day.

After dining at the palace, Steve, Fergie, and Salman went on to La Gavroche, the three-star restaurant in Chelsea, where a reception was being hosted by Tory party treasurer Lord Alpine. Fergie had been invited to attend with Andrew, but because he was away she said she would come to the party alone, after the dinner. The next day's papers reported the incident, exclaiming that when Fergie was about to be seated between the Tory treasurer and another government official, Steve grabbed her hand and proclaimed, "Mah woman and I sit together."

Oscar Wyatt had for some time been negotiating a deal to sell Saddam Hussein half of his American East Coast oil refineries. Oscar also purchased a quarter of a million barrels of oil a day from Iraq. Ramzi Salman was one of Saddam Hussein's closest confidants and a friend of Oscar's. Aware of this, Fergie hosted the dinner as a favor to Steve.

But when word of the dinner hit the papers, the Palace was aghast at Fergie's blunder. Saddam Hussein was the pariah of the international community. His regime was responsible for the murder of innocent victims, including his own people. The border dispute had become so dangerous that several members of the Kuwaiti royal family, including the Emir of Kuwait, were living in exile in Kensington Palace.

Suddenly, not only Fleet Street was interested in Steve and Fergie's relationship. Fergie's dinner with Salman aroused the interest of British Intelligence and, soon, the CIA in Washington. And the situation was about to worsen. In August, when Iraq finally invaded Kuwait, President Bush announced that the aggression would not stand. Suddenly, the world focused attention on Bush's anger at Saddam Hussein. No one was more interested in the growing furor than Oscar Wyatt.

21

O SCAR had the same opinion of the president of the United States as he had of his brother-in-law. George Herbert Walker Bush, like Robert T. Sakowitz, was the object of Oscar's scorn because of his unfair advantage in life, because he had been born into privilege and wealth.

"George Bush came down to Texas in 1948 in a private plane to go to work in the oil fields because his daddy was a director of Dresser Industries," Oscar charged. Notwithstanding the fact that the Coastal Corporation was a major contributor to Bush's 1988 presidential campaign, the disdain that Oscar had long felt for Bush turned to irrepressible fury when Bush began a monumental military effort against Saddam Hussein. It was an effort, Oscar suggested, that resulted from British prime minister Margaret Thatcher's telling Bush that such a war would correct the president's image as a wobbly wimp.

It was difficult for many Americans not to agree with Oscar's opinion. Bush insisted that the great nations of the world must form a "New World Order," to punish military aggression and tyranny, but there was a rich selection of other tyrants to choose from, some much more significant than Saddam Hussein. Bush, however, was determined to have his war, this war, despite the efforts of his critics, of whom the most outspoken included Oscar Wyatt and fellow Texan Ross Perot.

At first Oscar and Perot were more of an annoyance than a problem for Bush. But as summer turned to fall in 1990, both Ross and Oscar were becoming more and more adamant in the media against the increasingly inevitable war. Perot's analysis was the same as Oscar's, that Bush was pursuing a conflict in order to prove his manhood.

Like Perot — who, a decade earlier, had successfully rescued two of his employees from captivity in Iran — Oscar complained that Bush did not understand the Middle East. "If the U.S. makes the mistake of attacking [Iraq], we'll have every Arab, except the King of Saudi, the royal family, and the royal family of Kuwait, if they are royal, and the royal family of the United Arab Emirates, against us from time immemorial [sic], and those royal houses will fall.

"In nineteen years of trading with the Arabs, the one thing I've learned is to stay out of their chicken shit conflicts," said Coastal's chairman. "Let Arabs fight Arabs."

What most Americans did not know was that Oscar had a compelling personal reason for trying to avoid a U.S. war with Iraq. Coastal was at this very moment quietly negotiating to sell half of its East Coast American refineries to Iraq for $800 million. At the time of the August 2 invasion, a sale seemed very likely, but four days later, the U.S. put trade sanctions on Iraq.

"Now that's all on hold," Oscar said of the sale.

Shrewdly in step with changing world conditions, Oscar had moved in a big way out of production and into oil refining and marketing. Coastal's refining and marketing revenues were $5.3 billion, comprising 63.6 percent of Coastal's total sales.

Because Coastal needed an assured supply of oil, and Iraq needed an assured market, it was not surprising that two such sentimental romantics as Oscar and Saddam should be dreaming of a marriage.

"Guys like me like Iraq," Oscar said, when anti-Iraq sentiment was its strongest in America. "You don't have to go through any member of the royal family. You don't have to pay any princes. They operate like an independent oil company. It's just one price — take it or leave it."

While many observers considered Saddam a madman, Oscar said he found Saddam someone who "knows exactly what he's doing" even though he "might not morally be what people want him to be."

In addition to putting the refinery sale on hold, the sanctions included an embargo of Iraqi crude, of which Coastal was receiving 250,000 barrels a day, 10 percent of all the oil produced by Iraq.

According to the *Wall Street Journal:*

> Several companies, including Coastal, persuaded the U.S. to let them take delivery of Iraqi and Kuwaiti crude that had left the Mideast by [August 2]. But Coastal tried to take things further.
>
> Three days after the embargo went into effect, a Coastal tanker chugged into the Persian Gulf to pick up a shipment of Iraqi crude stored in a Saudi oil terminal. The crude had already left Iraq. "That oil is of no benefit to Iraq," a Coastal spokesman said at the time.
>
> Authorities didn't buy it. The tanker was turned back.
>
> Coastal immediately set its legal and regulatory experts to work to determine if there was a way around the embargo. . . .
>
> . . . On Oct. 10, Coastal got its exemption from the Treasury Department to bring the shipment of 2.6 million barrels of Iraqi crude to the U.S.
>
> A Treasury spokeswoman said, "It's the only instance of oil being allowed in that was covered by the general embargo."

Anyone who was appalled by Oscar's actions had only to look at his past successes at skirting sanctions against other countries. Years earlier, he had bought crude from Iran when there were sanctions against it, by, as the *Wall Street Journal* explained, "never bringing the oil or products refined from it to U.S. shores."

Oscar had been exploring for oil in Libya for a dozen years when the International Emergency Economic Powers Act, in 1986, imposed a virtually total ban on direct trade with Libya. These sanctions against Muammar al-Qaddafi were in response to the Libyan leader's terrorist activities, but Oscar shrewdly found a way to continue dealing with Libya. He set up a subsidiary of Coastal in Bermuda, which then in partnership with Libya bought a refinery in Hamburg, Germany, in 1988. Libya supplies the Hamburg refinery with crude at low prices in exchange for a greater equity interest in the future and for much-needed hard currency now.

While most companies and their executives shied away from any contact with Saddam Hussein and his country after the Kuwait invasion, Oscar maintained his ties with Iraq, reportedly "sending subtle and not-so-subtle signals that he wasn't jumping on the anti-Iraq bandwagon in the U.S."

In fact, Oscar flew to Baghdad in early December 1990, six weeks before a mid-January, U.S.-imposed deadline for Iraq to withdraw from Kuwait. Whether acting on his contempt for Bush, his anger at the derailing of his $800 million sale to Iraq, his lust for publicity, or a sudden surge of patriotic fervor, he flew to Iraq to rescue Americans being held hostage by Hussein.

The fact that Deputy Secretary of State Lawrence Eagleburger had sent word that President Bush was furious about the proposed rescue trip did not deter Oscar. He was a man who had always done what he wanted, and no one — including, and especially, this President of the United States — was going to stop him.

If his purpose in making the trip was not immediately obvious, some other things were — for example, his decision to take with him former Texas governor John Connally, who is as smooth and slick as Oscar is crude and obvious.

Tall, movie-star-handsome John Bowden Connally was born in 1917 in the Texas village of Floresville. He earned a law degree from the University of Texas in 1941 and served as Congressman Lyndon Johnson's assistant in Washington, D.C., from 1946 to 1949, but his most significant education came from being the lawyer of the mythic Texas oilman Sid Richardson during the fifties.

As Richardson's right-hand man, "Big John," as he was called, learned how big money is made and how it is spent, on politicians as well as on other investments. He learned how to ingratiate himself with the rich and powerful. On November 22, 1963, he became known throughout the world as the other man wounded in the assassination of President Kennedy.

By 1973, he had served as secretary of the navy, governor of Texas and secretary of the treasury, and he was widely considered to be the best possible Democratic nominee for president. But then he unexpectedly became a Republican and hitched his future to President Richard Nixon's, only a year before Watergate. As often happens to political turncoats, Connally was thereafter effectively debarred from politics, but this brought him back to Texas and the opportunity to make himself rich, like the men he admired. His business judgment, like his final political judgment, however, proved to be fatally flawed, and in 1987 he took Chapter 11 bankruptcy and left taxpayers with at least $65 million in bad loans from failed savings and loan companies.

Oscar was fond of Connally and thought he might be useful. So a month after Connally held a public auction of his personal belongings to help pay off his debts, Oscar put him on Coastal's board of directors.

On Saturday, December 1, 1990, Oscar and Connally left Houston in Coastal's Boeing 707 loaded with fifteen tons of medical supplies purportedly worth half a million dollars. They arrived in Amman, Jordan, on Sunday, where the medical supplies were unloaded for later distribution. Oscar and Connally then flew on to Baghdad and registered at the Al Rashid Hotel, a stay paid for by the Iraqis, as both Oscar and Connally repeatedly pointed out. In the kind of language that has endeared Oscar to reporters, he insisted, "We didn't furnish anything but our hat and our ass."

On Monday, December 3, both Connally and Oscar met with Industry Minister and Acting Oil Minister Hussein Kamel Hassan, Saddam's son-in-law, who listened but gave no indication whether hostages might be released or even whether Saddam would meet with the visitors.

Two men at least as expert at self-promotion as Oscar — former heavyweight champion Muhammad Ali and the Reverend Jesse Jackson — had already bartered medical supplies for American captives in Iraq. In September, Jackson had secured freedom for forty-seven Americans, and Ali had freed fifteen in early December.

Oscar and Connally each had a suite of his own, but the rescue headquarters where the work was done was in Oscar's three-room suite, where they revised lists of American hostages that included no Coastal employees but names supplied by American congressmen and senators, American corporations, and the Kuwaiti underground. Oscar and Connally sought no help from, indeed did not even contact, the American embassy but instead ran their own traps.

On Wednesday morning, a call came instructing Oscar and Connally to stay in their rooms, and only minutes later they were driven to the presidential palace. Escorted by Saddam's interpreter, a professor of English literature at the University of Baghdad, they were led to the meeting room where Saddam sat with his First Deputy Premier and the Parliament Speaker. Saddam was in full military uniform, including a holstered pistol on his belt.

He rose and shook hands with both Connally and Wyatt, then sat and listened to the carefully rehearsed pitches of two of America's greatest salesmen. Connally spoke first and stressed that Americans knew little and cared less about Kuwait but were outraged that fellow Americans were being held as hostages. Saddam chose to call these hostages "guests," but Americans were so revolted at Saddam's use of them as "human shields," Connally said, "that you are being called a modern-day Hitler."

When his turn came, Oscar, ever the practical businessman, pointed out to Saddam "how difficult it will be to handle all these detainees if war breaks out. For every two of them you've got, you're going to have to have at least one soldier guarding them. You'll have to feed them, clothe them, and house them, and all the time you have a war to fight."

No less practical than Oscar, Saddam asked through the interpreter, "Will the detainees discourage President Bush from attacking Iraq?"

"Absolutely not," snapped Oscar, "a few hundred hostages won't deter him for one minute."

When Oscar mentioned the fifteen tons of medical supplies, Saddam thanked him, removed his pistol, and put it on the table, which both Texans took as a sign that the negotiations were progressing favorably.

Forty-five minutes after the meeting began, Oscar and Connally rose to leave. Saddam shook hands with Connally and said, "Your plane will not go home empty."

Then, smiling broadly, Saddam put both his hands on Oscar's right hand and told his associates, "You see there are Americans who tell the truth. They are not diplomats."

Absolutely speechless, perhaps for the only time in his life, Oscar left the room knowing he had been successful but not knowing how successful.

A few hours later, the Texans received private word that Saddam had decided to release all foreign hostages, some three thousand of them, including one thousand Americans. On Thursday, December 6, Saddam himself announced the general release of prisoners.

With a gesture of false modesty that is an essential part of the Texas reputation for bragging, both Oscar and Connally said at first that they did not claim credit for Saddam's decision to release all the hostages. "Only he can say what persuaded him," said Connally. "It'd be inappropriate for us to take any credit. But I'm absolutely not convinced that he had made up his mind before we met with him."

Before long, Oscar would insist that he had been responsible for changing Saddam's hostage policy. "I firmly believe that Governor Connally and I were to a large degree responsible for the release of all the hostages."

The victory must have seemed especially sweet for Oscar, considering his view of Bush. Oscar, with no formal experience as a statesman, had made a mockery of the CIA and the President of the United States, who had tried for four months to win the hostages' release. Perhaps the sweetest moment came when the American embassy, which had not lifted a finger in Oscar's behalf, asked whether it might put three of its employees on Oscar's plane. "Okay," ordered Oscar, "but only if you get your ass moving and clear some of these other civilians for release."

The fuel tanks of Oscar's Boeing 707 were empty after the transatlantic flight from Houston, but he could not buy jet fuel without breaking the U.S. and U.N. sanctions. The Iraqi government solved this problem by making Oscar a gift of $35,000 worth of fuel.

Beginning at noon on Saturday, December 8, Oscar received several calls urging him to get out of Iraq while he still could, but he delayed leaving until eight o'clock in the evening, hoping for more hostages. Finally, with twenty-two American hostages, one British hostage, eight family members of hostages, and three diplomats formerly stationed at the U.S. embassy in Kuwait on board, he took off for Houston. Although his plane was far from full, he had begun the general exodus. Another 1,000 foreigners, including 175 Americans, departed Iraq the following day on Iraqi Airways jets.

Oscar walked up and down the aisles of his 707, questioning each man about the details of his captivity. The freed prisoners — including three U.S. embassy employees and several oil field workers — were fed sandwiches and Texas-style chili made in a Crockpot. Oscar had stocked the plane with champagne, and as the plane began its descent into Houston's Ellington Field at 4:00 A.M., on Sunday, December 9, Oscar popped the first cork and toasted his passengers, "Welcome home."

Oscar, in a tan raincoat, and Connally, in a navy raincoat, were the first to exit the plane and descend the stairs, reminding some in the crowd of the grand-opera-like entrances by the late General Douglas MacArthur. Oscar's demeanor was almost imperial, and he was perhaps not entirely oblivious of the phalanx of waiting photographers and reporters. Nellie Connally and Lynn were there among the crowd on the chilly tarmac, waving American flags at their husbands.

Once inside the terminal, the two men stepped up to a podium where dozens of microphones and television cameras awaited them. When a son of one of the ex-hostages handed Oscar a red rose and said, "Thank you for bringing my daddy home," Oscar burst into tears.

Their triumph was the lead story on the front page of newspapers across America, and Oscar, for the first time in his life, actually seemed eager for the good publicity. The articles provided a forum for speaking against the war, and, whenever possible, Connally delivered the message.

"If we become involved in a shooting war in that distant land, it will be tragic indeed," Connally declared. "We will incur the enmity of 200 million Arabs, including most of those in the lands we would be protecting."

But in the days that followed, Oscar and Connally's message often got drowned out by questions about Oscar's real motive in meeting with Hussein. While critics charged that he had gone to Iraq to do business with Saddam, Oscar found himself having to insist repeatedly that his mission was strictly "humanitarian."

He insisted that he had been negotiating the refinery sale not just with Iraq but with four other countries at the same time and that he was not trying to continue trade with Iraq.

The *Wall Street Journal*'s skepticism was evident when it put quotation marks around Oscar's "mission of mercy," whose purpose, the *Journal* said, was "ostensibly" to bring home the hostages. "The way Oscar Wyatt figures it, war or no war, embargo or no embargo, Iraq has at least 100 billion barrels of crude oil in the ground."

The United States Treasury Department also expressed interest in what Oscar was up to in Baghdad. Just five days after the mission, an anonymous Treasury source revealed that Treasury officials were investigating whether Oscar had violated trade sanctions against Iraq. Penalties for violating the sanctions included a fine of up to $1 million and up to twelve years in jail.

Oscar insisted that the rescue attempt was private; that he and Connally had not spent one dime in Iraq; that their hotel room and even the jet fuel for their plane was a gift of the Iraqis.

What the Internal Revenue Service may have thought about Oscar's private use of the company plane appeared to be secondary among Oscar's concerns, even though Oscar had reportedly battled with the IRS before. According to one press report in 1981, the IRS was "clipping the columns of *Houston Chronicle* society writer Maxine Messinger in an attempt to monitor Wyatt's business-and-pleasure junkets."

Oscar's chief concern was with the Treasury Department's and the Bush administration's views of the trip. Oscar and Connally wanted to avoid Bush's ordering their prosecution for breaking either the U.S.'s embargo against Iraq or the Logan Act, which forbids American citizens from dabbling privately in foreign policy.

In March 1991, the Treasury Department dropped its inquiry into Oscar's trip to Baghdad. But just four months later, following a year-long separate investigation of about fifteen Houston oil companies, the Treasury Department banned three Coastal affiliates from doing business in the United States after they were identified as agents of the Libyan government. The ban also included twenty-one individuals, among them officers and managers of Coastal's affiliates, which are 33 percent owned by Coastal.

In 1992, a former Coastal employee, reflecting on the flap over Oscar's trip to Iraq, says it was reminiscent of the controversy created in the early 1980s when Coastal was among the first companies to import crude oil after the Iranian hostage crisis.

If Coastal's chairman was a Texas-style hero when he stepped off his plane in Houston on December 9, he was not, thirteen days later, after a visit to Corpus Christi, where feelings about Oscar had long been mixed, at best.

Despite Lo-Vaca Gas's raping of Corpus Christi two decades earlier, Oscar was the town's richest, most controversial adopted son, and when the Chamber of Commerce needed a speaker to draw a crowd for its annual banquet, Oscar seemed an exciting choice. Tickets to the dinner were already selling well prior to Oscar's Baghdad mission, and within hours of his return to Houston with twenty-two hostages, the dinner was a virtual sellout.

The military is Corpus Christi's largest employer, and a contingent of military officers from the Navy Air Station and the Army Supply Depot were among the twelve hundred people who had each paid $39.50 to hear Oscar speak.

On the evening of January 22, 1991, just six days after American jets began bombing Iraq, when Oscar rose to address the banquet in a cavernous hall fronting the bay, he was greeted with applause fit for a hero. A huge American flag hung behind him, and above him the ceiling was decorated with red, white, and blue balloons.

But just minutes into his speech, the man who had so angered Corpus Christi before was doing it again.

"I want you to understand. I have five sons and I don't want them or any of your sons to be the white slaves of an Arab monarch," he railed. "The Bush administration has not come up with a reasonable explanation of why we should spill our blood for the Emir of Kuwait."

Chairs started screeching on the floor, as groups of diners got up and angrily marched out of the hall.

Not deterred in the least, Oscar brutishly and unapologetically continued to assail the Bush administration and its policies, predicting that, if the war continued, it would become a "meat grinder" for American troops. "The Kuwaiti defense force took less casualties than the coalition pilots have already lost. The mentality of the people we are defending is that they think they can buy their liberty with our blood."

By the end of his speech more than one hundred people, including a contingent of military officers, had marched out of the hall.

Later Oscar said of his reception, "You'd have thought I had AIDS, wouldn't you? Oh, well, I don't give a rat's ass. If they wanted to be entertained, they should have hired a comedian."

Chamber of Commerce officials no doubt wished they had — when they were bombarded with angry phone calls, some asking for a refund on their banquet tickets. Many Corpus Christians took the strident antiwar speech as a personal affront to their military town.

When Oscar heard that Corpus Christi mayor Betty Turner told the press that she was "disappointed, appalled, and embarrassed" by the speech, he sent back the key to the city she had given him.

"I told the mayor of Corpus she could take the key to the city and stick it up her ass," Wyatt later boasted to a reporter. In fact, he wrote an almost obsequious letter to the mayor returning the key.

Still, in the days that followed, Oscar took the tough-guy pose with reporters. He said he could not picture himself modifying his views to tell a group something it wants to hear. He said his tombstone should read, "He said what he thought."

One observer was reminded of the time Oscar said about OPEC's oil ministers, with whom he was on excellent terms, "It's pretty dangerous when 13 camel riders can set the energy prices in the U.S." When the American-Arab Anti-Discrimination Community called the comment racist, Oscar apologized and that was the end of it.

But the outrage in Corpus was less quick to die. Continued criticism prompted Oscar to take pains in a letter to the *Houston Chronicle* to explain that he supported U.S. troops even if he didn't support Bush's policy.

When the controversy continued, Coastal hired a public relations specialist. Doubtless on the advice of his PR man, at Coastal's May 1991 annual meeting, Oscar canceled what he had dubbed the "kiss at the pig," the news conference he traditionally held after the meeting.

But as Oscar left the meeting, he did manage to deliver one zinger. Asked whether Coastal stood ready to purchase Iraqi crude when it came to market again, Oscar said he doubted President Bush would allow the Iraqis to export it.

"He might starve them first," Oscar declared. "I don't put anything above him."

Such a comment, one reporter noted, explained why Coastal's PR man remained a chain-smoker.

Oscar's genius was not public relations, but making money, and whatever his shareholders' feelings about his brutish behavior, they could not help but be pleased with his 1990 job performance. At the annual meeting, he reported a fifth consecutive year of increased earnings with a record-setting net income of $225.6 million.

As a First Boston oil analyst explained, "The real attraction of Coastal is its unique ability to make good money, and serious amounts of it."

*   *   *

By early December 1990, Steve Wyatt had become more than just an annoyance to Britain's royal family. Not only was he growing too chummy with Prince Andrew's wife, but also, because of his father, Steve was becoming an embarrassment to the Queen in her relationship with the Kuwaiti royal family and President Bush. Oscar, after making a laughingstock of Bush over his inability to get hostages out of Iraq, took every opportunity in the press to lambaste Kuwait as an imperial regime for which American blood should not be spilled.

Nevertheless, on December 12, just five days after Oscar's Baghdad mission, Steve attended the royal family's most important celebration of the year, the collective birthdays of the Queen Mother, Princess Margaret, Princess Anne, and Prince Andrew.

The party for eight hundred guests was held in the gilded-domed Palace Picture Gallery amid the sophisticated sounds of a large string orchestra. It was difficult not to be awed on this momentous occasion in this historic gallery, but Steve could not have appeared more at ease. He lightheartedly bounced around the formal party, introducing himself to England's upper crust as "Sarah's friend."

Three nights later, Steve reciprocated by inviting Prince Andrew and Fergie to a bizarre fantasy party at an abandoned house in South London. Steve's offbeat party was much more to Fergie's taste than the formal Buckingham Palace ball, but if she hoped for future evenings with the refreshingly hip Texan, she would be disappointed. A report about Steve's party was filed at Scotland Yard and passed on to Buckingham Palace.

22

WITH CONTROVERSY swirling all around her family, Lynn Wyatt had always managed to come out unscathed. Neither her divorce from her first husband, nor the adultery and murder he committed, had bathed her in a bad light. Not even the dark side of Oscar Wyatt, whom *Texas Monthly* called "meaner than a junkyard dog," cast a shadow on her reputation.

"Terrible Oscar and wonderful Lynn" was the way Houston society described them, as though they were not a couple, but two very distinct, separate business entities. It was Lynn's ability to distance herself from scandal that had won her the kudo "the Teflon Socialite."

But as 1991 began, there appeared a number of threatening portents. The fact that her husband was being called a traitor and a scoundrel because of his position on Iraq was the least of her problems. Far more frightening was Douglas's lawsuit, which was approaching trial and which now involved her outright.

On February 7, 1991, Robert did what Lynn had staunchly and repeatedly refused to do. He sued his only sibling. The suit, which was delivered to Lynn at Allington by a process-server, charged that Lynn, as a member of Sakowitz's board of directors, was jointly liable with Robert for the corporate decisions that she had voted for and that Douglas's suit alleged were wrongful. While denying any wrongdoing on his own part, Robert's suit claimed that if there had been any breach of fiduciary duties to the estate, Lynn was guilty to a much greater degree than he was because "she made no effort to help the company."

Robert's suit against his sister was quickly thrown out by the judge, but the allegation would be the core of Robert's defense.

After nearly three years of trying to defend himself against Douglas's courthouse attacks, Robert had taken the offensive. This was due in large part to a very smart, very scrappy, relentlessly tenacious criminal lawyer named David Berg.

Robert had known Berg casually since the early 1980s, when their sons were in school together. Although their paths rarely crossed socially, Robert had from time to time called Berg to tell him about problems he was having with Oscar.

"He would be very upset and want to talk," David recalls. One night, around midnight, David got a telephone call from Robert asking David to meet him right away, that night. David was terrified: "I thought, *Oh, my God, he's killed Oscar!*"

David had given Robert free legal advice from time to time, even though David's specialty was criminal, not civil, law. But mostly the two had just talked as friends.

The more Robert talked with David, the more he thought seriously about hiring him to represent him against Douglas. But to do so was a risk. David had brilliantly defended alleged criminals, but this was a civil case. Could he handle the subtleties and intricacies of probate law? Could he sort through the mountain of financial records — there were three hundred volumes on the store's bankruptcy proceedings alone — and piece together a convincing explanation for why Robert had done what he did?

Hiring David also presented an image problem for Robert. David Berg did not have a lavish office in the best downtown skyscraper. He owned a two-story semi-rundown brick building on the edge of downtown. David was not fashionable, but he was successful.

After graduating from the University of Houston Law School, Berg opened his practice in Houston in 1968 defending antiwar protestors and cases involving illegal search and seizure. His first big break came his first year in practice, when twenty-two-year-old Danny Schacht was arrested and put in jail for wearing a military uniform to an antiwar protest in downtown Houston. Schacht's father enlisted the help of Berg, who took Schacht's case all the way to the United States Supreme Court and argued it successfully. At age twenty-seven, Berg became the youngest lawyer since Daniel Webster to win a reversal from the Supreme Court.

In 1978, Berg again gained national attention when he successfully defended a woman against charges that she had shot her common-law husband, cut him into five parts, and then driven the dismembered corpse across the country in her Cadillac. Berg employed the "battered wife" defense for the first time in Texas, and he won. The *New York Times* lauded Berg in a front-page story on cases employing the battered wife defense.

As the eighties drew to a close, Berg had decided to expand his practice to include civil law. In his first solo civil case, he represented the family of a black woman who was killed in a collision with a train at a railroad crossing in Sweeney, Texas, a small town outside Houston. Berg argued that the Missouri Pacific Railroad Co. had ignored repeated requests for signals at the crossing.

"People said we'd never get a favorable judgment in a rural courtroom for a black family," Berg recalls. When he had finished arguing his case, the jury awarded a record $12.5 million verdict. Again, he made national news.

Convinced by that verdict that Berg could handle the Sakowitz case, Robert hired him in January 1991 with the payment of a six-figure flat fee that he had to borrow from a bank. Although Berg was trying to shake the label "criminal lawyer," he still followed the practice of criminal lawyers — clients pay in advance.

"Growing up, I didn't know the Sakowitzes, but I knew of them, and what I saw was their elegance and that they had assimilated," says Berg. "I grew up very proud that a Jewish family in this Southern town could have achieved so much eminence and power."

In addition to defending Robert financially, Berg says, he was determined to stop Oscar from destroying the Sakowitz name.

Like his high-profile client, Berg relished publicity and had gotten a large share of it through the years. But even he could not have imagined, much less created, a story that would generate the degree of publicity that fell in his lap in July 1991, just two months before the scheduled trial date.

After Roger Hall broke off his friendship with Douglas Wyatt in January 1991, he demanded that Douglas help him get his money back for what two Houston appraisers said were overpriced gemstones. He repeatedly asked Douglas to get his mother, Lynn, to buy the Eternal Values stones, but Douglas refused.

One day Roger called Lynn himself, but his reason for calling, he says, had nothing to do with the stones. "I called and told her that I didn't have any interest in the Doug Wyatt/Bobby Sakowitz war, but that she needed to get Douglas out of [Eternal Values] because they were sapping him for every penny that he had."

Lynn and her other Oscar (designer Oscar de la Renta) by day. (*Phyllis Hand*)

Lynn dressed in Dior but with the designer Valentino in 1985 in New York. (*W*)

Lynn with Oscar de la Renta (and de la Renta executive Boaz Mazor, at left) by night. (*Robin Platzer*)

Andy Warhol, Lynn, Diane von Furstenberg (standing), and Oscar at the world premiere of the movie *Urban Cowboy* at Houston's honky-tonk Gilley's. (*Houston Chronicle*)

Joan Collins and Lynn, facing off at Lynn's July 1988 birthday party, Flower Power, at Villa Malbousque in Cap Ferrat. (*W*)

Two international charmers, Lynn and Ivana Trump, in 1991 in Houston. (*Sheila Cunningham*)

Lynn and Oscar with New York cabaret pianist Bobby Short. (*Phyllis Hand*)

Ann Sakowitz and her two glamorous children — when Lynn and Robert were still on speaking terms. (*Phyllis Hand*)

Father and son each sued Robert Sakowitz. (*Phyllis Hand*)

Trey and Douglas Wyatt at the plaintiffs' table during *Wyatt v. Sakowitz*. (*Houston Chronicle*)

Lynn, Oscar, and son Trey leaving the courthouse before the verdict in *Wyatt v. Sakowitz.* (*Houston Chronicle*)

Robert and Laura in the courtroom waiting for the verdict. (*Houston Post*)

Robert Sakowitz's brilliant defense attorney, David Berg, talking with jurors after the verdict. (*F. Carter Smith*)

The man *Texas Monthly* called "The Meanest Oilman in Texas," in Coastal's boardroom in 1991. (*Pam Francis*)

A weeping Oscar meets with reporters
after arriving in Houston with hostages
he rescued from Iraq in 1990. Far left is
former Texas governor John Connally.
(*Houston Post*)

Playboy Steve Wyatt
doing what he does best.
(*Phyllis Hand*)

Steve Wyatt and Fergie at
a polo match in Houston
when the Duchess visited
Lynn in 1989. (*Wide
World Photos*)

The Duchess of York and the celebrity socialite at a black-tie gala in Houston when Fergie visited Lynn in 1989. (*Sheila Cunningham*)

Roger says that Lynn listened but said very little. He had no indication of whether she acted on his advice.

Roger continued to demand that Douglas get his money back for the gems and at least once told Douglas that he was considering talking with Robert Sakowitz about the cult. It was late spring and the *Wyatt v. Sakowitz* trial was nearing.

When Douglas continued to ignore him, Roger made good on his threat and called Robert. Roger told Robert that Douglas's lawsuit was motivated by anti-Semitism stemming from his Eternal Values beliefs.

Although David Berg had an inkling of Douglas's involvement with the cult, chiefly as a result of Marie Brenner's *Vanity Fair* article of a year earlier, neither he nor Robert had any idea until that day just how valuable Douglas's cult involvement could be to their case.

Roger recalls, "[Robert] acted like the guy who'd just gotten the biggest break of his life. He kept asking questions about Doug. At one point during breakfast, Robert said to me that Doug had told him and Lynn, 'You guys are just dragging me down.'"

This line was a common Von Mierers refrain: *the Jews will drag you down.*

Soon after the breakfast meeting, Roger met with Berg. While Berg took careful notes, Roger told him about Eternal Values. After their conversation, Berg notified the court that Roger was a witness with facts relevant to *Wyatt v. Sakowitz.*

Douglas's attorney, Andy Vickery, anxious to find out just what those facts were, took Roger's deposition in July 1991. It promised to be the most potentially explosive deposition in the high-profile case.

"Every single thing in his life is driven by his beliefs in Eternal Values," Roger Hall testified about Douglas. "Every single thing."

Hall explained in his deposition that Douglas shared the cult's belief in reincarnation. Specifically, Hall testified, Douglas was convinced that, in a previous incarnation, Robert Sakowitz was an evil gunfighter in the Old West and Oscar Wyatt was the sheriff, that they hated each other back then, and that they had come back to fight it out in this life. In this same scenario, Douglas's grandmother, Ann Sakowitz, ran the local saloon.

Hall said that Douglas shared the group's view of the Holocaust as a scam. "They specifically recruited wealthy people . . . and people with good social connections because one of their ultimate goals was to place their membership in a position to fight Jews in government and business," Hall said.

When Hall's deposition made its way into the hands of the press just a month before the trial, tales of homosexuality and group sex, anti-Semitism, and occultism splashed onto the pages of newspapers from Texas to New York. This was a case where the court of public opinion mattered greatly to all participants, and Berg was winning the publicity war.

Whether or not Berg actually believed that Douglas's involvement with Eternal Values played a role in his fight against Robert is difficult to know. What was certain was that Roger Hall's misfortune over the gemstones was David Berg's good luck, and he played his luck brilliantly. The explosive allegations about Douglas's involvement in the cult saturated Houston, then spread across the country. On September 25, five days before the trial began, the *New York Post* blasted in a large headline, RICH UNCLE PINS KIN'S SUIT ON BIZARRE CULT.

While Berg was putting his spin on the story, Douglas's attorney, Andy Vickery, had a few surprises of his own. He filed a motion in Probate Court II, where the case was soon to unfold, requesting that the judge screen any evidence relating to the cult. Buried within his motion was a line that no Houston journalist missed. Among evidence the plaintiff wanted screened was "anything concerning the sexuality or sexual preference of any party."

The judge said he would not rule on whether to allow the cult evidence until the matter came up at trial. But this mattered little to David Berg. What, if anything, came out in court might be anticlimactic. The newspaper stories had already colored the impressions of a large number of potential jurors. In the court of public opinion, David Berg was far ahead and the trial had not even begun.

Robert could only imagine the public damage the cult evidence had already done to Lynn. She was the one who had refused to intervene for Robert and stop Douglas's suit, and she was the one who had made the suit possible in the first place.

But if Lynn was devastated by the latest turn of events leading up to the trial, she did not show it in public. It surprised no one when, on the eve of the trial pitting her brother and mother against her sons and husband, Lynn triumphantly swept to the stage in downtown Houston's Wortham Center. Her family may have been tearing itself apart, but she dressed herself, for a performance by

Placido Domingo celebrating the twentieth anniversary of the Houston Grand Opera's director, in a shimmering satin gown that Yves Saint Laurent made especially for her, held her head high, and momentarily pulled herself out of the center of the storm.

After being toasted for chairing the gala, Lynn stepped up to the podium and graciously thanked the evening's guests, who had paid between $500 and $5,000 each to attend the concert. Lynn, herself, was largely responsible for the big turnout. Even the most cynical guests — who snickered at her seemingly blithe manner as her family prepared to blast itself apart in court the next day — found it difficult to criticize the woman who, in this one evening alone, netted $200,000 for the Grand Opera.

After the concert, guests were invited to share pecan waffles and chocolate mousse cake with the world-famous tenor, at tables set up in the Wortham Center's dramatic foyer — a space so grand and cavernous that it more closely resembled a train station than a concert hall. Oscar Wyatt led Domingo to a table where Lynn waited with sweets. But as the flow of opera patrons converged on the Wyatts' table, it seemed that just as many black-tied gentlemen and bejeweled ladies had come to greet Lynn as Placido. Perhaps the acrimonious lawsuit and its many salacious rumors had changed nothing.

23

B Y SEVEN O'CLOCK in the morning on Tuesday, October 1, 1991, more than a dozen reporters and television cameramen had already lined up outside Courtroom Two on the fifth floor of the Family Law Center Building in downtown Houston. Within an hour, another two dozen would jam the hallway. When Robert, Laura, and Ann Sakowitz stepped off the elevator at 8:02 A.M., the mass of reporters pushed toward them, shining bright television camera lights in their eyes.

But then, a very unusual thing happened. Instead of shouting the usual volley of questions, the crowd of reporters parted like the Red Sea and politely watched as the Sakowitzes, hand in hand, walked down the long hallway to the courtroom.

Robert, only fifty-two, had aged considerably since the closing of the store little more than a year earlier. Gone were the clever throwaway line, the cheeky smile, and, most obvious of all, the cowboy hat for which he was known and ridiculed in Europe and America. Today there was none of the usual pretense. For once, Robert Tobias Sakowitz, his face drawn and his brow wrinkled, looked exactly like what he was — a man humbled by the loss of his family's eighty-eight-year-old store and about to face his fiercest and most feral enemy.

His efforts to smile only made him appear more terrified. According to David Berg, nothing Robert had been through before had frightened him as much as this — not the fear of losing the store his grandfather founded, not the fear of massive lawsuits by creditors, not even losing the great bulk of his personal fortune. What frightened Robert most was his brother-in-law. In the words of David Berg, Oscar was the "evil Goliath who was not going to be happy until he brought Robert to his knees."

And perhaps that was the real reason why *Wyatt v. Sakowitz* had all the passion of a murder trial, why the emotion on both sides had grown so far out of proportion to the financial stakes. To see the fear in Robert's eye and the cruelty in Oscar's, one would never believe that this case was simply a fight over a few million dollars, which, after all, was an insignificant sum in the circles where this family traveled. "Not enough to pay the help for a year," scoffed one River Oaks matron.

Once all the witnesses were seated in the first few rows of the spectators' benches, some thirty reporters — excluding cameramen, who were kept outside the courtroom — crowded into the remaining rows behind the witnesses. The Sakowitzes had already taken their place at the first of two parallel tables facing the jury box, situated against the east wall at a right angle to the gallery.

The courtroom was new and modern with recessed lighting, clean, beige carpeting, and walls of light pine paneling. Light polished-wood benches took up half the courtroom, on either side of the center aisle. The raised witness stand was to the right of the judge's bench. The court reporter sat directly below the witness stand, facing the gallery and barely a yard from the defense table.

Although Robert tried to hide his maverick image by dressing ultraconservatively in a perfectly tailored, navy, pin-striped suit, there was at least a hint of the maverick Texan. When he sat down at the defendant's table and crossed his legs, his signature brown lizard cowboy boots stood out. To the many transplanted Yankees living in Houston, cowboy boots with a business suit looked hokey even if the wearer was Houston's leading fashion plate.

Seated on Robert's right and clutching his hand was his blond, blue-eyed wife, Laura, wearing a loose-fitting, knee-length, plain black dress. She wore very little makeup and no noticeable jewelry other than a wedding band. Her long, straight hair was pulled back into a ponytail and tied primly with a small black ribbon. All of this was in striking contrast to page after page of sexy, glitzy photographs of her in the most recent issue of *Town & Country*. In addition to the color photographs of Laura in tight, short skirts, plunging necklines, and even a thong body suit, she was pictured in a full-page color shot with Robert — he in white tie and tails, she in a red, beaded, floor-length Bob Mackie gown, her thick, shoulder-length blond hair loose and flowing.

Robert had not consulted David Berg before accepting *Town & Country*'s offer to be photographed for the issue, but he should have. Barely had the trial begun when the issue of *Town & Country*, "baring the *real* Laura Sakowitz," sailed over and across the press benches. Reporters ripped through the pages, snickered at the miraculous transformation of Laura from a sophisticated, sexy young blonde kicking up her heels in the slick national magazine to a woman who looked as though childbearing and churchgoing were her only interests.

Berg wanted to show the ordinary men and women on the jury that Robert and Laura and Robert's mother, Ann Sakowitz, had lost most of their fortune in the Sakowitz store's bankruptcy, while explaining that the Wyatts had remained "very powerful people . . . one of the wealthiest families on the face of this earth." It was Lynn Wyatt, not Robert Sakowitz, Berg would point out, who, despite the family's terrible ordeal, chaired Houston's glittery Opera gala on the eve of the trial.

The fact that the Sakowitzes had been seated for more than half an hour before the Wyatts arrived was not accidental. Berg, wanting to capitalize on the Sakowitzes' appealing looks, got to the courtroom first in order to claim the table closest to the jury box. The jurors would be seated in two rows of six. While Robert, Laura, and Ann Sakowitz looked terrified and held hands, the Wyatts, who had now taken the table just a few feet behind the Sakowitzes, could not have appeared more confident. Douglas stood with his hands in his pants pockets, smiling, chewing gum, and chatting with his attorneys and his half-brother Trey Wyatt, who seemed eager and excited for the trial to begin.

Tall, thin, and dressed in an elegant gray suit, Douglas appeared very much the scion of a once-great retail store. In fact, while Robert occasionally looked too slick or too cowboy, Douglas always appeared to be straight out of the pages of *Gentleman's Quarterly*. With his mesmerizing violet-blue eyes, hard, angular features, and sexy five-o'clock shadow, it was easy to understand how both women and men were attracted to him.

What was not as easy to believe was that this handsome, soft-spoken, clean-cut young man could be involved in a bizarre New Age sex cult. It seemed absurd that Douglas Wyatt, whose mother was a Sakowitz, the most high-profile Jewish family in Houston, could be involved in an anti-Semitic cult. Or that he — a graduate of Washington & Lee University and a practicing lawyer — actually believed that the world would spin off its axis in 1999, at which point he would become the leader of the Eternal Values cult, which would rule the world. Or that he believed that homosexual men are the highest form of human evolution.

The trial was the hottest ticket in town, yet Houston society stayed away. Even gossip columnist Betsy Parish refused to show her face in the courtroom. "People don't want to be seen taking sides," she confided.

Conspicuously absent from the courtroom was Steve Wyatt. He was not at the trial because he was "out of the country," Douglas's attorney, Andy Vickery, said. Houston society wondered what the real reason was that Steve did not show up.

Shortly after 8:30 A.M., Oscar burst into the tense courtroom. Frowning and walking at a determined pace toward the front of the courtroom, Oscar appeared to be heading toward his brother-in-law. But when he got within a few feet of Robert, he spun to the left and marched up to Douglas. After mumbling a few words to his son, Oscar took a seat against the west wall. Attention in the courtroom immediately shifted from Robert to Oscar. Slouched in his chair, Oscar projected a palpable menace.

No one in the courtroom doubted that, at sixty-seven, Oscar Wyatt still cared about winning. Five months earlier, Oscar had told a reporter that what motivated him in life was fear of failure. "Failure is the only thing I'm terrified of," he confided.

Most reporters and other spectators, as well as most of Houston society who did not show up for *l'affaire Sakowitz*, had cast Oscar in the villain's role. Douglas was merely his father's instrument, they believed.

Although Oscar had already won his own major victory against Robert in March 1990, when Robert agreed to pay Oscar $912,000, just a fraction less than the $1.2 million his suit had sought in damages, Oscar now regretted letting Robert off.

"I shouldn't have settled that case with him," Oscar told *Vanity Fair.* "I would have killed him in court."

Oscar had been represented in his lawsuit against Robert by Tom McDade, who not so surprisingly showed up on this morning for the opening arguments in Douglas's extravaganza. A dapper, white-haired man who handled much of the legal work for the $9 billion Coastal Corporation, McDade was so shrewd and so tough that observers could not help but wonder why Douglas hadn't used him to finish off Robert.

In fact, McDade's law firm, Fulbright & Jaworski, had originally filed Douglas's lawsuit against Robert. But to carry out the task, Douglas and his three brothers, for whom Douglas served as trustee, hired forty-four-year-old, Yale-educated Andrew Anderson Vickery.

Although Vickery came from modest beginnings, he had the smell of privilege. Tall, blond, and well-dressed in dark, conservative suits, he appeared youthful and at ease. It appeared that life had been easy for him, in contrast to David Berg, who seemed aflame with anger.

The long-running suspense leading up to this trial increased when probate judge Pat Gregory entered the courtroom. Fifty-seven years old, tall and fat, with a completely round face topped by a thick crop of dark hair, Judge Gregory panted when he trudged up to the bench, as though in addition to his own body mass, his black robe was filled with weights.

As he sat down heavily, the six male and six female jurors filed into the courtroom, took their seats in the jury box against the east wall, and the trial, which had been nearly four years coming, was under way.

Andy Vickery stood in front of the witness box and wore a serious expression. "This is a case about a man who, unfortunately, because of his greed, betrayed the trust of his father and of his family," he began softly in his small-town Georgia accent. "This case involves a son who was given a great deal, a great deal, and from the age of nine, an opportunity to mark shirts at ten cents an hour; an opportunity to see what would become his legacy."

Vickery said he intended to show that Robert was guilty of commingling funds and self-dealing; of increasing his personal wealth by taking money belonging to the family business and to the other heirs of Bernard Sakowitz.

A self-professed frustrated Baptist preacher, Vickery delighted in the opportunity to incorporate religion in the law. "I'm not talking about a mere prodigal son," Vickery preached, "I'm talking about a profligate. At almost each and every instance where there was a chance to make a side deal, that's what he did."

As Vickery spoke, Robert showed very little emotion, but the way he bowed his head slightly and looked up at Vickery made him appear guilty. His receding hairline, dark, shifty eyes, and long jaw also made the man who had once closely resembled James Dean now look oddly like Richard Nixon.

While Robert tried to mask his emotion, Ann Sakowitz made her feelings very clear. Her full head of fluffy blond hair made her look younger than her years, but the deep circles under her eyes told another story. Leaning back in her chair with her arms folded, she moved her head slowly and deliberately from side to side, like a pendulum, and mouthed the words "No. No. No."

Ann's reaction and her seat at the defendant's table next to her son could not be ignored. Vickery had no choice but to acknowledge it and try to play down its significance. "[Ann] is the very lovely and charming lady that is sitting over here at the table with her son," he volunteered gently. After pausing briefly, he added, "where I would expect her to be."

Many observers questioned this last line. Why would she be with her son rather than her daughter? Why had she not remained neutral?

About ten minutes into Vickery's opening statement, Robert started scribbling notes on small, yellow slips of paper and passing them to his mother, who handed them to David Berg. The notes contained questions Robert wanted asked. This had been an especially annoying habit of Robert's at the store, to fire off an endless barrage of notes all day to employees on the most minute matters. But now Berg was in charge, and the notes were very distracting. Berg once wrote, "If a lawyer or anyone at your table hands you a note that says, 'Ask this question,' you should pull out a 357 and shoot whoever hands you that note." Berg did not have a gun, but he did finally shoot a note back to Robert: "Quit writing notes."

Vickery said that the Wyatts wanted more than $8.5 million, allegedly taken by Robert, put back into the estate of Bernard Sakowitz, and as much as four times that in punitive damages. They also wanted Robert removed as trustee of Bernard's estate. "The question is, should this fox get to stay in the hen house?" Vickery charged.

To Berg, the most galling of all the Wyatts' demands was that a constructive trust be imposed on Robert's house, which Vickery alleged "was bought with profits that he derived from family money." Since the day Robert bought the house on the sly, just nine months before the store filed for bankruptcy and put hundreds of longtime employees out of work, he had been making excuses for the house. Even now, attempting to play down his high lifestyle, he insisted that he was trying to sell the two-story, 8,236-square-foot mansion, which sat on nearly two acres of Houston's most prime residential real estate. The asking price was $2,950,000 — approximately $1,220,000 more than the county tax appraiser said it was worth.

Following the store's bankruptcy and the closing down of a lucrative oil well in 1986, Robert's wealth had dwindled to about $2 million, most of which was in the house. Robert was terrified that the Wyatts would take this chief asset, where he lived with Laura and his four children, three under the age of seven.

It was difficult not to feel sorry for Robert, a man who cared desperately to have a public image of success. Even if what he had done was wrong, hadn't the private shame and public humiliation of losing an eighty-eight-year-old store been punishment enough?

Vickery concluded his opening statement by explaining that, as a fiduciary of his father's estate, Robert had a special obligation to uphold his father's trust and deal fairly, and it was therefore Robert's burden to prove his innocence. When Vickery said this, his words surprised the audience. To many, that equation sounded wrong. Wasn't a defendant presumed innocent until proven guilty? Didn't the Wyatts have to prove Robert guilty beyond a reasonable doubt? Or was the Wyatts' power so great that they could invert the law?

In every trial, there comes a moment, often least expected, when something happens that defines the trial, and this was that moment in *Wyatt v. Sakowitz.* What the observers, and some of the participants, had lost sight of in the blur of explosive hype was that this was not a criminal case. It was a civil case. While Douglas had the burden of proof, he did not have to prove that Robert was "guilty beyond a reasonable doubt" — a concept that applies only in criminal cases where the consequences of losing are so grave. To win the case, Douglas merely needed a "preponderance of the credible evidence." He needed only to tip the scales in his favor.

Observers who noted that this trial was not a murder trial insisted that at the very least it was an *attempt* at murder — an attempt by Oscar Wyatt to kill his brother-in-law. Robert's reputation, lifestyle, and aura all depended on having a great deal of money. So if you destroyed his money, you destroyed his life. As Oscar knew from his most terrified nightmares, it was worse to be poor than to be dead.

As soon as Vickery finished his opening statement, David Berg shot out of his chair and approached the jury box. Berg, at forty-nine, had short, flat, gray hair that came to a point above his brow, a strong curved nose, and tired eyes behind steel-rimmed glasses. Berg's life had been tough, and it showed. Like his client, Berg was small — only five feet seven and 140 pounds — and he too wore cowboy boots with his dark business suit.

After preparing for nine months, Berg was anxious to take on the most high-profile case of his career. The fact that he had had only four hours' sleep in two days and that he was filled with anxiety did not detract from his energy or forcefulness.

"I've been up against the government and I've sued the Ku Klux Klan," he told the jury, which included five blacks and two Hispanics, "but never have I met the power of the Wyatt family."

Berg believed he could destroy every charge against Robert by showing that everything Robert did in connection with the store had the approval of Sakowitz Inc.'s board of directors, which included Robert's sister and his mother — even though Vickery insisted that Lynn was merely an "honorary" member.

"They are going to try to make you believe Lynn Wyatt is some airhead," Berg shouted, the words exploding from his mouth. "She's not. She's amassed a personal fortune. This lady is sharp as a knife."

Berg blistered Lynn as a manipulative, insensitive woman who did not lift a long-nailed finger to help her brother and the family business when tough times hit Houston. "Robert tried diligently to make his sister, Lynn, aware of everything that was going on at the company," Berg intoned. Then came an off-the-cuff line that was repeated at cocktail parties from Houston to New York to Paris: "But it's difficult to explain deals to a woman who's always under the hair dryer or jetting off to the south of France."

By assigning her inherited shares in the store to her sons, Lynn made the lawsuit possible, Berg told the jury. He decided to paint Lynn as Daisy in F. Scott Fitzgerald's *The Great Gatsby*, who "creates a problem and then retreats." Borrowing an idea from the novelist, Berg blasted, "She lights the fuse and then steps back into her vast wealth where she can't hear the explosion."

Robert suddenly straightened up in his chair and raised his head. After years of having charges hurled at him, someone was finally speaking in his defense — and that someone was a master at the art, powerfully enunciating, at times almost spitting out, the words. Great lines, some that were planned and others that were spontaneous, kept coming.

"I don't know if this suit was filed for sport or spite: the sport of rich men or the spite of little men," Berg shouted, and then paused. No one in the courtroom thought he was referring to Douglas.

Oscar Wyatt sat quietly against the west wall and showed no reaction. His face did not turn red the way it did when he became really angry. Oscar did not look angry at all. He looked satisfied. He had waited nearly four years for this showdown; waited to see his brother-in-law dragged through the pain and expense of a trial certain to damage Robert's reputation even more than Oscar already had. What must have made the trial especially satisfying for Oscar — a man who bragged during America's war in the Middle East that he liked doing deals with Iraq — was the challenge of a tough opponent.

"I don't put anything past him," Oscar once said of Robert. "He has the testicles of a brass monkey."

Everyone wondered how the quick-tempered Oscar would handle himself on the witness stand. Although Vickery told reporters he planned to call Oscar as a witness, Berg doubted Vickery would do it. "It would be suicidal," Berg said.

When the opening arguments ended, Oscar got up, kissed Douglas on the cheek, and bolted out of the courtroom. Reporters raced after him to the elevator, asking for his comments. As the elevator doors opened, he turned and faced the bright television camera lights: "Don't you think it's interesting," he said, smiling, "that Robert Sakowitz hired a well-known *criminal* attorney to represent him?"

When reporters rushed over to Berg's co-counsel, James Patrick Smith, and repeated Oscar's comment, Smith replied, "Mr. Wyatt knows a lot of criminals, so we'll defer to him."

Late that night, Smith was awakened by a phone call from Oscar's attorney, who said that Oscar had seen Smith's comment on the evening news and swore to punch Smith in the nose the next time he saw him.

24

THE MORNING was hot and muggy, a final, lingering reminder of Houston's insufferable but almost-ended summer months. Because the start of the trial coincided with Lynn's traditional end-of-September return from the south of France, she had managed to keep her promise to Douglas's attorney to be back in Houston for the start of the trial without missing a single party on the Riviera.

Now, as she hid behind the high, clipped hedges of her Houston estate, a firestorm was raging downtown at the Family Law Center of the Harris County Courthouse — and she was at its core.

Andy Vickery had stated firmly in his opening statement that he would not put Lynn through the pain of coming to the courthouse to testify. "I'm just not going to do it," he insisted. The fact that she was the first witness called to testify in *Wyatt v. Sakowitz* and that she did not appear in person, but instead testified by videotape, did not lessen the interest in Lynn and her role in the lawsuit — it merely heightened the drama.

As the court bailiff lowered the lights, Andy Vickery switched on a videotape of parts of Lynn's deposition taken by David Berg four months earlier. The video was shown on the courtroom's three television monitors. Lynn was not asked to state her age for the record, and no one who did not know her could have guessed that she was fifty-six. She looked not a day over forty. Her full mane of buoyant blond hair framed her white-powdered face, and she wore an elegant and obviously expensive red Chanel suit. Sitting erect in a chair at her attorney's office, she looked as ravishing as she always did in *W* and the *New York Times* and *Town & Country*.

At first she verbally held the attacking David Berg at a distance. Although her taped testimony being played in the courtroom was presented by Vickery, she seemed to be genuinely torn between loyalty to her husband and her brother. She began by saying that she and her brother had been very close before she married Oscar and that she had been reluctant to accept Oscar's suspicions that her brother was mishandling the family store. "I was in denial for a long time because I love my brother," she said, building suspense.

"I was getting from [my husband] the feeling that there was some wrongdoing, like conflict of interest or self-dealing. But I didn't want to know this and when he would talk to me about this thing, I would literally walk out of the room."

For a few moments, the audience seemed to sympathize with her.

"Do you know that your husband has gone around this city saying terrible things about your brother?" Berg demanded.

"Well, yes, some things."

"Are Sakowitzes in the habit of going around bad-mouthing blood relatives, or anyone else for that matter?" Berg asked angrily.

"No," Lynn cried. "That's why it's so painful for me. I pleaded with them not to bring this suit. In my mind, for someone to sue someone in the family was horrifying to me."

"Is this lawsuit horrifying to you?" Berg asked.

Lynn stiffened. "I sure don't like it."

"Is it worth the money?"

"I don't think it's ever been worth the money. I think it's worth the principle . . . Listen, I loved my brother. I trusted my brother. If my brother is wrong in all these things" — she stopped and noticed that Berg seemed distracted.

"Now look at me when I'm talking to you," she demanded. The video camera remained on Lynn.

"Oh, pardon me, Mrs. Wyatt," Berg replied courteously, off-camera. "I had to look down at my notes."

"I'm saying something to you that's meaningful to me and you act like you're just not interested. You didn't even let me finish my darn statement. I'll wait until you can listen to me and then I'll tell you," she snapped, folding her arms and leaning back in her chair.

It was not normal for a man — any man — with whom Lynn was speaking to take his eyes off her. But the scolding did not help make her the sympathetic character she clearly wanted to be.

After the trial, Berg recalled the exchange with delight: "That was everybody's first-grade teacher or wicked stepmother up there on the stand."

As Lynn's videotaped deposition progressed, it became clear whose side she was on. "I love my brother," she said, "but I don't trust him."

It was this comment of Lynn's that, for months after the trial, would seem to haunt Robert the most. In December 1992, he reflected sadly, "I don't think she understands the definition of love. You can't love if you don't trust. It's a very telling statement about [Lynn's] ability to trust."

Berg hammered away at Lynn until she was forced to say she had never objected to anything that Robert did when she was on the board. But she repeatedly maintained that she was not "a businesswoman," did not discuss business with her family, and was not in a position to understand the workings of the board.

"My relationship with my father was not about business. It was about clothes . . . about what people like to wear, what the fashion is," she said earnestly.

At times, Lynn seemed clearly confused, complaining, "You just keep asking me about specific things and I'm not good at specific things."

As Berg's questions dragged on, she seemed to grow weary. "Nobody understands this conflict," she cried.

Berg was fuming in his chair as he watched the videotape. Because of the way Vickery had edited the tape, Berg charged later, Vickery was presenting half-truths. But rather than fire court objections now, Berg would wait for his turn to play his own edited version of the tape.

The videotape was like a soap opera, with twists and turns that left viewers excited, amused, shocked, but, most of all, curious. Had Oscar threatened Lynn with divorce if she did not turn her stock over to her sons, enabling them to sue her brother? Had Lynn assigned the stock to her sons to get back at her brother, who had always been given more by their father than she? Had Douglas Wyatt sued his uncle because he desperately wanted to please his oil-rich father?

Toward the end of Lynn's deposition, she said that Douglas had brought the lawsuit because "he thinks it's right . . . and it's not for the money. It's for the principle of the thing."

When she said this, Berg saw his chance to introduce Frederick Von Mierers and the Eternal Values cult. He would show that the so-called principle was, in fact, that Douglas was motivated by a bizarre cult that hated Jews and women. When Vickery had completed his presentation of the tape and had switched it off, Berg asked the judge to allow for a Motion in Limine, the legal term for a motion to discuss, outside the presence of the jury, evidence not yet introduced.

Once the jurors had left the courtroom, Berg approached the bench and asked Judge Gregory to allow him to play a segment of the tape in which Lynn discussed buying jewelry from Eternal Values' leader Frederick Von Mierers. In her deposition, Lynn said that she had purchased $70,000 worth of gems with mystical powers. Among other jewelry, she had bought a ring which she was wearing at that very moment, during her deposition. She even explained to Berg that the gems' effectiveness depended largely on whether they touched the skin. If worn correctly, the gems were supposed to give the owner protection from evil forces.

Berg planned to use this testimony by Lynn to introduce Douglas's involvement with Eternal Values.

It was the most suspenseful moment thus far in the trial. Reporters — who sat on the edge of their seats, ready to race to the pay telephones outside the courtroom — listened carefully for Judge Gregory's ruling. Berg's evidence about the cult was so potentially explosive that it was certain to catapult all stories onto the front pages of even the most conservative journals. But reporters and spectators would have to continue to wait for the juicy details of Eternal Values' lock on Douglas Wyatt. For now, Judge Gregory ruled against allowing the testimony. But the matter was certain to come up again.

Berg's turn had come, however, to play his own version of Lynn's videotaped deposition, which showed that Lynn was well aware of some transactions that took place when she was on the board of Sakowitz but that Vickery had edited out of his version.

However Lynn came off, she had managed to steal the spotlight, as she did at parties around the world. But this time she had pulled it off not in some Venetian palazzo or lavishly decorated New York ballroom but in the bare-bones courtroom of the Family Law Center in downtown Houston, and she had done so without even being there.

Houston Post society columnist Betsy Parish reported that when one of her high-society readers was asked by a reporter "why there wasn't a bevy of society types sitting in the courtroom," the response was "I guess if Lynn Wyatt thought she didn't have to show up, they figured they didn't have to either." Parish has a chatty way of talking to her readers and, as if addressing them directly, she ended the item saying, "No, and shame on you for asking, they didn't send their own videotapes instead."

When asked who she thought would win the case, Parish worked at appearing neutral. "People are sending bouquets of flowers to both sides of River Oaks Boulevard," she said, "since no one can predict the outcome."

By noon on the second day of the trial, the streets around the Family Law Center, on the seedy southern edge of downtown Houston, were clogged with television vans and masses of people who gathered to see who or what was causing all the media commotion. The curiosity seekers were attorneys, office workers, and secretaries, as well as a large number of ragged homeless people who slept around the once elegant but now boarded-up Rice Hotel a few blocks away and who spotted the area's sidewalks with puddles of urine.

With a population of 1.6 million, Houston was the fourth-largest city in America. It also had the fourth-highest murder rate in the country. In Texas, the most violent state in the nation, Houston's crime rate was nearly double that of any other city, including Dallas and Fort Worth. On October 1, 1991, the day of opening arguments in *Wyatt v. Sakowitz*, Houston reported its 500th murder, making 1991 one of the eight bloodiest years in the city's history. The media provided a daily diet of detailed reports on murders, criminal gang activity, and other crack- and cocaine-related crimes, leaving terrified citizens desperate for solutions. It was no surprise that quick and simple solutions to the crime problem led the agendas of all three politicians who were at that moment battling in a hotly contested mayoral race.

For decades after World War II, Houston had been one of America's fastest-growing cities, but in the 1980s the city's buildings and its population exploded. New arrivals were attracted by the city's petrochemical industries and the building boom. Blacks, Hispanics, and whites came from the failing industries of the Rust Belt, the family farms of the South and the Midwest, and the border towns and barrios of Mexico.

This growth was at every economic level. At the top were the executives of the many major companies that moved their headquarters to Houston. They raised the prices of River Oaks mansions, country club memberships, and fancy caterers.

The Texas tradition of independence, of minimal government interference, resulted in Houston's becoming the only major city in America with no zoning laws, so that a tawdry topless bar or a barbecue stand could operate next to expensive residences. Houston ceased to be a genteel Southern city and became the same kind of violent, variegated metropolis as Chicago or Philadelphia. Even a police force internationally recognized for its brutality could no longer keep blacks and Hispanics in their historic subservient state as the economic bust that followed the boom increased the city's unrest.

In the early eighties, when the price of oil and gas plummeted and the pell-mell construction of office towers and apartments suddenly stopped, there appeared the modern equivalent of the ghost towns of the Old West where empty saloons, brothels, and boardinghouses lined the deserted streets. But in Houston, at the end of the eighties, the modern equivalent was not empty one-story wood buildings but empty high-rise office buildings and apartments and stores. No building in Houston better represented the end of the economic era than the store at 1111 Main Street. Located just nine blocks from the Harris County Family Law Center, the once glorious five-story Sakowitz store that covered nearly an entire city block was finished — shuttered, closed, empty, and forgotten.

The first live witness to take the stand was twenty-six-year-old Bradford A. Wyatt, Oscar and Lynn's youngest child. Had he not stated his name under oath, it would have been difficult to believe that this obese young man in a tan police officer's uniform was the child of Lynn Wyatt. To the astonishment of many in the courtroom, Brad explained that he was a Harris County patrolman and that he planned to make a career of law enforcement.

His pudgy, red, chapped cheeks, burr haircut, and blunt "Yes, sir" and "No, sir" answers made him appear a caricature of a rookie police officer in some small Texas town.

Brad testified that he had once had a small landscape business and that he received checks from Sakowitz Inc. for work done at his Uncle Bobby's home. Vickery wanted to show that the company had wrongfully paid for this personal expense of Robert's.

The charges stung, but only for a moment, until Berg, on cross-examination, said that when Sakowitz Inc. paid for work done at Robert's home it was for work done in connection with store-related parties. As Berg challenged virtually everything this witness said, Brad's posture began to sag, until he was slouching in defeat, his mouth hanging open.

Berg had a parting shot for Brad, whose landscape firm had employed a number of Hispanics. "Here's a letter signed by you," Berg said, biting off the words harshly so the jury could understand all of them. "You write 'Head Honkey in charge of Wetbacks.'"

When Brad pulled his large mass out of his chair and lumbered down from the witness stand, he did not look at the jurors, who were seated on his left. "He looked [especially to the minority jurors] like every highway patrolman who had ever stopped them for no reason," Berg said after the trial.

Although many spectators hoped that Steve Wyatt would take the stand next, he never came near the courthouse. Steve wanted nothing to do with the trial. "He was more like my mother on this," says Trey Wyatt. "I think he felt it was wrong. He didn't want to do it."

Steve had had more than his share of publicity in recent months as the Texas playboy who dared to have an affair with Fergie, the Duchess of York. Buckingham Palace was so outraged by the stories about Fergie's alleged affair that it had ordered an embargo on the Texas Lothario. Little did anyone on either side of the Atlantic realize, at this point, how much more scandalous the Fergie-Steve stories would soon become.

Next to take the stand for the plaintiff was Val Renken. A tall man in his late sixties, wearing a double-breasted suit and a white wig, this longtime family retainer knew more secrets about the Sakowitzes than anyone else.

In a timid voice, Val told how Ann traveled the world with him on buying trips for the store and how Bernard had died in his arms at the Sakowitzes' winter home in Arizona. When Vickery asked whether Robert took things for himself that were bought for the store, Renken thought a moment and replied, "On the last trip when we were in China, I believe there was an urn" — hardly explosive evidence of looting the family business. But Val was waiting to describe how Robert had instructed him to do an inventory of the store's decorations and fixtures — paintings, chairs, an armoire — which, Val says, Robert then had sent to his home. Douglas had earlier tried to get a warrant to search Robert's house, and Douglas told Renken it was important he testify about these allegedly stolen items. But Vickery did not pursue the angle further. After the trial, Vickery said he made a "tactical decision" not to pursue the allegations that Robert took things from the store, explaining, "It's relatively small potatoes compared to some of the other things [Robert was charged with]."

Another reason Vickery did not pursue this angle further may be that Oscar had charged the very same thing in his 1986 lawsuit, which had been widely publicized and settled out of court. Berg was already complaining that Douglas's suit looked like Oscar's all over again.

When Berg got his chance, he quickly pulled the focus off Robert and onto Renken. He began by forcing Renken to admit that he had been fired from Sakowitz. By the time Berg had finished with him, many in the audience assumed Renken was just a bitter former employee, there to get back at his former boss.

Before the trial, Robert had gone to Renken's gift shop in Houston's Galleria area and tried to frighten him out of testifying. In an interview after the trial, Renken said that before the trial, "Robert came in [to my shop] and said, 'I know you're Douglas's friend. If you testify I'll destroy you.'" Renken, who had been with the store for twenty years before he was fired, says he responded, "What could you possibly do to me that you haven't already done?"

Before the trial, at the courthouse, says Renken, "David Berg said to me, 'What Robert meant to say was he'll destroy your testimony, not you.'" On the stand, Renken altered the exchange with Robert to: "I got a call from Robert saying that if I testified he would destroy my testimony and anything I had to say," a statement substantially less damning than Renken's original recollection.

Douglas was absolutely motionless as he watched the proceedings. Unbending and lifeless, he looked like a mannequin from Sakowitz's third-floor men's department. He sat back in his chair, with his head tilted back, his long legs crossed at the knees. He wore no expression and rarely even blinked.

Berg had momentum, and he did not lose it when another son of Lynn and Oscar's, twenty-seven-year-old Oscar S. Wyatt III, took the stand. Called Trey by friends and family members and "Little Oscar" behind his back, this third child of Lynn Wyatt had inherited his father's brusque cockiness and rough tongue. Chunky and pale-cheeked, Trey also looks like a younger version of his father. As one reporter put it, he's "built on the basic Wyatt bulldog master plan."

Unlike his older brother Douglas, Trey fidgeted constantly at the plaintiff's table. Dressed in a boxy Brooks Brothers–style suit,

Trey shifted in his chair, ran the palms of his hands over his hair, and strummed his fingers on the table.

On the witness stand, Trey explained that, like his brother Brad, he also was interested in law enforcement. In addition to working as a "banking representative" in Corpus Christi, he was a reserve deputy in Corpus. Trey fell somewhere between the extremes of his next older brother and his younger brother. He was not quite the redneck cop Brad appeared to be, but neither was he the sophisticate Douglas was.

Berg began his cross-examination of Trey by reading aloud portions of a *Texas Monthly* article that quoted Trey as saying, "I have more respect for some of the common criminals I have arrested than I have for Robert Sakowitz."

When Trey admitted that he had made the statement, Berg slowed his cadence and lowered his voice. "Do you know how you broke your grandmother's heart with what you said in the article? Do you care?" he demanded.

Trey, his head bobbing up and down affirmatively, said he did know and he did care. Then he pushed to get into the court record that his grandmother had disowned him and his brothers.

"My grandmother told me that because we filed this lawsuit, regardless of whether Uncle Bobby was guilty or innocent, we are no longer her grandchildren," he said, pausing and looking around the room for an explosive reaction. He then added, "She told me on a phone conversation in 1988 that she does not want any of us at her funeral."

Because she was a witness, Ann Sakowitz, after opening arguments, was made to wait outside the courtroom until she testified. As her grandson Trey testified, Ann sat in a room across the hall, reading a Dick Francis mystery novel.

By the time Trey bounded down heavily from the witness box and retreated to the plaintiff's table, it was clear that Berg had taken control of the courtroom. One by one, he had tactically destroyed the testimony of each of the first four plaintiff's witnesses. Quick, forceful, and armed with a massive amount of documentation, Berg showed he had a complete understanding of the Sakowitzes' Byzantine background. He demonstrated early that this was *his* case, not the Wyatts'. "They brought the lawsuit," he said later, "but I was going to tell the story."

On cross-examination, his timing was impeccable. He knew

precisely when to attack and when to back off. He connected with the jury because he spoke with conviction. When he talked about injustice, it was obvious that he was a man who had experienced it, who understood it, and who could get very angry about it. Not many years earlier, Houston's legendary criminal lawyer Percy Foreman, in a packed courtroom not unlike this, won the acquittal of a man accused of murdering Alan Berg, David's only brother. Privately, David said that he took Robert's case because "I cannot abide the destruction of a family."

25

A T 11:30 A.M. on Wednesday, October 2, Robert Sakowitz took the stand. Dressed in a plain blue suit, light blue shirt, and a striped blue-and-white tie, he was considerably less flashy than when he had sashayed around Houston in tight black leather pants and a black leather shirt open to his navel.

J. P. Smith, Berg's co-counsel, was pleased that his client had obviously listened when Smith told him to sit slightly forward of the midline, which, according to Smith, makes the witness look interested and physiologically causes attentiveness. Smith also had instructed him to look six inches over the head of the juror sitting in the middle of the back row when he spoke and to put his hands in his lap and keep them there.

Smith knew his way around the probate courts, and around Judge Pat Gregory's courtoom in particular. Gregory had, in 1980, appointed Smith to the very lucrative guardianship of Ugo di Portanova, one of the Cullen oil heirs, who was judged to be mentally incompetent. Robert says he hired Smith to represent him because Smith "was held out to be a probate attorney who knew Judge Gregory very well."

Vickery began by accusing Robert of plotting the store's expansion program in Houston, Dallas, San Antonio, and Tulsa, Oklahoma, to benefit his own real estate holdings, and then asked Robert to read aloud from the will of Bernard Sakowitz. He then asked if the will called for Robert to engage in self-dealing in regard to his father's estate.

"No, sir," Robert answered softly.

Laura Sakowitz listened intently to Robert's testimony and rarely shifted in her hard chair. To most spectators in the gallery,

who saw only her back, Laura appeared merely the dutiful, concerned wife, loyally at his side. But to J. P. Smith, who saw her from
the same angle that the jurors did, she looked terrified. At each
break, Smith pleaded with Laura to change her expression.

"I kept saying to her, at recess, 'Try not to look like you're
scared to death,'" recalls Smith. "'You want to look concerned, but
you don't want to make it appear that the defendant is guilty.'"

In only half an hour on the stand, Robert had several times
answered Vickery with "I don't know" or "I don't understand your
question." These evasive responses made him appear far too defen-
sive and, at the same time, arrogant and aloof. Because Robert's
facial expressions continued to paint him as guilty, it was difficult
to believe that it had been Douglas, not he, who had repeatedly
tried to settle the case before trial.

Douglas had offered to settle for a million dollars. Robert
refused. Douglas had then said he would settle for half a million.
When Robert refused again, Andy Vickery suggested mediation
with a third-party lawyer and suggested the mediator be Jewish.
Vickery says this was an attempt to trump the charge that Douglas
was anti-Semitic, but Berg took it as an insult to his "humanity."
Robert agreed with his attorney, explaining, "Oscar doesn't have a
great love for my co-religionists." The fact that Lynn is Jewish, says
Robert, is merely "part of the irony."

With Robert making such a weak performance, Berg decided it
was time for Ann Sakowitz to break her silence. Ann, whom her
grandsons called "Dede" and whom Berg referred to as "Mama
Ann," was the defense's star witness, and although she had not yet
testified in the trial, there was not a woman or man in the courtroom who did not speculate about what would happen when she
told her version of the events.

At the recess, Berg sent Ann out to meet the crowd of reporters
in the hallway. She wore an elegant navy suit, cut an inch above
the knees, dark hose, and very high-heel, open-toe, sling-back
shoes, on which she weaved slightly. For all her elegance on the
outside, she appeared torn up inside. Bowing her head and dabbing
at her mascara with a handkerchief, she whispered that her grandchildren had betrayed her. "It hurts deeply that they have turned on
me this way," she cried.

In the months leading up to the trial, Ann spoke to the
national press about the pain the Wyatts had caused her. She said

she saw her daughter only when "that man," meaning Oscar, was not at home. But most of her hurt seemed directed at Douglas. How could he bring such a suit — after she had been like a mother to him when Lynn divorced Robert Lipman and moved back home with Douglas and Steve.

Among the reporters covering the case was Tim Fleck, editor of the weekly tabloid *Houston Press*, who kept all of Houston abuzz during the trial with his often witty, sharp-tongued commentary on the family feud.

His story about the trial's first day was headlined: YOU SCRATCH MY FACE AND I'LL SCRATCH YOURS. Accompanying the story were two photos pieced together of Laura and Robert on the left and Lynn and Oscar on the right. The caption read, DINNER PARTY FROM HELL: IF THESE FOUR SHOW UP, BETTER RUN FOR YOUR LIFE.

Judge Gregory seemed to enjoy the media extravaganza. He smiled as he looked over the tops of his glasses and interrupted the proceedings to scold talkative reporters: "The acoustics are very good in this courtroom. We can hear what you're saying in the back row."

Gregory first ran for Houston's Probate Court II in 1968 and never had a political opponent. Bright and exceedingly well versed in the probate code, he became presiding judge of the state's fourteen-member probate bench and, with a $99,433 annual salary, the highest-paid elected judge in Texas.

He also became one of the state's most visible probate judges, handling in addition to the Wyatt/Sakowitz case, the will of multimillionaire Howard Hughes and the famed Cullen/di Portanova guardianship case. In the latter, Gregory not only became highly visible, his reputation was touched by scandal when he was accused of accepting favors from attorneys on one side of the case.

It was in the 1980s that Ugo di Portanova, the younger brother of Houston's socially prominent Baron Enrico di Portanova, sued Quintana Petroleum Corporation and members of the family of the late Hugh Roy Cullen, who built the Wyatt mansion. The suit claimed that the mentally incompetent Ugo di Portanova should have gotten one-eighth of his mother's stock in the corporation.

When Gregory came under fire from accusations that he had been involved with improper financial dealings with one law firm connected to the case, he recused himself from the case, but in 1990 he quietly returned the case to his court.

As a *Houston Chronicle* article, titled "Judge's Ethics Called into Question," reported just five months before *Wyatt v. Sakowitz* went to trial, the di Portanova case proved "a treasure trove for a covey of attorneys who helped Gregory with financial and personal needs."

When Robert took the stand again after lunch, Vickery began to paint a picture of Robert's extravagant personal life. He made Robert divulge that his compensation as chairman of Sakowitz Inc. had included a $200,000 annual salary, membership fees for numerous social clubs, temple dues, two automobiles, extensive travel expenses, and a full-time housekeeper. Robert admitted that he had spent about $1.2 million so far refurbishing his River Oaks mansion. He estimated his art collection's worth at $500,000 and his wine collection at $250,000.

Vickery proved that Robert lived extravagantly, but he never proved that the last of these luxuries — the home, the art, the wine — were bought with "funds wrongfully obtained through his manipulation of Sakowitz, Inc. and its related entities," as the lawsuit alleged.

Vickery's propensity to blast Robert's style rather than prove his alleged wrongdoing reached its peak of foolishness when he questioned Robert about the cowboy hat he wore to Paris couture shows.

"Didn't you wear a cowboy hat in Paris to promote your maverick image?"

"I wear that hat for two reasons," Robert retorted, without missing a beat. "One, it rains a lot in Paris; and two, it is easy for my associates to spot me in a large crowd in that hat."

Robert had made Vickery look silly and petty for asking the question. Worse, Vickery sometimes asked questions to which he did not know the answer — a dangerous game for a trial lawyer. At one point, while Robert gave the impression that fighting the lawsuit had kept him from finding a job that would provide desperately needed income, Vickery snapped, "You've got a job with the Greater Houston Visitors Bureau."

On cross-examination, Berg asked what Robert's job as chairman of the Visitors Bureau paid. "I'm paid zero," he replied.

Still, Berg had a monumental challenge in making Robert, a man known for his wealth and flashy lifestyle, appear the poor boy up against the heartless rich Oscar. Berg had felt, going into the trial, that he could accomplish this by seating a jury that was of a lower economic class and one that worried about money.

"What made it easy in jury selection was focusing on Robert's economic plight," says Berg. "You ask the question in jury selection, 'Has anybody here ever lost a business? Anybody here ever been late on debt?' And then they start to say to themselves, 'Uh, huh, this guy's like me, only on a bigger scale.'"

J. P. Smith, who selected the jury for the defense, believed their side had a great advantage in jury selection. He viewed the defense as the underdog, and juries typically side with the underdog. Most jurors like people they can relate to, and most jurors, like most citizens, are not multimillionaires.

Berg wanted minorities on the jury — people who would be angered by the racist way in which Brad Wyatt signed his letter — and he also wanted women. If he was able to introduce the cult evidence and show that Douglas was a misogynist, the effect on women jurors could be explosive. Even if the judge disallowed the cult evidence, news of Douglas's involvement in the woman-hating, anti-Semitic cult had been all over the papers in the weeks leading up to the trial. At least some of the potential jurors could well have seen the articles.

But when Robert saw the complexion of the jury — five whites, five blacks, and two Hispanics — he was shocked and horrified. "I thought he was going to have a coronary," says J. P. Smith. "He said, 'There's no way this jury's going to be intelligent enough to follow this evidence.'

"And I said, 'Bobby, we're not giving them an IQ test. All they gotta do is vote for you.'"

Although more than half of the pool of potential jurors said they had had a Sakowitz charge account, the jury that was selected looked more like J. C. Penney or Walmart customers than Sakowitz. The jury included two city equipment operators, a floor worker at a manufacturing plant, a pastor in a lower-income church, three nurses, an assistant to a medical examiner, a bookkeeper, a school counselor, and two engineers.

In the minds of these working-class men and women, whether or not Robert had lost his money and Oscar had come from humble roots was immaterial. To the jurors, both sides looked and acted rich, very rich.

"The attorneys kept referring to Mr. Wyatt's house on River

Oaks Boulevard being located right next to the River Oaks Country Club and then Mr. Sakowitz's house on River Oaks Boulevard, which was for sale," a juror said after the trial. "No one on the jury could even imagine what it was like to live in that part of town."

If Berg thought he scored points when he blasted Lynn for jetting off to the south of France, he was wrong. True, the jurors did not have summer homes anywhere, much less in the south of France, but, similarly, neither did they own quarter-million-dollar wine collections or half-million-dollar art collections, as Robert Sakowitz did. Five of the six male jurors never wore a suit to the trial, probably because they did not own one.

What happened in the audience was at times even more exciting than what was taking place on the witness stand. As Robert testified about his lifestyle, two handsome Aryan-ideal men with sharply chiseled features and ice-blond hair came in and sat down. When one caught Douglas's eye and winked, Douglas ever so slightly nodded back. Douglas then reached into his pocket and applied lip gloss. This moistening of his lips, which he did several times a day, was the most he deviated from his motionless, mannequin pose.

By late Wednesday, it was clear that Vickery was in trouble. Not only had Berg neutralized or destroyed the plaintiff's witnesses of the day before, but also Vickery's cross-examination of Robert was ineffective. Part of his problem was that his tone was sarcastic. He sometimes sounded like a high-school debater who, instead of preparing the night before, tried to whine and stamp his foot until he got his way.

When it appeared that Vickery had clear evidence of self-dealing and commingling of funds by Robert, the reporters sat up and got ready to take down his arguments. But then he invariably went off on a tangent far from the point. On many occasions, he failed to ask the crucial questions, nail down the facts, and make his points so that the jury could understand them.

Oscar, though not present after the opening arguments, reportedly was not impressed with Vickery either. A friend of Douglas's who was involved in the case says Oscar frequently referred to Vickery in an insulting manner that implied Oscar thought Vickery was not nearly tough enough.

Because the plaintiff's chief problem seemed to be Vickery, reporters began to question why Douglas had hired him. In fact, Vickery was the third attorney to handle the case, and in a sense he had come on the case by default. The lawyer who brought the case in 1987 resigned a year later, and the lawyer who took over for him was forced to resign due to illness just three months before trial. So while Berg had nine months to prepare his case, Vickery had only nine weeks to learn the family's Byzantine history well enough to fight Texas's most publicized courtroom battle.

In 1976, Vickery had joined Fulbright & Jaworski, which was chief counsel for Oscar Wyatt and his Coastal Corporation. Vickery had left Fulbright & Jaworski by 1987 and started his own small firm when Douglas Wyatt approached him about taking the case.

"It's terrible what happened to all those longtime devoted employees of the store," Vickery recalls thinking when Douglas came to him. "I don't take just every case that crosses my desk. I took this because I wanted to see wrongs righted."

The most crucial evidence in the trial came on Thursday, when Robert gave his version concerning the disputed $1 million that the Wyatts claimed he took from the store in 1983 and did not repay. Under careful questioning from Berg, Robert testified that a company he owned, Shamrock Shops, had loaned the store $1 million in 1981 and he was merely taking that $1 million back when he moved it back into Shamrock Shops in 1983.

Robert's transaction was not quite as acceptable or simple as he characterized it to Berg because at the time that he moved the money into Shamrock Shops, the store was desperate for funds. But Berg and Robert's explanation once again appeared to satisfy the jury.

Their satisfaction was obvious from the way they smiled at Robert and nodded their heads when he spoke. He had loosened up after the first day and had established a rapport with the jurors. "The way he tilted his head and smiled at us," recalls juror June Hewling, "you just felt so deeply for him, you wanted to speak out and at least say, 'Hello, how are you?'"

The more confident Berg became, the more he hoped Vickery would not call Oscar to the stand. Berg was increasingly fearful that Oscar, with his quick and vicious tongue, would say something that would cause a mistrial, either accidentally or deliberately. During his deposition, Oscar had been a loose cannon, hurling charges that were often unresponsive to Berg's questions. When Berg asked specifically about an alleged side deal of Robert's, Oscar responded: "The good deals always fell in his pocket. The bad deals always fell on the store's pocket. . . . If I'd been on the board he'd have been stopped in his tracks very early."

Irascible, uncontrollable, Oscar Wyatt was the antithesis of slick and careful Robert Sakowitz, who, after spending six hours on the witness stand Thursday, breathed a sigh of relief and told the press, "It's not over yet, but I am very pleased after all these years to be able to take the stand and speak my piece."

As the trial moved through its fifth day, Friday, the defendant made his most impressive showing yet. Robert explained the events leading up to the store's bankruptcy and the subsequent takeover by the Hooker Corporation. Before he began, Robert asked if he might come down from the stand and draw the merger on a large cardboard exhibit.

With no objections from the judge or Vickery, Robert left the witness box, walked over to an easel in front of the jury box, and began to draw.

Looking the jurors in the eye, Robert felt as though he was back at Sakowitz, talking to his sales force on the fifth floor of the downtown store. Not since the store had closed had Robert had this kind of audience. In fact, for those few minutes, he looked as though he was actually enjoying himself.

With Robert on the floor hypnotizing the jury, Vickery squirmed in his chair. His discomfort was palpable. As most trial lawyers know, often more important than what a witness says is how he says it — and not just the tone of his voice, but his body language, as well. Finally, Vickery shot out of his chair and insisted that Robert get back up in the witness box. Judge Gregory agreed with Vickery and ordered Robert to do so, but by now Robert's intimacy with the jury had been established.

Robert took the witness stand again Monday morning but only briefly. After an hour of questioning by Vickery, Berg had the final word with his witness. He had Robert read documents from company minutes that approved of Robert having a personal interest in store real estate deals. Berg's last move was to introduce into evidence a framed photograph of Robert with Bernard. The master criminal lawyer pointed out that the frame was engraved "Partners for Life."

The irony that perhaps only Robert and Ann caught was that Bernard had been guilty of many of the same general accusations Robert now faced. Robert had learned to use corporate funds as though they were his private funds from watching his father do it again and again.

At 10:40 A.M., after nearly three days on the stand, Robert stepped down and returned to his chair at the defendant's table.

On the heels of Robert's impressive showing, at 1:30 P.M. Monday, the court finally got to hear from the very handsome and highly controversial litigant who had drawn many of the curious spectators into this courtroom.

"State your name."

"Douglas Wyatt."

"How old are you?" Vickery asked.

"Thirty-four today."

"Today's your birthday?"

"Yes, sir," Douglas smiled politely.

Dressed in a perfectly fitted gray suit, Douglas wore a sleek black watch on his right wrist, his only visible jewelry. In a deposition taken weeks before the trial, Douglas had said that he never wore his protective Eternal Values gems to court, but even if he had worn them today, the gems, which dangled from chains around his neck, would have been concealed under his shirt.

Led by Vickery, Douglas explained the sequence of events leading to his mother's stock assignment to him in 1987 in the south of France. Douglas insisted that he was only trying to help his mother by taking the assignment. "I am the lawyer in the family," he said softly. "I see this as my duty."

When Vickery had finished with his witness, Berg stamped to the stand and shouted, "Today's your birthday. Do you remember on your uncle's forty-ninth birthday, you had your uncle served [with this lawsuit] at his home when his wife and children were there with him?"

After a long pause, Douglas said that his timing was not deliberate.

"He was a surrogate father to you, wasn't he?"

Douglas hesitated.

Berg blasted his question again.

"Yes, he was."

Looking very relaxed and speaking softly, with no hint of vindictiveness, Douglas said that Robert committed fraud when he moved $1 million out of Sakowitz and invested $750,000 in a personal oil deal and $250,000 in the real estate that included Sakowitz's Dallas store.

Berg cross-examined: "In 1978, did your uncle disclose the transaction of the Dallas deal?"

After first saying that Robert had not made full disclosure, Douglas conceded that, in fact, the Dallas deal was on the company's books and records. Berg did not ask him whether the store's books included the oil deal — in which Robert had invested $750,000 in funds that came out of the store and which eventually made him $6 million.

Berg asked a series of questions to which Douglas's answers should have been solid but instead were vague.

Those in the gallery waited for Douglas to take charge, to show some anger or sadness or conviction, some sign of why he had brought the lawsuit. But none was forthcoming.

During Douglas's testimony, Oscar's attorney Tom McDade disrupted the courtroom when he bolted through the door, swept up to the front of the room, and took a seat against the west wall. Trey Wyatt was then further disruptive when he got up from the plaintiff's table and walked over to converse with McDade. If Oscar was not a force behind this lawsuit, why was his chief attorney now sitting in on the proceedings? Most people assumed that the chief counsel for the Coastal Corporation had better things to do than watch Douglas Wyatt humiliate himself on the stand.

When Berg charged that one of Douglas's allegations in his suit was "the opposite of what happened" and Douglas was unable to defend the charge, Berg saw his chance to finish off Douglas once and for all. He swung around to face Robert and made a sweeping gesture with his arm that encompassed the entire courtroom. "Do you want to apologize to your uncle right now in this courtroom?" he asked.

"Yes, if it's wrong, certainly so," Douglas replied softly.

Outwardly, Robert appeared unmoved by the apology. But, like Berg, he could imagine the effect this had on the jury.

Douglas's vague understanding of his own charges made spectators wonder what Douglas had been doing for the last four years since he filed the suit. He seemed like a naive child, possibly weak enough to be controlled by a cult; certainly desperate for approval from his father; and, from the tone of his answers on the stand, ultimately fearful of what his suit had wrought.

Under rough questioning by Berg, Douglas admitted that he knew little about how the stores were run and he even agreed with Berg's statement that the expansion program that Douglas had blamed on Robert had been initiated by Bernard. At each turn, Berg showed that Douglas's allegations were either wrong or could not be proven. When Berg made him admit that each deal Robert executed was approved by Sakowitz's board, a handful of jurors needed to hear no more.

At 4:05 P.M. on Monday, after just two hours and thirty minutes on the stand in the lawsuit he had filed, Douglas Wyatt stepped down and the plaintiff rested its case.

26

B ERG'S QUESTIONING of the plaintiff and his witnesses had been so expert and he was so clearly ahead that, when it came time to present his case, the audience assumed it would be a short coup de grace. But he got off to a terrible start when he called an accountant to the stand. As the accountant droned on about intercompany accounts and estate taxes, Berg read the eyes and body language of his jurors, who were telling him they had heard enough. So after the accountant and a quick examination of the store's longtime controller, Berg turned toward the jury and said softly, "Your honor, at this time I would like to go get my next witness."

Right on cue the courtroom doors opened and in walked Ann Sakowitz. She moved toward the stand, clutching in one hand her black handbag and in the other the bottom of her black sweater, which she wore draped on her shoulders, grandmother-style, over a purple wool dress.

Ann pitched forward slightly when she walked, as much from the slope of her three-inch heels as from her slightly curved back. She stepped carefully up into the witness box, sat down slowly, and took a deep breath. Ann knew that her testimony was crucial, but she hated being here. She put the pain of testifying on a level with attending Bernard's funeral.

After smiling delicately to the jury, she softly stated her name for the record. She was just two years from her eightieth birthday but looked sixtyish at most. She wore plenty of mascara, heavy blue eyeliner, and bright orange lipstick. Her honey-blond hair was full and loose, swept back from her high forehead. Her high, half-circle eyebrows gave her a bright, youthful look.

Berg pulled a chair up to the witness stand, sat down, and gently began asking her about her life. He never took his eyes off her; her eyes were fixed on him. The two began a duet, and the rest of the courtroom seemed to disappear.

After giving a brief family history, Ann said, "We had one of the closest families." Pausing just the right amount of time, she added wistfully, "Bob would say, 'If we can't do it together, we won't do it at all.'"

"Did something happen that changed your family?" Berg asked.

"Yes," Ann said slowly but assuredly, taking a deep breath, "Lynn married Oscar Wyatt." Then, frowning for the first time and rushing her words, she added, "Oscar never did like Bob. Why, we don't know."

"Objection," shouted Vickery, jumping up from his chair. "This has no bearing on the case."

"Your honor, there is a great deal of bearing," Berg retorted, now also out of his chair. "I'm trying to show a possible motivation for the plaintiff's filing this lawsuit."

It did not matter that the judge sustained Vickery's objection and told the jury to discount Ann's last comment. The defense had made its point.

Responding to Berg's leads, Ann said firmly, "We encouraged [Bob] to get into his own business deals. Bernard said he didn't want what happened to him to happen to Bob where he had all his eggs in one basket at the store."

Ann faltered only once during Berg's questioning, but it came at a moment when her testimony was crucial.

"Were you aware of the sale of Fairview Farms?" he asked.

"Yes."

Berg wanted to prove that Ann, a Sakowitz board member, was fully aware of the now-disputed million-dollar transaction. The sale of Fairview Farms, Robert had already testified, had produced for him the million dollars that Robert said he loaned the company in 1981.

"Do you recall where those monies went?"

"Yes," she said tentatively. But then, after hesitating a moment, she said, "Well, no." Finally, she said, "Well, I'm not sure."

She appeared to be trying to remember how to answer the question, as though Berg had asked it of her many times before and she had simply forgotten her planned response. Berg moved on quickly.

Vickery had argued earlier that Ann could have sold her ranch in East Texas to raise money to pay the inheritance taxes on Bernard's estate. This, in turn, would have enabled the estate's trusts to be funded, which Douglas wanted.

"What about selling the ranch?" Berg asked.

"There was some discussion about selling it, but I didn't want to." Her voice cracked. She paused for a long time, bent her head back, and looked at the ceiling. "If I sold the ranch," she whispered, about to burst into tears, "that was a part of Bernard I didn't want to let go."

When she brought her head down and began sobbing, Judge Gregory broke in and said, "Ladies and gentlemen, we'll take a fifteen-minute recess."

When the trial resumed, Berg began slowly, as if to emphasize how very delicate his client was.

Ann explained that when her grandsons filed the lawsuit, "It killed me. It broke my heart."

Her voice, which had earlier portrayed her as the sexy, feminine matriarch, began to take on a hard edge. It became slightly argumentative even though Berg was still doing the questioning. Finally, she appeared anxious and determined to make one last point. "Lynn betrayed her father's trust by giving away her birthright before her death," she bristled.

Virtually everyone in the courtroom was stunned, as Ann Sakowitz's harsh words hung in the air.

Berg decided to end her examination with a discussion about a hotly disputed promissory note on which Robert owed his father $499,000. The note was forgiven at Bernard's death, but Douglas's lawsuit claimed that the note should not have been forgiven. "Bernard wanted that note extinguished at his death," Ann said matter-of-factly. "I did so because he wanted me to."

When Berg finished questioning Ann, Judge Gregory called a recess, and both Berg and Vickery repaired to the men's room.

"Okay, now go jump all over her," Vickery says Berg told him.

Vickery may not have been the brilliant strategist Berg was, but neither was he a fool.

"Right," Vickery replied sarcastically.

Both Berg and Vickery, of course, had been around the courthouse long enough to know that an attack on Ann, a seventy-eight-year-old devoted mother, would be counterproductive. Vickery believed his wisest move was to get this emotionally compelling woman off the stand as quickly as possible. And so he had planned to ask Ann just one question: "You love your son, don't you, and you'd stand behind him no matter what?"

But when the time came, Vickery got carried away and asked several questions. After introducing himself politely to Ann, his first question brought about one of the few genuine peals of laughter heard during the trial. Vickery wanted to prove that although Ann testified that Oscar Wyatt had somehow split the family, in fact, the family initially embraced the wealthy oilman.

"Was Oscar Wyatt best man at your son's first wedding?"

"Probably," she began, as Robert glared at his mother and ever so slightly shook his head. "Well, I don't know," she continued, obviously confused, "that wedding was so bad I have tried to block it out of my mind."

For once during the trial, everyone — including a very red-faced Robert — laughed heartily.

"You still communicate with your daughter, don't you?"

Ann admitted that she did, but said that she squarely placed the blame for the suit on Lynn.

"I have returned presents she and Oscar have given me," Ann said pointedly. "I felt they have taken so much from me already they weren't going to take my conscience also."

But Vickery forced her to reveal that after the store bankruptcy, Lynn and Oscar each gave her $10,000, the amount that each spouse can give away without having to pay gift tax. A more careful lawyer might have left it at that, but Vickery added, "And that helped you out, didn't it?"

A smug look crossed her face. "In fact," she snapped, "I paid some of my legal fees with it."

While bittersweet laughter broke out in the courtroom, Vickery wished he could have that last question back.

But Ann's testimony quickly turned very sad. Asked if it was true that she had disinherited her grandsons, Ann cried, "Believe me, I didn't want my grandsons to be split away from me."

Ann's stunning performance was exactly what both Berg and Vickery had predicted it would be. She smiled carefully as she climbed down from the witness box and Berg led her to a chair next to her son.

One of Robert's secretaries from his days at the store said after the trial, "Ann Sakowitz should go on the stage to supplement her income."

After putting only three witnesses on the stand, the defense rested its case at 4 P.M. Tuesday.

Judge Gregory then asked the jurors to leave the room, and when they had gone, Vickery and Smith approached the bench. Vickery, against Berg's strong objections, convinced Gregory to allow Lynn to appear as a rebuttal witness. Vickery had said at the start of the trial that he would not ask Lynn to come to the courthouse in person. But his case had become so desperate that he now needed a blockbuster witness to turn the jury around.

When the jurors returned, Vickery announced, "We call Lynn Sakowitz Wyatt."

The audience gasped and collectively turned to the door. For nearly two minutes the doors at the rear of the courtroom remained closed. Finally, they swung open and Lynn Wyatt swept into the room, her entrance illuminated by television cameramen who tried desperately to capture the moment from their post in the hallway. Dressed in a charcoal gray Yves Saint Laurent suit, she carried herself like a queen.

As she approached the witness stand, she passed within four feet of her mother and her brother. She did not glance at them, and they did not glance at her.

In the witness box, Lynn crossed her legs, sat very erect, and dressed her face in a serious expression, a look she rarely exhibited in public. She wore bright orange lipstick that looked the very same shade as Ann's. The white powder on her face was especially heavy today, perhaps an attempt to mask her emotions, but her deep green eyes betrayed her fear.

The packed courtroom was frighteningly silent as all eyes were focused on Lynn.

This was not the first time in her life that Lynn had upstaged her mother. Once, when Ann visited Lynn at her villa in the south of France, Ann cut short the length of her stay and confided to a friend on her return to Houston that she felt uncomfortable among Lynn's grand friends.

Finally, Vickery began, "Is your name Lynn Wyatt?"

"Yea-yus," she said, her smoky voice laced with a deep Texas accent.

Just how nervous she was became evident when she interrupted Vickery's next statement.

"A few minutes ago, the jury was told that you have somehow betrayed your father by signing over your birthright . . ."

"No. I do not," she replied.

Spectators in the gallery looked at each other and arched their eyebrows.

Without prompting from Vickery, she continued, speaking very fast, "I came from a wonderful, close-knit family. I was on the board only because of the love of my father who put me on that board."

She then turned and looked at Judge Gregory, let out a deep breath, and said helplessly, "I'm very nervous. I'm sorry, your honor."

Now led by Vickery, Lynn told the jury that she had been a loyal member of the Sakowitz family. "I was a Sakowitz," she said. "I am a Sakowitz," she corrected herself. "Did I betray my father in any way? No. I had a special relationship with my Daddy."

When Vickery asked her to explain why she made the stock assignment to her sons, her answer moved the audience as well as the jury: "All the people that I love were opposed to each other, and I felt that if I could divest myself of this, I could relieve some of this pain."

The most memorable moment in her testimony came when Vickery asked her to defend why she went to the party benefiting the Houston Grand Opera the night before the trial began.

"I had made a commitment to the Houston Grand Opera," she said with a degree of aloofness, "and I believe in keeping my commitments." Then, without missing an opportunity for publicity for the Opera, she added, "And we were very successful."

There was muffled laughter in the courtroom.

During a short cross-examination by Berg, Lynn admitted that Oscar had said things to her that undermined her relationship with Robert, but she argued yet again that she did not turn her inheritance over to her sons with instructions to sue her brother. When Berg tried to end powerfully by asking Lynn if she knew how painful the trial had been for her mother, Lynn fired back, "This is painful for all of us, Mr. Berg."

When Lynn finished testifying and joined Douglas at the plaintiff's table, he stood and uneasily kissed his mother on the cheek. A few minutes later, Judge Gregory called a recess until the following morning, when the court would hear closing arguments.

As soon as Gregory brought down his gavel, Lynn stood up and the court bailiff escorted her through a side door of the courtroom and down a private elevator reserved for judges. Reporters caught up with her as she reached her chauffeur-driven car, waiting for her in front of the courthouse. It was rare for Lynn not to have a witty comment for the press. But on this day, she hid behind her dark glasses and quietly climbed into the front passenger seat. The Wyatts' chauffeur closed the door after her, and the car sped toward River Oaks.

27

CLOSING ARGUMENTS were to begin at 10:30 A.M. Wednesday, but because Judge Gregory decided to allow television cameras in the courtroom on this day only, the logistics involved in doing so set the trial back nearly an hour. A few hundred lawyers, spectators, and members of the press had already waited impatiently and noisily outside the courtroom for nearly two hours. The moment the doors opened, the crowd pushed and surged forward. But once inside, they became very quiet. The atmosphere was somber; the scene resembled a wake.

The Wyatts were already seated on the front row of the spectators' benches on the left side of the gallery. Oscar sat as far to the left as he could without hitting the tripod of a large television camera. A camerman stood behind it with his back to the wall. The camera was usually directed at the jury box, but when it panned the audience, the camera lens came within a foot of Oscar's face. Curiously, the man who did business with Iraq and Libya and who said he hated to have his picture appear anywhere, lest Israeli terrorists see it, seemed not to mind the camera.

Seated on Oscar's right was his youngest son, Brad, and on Brad's right was Trey. All three men appeared to have a rubber inner tube hiked up under his arms under his clothes. They bore a striking contrast to Douglas, on Trey's right, and Lynn, who sat at the far right, next to the aisle.

Douglas, wearing a light gray Italian-cut suit, rested his arm on the back of the bench and cupped his long, slender fingers ever so slightly around his mother's shoulder. Lynn wore a white silk blouse under a gray suit that was only slightly different from the Saint Laurent suit she wore the day before. She sat absolutely erect and motionless, staring straight ahead, as though waiting for her portrait to be painted.

Ann, Robert, and Laura Sakowitz sat at the defendant's table with their backs carefully turned to the Wyatts. They were dressed much as they had been for most of the trial — Laura in a simple navy suit, Ann in a nondescript wool dress, and Robert in a navy suit with a white shirt.

The fact that the two families did not speak or even acknowledge each other made the scene all the more tense. Finally, the jurors filed into the courtroom and took their seats, and Judge Gregory began reading the jury charge. He explained that Vickery would open the closing arguments, followed by Smith, then Berg, and, finally, Vickery would have the last word in rebuttal.

Vickery knew that every bit of sympathy and emotion in the courtroom was on his opponent's side — especially with the heart-wrenching testimony of Ann Sakowitz still fresh in the jurors' minds from the afternoon before. At this point, any attempt to engender sympathy for the Wyatts would be a waste of time. Instead, he would argue as best he could that while the Sakowitzes had cornered the market on sympathy, the Wyatts owned all the rights to the law and the facts.

"The law respects Bernard Sakowitz' will . . . and will not permit, no matter how much they might like it, other people to put words in the mouth of the testator," Vickery said. "There's no provision [in that will] that says you can engage in self-dealing; that you can engage in commingling."

In the first round of his closing arguments, Vickery used the words "the law" thirty-four times, slightly more than once every minute.

The only real drama provided by Vickery thus far, however, came when he reached into his left pants pocket and said, "Shamrock Shops was in the red every year, always owed the family money. What he'd like to say is, 'Well, this money is all in the family coffers and you know two years ago, I put in a ten dollar bill that now looks a lot like this one,'" Vickery said, pulling out a bill. "'I think I'll take that one out now and put it in this pocket,'" he said, putting it in his right pants pocket.

But as he did during most of the trial, Vickery rambled, skipping from one point to another. After what seemed a very long time, he finally turned the floor over to J. P. Smith, whose job was to read the questions in the jury charge and instruct the jurors how, in the defense's view, they should answer.

When his time came to speak, Smith shouted, "They want to say Lynn Wyatt is just not a sophisticated businesswoman. That is simply not true. There is no citizen in Harris County, Texas, who has more access to lawyers and accountants, including the law firm of Fulbright and Jaworski, who coincidentally happens to be the law firm of Mr. Oscar Wyatt."

Jurors frequently looked out into the gallery at Oscar, but he never looked back at them and showed no emotion whatsoever. Oscar sat slouched over on the bench, his eyes fixed on whichever attorney had the floor.

For someone who had not filed the lawsuit, who had not been named in the lawsuit, who had not appeared as a witness, who had not even come as a spectator — except during the opening and closing arguments — Oscar had throughout the trial maintained an almost mystical presence in the courtroom. He may not have been there in person, but he was there in spirit — and, in the words of Berg, "as an evil spirit."

After twenty-five minutes, Smith turned the floor over to Berg.

In his nearly thirty years as a trial lawyer, in all the times he had prepared closing arguments — even where a client faced prison — Berg had never prepared harder than he had for this moment.

He began with a line that coming from anyone else might have seemed insincere, but Berg made it believable. "It never occurred to me until this very minute," he said very softly, moving close to the jury box, "that the greatest asset this family had was what? Their family.

"But it has been torn apart by a lawsuit, filed by that man," he shouted, pointing at Douglas, "fueled by that man," he shouted louder, pointing at Oscar, "and made possible by Lynn Sakowitz Wyatt.

"I noticed that she didn't look at her mother when she came in this courtroom yesterday, and you know what? I don't blame her.

". . . Lynn should have said, 'Douglas, this is wrong. *We-have-to-stop!*'" Berg shouted, knocking hard on the wooden railing of the jury box, once for each word. "'You're killing my mother, you're hurting my brother, he can't even get a job because of you.'"

Oscar never once flinched or cleared his throat. He seemed not in the least bothered by Berg's angry charges. Trey, however, must have feared his father's temper because, from time to time, he bowed his head and looked up at his father out of the corner of his eye, as though waiting for the old man to explode.

Berg turned toward the gallery and stared at Douglas with a pained expression before turning back to face the jury.

"There'll come a day, and it won't be long, when Douglas Wyatt looks across a room and sees a woman who looks like his grandma, Dede," Berg said, his eyes filled with hurt. "It happens to all of us. I would give anything to see my grandma again . . . anything."

Berg looked up and could see tears streaming down juror Gregory Rodriguez's cheeks.

"There'll come a day. Those of us who know a little something about death will tell you there'll come a day, though you might not believe it, Douglas, when you'll see a woman who looks like your grandma. As we grow older, we remember those things that brought us great comfort and joy when we were children. As the pressures of what is sometimes a very difficult life mount, as the pain mounts, as the losses mount, as we get older, when friends die, when relatives die, when businesses go bad, we begin to remember those things that brought us comfort and joy and peace when we were children."

Berg took a deep breath and continued, "I submit to you that there will be an older Douglas Wyatt, perhaps seated at a mansion that he'll inherit from his mother next to River Oaks Country Club. He'll be seated at perhaps an empty dinner table lavishly set and he will remember with blinding force an uncle who taught him how to throw a football. It happens, Douglas. And in that moment, and it won't be long, he'll know that he was wrong."

Now there were many tears and sniffles in the courtroom.

"There's this great folk singer, Leadbelly. He sang this great ole blues song, 'Wasn't it a mighty storm that blew the children all away?'

"And that's where we ought to start our inquiry about this case. Wasn't that a mighty storm in Galveston that blew away the Sakowitz family business? And didn't they rally around and move north right up here to Houston and begin a one-hundred-year tradition? And didn't another storm come in the 1980s? The worst urban depression in the history of this country. There have never been a number of bankruptcies such as what we experienced in

Houston, Texas. And when they blew Robert Sakowitz' business away, when they blew Lynn Wyatt's business away, when they blew Ann Sakowitz' business away, instead of rallying around like Tobias and Simon and their families, they turned on him. They abandoned him. They bad-mouthed him. Oscar Wyatt, according to the admission of Lynn Wyatt, bad-mouthed him all over town."

Berg wanted to counteract any advantage to Douglas of Lynn's dramatic eleventh-hour trip to the courthouse.

"This woman is sharp as a knife," he shouted, "when she raises funds all across the city for various charities." Then, changing his voice to mock femininity, he added, "It's too late to portray her as some devastated southern belle who didn't know anything about business."

Lynn did not move an inch in her seat. Nor did any of the Wyatts. They appeared as mesmerized by Berg as every other spectator in the courtroom.

Berg went on to describe Oscar Wyatt, "who I would suggest to you is the brooding presence that hovers over this trial, whose venom against Robert for whatever reason has poisoned his sister's trust and love and has poisoned his children.

"You heard their testimony, you saw the Wyatts. This is not the Partridge family, folks."

There was long, loud laughter in the courtroom. Judge Gregory appeared ready to bring down his gavel and call for order. But the spectators, anxious to hear Berg's every word, fell silent the moment he continued.

Berg's next move was perhaps his most brilliant in the trial. Standing before the twelve men and women of the jury, he brought back the ghost of Robert's father, Bernard Sakowitz.

"I almost feel Mr. Bernard's presence here in the courtroom," Berg said softly, carefully naming Bernard in the way store employees had. "Mr. Bernard would say, 'I wanted my son to have some liquidity that I don't have.' Mrs. Sakowitz told you that yesterday. And Bernard would say, 'Shame, Douglas, shame.'

"And you know what else Mr. Bernard would say?" Berg whispered, just barely louder than the courtroom sniffles.

"'Robert, you have the family respect and love. . . . You did exactly as you were supposed to do. You have never betrayed me. And so you lost a business. Start another one. Start another.'"

Bernard was the perfect witness because Berg wrote all his lines.

The jurors would be asked, he told them, reading from the jury charge: "Was Robert Sakowitz' breach of his fiduciary duty, if any, to the estate of Bernard Sakowitz or the trusts, excused?"

He continued reading from the charge, "The acts of Robert Sakowitz are excused if the actions of Robert Sakowitz were ratified by the plaintiff or Lynn Sakowitz Wyatt."

Then, looking up, he pleaded, "Remember what Mrs. Wyatt said. Robert never hid anything from her.

"[The Wyatts] have had entree all their life to whatever they wanted. There have been no nos in their life; no impediment to their power. They've gotten what they wanted." Turning and walking toward the jury, Berg pleaded, "Only you can tell them no. Only you, for the first time in the history of this family, can say, 'You've gone too far this time. You've gone too far.'"

When Berg finished, the courtroom was silent. Reporters, spectators, and even the jurors appeared stunned. Berg had given the best closing argument of his life. Whatever the verdict, he believed that he had so effectively argued Robert's case that he had personally restored the Sakowitz name.

But the trial was not over. Vickery had one last chance. In his final arguments, Vickery would once again ask jurors to make an example of Robert, the conniving trustee who cheated his relatives. Maybe Douglas had not suffered greatly, but there were plenty of families who had been hurt by dishonest trustees. Let their verdict send a message loud and clear. That was the purpose of exemplary damages. Make an example of this defendant who had betrayed his family.

"What you say will be heard by many people," Vickery told the jurors, "not just those here but by many outside of here and it will go far and wide and it will help to establish rules of conduct for other families, many families across Houston, across Texas, up in Tulsa, out in Midland, where all these stores were."

He concluded with the biblical story of Rebekah, Jacob, and Esau.

"I mean this with no harshness for Mrs. Sakowitz but I'm reminded of the story of Rebekah, Isaac's wife, who favored her younger son over her eldest child; who persuaded her younger son that he ought to have more than his fair share. [Rebekah] enabled her younger son to deceive his father and said, 'We're in this together. Whatever you do, I'll back you up.'"

Vickery explained how Jacob then got what was not rightfully his and prospered. Jacob eventually realized that he had wronged his brother and sent his brother gifts, asking for forgiveness.

In the end, however, the Sakowitz story differs in one way, Vickery explained. "We do not have in this case the prodigal son returning home, or the contrite Jacob asking for the forgiveness of his family. We have here instead a man who's not merely a prodigal and hasn't returned home to family, but at this point is an unremitting profligate."

After eight days at trial, the jury went out at 1:30 P.M. on Wednesday and, after lunch, began deliberating at 2:10 P.M. Berg beamed as he paced the halls and continued to answer reporters' questions, and whatever Vickery's feelings might have been, he too wore a happy expression and made himself unusually accessible to the press. As the minutes and then hours ticked by, reporters paced the hall anxious to make evening deadlines.

When word came shortly before six o'clock that the jurors were close to a verdict, Laura and Robert and Ann took their seats again at the defendant's table. Robert stared at the empty jury box, his hand cupped over his mouth, as though trying to refrain from either screaming or vomiting. Ann sat facing her son, at times looking toward the ceiling to keep tears from rolling down her face. Looking at her, an unknowing spectator would have assumed that this woman's son, the defendant, faced life in prison.

By now, many of the spectators had gone home, and among the Wyatt family only Douglas and Trey remained. They sat quietly and unemotionally at the plaintiff's table surrounded by their lawyers. Douglas, looking sad and alone, may have wondered why his parents, who had had such integral roles in the suit, had not stayed to hear the verdict. As the jurors filed into the courtroom, the Sakowitzes huddled together, exhibiting a united front.

Berg looked at the clock. It was 6:10 P.M. The jury had deliberated exactly four hours. Enough time had passed to indicate that the jurors had difficulty reaching a decision. Still, Berg looked and felt confident. He put his hand over Robert's on the table and clutched it tightly.

"Question number one," Judge Gregory began, "Did Defendant Robert Sakowitz breach one or more of his fiduciary duties to the estate of Bernard Sakowitz and/or the trusts created by Bernard Sakowitz' will?"

After a short pause, the foreman answered, "No."

A loud, collective groan filled the room.

As the judge read on, everyone in the courtroom listened intently, except for Berg, who knew it was all over. Smiling and nodding his head, he looked into Robert's eyes as if to say, "We won. You don't need to listen anymore."

A "no" on the first question meant the jury did not even have to answer questions two and three. The jury also answered no to question four, "Has the defendant Sakowitz misapplied the property committed to his care and/or engaged in gross misconduct or mismanagement in the performance of his duties as an independent executor of the estate of Bernard Sakowitz?"

The last question was "What sum of money, if any, should be assessed against the defendant in exemplary damages?"

The foreman answered, "Zero."

Robert hugged Laura and then began to sob, tears streaming down his cheeks. As soon as the judge dismissed the jury, Robert and Laura jumped out of their chairs and rushed over to the jurors. Ann bolted around the other side of the table.

"Thank you for seeing the truth," Laura cried as she hugged jurors and even reporters. "My faith is restored in everything."

Robert embraced the black women and Hispanic men of the jury, several of whom were crying by now, as well. Juror Gregory Rodriguez, an equipment operator for the City of Houston, cradled Robert Sakowitz's head against his shoulder and told reporters what an honor it had been to serve on the jury.

Juror June Hewling, a nurse, said, "This is probably the only time in my life I'll hug a millionaire." But Hewling, who was born one of nine children in Antigua, West Indies, added that she had no desire to trade places with the defendant. "I come from a very close family, and I thought, if this is what happens to your family when you're really rich, let me struggle along on my income."

Some jurors said that Douglas was his own worst enemy when he took the stand and acknowledged he was not aware of some facts in the case. Other jurors said the board minutes of the company convinced them that whether Robert's actions were right or wrong, he had his family's approval for all the deals he made and therefore was innocent of the charges.

Outside the courtroom, reporters gathered around a podium in the hallway and waited for the family. Robert came out first, and after shaking off his weeping relatives, he approached the podium. "I am elated," Robert boomed, flashing his sexy smile under the bright glare of television lights. "I have been able to clear the name of Robert Sakowitz and the Sakowitz family." Then, in a deeply serious tone, he added, "I think what became clear is that these allegations were not based in fact. I thank the jury."

A reporter asked, "What about your sister? Do you think she'll embrace you again?"

"I really don't think that's in the cards," he said sadly. "When she came down at the end [of the trial] and added insult to injury, that made the disappointment all that much greater."

Then pausing a moment, Robert added, "Mr. Wyatt — and I don't mean Douglas — has his own agenda."

A reporter then shouted, "Mrs. Sakowitz, how do you feel about your daughter?"

Ann, who had been standing behind her son, moved up next to him. "I think Lynn has sold her soul and her family to greed and power," she snapped. Once again, it was shocking how easily this small, delicate lady silenced a boisterous crowd of reporters.

"What was the turning point?" a reporter asked Berg.

"When they filed the suit," Berg fired back.

Holding the spotlight a moment more, he added magnanimously, "Robert Sakowitz is a very special man filled with the kind of integrity that results in a twelve-man verdict."

Once the victors had moved down the hall and around the corner to the elevators, Douglas and his lawyers came out of the courtroom and approached the podium. Even Trey was gone now.

"What was it that turned the case in their favor?" a reporter asked.

"The board minutes going back year after year," Vickery said. "There's no question that the minutes contain approval of many of [Robert's] deals."

Douglas, thin and unbending, stood tall with his hands behind his back and said softly, "This has been a very difficult case for the whole family. My brothers and I felt we had to go forward with the case. I certainly was not interested in the financial outcome. I was interested in some wrongs being brought out."

A reporter asked, "What about Eternal Values?"

"That has nothing to do with this case," he answered numbly. "It's been so sensationalized. Everything I've read about it is wrong. It doesn't warrant discussion here . . ."

Outside in front of the courthouse, a friend of Robert's invited the Sakowitz family, Robert's lawyers, and a number of jurors to a celebratory dinner at a fashionable Mexican restaurant in River

Oaks. But not until he accepted the invitation did Berg learn that jurors also were going. Had he known this when the invitation was made, he said, he would not have gone.

Upon arriving at Armando's, a nondescript wood building that has no sign in front, the entourage was met with loud applause. Two diners who were not among the revelers but who had followed the trial closely sat only a few tables away. They were Houston reporter Michelle Smith and New York writer John Taylor. Michelle had been covering the trial for *Women's Wear Daily,* and Taylor had been in town all week writing an article for *New York* magazine. Berg thought it curious that, of all the restaurants in Houston, Michelle and John showed up at Armando's. Whether or not it was a coincidence, in the coming months Berg would come to believe that Michelle's involvement in the Sakowitz family feud extended beyond merely covering the trial.

As Berg's suspicions festered, Robert was inundated with congratulations that came in the form of phone calls, flowers, and even champagne. On the Sunday after the trial, he celebrated his fifty-third birthday, told the press that he felt "freedom after six years" of legal battles, and was hoping to get a book contract.

Around Houston, many hypotheses were put forth about how the Sakowitzes won the case.

"Our feeling is we were out-lawyered," said Trey Wyatt. "I think Vickery did the best he could, but he was in over his head. He didn't understand the facts."

In a strange way it seemed Douglas was content with the verdict. A week after the trial, he wrote Andy Vickery a thank-you note in which he said that despite what Robert might feel he had gotten away with, Douglas felt he had accomplished his principal objectives in the case.

The *Houston Chronicle,* the morning following the verdict, quoted Oscar as saying, "You win some, you lose some," but many familiar with the case found it difficult to believe he felt that casual about it.

And when word got out that Steve Wyatt, soon after the verdict, telephoned his grandmother, Ann, to apologize for all that had happened, Trey Wyatt confided to a reporter: "Steve's phone call may have been premature."

28

FOR WEEKS after Robert Sakowitz and David Berg won their courthouse victory against the Wyatts, they were euphoric. Their victory tasted especially sweet because it was such an upset. Oscar was widely believed to be invincible, with his unlimited funds to pay for his fights, his apparently unslakable thirst for fighting, and his long history of supporting judges in their political campaigns.

So great was Robert and Berg's surprise victory that they acted as though, having triumphed over Oscar, nothing could ever defeat them again.

But as October turned to November, the glow of victory that Berg and Robert had felt so strongly began to fade. Berg was increasingly troubled by Judge Gregory's delay in ruling on what at first seemed merely a routine motion. The Motion for a New Trial, a prerequisite for appeal, filed by Andy Vickery on October 23, 1991, charged that the jury finding went against the overwhelming weight of the evidence in the case.

At first, Berg publicly brushed off the motion as little more than a formality, a right of the plaintiff. When asked in October about the likelihood of a new trial, Berg had said convincingly, "There will never be another round. The chances of it are one in a thousand."

Ann Sakowitz, a woman who knew her son-in-law far better than David Berg did, was less confident. In November, six weeks after the verdict, she, Robert, Laura, J. P. Smith, and Berg went to dinner together. During dinner, Ann said, "I've got a terrible feeling [Gregory's] going to grant a new trial."

"Ann, that's crazy," Berg snapped.

But by early December, Berg confided that he too was concerned over the court's delay. Everyone on the Sakowitz side seemed to grow more and more nervous by the day. "Laura is just convinced that Oscar is not going to be satisfied until Robert is destroyed financially," said Berg. "She is very upset over what the Wyatts are doing to her husband, and it has put a tremendous strain on Laura and Robert's marriage."

What had brought the Sakowitz family and other families like theirs from the fearful ghettos of Russia to riches in America was intense blood loyalty. Where had it gone now?

There was at least some consolation for Robert in that his three daughters were too young to understand what was happening to their father. "Robbie knows about it because he's seventeen," Robert explained, "but I don't think the other kids know anything except that daddy has a sister who is married to a man and that [they] are having their problems."

But it was Berg who became the most paranoid of all, and in his mind Oscar was not the only player in this complicated chess game. Berg began to piece together bits of information about *Women's Wear Daily* free-lance writer Michelle Smith, who covered the trial, and how she might fit into the tangled web of events.

As Berg began to think back about the trial, he recalled that Michelle had shown up at the Mexican restaurant right after the trial ended. Berg was there with his victory party, but what was Michelle doing there?

As Christmas neared and there was still no ruling, Robert said in jest to Berg, "I wonder whether Gregory spent part of his Christmas holidays on a deer lease of somebody we know."

Robert says he was very suspicious about Oscar's role in influencing Gregory.

The New Year brought more bad signs for the defendant when Berg attended a Democratic fund-raiser at the downtown Houston Club. "As I was entering," he said, "Oscar was leaving. Once I got inside, I saw Michelle Smith there locked in conversation with Judge Gregory." The more he thought about it, the more curious he became about Michelle and her relationship with the Wyatts and Judge Gregory.

A former Sakowitz executive said Robert was as depressed as she had ever seen him: "I've watched Robert suffer through an awful divorce and the store's bankruptcy, but never has he faced anything this terrible."

In spite of the tremendous emotional and financial expense inflicted on him by his nephews' lawsuit, Robert exhibited an extraordinary ability to forgive. When Robert was skiing with cosmetics executive Leonard Lauder in Aspen a few months after the trial, they saw Steve Wyatt on the mountain.

Lauder said to Robert, "Bob, here's an opportunity to make peace in the family. Why don't you ask your nephew to join us."

Robert did, but Steve declined.

"It's just so awkward for me," Steve told Robert. "I just can't."

During the Christmas holidays, Lynn Wyatt also was suffering, not only about the vicious family fight, but because just a few days before Christmas, some jewelry and her address book were stolen.

The jewels were replaceable, but the address book was not. It contained her life's work; it was among her most valuable assets, her guidebook, and now it was gone. The incident occurred at New York's La Guardia Airport when — as often happened when she traveled commercially — she stepped up to the airline counter to pay overweight on extra luggage. When the airline clerk handed her five $1 bills, her change from the overweight she paid, she carefully folded the bills and stuck them in her pocket. She placed her black *necessaire*, containing her address book and several pieces of jewelry, on the counter.

A few minutes later, a man with a moustache who was standing behind her said, "You dropped your money." When she looked down, she saw five $1 bills on the floor.

"It flashed through my mind that I had folded the money and how could they pop out like that," Lynn told *New York Post* columnist William Norwich. "But I said, 'Thank you,' and leaned over to pick up the money. When I stood up my black bag was gone."

With it went an estimated $198,000 in jewels, including an eight-carat diamond ring reportedly worth $75,000, an $85,000 ruby-and-diamond ring, and a $30,000 sapphire ring, none of which were, in Lynn's words, her "big-time jewelry."

Privately, friends say, she was devastated. Lynn's close friend Jerry Zipkin, the New Yorker who became known as the "social moth" escorting Nancy Reagan and Betsy Bloomingdale during the Reagan Eighties, ran into Lynn at La Guardia immediately following the robbery.

"What really killed her was losing that address book," says Jerry. "If this had happened to me, I would have gone into cardiac arrest. My book can tell you the telephone number of the second guest bedroom at so-and-so's beach house in Acapulco.

"When I saw Lynn, she said, 'My address book was stolen. What am I going to do?'

"We decided that I'd read mine on the phone to her. So she got me on the phone, and when we began she said, 'Your *As* are more than my whole book.'"

In the international circles Lynn and Jerry frequent, there is little time for close personal relationships to develop. One does not spend too much time in any one place or with any one group. It is necessary to get around quickly, and the address book makes that possible.

"There isn't a country in the world I couldn't go to and be accepted," brags Jerry. "Same is true of Lynn. She's part of the milieu. She can fit in anywhere."

On January 30, 1992, eighty-one days after the jury had found for Robert and against Douglas, Judge Gregory declared that the jury's verdict was faulty and that the case would have to be tried again from scratch. He gave no explanation for his decision, other than simply approving a motion by Andy Vickery claiming that the jury ignored the law in reaching its judgment and that Judge Gregory himself made a mistake in an instruction to the jurors.

Vickery said that he had asked for a new trial because the burden of proof had incorrectly been placed on Douglas. Judge Gregory had instructed the jury that Douglas had the burden to prove that Robert mismanaged the Bernard Sakowitz estate. In fact, says Vickery, the law states that it should be up to Robert, as trustee, to prove that he was managing it properly. He also said that two facts were established at trial that, as a matter of law, showed Sakowitz breached his fiduciary duties: Robert admitted that his funds were commingled with estate funds in June 1981; and evidence established that a transfer of funds from Sakowitz Inc. to Robert's company Shamrock Shops in June 1983 was a loan.

David Berg bristled with anger and swore that he would "try the case ten times, and I'll get the same verdict each time." He also announced that he would "dedicate the resources of my firm to represent Robert and his mother until this case is finally resolved, no matter how long it takes."

Berg wanted to make clear to the Wyatts that they were not going to win simply by putting financial pressure on Robert. This was not a hollow promise. Berg would not charge Robert any further fee.

Houston society was stunned by the headlines: WYATT VS. SAKOWITZ: ROUND 2, screamed the conservative *Houston Chronicle.*

How could Robert's sweeping victory be taken away from him? Was the Wyatts' power really that great? Why would either side want to repeat the scandalous courthouse spectacle of four months earlier?

One thing was certain about Round Two: it was a case that would be tried in the press.

Just a couple of days after the Motion for a New Trial was granted, Michelle Smith told the *Houston Press* that she had talked with Judge Gregory about ghostwriting a book on his high-profile cases. In the article, Michelle explained that Gregory had ruled in some of the biggest trials in Houston, including the will probate of Howard Hughes. "The working title," she said, "is something like *Candy, Counts and Casinos.*"

Michelle later said she talked with the *Press* on the advice of an image consultant she had contacted after she heard that rumors were circulating that she and Judge Gregory were having an affair. Michelle believed that David Berg had started those rumors.

But while the book in progress explained why Michelle was seen in public in the company of the judge, it did not take her out of Berg's firing line. Instead of diffusing the issue of her relationship with Gregory, her admission gave Berg just the ammunition he wanted.

On February 13, eleven days after the article about Michelle appeared, Berg fired the opening shot in Round Two when he had Michelle served with a subpoena for her deposition. He wanted to learn the extent of her relationship both with the judge and with the Wyatts and how the Sakowitz case figured into the book that she and the judge were writing. Michelle's first move after receiving the subpoena was to place a call to Judge Gregory.

In her deposition, Michelle admitted that the Sakowitz case might be included in the book but she said that her conversations with Gregory about *Wyatt v. Sakowitz* had been "extremely limited because the matter was not resolved." She also said that some of her discussions with Gregory, who is married (Michelle is not), took place at her home.

What further piqued Berg's curiosity was her admission that she had spoken with Douglas soon after the trial about writing an article about his law firm, Looper Reed Mark McGraw, for the journal *Texas Lawyer*, for which she would expect to be paid a fee by Looper Reed. She also said that she had dined alone with Douglas after the trial and that, on one occasion, before the new trial was granted, she had discussed with him his Motion for a New Trial.

Was Michelle going out alone with Douglas one night and discussing the case and then working on her book and discussing it with Gregory alone on the next? The appearance — if not the fact — of impropriety was potentially enormous.

If the Wyatts, Michelle Smith, and Judge Gregory were upset over Berg's deposition of Michelle, they were not alone. Robert's lawyer J. P. Smith, who had long been a friend of Gregory's, so objected to Berg's attack on Michelle and, therefore, on Judge Gregory that he resigned from the case.

Later, when J. P. Smith had trouble getting Robert to pay his fee, he sued his former client. Robert responded by threatening to sue Smith for malpractice, charging that Smith's loyalties had been divided between Robert and Judge Gregory, as well as two other attorneys who were peripherally involved in the case. Robert was upset that, in his view, Smith — his own attorney — had gone around Houston declaring that the burden of proof had been improperly placed on Douglas and that the judge was correct in ruling for a new trial.

Robert also charged that Smith's fee was much higher than Smith had estimated when Robert hired him. Soon after Robert threatened malpractice, he and Smith settled their dispute.

No one knew better than Berg what a big risk it was to attack Gregory. But despite the potential damage to his legal career, Berg had decided to try to get Gregory removed from the case, explaining: "Knowing what I know now about Michelle Smith and Gregory, I cannot *not* pursue the rumors. As a lawyer it's my duty to explore a conflict of interest such as this. If I didn't, it would be malpractice on my part.

"The judge is so predisposed against Robert anyway that we've got nothing to lose by trying to get another judge. If we go back to Judge Gregory's court, he is going to say, 'As a matter of law, there is commingling, and the only issue that the jury's going to have to decide is how much money does Robert Sakowitz owe the estate.' If we go back to his court, we don't stand a prayer."

Despite his near obsession with the case, Berg never lost his wry humor. Asked about the difficulties of the Sakowitz case, he grinned and said, "I spent most of my life in the relatively pristine world of criminal law where all that's at stake is you go to prison for life. In civil cases, people are willing to do and say anything for money."

At about the same time that Berg deposed Michelle Smith, Andy Vickery was busy preparing a motion asking Gregory for a summary judgment of $7.5 million in damages to be paid to Douglas and his brothers. But Berg beat him to the courthouse.

On Wednesday, March 11, Berg raised the stakes in *Wyatt v. Sakowitz* when he drew a bead on his newest adversary. "Defendant Robert Sakowitz moves to disqualify and/or recuse Judge Pat Gregory from any further proceedings in this case and to void his order granting a new trial," the motion read.

"Judge Gregory has both a personal and financial interest in the outcome of this case, and he has displayed personal bias in favor of the plaintiff. During the period that followed the verdict, and while the Plaintiff's Motion for New Trial was pending in his court, the judge actively pursued writing a book about high profile cases tried in his court, including this one."

In trying to recuse Gregory, Berg had ensured an exciting next step to the saga, but no one dared to predict that it would be the last. Many observers thought the case had already enjoyed too robust a life. It was time to end *Wyatt v. Sakowitz.* The question was how.

29

N O ONE WANTED the case to die more than Lynn Wyatt. Oscar may have been thrilled about Round Two, but not Lynn. The press reports about her family were taking a terrible toll on her. In public, she seemed to have lost her elegant joie de vivre.

"She just wants all the bad publicity to go away," a friend of Lynn's confided in January 1992. "She thinks she can control what is written about her, which is ludicrous, but that's what she wants — for her press to be as glowing as it used to be."

But Lynn is, above all, a realist. She knows that adaptability is the key to happiness, indeed to survival. Whatever cannot be changed — being less important to her parents than her brother; Oscar's ways — must be accommodated rather than uselessly and endlessly resented.

So she decided that if she could not control or shape her publicity for the moment, she would not pursue it. A former editor of *Town & Country* says that he noticed this change in Lynn. "I think she's trying to become much quieter."

In public, she looked almost timid, compared to her former, sparkling self, as though she believed she had lost her right to be a star. Nowhere was this more obvious than in her dress, which became more subdued and refined.

"Lynn is very upset about the new trial," Jerry Zipkin confided in early 1992. "She told me it upsets her terribly. That's Oscar. If she objects too much to him, I think he'll tell her to get out. He makes her life very tough."

What must have seemed bitterly ironic to Lynn was that, had she not made the stock assignment to Douglas in 1987 at Cap Ferrat, the lawsuit might never have happened and she would not now be faced with the resulting explosions of bad publicity.

In addition to the possible new trial and David Berg's allegations against the judge, there was also the terrible likelihood that the worst had not yet been revealed to the public about Douglas's involvement with Frederick Von Mierers and Eternal Values.

The day after the *Wyatt v. Sakowitz* verdict, Douglas's former friend Roger Hall sued the *Houston Chronicle* for libel, alleging that a front-page article had portrayed him in a false light when it said he was a member of Eternal Values. Hall said in the suit that he was recruited by the cult but never joined it or adhered to its beliefs and practices.

Hall's deposition in *Wyatt v. Sakowitz* had smeared Douglas's reputation, but it also backfired on Hall when the juiciest parts of his deposition found their way into Houston's newspapers. The *Houston Chronicle* ran a front-page banner story, in which Hall was described as having left the cult, but that two years earlier he was "meeting cult leader Frederick Von Mierers in New York apartments, adhering to a special diet, wearing unusual jewelry to cure character defects and studying New Age tapes."

In the weeks and months that followed the *Chronicle* article, Hall says, his commercial real estate business disappeared. "I lost all my clients in Houston because they thought I was a homosexual who took psychedelic drugs and hated Jews."

What bothered Hall most were the effects his cult involvement had on his family. "My wife was forced to resign her position in pediatric medicine because of this cult stuff," says Hall.

At his son's Little League games, Hall noticed that the other parents who used to be so friendly to him and his wife now stayed away. Other parents also pulled their children away from Hall's son and daughter.

What Hall may say at his trial against the *Chronicle* is potentially far more explosive than his deposition in *Wyatt v. Sakowitz* because then Hall's account of Douglas's involvement with Eternal Values will be absolutely germane to the trial. Douglas was Hall's closest link to the cult. Most of what Hall knows about the cult, Douglas taught him.

As if Lynn were not facing enough problems with a new *Wyatt v. Sakowitz* trial and the likelihood of Roger Hall's lawsuit coming to trial, her son Steve now added an international scandal so big that it pushed the stories about Robert and Oscar's feud off the front pages.

This time, too, Lynn must have wondered whether the negative press was her fault. Wasn't she responsible for her eldest and favorite son Steve's relationship with Sarah Ferguson, the Duchess of York? Hadn't she introduced them and pushed them together when Fergie came to Houston in 1989? Wasn't she then also responsible in part for the breakup of the Duke and Duchess's royal marriage?

Her plans had gone so terribly awry. On those lonely nights at Allington, when Oscar was in the Middle East, when she walked the halls and climbed the swirling marble staircase alone, when she thought about Douglas and Eternal Values and the new trial and Steve and Fergie, she must surely have wondered how much she had herself to blame.

The press had made Lynn Wyatt. Could it now destroy her?

The gossip about Steve and Fergie did not break in the United States until almost a year after their Moroccan trip. It was the cover story in the March 1991 *People:* "FERGIE AND THE TEXAS PLAYBOY: While Andrew is at sea, the Duchess of York hikes her hemlines and, amid whispers of scandal, parties with a Texas millionaire."

Lynn, at first, seemed not to view this as a negative story. In fact, she seemed to boast about Steve's relationship with Fergie. Allington was filled with photographs of Wyatt family members with famous friends. Instead of putting away her framed, signed photograph of Fergie, she left it out for all her guests, including a *Town & Country* reporter, to admire.

"People who remembered how Lynn promoted the rumors about herself with Rainier thought she also liked the rumors about Steve and Fergie," says a friend of Lynn's. "Even though the affair with Fergie and Steve was scandalous, it proved how close she and Steve were to royalty."

But Jerry Zipkin says Lynn tried to discount the rumors. "She said, 'Most of what's been printed about Steve and the Duchess is not true,'" says Zipkin.

Whatever the truth of Steve's relationship with Fergie, for months it had not sat well with the Queen and she finally issued a moratorium on Wyatt.

Fergie's mother, Susie Barrantes, was quoted as saying that the Queen told her daughter-in-law to "chill out Steve Wyatt."

This became apparent to Steve when a close friend of his and his wife hosted a party that Fergie had planned to attend with Steve.

After accepting the party invitation, at the last minute Fergie wrote a letter of regret. The hostess, who says she believes Steve and Fergie "must have" had an affair, says Fergie's letter "showed jealousy of Steve and his relationships with other women."

Another female friend of Steve's from Houston, Karen Fertitta, says that when she visited Steve in London and Fergie joined them for dinner, Fergie expressed concern over Karen's relationship with Steve. "Sarah was worried that I was in love with Steve and going to get my heart broken. I think she, like I, had seen a lot of women fall in love with Steve and get their heart broken."

Whatever Steve's feelings for Fergie were, he was not about to fight Buckingham Palace. During the fall of 1991, he left England and moved to Alexandria, Virginia, to work for one of Oscar's Washington-based oil companies. But London had not heard the last of Steve Wyatt.

In January 1992, Steve single-handedly turned Britain's gossip mongers upside down and gave the world what promised to be the biggest society scandal of the year. When he moved out of his apartment at 34 Cadogan Square, he left behind 120 snapshots of himself with Fergie during their Moroccan vacation, and the maid who came to clean the flat found them. Within hours, the *Daily Mail* broke the story.

The photographs were not published, but the *Daily Mail* described them carefully and even ran a rendering from descriptions of one of the photos depicting Fergie and Steve, dressed in sweatshirts and shorts, sitting on a swing together with their arms around each other. In the drawing, Fergie and Steve are innocently looking at the camera smiling. Because these were taken not by a newspaper photographer behind a bush with a telephoto lens, but *en famille*, they had a certain innocence.

Although there was much talk that Steve had intentionally left the photographs, hoping they would be discovered, it is far more likely that Steve, whose strong point has never been intellect, simply walked off and forgot them.

When the story hit America, the ever-Wyatt-faithful Betsy Parish at the *Houston Post* tried to play down the issue, insisting that the photographs were "much ado about nothing."

After she said the same to a throng of British journalists at a group interview that ran on the evening television news in Houston, Betsy received a bouquet of flowers from the Wyatts.

Lynn, meanwhile, was trying to fight off the barbarians at the gates of Allington, and Steve went into hiding. Some reports had him living at a Buddhist camp in the Far East. Others had him hopping from one city to another in England, France, and Italy, trying to keep ahead of Europe's tireless paparazzi. With the press on his tail, Steve confided to a friend that he knew that at some point he would have to make a statement about the allegations.

His disappearance to Alexandria, Virginia, where his address and phone number were carefully guarded secrets, did not end the stories about him. The London *Sunday Times* article DALLAS MEETS PALACE rehashed those overexposed Kodak Morocco moments and sent the fax lines between London and Houston into overdrive.

America's tabloids, not to be outdone by their British counterparts, put their own twists on the story. The *National Enquirer* screamed in a headline, FERGIE LIES TO HUBBY: MY BOYFRIEND IS GAY!

This, after the American press had just had a field day with Douglas Wyatt's connections to the homosexual Eternal Values cult, sent new rumors flying.

Lynn, apparently no longer charmed with the gossip, described Steve's predicament as "a tabloid hell."

Fergie did not help diffuse the rumors when she fled to the basement apartment of London mystic Madame Vasso. The press reported her visit to Madame Vasso, during which Fergie, according to the press, sat under a blue plastic pyramid to cleanse her soul. If Andrew read of his wife's excursions, did he also know about the blue plastic pyramid above Steve Wyatt's bed?

Just how broad Buckingham Palace's ban on Steve Wyatt had become was obvious when the Queen forbade Fergie and Andrew to attend the opening of London's newly refurbished Lanesborough Hotel. Dallas billionaire Caroline Hunt owned Lanesborough's management company, and she was bringing with her a planeload of Texans for the opening. It did not matter that neither Steve nor his parents were invited to the party; the Palace did not even want to risk guilt by association. All Texans, it seemed, fell under the ban.

Stories about Fergie's unhappiness with Andrew had circulated for months, just as Princess Di's marriage to Prince Charles had long been rumored to have its troubles. Rumors about Di and Charles were proven true in 1992 when Buckingham Palace announced that they would separate. When word leaked to the press in mid-March that the Duchess had spoken with the Queen about the possibility of a divorce from Prince Andrew, the tabloids made it a foregone conclusion.

FERGIE: I CAN'T STAND IT ANYMORE, shouted the *Daily Mail*. ANDREW AND FERGIE ARE SET TO PART, proclaimed the *Sun* in three-inch-high letters. A half dozen of London's other newspapers carried similar headlines.

Finally, on March 19, 1992, Buckingham Palace formally announced that a separation was under consideration.

For the first time since the Moroccan photographs were made known to the world, Steve issued a statement to the press. "I have never had any romantic liaisons, ever, with the Duchess," he said from his Washington office. "We are still friends, but it is just a platonic friendship."

He also commented on the Palace announcement that a separation was being considered. "If the rumor is true, I am deeply saddened by the news, and I wish the Duke and Duchess of York the very best of luck in these trying times."

The media's fascination with Steve, however, would soon end. With Steve thousands of miles away, Fergie focused her attention on a new playmate, Johnny Bryan, to whom Steve had introduced the Duchess months earlier. In an ironic twist, Bryan, a high-school classmate of Steve's, is connected to Steve by marriage. Johnny is the son of Tony Bryan, whom Pam Zauderer Sakowitz left Steve's uncle, Robert Sakowitz, to marry in 1978.

When Pam learned of the alleged affair between Fergie and Johnny, she was not surprised. "I think Johnny probably went to the top and started down," says Pam of her stepson, whom she still adores. "Queen Elizabeth didn't appeal to him and Diana was taken."

Pam says Steve Wyatt and Johnny Bryan have two things in common: "Both are very, very sweet, and both have a sophistication well beyond their years."

Like Steve, Johnny was about to experience his share of, in Lynn's words, "tabloid hell." Fergie apparently could not resist going away with her Texas beaux and frolicking in the Mediterranean sun. With Steve, it had been Morocco and Cap Ferrat; with Johnny, it was Saint-Tropez. A photographer in the bushes outside their villa in Saint-Tropez captured her in various poses. There she was, sitting on Johnny's shoulders in the pool, her thick pale legs wrapped around his bronze, bald head. And here she was bouncing around the pool in a topless bikini, bending over to kiss Johnny as two-year-old Princess Eugenie watched.

Most scandalous of all, there would appear all over the world a photograph of Fergie, once dubbed a "royal slouch," sprawled on her back on a mattress in the sun, one leg extended in the air, at the end of which was Johnny, sucking her royal toes.

Days later, when the photographs appeared under the headlines TOE-JOB FERGIE QUITS CASTLE, KICK HER OUT, and DIVORCE AND NOW, ANDREW, Fergie was, of all places, at the Queen's castle in Balmoral, where she was allegedly considering reconciliation with Andrew.

The world can only speculate about the resulting conversation between Fergie and the Queen. But one thing was clear — public favor was with the Queen and Andrew and against her.

Fergie's popularity reached an all-time low. Even those who had stuck with her through the Steve Wyatt rumors now turned on her. The public charged her with showing scant consideration for the standards set for her by the British people who subsidize her, and even less consideration for the family into which she married.

In early 1993, a divorce from Prince Andrew seemed imminent, her future with Johnny Bryan up in the air, and her past with Steve Wyatt, just that.

Whether Steve caused Fergie's split from Andy or merely helped it along will probably never be known — perhaps not even by the subjects themselves. But if Steve's name is recorded in history, it will be as the first widely known cause of the breakup of the marriage of Queen Elizabeth's second son, fourth in line to the British throne. In the world of international scandal, Steve has already surpassed even his natural father and his stepfather — and he is still young.

The stakes changed dramatically when David Berg filed his motion to remove Judge Gregory from *Wyatt v. Sakowitz*. No longer was this simply a war between two high-profile branches of a wealthy family. The case, which Berg had earlier described as a "showcase" for his talents, now put his entire career at risk. The scrappy, youthful Berg was no longer taking on only the evil Goliath, Oscar Wyatt; he was now in addition taking on one of the most powerful giants in the Texas judicial system within which his future lay.

A recusal motion against any other probate judge would have gone before Gregory because he is the state's chief presiding probate judge. But because Gregory could not rule on whether or not to disqualify himself, he asked the state's assistant chief presiding judge, Anthony Ferro of San Antonio, to decide the question. Ferro, in turn, assigned it to Austin judge Guy Herman.

Angry that the decision was now in the hands of a subordinate of Gregory's, Berg filed a petition calling for Gregory to set aside all proceedings in the case and turn the recusal motion over to the Chief Justice of the Texas Supreme Court, Tom Phillips, who could either make the recusal decision himself or select a judge to hear it. When he immediately got his stay, Berg predicted confidently, "This is the beginning of the end for Judge Gregory."

If Robert wanted to play that tough, so could his opponents. Just days after Berg got his stay, Vickery was off the case, and in his place came Oscar's tough and brilliant litigator Tom McDade.

Then came a surprising turn of events. On May 11, Judge Gregory called a press conference announcing that he was recusing himself from the case. He accused Berg of creating a "sham issue" and said there was no valid basis for recusal, but that nonetheless he asked that the case be transferred to another judge "in the best interest of judicial economy and to eliminate that sham issue."

A few days later, a new judge, Robert Burnett, was selected. Because Berg believed that Burnett was a close friend of Gregory's and because Burnett's venue was two hundred miles north of Houston, at Fort Worth, Berg may have inadvertently made matters worse for himself. If the case had to be retried, Berg wanted it tried in Houston, where, he said, the Wyatts would "have hell finding a jury that doesn't know about the first verdict."

But what he really wanted was to avoid a new trial altogether, and in May he did what he had long said was unthinkable. He sent a settlement proposal to the Wyatts. The letter, Berg says, explained that Robert would be "willing to split the assets in the estate."

The notion that prideful Robert would consider any form of settlement was shocking. Never mind that the case had gone on for seven years or that Robert was too embarrassed to specify how much he had spent fighting the suit, except that it was hundreds of thousands of dollars.

Robert made the offer but was dubious about the likelihood of a settlement. "Oscar takes great pride in his reputation of being so ruthless, and he uses that to his advantage when he's negotiating," said Robert. Robert could as well have been talking about himself when he added, "I'm not sure that Oscar would ever want to settle, lest someone say he gave in."

Lynn Wyatt, meanwhile, made her annual trip to Cap Ferrat. On this birthday, her fifty-seventh, her party's theme was Diamonds and Denim, which received the usual laudatory coverage in *Women's Wear Daily.*

But her trip was interrupted when she discovered that she had an ovarian tumor. Oscar sent a plane to pick her up and take her first to a hospital in Switzerland, where tests were run, and then home to M. D. Anderson hospital in Houston for surgery.

Lynn called her mother from the hospital and said she wanted Ann to know before she heard it from someone else that she was at M. D. Anderson hospital, had had a cancerous tumor removed, and was doing fine.

When Ann relayed the news to Robert, he decided to visit Lynn at the hospital. Ann and Laura went with him. "We didn't say anything about any situation," says Robert. "We just talked about her health. When I was leaving she wanted me to come over and give her a hug but it was extremely awkward."

When word spread quickly throughout Texas and New York that Lynn was at M. D. Anderson, world renowned as a cancer hospital, friends on either side of the family suggested that Lynn's illness should be a lesson to both sides of the battling family.

"I hope Oscar realizes he brought on Lynn's sickness," said a close friend of Steve Wyatt's. "This is what Oscar has put his wife through and his family through."

A friend of Robert's insisted, "This is what she gets for allowing Oscar to sue her brother."

Lynn, meanwhile, was quickly up on her feet, talking about her "clean bill of health," and headed back to Cap Ferrat. "My doctor wants me to get some rest there."

Her doctor is obviously not a follower of the world's society columns.

Judge Burnett in Fort Worth set an October 26, 1992, date for the new trial, while Berg continued to seek a remedy to what he termed "the squirrel cage Robert is in where he can't get away from Judge Gregory and his minions."

In September, Berg filed his last motion to have a federal court judge stay the proceedings in state court and halt the scheduled retrial. The motion asked Federal Judge Melinda Harmon to rule unconstitutional the manner in which the case had been moved from Gregory's court to Burnett's, and to send it back to Texas Supreme Court Justice Phillips for a fair hearing on whether to recuse Gregory.

Berg believed that a favorable ruling by Harmon was his last chance to stop the case from being tried in October. If Judge Harmon ruled against Berg's motion, there was a good chance the case would be tried in Burnett's court, where Berg was convinced he would lose "on an unlevel playing field."

But Berg was not relying only on Judge Harmon. In October, Robert and Douglas and their attorneys entered into settlement discussions through a third-party mediator. At issue was Robert's refusal to step down as trustee of Bernard's estate.

"If we can reach some settlement that gives my mother her property she's been waiting for for eleven years, I'll do it," Robert said. But he added, "Oscar and Lynn won't agree to the probate of the will because then I'd have to be the trustee."

In October, Douglas's attorney Tom McDade had made very clear his position on Robert as trustee of Bernard's estate: "I would never allow any client of mine to do anything with or have anything to do with a situation where Bobby Sakowitz was in a fiduciary position. Period."

J. P. Smith, now watching from the sidelines, said he understood why a settlement was so difficult. "The Wyatts' constant refrain is that when Bobby gets around money it always ends up in his pocket. Ergo, we don't want him to have any more.

"Robert thinks that [if he resigns the trusteeship] and walks down the street people will point at him . . . that he will have sullied the Sakowitz name."

But by October 13, Robert's fifty-fourth birthday, McDade and Berg had drawn settlement papers, and Berg spoke as though a settlement was likely.

From the start, this case had played in the court of public opinion, and that was not likely to change. Two seemingly innocuous sentences that appeared in Betsy Parish's society column in the *Houston Post* were all it took for Berg to cry foul and threaten to call off settlement negotiations.

On October 18, just eight days before the scheduled trial date, Parish wrote: "Whether a recent out-of-court settlement did or did not include legal instructions not to disclose details of the transactions is not the question, folks. It's whether the payor knows the payee is blabbing it all over town."

It was up to the reader to decipher what she meant. Berg, who seemed increasingly to see a bogeyman under every bed, thought he understood Parish perfectly.

Berg feared that Judge Harmon might assume the case was settled and not make a ruling. He wanted her to issue a stay because, although settlement discussions were well under way, they could still fall apart. But just four days later, on October 22, Berg was notified that Judge Harmon had made a decision. Berg telephoned Robert to pick him up at the Federal Court. Robert was waiting in his big Sakowitz-green BMW in front of the courthouse when Berg walked out, still reading the order. "I looked up at him," recalls Berg, "and said, 'We got it.'"

Robert started shouting, "No lawyer would ever have stuck with me this long. You're unbelievably tenacious."

Then, suddenly, both men started crying. "It was just such a huge relief," says Berg.

The Thursday-afternoon ruling stayed all proceedings in the case, which had been scheduled to go to a new trial the following Monday. The ruling sent the case to the Texas Supreme Court Chief Justice, who would then send the case to a district judge for another hearing on Robert's motion to disqualify Judge Gregory. Harmon said in her ruling that there is "a substantial likelihood that Sakowitz can show at a hearing in an unbiased forum that Judge Gregory was disqualified from granting a motion for a new trial."

The stay gave Berg new leverage to get a settlement acceptable to Robert, and by January 3 both sides had signed secret settlement papers. Finally, on February 18, 1993, the lawsuit that had been filed five and a half years earlier was dismissed by the court.

Under the confidential agreement, the assets of the Bernard Sakowitz estate were to be divided and the estate dissolved. Robert avoided the humiliation of stepping down as trustee (since there was no longer an estate), something Berg had sworn his client would never do. And he would not suffer the penalties that might have been assessed had *Wyatt v. Sakowitz* gone to trial again and he lost.

But while the case was settled, no one — most especially Robert — expected the conclusion of *Wyatt v. Sakowitz* to put an end to ill will on both sides. Robert had said at the end of the trial in 1991 that a reuniting with his sister was not "in the cards," and after the settlement he insisted that his once loving relationship with Lynn was "irrevocably shattered."

Nor did Robert expect the conclusion of *Wyatt v. Sakowitz* to end what he calls Oscar's attacks on him. Prior to the settlement, Robert said he suspected that even if this case were settled, Oscar will "try and trump up something in the future" in another court. "He wants to destroy me, and all I'm trying to do is defend my family."

David Berg tried to put a happier face on the settlement: "The families aren't going to Bar Mitzvahs together, but they're not fighting anymore," he quipped.

But if Lynn and Robert sighed with relief over the settlement, hoping that finally they could put this lawsuit out of their minds once and for all, they were wrong. In a chilling turn of events, in January 1993, the same month that *Wyatt v. Sakowitz* was settled, Judge Pat Gregory was indicted on state theft charges and federal money-laundering charges.

The charges, which were unsealed in March 1993, stem from a 1988 transaction in which Gregory allegedly deposited a $5,000 check from a charitable foundation into his personal bank account when, in fact, the check was intended for a probate school Gregory operates. The state charge, which pertains to the theft itself, carries a penalty of ten years in prison and a $10,000 fine; the federal charge, which pertains to what Gregory allegedly did with the money, carries a maximum punishment of twenty years in prison and a $250,000 fine.

In addition, according to the *Houston Chronicle*, "Sources said that the federal investigation involves allegations that Gregory provided or offered to provide preferential treatment to parties involved in cases before his court in exchange for financial consideration. Investigators found that Gregory had 41 bank accounts, sources said."

David Berg has long suspected that the Wyatts influenced Gregory to throw out the verdict in *Wyatt v. Sakowitz* and grant a new trial, and he now says he will wait and see what if any charges may be made involving Gregory's handling of the Sakowitz case. If it were proven that Judge Gregory had acted improperly in the Sakowitz case, a new trial could be granted. But Berg says that because the case has been settled, the chances of Berg's agreeing to a new trial are "zero."

How ironic it must seem to Robert, after spending seven days defending himself in Gregory's courtroom against charges of abuse of power as a corporate officer and as a trustee, that the man who sat in judgment of him has been accused of overstepping the boundaries of his own enormous power by taking funds that were not his.

Asked how he felt about Gregory's indictment, Robert was uncharacteristically concise. Paraphrasing Neville Chamberlain, Robert called it "Justice in our time."

While the lawsuit may soon fade from public memory, no one expects that its participants' names will disappear from the press around the world.

After Steve Wyatt's scandal in January 1992 — when the photographs of him and Fergie were discovered in his London flat — he was careful to keep his name out of the papers. But a year later, he was back on the front pages. On February 7, 1993, London's *News of the World* in two-inch headlines announced, WYATT DID HAVE A FLING WITH FERGIE.

The newspaper, in an excerpt from a new book, quoted Fergie's father, Major Ronald Ferguson, saying to the author, Lesley Player, who was also his mistress at the time: "Sarah is unhappy and I am going through hell with her. I told you she wasn't having an affair with Steve Wyatt. Well she is — and she doesn't want to be with Andrew anymore."

In the book, *My Story: The Duchess of York, Her Father and Me*, Player says that when she asked Ronald Ferguson how long Fergie and Steve's affair had been going on, the major replied, "Several months."

Lesley was deeply hurt to learn that Steve had been seeing Fergie at the same time he had been seeing her. "It meant that all the time Steven had been saying those beautiful things to me, creating my trust, building my hopes," writes Lesley, "he had been two-timing me — and indeed Sarah too, no doubt whispering the same words of romance and intimacy into her ear as they lay in that same room and that same bed."

Player goes on to say that around this same time, Major Ferguson told her that Steve had asked for a lunch with him at

London's tony hotel Claridge's. According to Player, Major Ferguson told her, "It was the oddest thing [about Steve]: he kept saying how wonderful I was, and how much he had heard about me. He was being very open about his love for Sarah, and talking to me as if I was a future father-in-law!"

Having made his reputation in London, Steve was already on his way to becoming a celebrity in Washington and New York. When Lynn threw a party for Steve at the fashionable restaurant Mortimer's, it was carefully chronicled by the society press. And his sighting at Elaine's one weekend with a woman other than the Duchess was picked up by *Newsday* in an article titled "Fergie Forsaken?"

Douglas Wyatt's name too seems likely soon to explode in the press. Wyatt watchers are eagerly awaiting his testimony about Eternal Values when Roger Hall's case against the *Houston Chronicle* — scheduled for October 1993 — comes to trial.

Hall said in March 1993 that his lawyers, in addition to involving Douglas in his suit against the *Chronicle*, also plan to take Lynn's deposition.

Oscar's speeches at oil industry events will doubtless continue to build his reputation as the most outrageous and outspoken man in the oil patch. Some thought he would have difficulty again offending as many people as he had in 1991 in Corpus Christi, but he may have surpassed himself in late 1992 in a speech accusing the Bush administration of colluding with Persian Gulf "potentates" to keep oil prices down. "I hope this winter is so cold," he snapped, "that people in the north, when they let their dog out will have to use an ice pick to chip him away from the tree."

Oscar's long history of business dealings with unpopular Middle East countries will also continue to place him at the center of controversy — as evidenced in March 1993, when Coastal Corporation's vice president and general counsel, Michael Beatty, withdrew his nomination to become the Clinton administration's deputy energy secretary. Although Oscar had campaigned long and hard for Bill Clinton for president — and against George Bush — and Beatty is a personal friend and supporter of Clinton's, Beatty's bid for the energy post ran into strong opposition from relatives of Pan Am Flight 103 bombing victims who were angered because of Coastal's business ties to Libya, which is suspected of complicity in the bombing.

Even if Oscar's trip to Iraq to free the hostages was for human-itarian purposes, as Oscar has maintained, in the long run the mission had failed to make him a hero — at least in the eyes of some Americans.

Nevertheless, Oscar still works as tirelessly as always and can be expected to continue to build Coastal by devouring other companies, as well as in other ways, designed, as he points out, not to make friends but profits.

At home and abroad, few are those willing to bet against Oscar's future. Since he entered the oil business half a century ago, he has grown tougher, more surefooted, and richer despite the staggering setback of Lo-Vaca, which would have destroyed most other men. As the new century is about to begin and major companies of all kinds — Exxon, Chevron, General Motors, and Sears — are run by committees, Coastal is still run by one man and will continue to be until he decide otherwise. Like Lynn, Oscar Wyatt is a winner, which is what both of them determined to be from the beginning.

Although Lynn had been fearful that the family fight would hurt her image and lessen her publicity, it has, in fact, made her even more widely known, and press interest in her continues unabated. She will probably continue her major international fund-raising activities and top herself again in 1993 with her Cap Ferrat birthday party in July.

Robert Sakowitz, throughout *Wyatt v. Sakowitz,* as throughout most of his life, had the press on his side, and there seems little likelihood that this will change. He continues to live in his River Oaks Boulevard mansion, which continues to be listed for sale. A bigger problem for the man who once complained of not having a "big pencil" and now has no pencil at all seems to be what he will do with the remainder of his life. He could take a page out of his grandfather Tobias's book, who when his Galveston store was wiped out in the 1915 hurricane built a business many times bigger. It is obvious that Robert still has much of the drive and ambition he had when he first began at Sakowitz more than three decades ago.

The Wyatts and the Sakowitzes seem destined to remain public figures because they illustrate significant aspects of America's history in the twentieth century: the beginning and the end of important, privately owned, local businesses in America; the importance of the oil business to America, both financially and politically; and the inextricable symbiosis of fashion, society, philanthropy, and publicity.

As 1993 began, each of the three main participants had reached a significant moment. Oscar was nearing his seventieth year. Lynn's ovarian cancer had given her a brush with mortality. Robert, like his grandfather, now knew what it was to lose a business and have to start again.

Fierce interfamily feuds, greed for riches, and strong sibling envy exist, of course, in all families, but in rich families there are both the power and the time to indulge these passions prodigiously. For three generations, members of the Wyatt/Sakowitz family have — sometimes with volcanic force — illustrated both the best and the worst in human nature.

One particular family lawsuit has been settled, but its underlying psychological causes, on both sides, may be stronger than ever. For the moment, an ocean separates Steve and Fergie, and United Nations sanctions against Iraq prevent Oscar from dealing with Saddam Hussein. But this blood rich family's successes and scandals have for generations made international headlines and they will again. The story has not ended.

Notes

The following abbreviations are used throughout the notes:

Berg — David Berg
Bryan — Pamela Zauderer Bryan
DEPO — Deposition
HC — *Houston Chronicle*
HP — *Houston Post*
INT — Interview by Jane Wolfe
Johnson — Gaylord Johnson, Jr.
LSW — Lynn Sakowitz Wyatt
OSW — Oscar Wyatt
OSW v. RTS — Oscar Wyatt's lawsuit against Robert Sakowitz
Renken — Val Renken
RTS — Robert Sakowitz
Sackton — Alexander Sackton
Smith — James Patrick Smith
TM — *Texas Monthly*
VF — *Vanity Fair*
Waldrop — Carol Waldrop
W. v. S. — *Wyatt v. Sakowitz*

CHAPTER 1

3 "She was being torn apart": LSW DEPO, *W. v. S.*, 5-14-91.
5 "while cheating his family": *OSW v. RTS.*
5 "she walked out of the room": LSW DEPO, *W. v. S.*, 5-14-91.
5 "Bobby's 'plunder'": Ibid.
6 "considering resigning her directorship": LSW DEPO, *W. v. S.*
6 "the stock assignment . . . appealed to her": Ibid.
6 "He refused the stock assignment": LSW DEPO, p. 115.

9 "Douglas Wyatt was scrambling to block it": INT Joan Kehlhof.

9 "a process-server slapped him with a lawsuit": INT RTS.

9 "he should talk with Douglas . . . she told her brother": INT RTS.

9 "thought himself more like an older brother": Ibid.

CHAPTER 2

13 "Leib . . . to make their home in Galveston": Much information about Leib and Leah comes from Alex Sackton.

16 "he and Simon . . . able to pay off the balance": INT Sackton.

17 "just-opened Houston Ship Channel": Houston history from *Houston: A Student's Guide to Localized History*.

20 "never in serious danger of losing the store": INT Sackton.

21 "Tobe felt safer having the farm": INT Toby Sackton.

CHAPTER 3

23 "pressured him not to marry her": INT Margaret Sackton Rosan.

24 "Bernard didn't like Ruth": INT Johnson.

25 "thought his salary was less than it should have been": INT Sackton.

25 "changed his name from von Birnbaum": INT Dora Baum Axelrod.

26 "when Ann first met him she was not immediately attracted": Ann Sakowitz's testimony, *W. v. S.*

26 "Mommy, let me do it this way": *HP*, 11-13-88.

27 "Alex changed his last name to Sackton": INT Sackton.

27 "theirs was an acrimonious relationship": INT Johnson.

29 "you had become part of that family": INT C. C. Eckhoff.

30 "institute a similar policy at the University of Houston": INT Johnson.

31 "founders of the Houston Country Club": INT Harriet Bath.

CHAPTER 4

34 "young Bobby his first retail idea": INT RTS.

35 "classmates called him anti-Semitic names": Ibid.

35 "to defend himself, he learned to box": Ibid.

35 "think of all the dresses you would get": INT Bryan.

36 "we were more partial to [Robert]": testimony of Ann Sakowitz at *W. v. S.*, 10-8-91.

36 "not bring himself to hit her back": Ibid.

36 "she was my baby sister": INT RTS.

36 "one summer at camp in Maine": *W*, 9-9-83.

37   "her most attractive traits were already developed": INT Jackie Pope Aldredge.

38   "stereotypical New Yorkers": INT RTS.

39   "married somebody that nobody in the family thought was good": INT Toby Sackton.

41   "counted the cars that went by": INT RTS.

42   "everyone at Harvard had heard of Neiman-Marcus": INT Peter Miller.

42   "was vexing to Bob": INT Richard Marcus.

43   "Rockefeller, especially, had an impact": *TM*, "The Fraying Empire of Robert Sakowitz," Alison Cook, 12-85, p. 232.

43   "did everything — art, architecture": Ibid.

43   "He was drinking when we got married": *VF*, "Oscar Wyatt's Private War," Marie Brenner, 4-91, p. 218.

44   "that is where Bobby Lipman began hanging out": INT Donald Waugh.

44   "She looked like a hooker": INT Bill Flemming.

45   "Lipman was really treating her badly": *People* magazine interview of RTS by Ann Maier, 10-10-91.

45   "weren't very happy to have her back": INT Raymond Howard.

45   "Bernard put a stop to his visits": INT RTS.

46   "I'll get married and get enough money for both of us": INT Raymond Howard.

CHAPTER 5

48   "mechanic for the local Gulf States": *VF*, Marie Brenner, 4-91, p. 219.

48   "scrimped and saved": Ibid.

49   "He was a tough, aggressive kid": INT Robert Nemir.

49   "the only time Eva would get out": INT Elizabeth Lucas.

49   "leaving home in the middle of the night": INT Leonard Coleman.

51   "my father-in-law acted the same way Oscar does": INT W. S. Conklin.

51   "always flying off at the mouth": INT Neblett Davis.

51   "Everyone called him 'Chink'": INT John Ratcliff.

51   "not be uncomfortable breaking the rules": Ibid.

52   "frequently called for holding": INT C. W. Lucas.

52   "I'm going to get an education . . . give my mother everything": INT Jessie Mae Chappell.

54   "If he can get into heaven . . .": INT Leonard Coleman.

54   "In Okinawa, I had been ordered": *VF*, 4-91, p. 220.

55   "learned the history of virtually every gas field": *TM*, "Power Politics," Paul Burka, 5-75.

55   "Hole after hole": *San Antonio Express-News*, 8-25-74.

56   "Wymore was sued twice": *San Antonio Express-News*, 9-29-74.

57   "pipeline companies . . . their own rationing": *TM*, 5-75, p. 71. Paul Burka's article "Power Politics" is a major source of information on much of Oscar's early years in the gas business.

57   "town lot operator was still much better off selling gas . . . to Oscar": Ibid.

58   "Charges of meter tampering": Ibid., p. 72.

58   "Mr. Wyatt was a go-getter": INT Guy Thompson.

59   "a mattress strapped to his back": *TM*, "Dog Eat Dog," Jan Jarboe, 4-91, p. 154.

CHAPTER 6

61   "how badly CPS wanted cheap gas": INT Leroy Denman.

62   "Board watched nervously": Ibid.

63   "aimed a loaded shotgun": *Corpus Christi Caller-Times*, 8-5-60.

63   "Oscar developed a larger block of voters": *TM*, 5-75, p. 75.

64   "started their motor during the race?": *TM*, 4-91, p. 158.

65   "guests of the Mexican Oil Company": INT Jack Manley.

65   "Bonnie and Jack had had a stormy": Ibid.

66   " 'a dollop of honey' before making love": *Chicago Tribune*, 9-16-73.

66   "it was Oscar who had bugged his room": INT Jack Manley.

67   "Oscar filed a divorce document": *O. S. Wyatt Jr. v. Bonnie Bolding Wyatt*.

67   "Oscar and Bonnie were mad": INT Patty Taliaferro.

68   " 'We're leaving,' he shouted": Ibid.

69   "pleaded guilty to being drunk": *Austin American Statesman*, 7-9-78.

69   "whose house I tore up one night": INT Patty Taliaferro.

69   "bug in Bonnie's station wagon": INT Jack Manley.

70   "settlement of $1 million": INT Bill Hudson.

70   "give me the rights to your life story": *VF*, 4-91, p. 218.

71   "I just love oil and oilmen": *Chicago Tribune*, 9-16-73.

CHAPTER 7

72   "People would come up and volunteer to my father": INT RTS.

73   "you've never proposed to me": *VF*, 4-91, p. 218.

73   "demanded that Oscar give her $1 million": LSW DEPO, *W. v. S.*, 5-14-91.

73   "Oscar's young company made a $9 million profit": *Forbes*, 11-15-63.

74 "reportedly for $400,000": *Corpus Christi Caller-Times*, 11-26-63.

75 "Oscar had given her the house as a wedding gift": INT John Astin Perkins.

78 "Oscar started really cutting down Lynn": INT Tom Marsh.

78 "sex with Palm Beach's old grandes dames": INT Donald Waugh.

79 "He loved to mention his penis": INT Philip Van Rensselaer.

CHAPTER 8

80 "talk of a buy-out began": INT RTS.

81 "$4 million for the stock": INT Johnson, INT RTS.

82 "store could afford to pay dividends": INT Toby Sackton.

83 "where they lunched with Richard Burbridge": *TM*, 12-85, p. 234.

84 "'André, wait just a minute'": *Houston City*, "Robert Sakowitz: The Man Behind the Name," Jan Short, 8-83, p. 49.

86 "They . . . resented the fact we moved to Houston": INT Lawrence Marcus.

87 "Marcuses became fearful that with a death": INT Richard Marcus.

88 "We didn't know a rabbi": INT Bryan.

90 "the most opinionated son-of-a-bitch": Ibid.

91 "Oh, serene cowboy": *HC*, Maxine Messinger, 1-30-69.

92 "there was the deed to this beautiful house": Oscar deeded the house to Lynn in November 1969. This quote comes from the book *Only the Best* by Stuart Jacobson (published by Abrams, 1985).

93 "My father thought the world of Bobby": INT Sackton.

94 "Mr. Tobias . . . moved by the gesture to close the store": INT Waldrop.

CHAPTER 9

96 "cerebral hemorrhage": (London) *Evening Standard*, 9-20-67.

96 "editors would refrain from publishing": Press Association memo, 9-24-67.

97 "didn't recollect anything about the murder": INT Paul Orth.

98 "a very tall man had been prosecuted": (London) *Daily Telegraph*, 10-11-68.

99 "trip to hell on . . . STP": (London) *Evening News*, 10-7-68.

99 "I felt myself shooting out into space": (London) *Daily Mail*, 10-8-68.

101 "I was so removed from Bobby Lipman": *VF*, 4-91, p. 218.

101 "Van Rensselaer and Robert first met in Athens": INT Philip Van Rensselaer.

102 "Sakowitz family has told conflicting stories": INT Nigel Dempster.

102 "it suits Oscar and Lynn to say that Lipman is dead": Ibid.

102 "In a book published in 1993": the book is *The Duchess of York, Her Father and Me* by Lesley Player.

CHAPTER 10

103 "he obtained a $75 million line of credit": *TM*, 5-75, p. 81.

103 "1966, Coastal warned publicly": *TM*, 5-75, p. 82.

104 "1968, when Coastal curtailed delivery": Ibid.

104 "He's a master at bluff": INT Leroy Denman.

105 "By 1972, Coastal was selling . . . interstate pipeline": *TM*, 5-75, p. 86.

105 "also making lucrative brokerage deals": Ibid., p. 87.

106 "That was an absolute lie": INT Lowell Lebermann.

110 "He 'would just wander through the house'": *VF*, 4-91, p. 223.

110 "kept the judge 'on a retainer fee as a lawyer'": *Corpus Christi Caller-Times*, 1-15-77.

111 "Oscar was interested in buying Alex's shares": INT Sackton.

111 "the estate would be split fifty-fifty": INT RTS.

111 "he was an honorable man": Oscar Wyatt DEPO, *W. v. S.*, 9-21-91.

112 "the store was so overextended": INT Harry Berkowitz.

113 "Bailey visited Robert at his office": INT Waldrop.

CHAPTER 11

120 "Pam was still deep in mourning": INT Bryan.

123 "It had been a wedding gift from her mother": Ibid.

124 "how to reach the detective": RTS DEPO in *Sakowitz v. Sakowitz*.

124 "Robert secretly planted the bug": Ibid.

125 "together they removed the tape from the phone box": Ibid.

126 "So come live with us": INT RTS.

127 "so prejudiced the jury that he called for a mistrial": INT Bryan.

127 "investigation into the legalities of his wiretapping": Ibid.

CHAPTER 12

130 "Robert would come out with beautiful speeches": INT Albert Lidji.

133 "he personally had a stake in . . . deals": RTS testimony *W. v. S.*

133 "never told Berkowitz . . . he had a . . . stake": INT Harry Berkowitz.

133 "Every time I go to the bathroom": Ibid.

134 "stock was by giving us the store's [customer] list": INT Gary Easterly.

136 "we would never ... have gotten internationally known": Ann Sakowitz DEPO, *W. v. S.*

138 "a bankrupt Oscar Wyatt than have a warm home this winter": *Corpus Christi Caller-Times*, 12-5-76.

138 "$115 million in Valero preferred stock": *Forbes*, 8-21-78.

139 "Oscar retained his $262,000-a-year chairmanship": Ibid.

139 "Coastal collected a $60 million profit from crude oil trading": *TM*, "Oscar's Follies," Harry Hurt, III, 12-81, p. 198.

CHAPTER 13

148 "thousands of paparazzi": Pat Hackett, *The Andy Warhol Diaries*, Warner Books, 1989, p. 292.

149 "criminal indictments against four major energy": *TM*, 2-78, p. 57.

150 "entering this plea of guilty freely": *United States of America v. Oscar S. Wyatt, Jr.*, Criminal No. H-80-3, 9-25-81.

150 "paid the government a refund of $9 million": *Corpus Christi Caller-Times*, 1-12-80.

151 "ironclad $19 million contract": *Austin American Statesman*, 7-9-78.

151 "spent $3,000 suing the government": *WSJ*, 2-2-84.

152 "Wyatt enjoyed the respect, confidence and esteem": *Oscar Wyatt v. James R. Pierobon.*

CHAPTER 14

154 "contrary to the agreement he had made with Bernard": OSW DEPO, *W. v. S.*, 9-21-91.

154 "share and share alike": Ibid.

156 "Sakowitz has gone into the furniture business": INT Chuck Griffin.

157 "continued to do most of my shopping at ... Neiman's": INT Nancy Lemmon.

157 "Oscar changed into red flannel pajamas": INT Betty Ewing.

159 "I was just waiting for Fred Astaire": *ULTRA*, "Riviera Retreat," Joetta Moulden, 7-89.

160 "he shouted obscenities and slugged": *New York Post*, 2-23-83.

160 "You little bitch bastard": *New York Post*, 2-24-83.

161 "he did not hit him": Ibid.

161 "Lynn should have ... stayed in Houston": *New York Daily News*, "By Suzy," 2-25-83.

161 "When my wife is in New York": *HC*, 3-17-83.

164 "She is a small size 4": INT Bill Blass.

CHAPTER 15

168 "the Alfalfa Club has never asked me": *VF*, 4-91.

170 "Oscar had personally written a check to Texaco": INT George Parker.

170 "U.S. Steel is the most immoral fucking": INT Jeff Dorrell.

170 "I know some Greek guy you fucked": INT Christina Zilker.

171 "Cancer? Hmmm": *TM*, 4-91.

171 "He has a powerful sexual magnetism": INT Nancy Holmes.

172 "Oscar screwed him to the wall": INT William Garrett.

173 "I do all that jet-setting horseshit": *TM*, 4-91.

176 "My mother is the sexiest": Douglas Wyatt's comments to the author.

176 "Lynn . . . described Steve as her 'love object'": *Tattler*, by Christa D'Souza.

CHAPTER 16

178 "Is that all we make?" INT RTS.

179 "We rewrote the script every day": INT Waldrop.

179 "whoever got to Robert last": Ibid.

182 "bankers and advisors told him not to open in Tulsa": INT Renken.

182 "He first moved the million dollars out of Sakowitz": RTS testimony, *W. v. S.*

182 "knew how to cut a fat hog": *New York* magazine, "Texas Crude," John Taylor, 11-4-91.

182 "don't have to worry about say, quarterly reports to shareholders": *Southwest*, 10-81.

183 "if we all vote for him to murder somebody": LSW DEPO, *W. v. S.*, 5-14-91.

184 "fairy tale for a girl from Deer Park": *HP*, 7-27-86.

185 "She just stood there onstage": INT Waldrop.

186 "He bought a mansion": The house was purchased in the name of attorney Fred S. Murray, according to the deed to the house, which was filed with the Harris County Clerk's office in November 1984.

186 "The store paid for some of it": INT Gary Easterly.

187 "had to return $600,000": INT Waldrop.

187 "hard to get along with": INT Mark Carnes.

189 "dispatched two corporate detectives to trail him": *WSJ*, 2-2-84.

189 "$26 million when CSX gave Coastal": Ibid.

189 "with a $42.1 million 'peace payment'": *WSJ*, 2-15-84.

190 "ANR resisted the takeover bid": *New York Times*, 3-4-85.

191 "Oscar may do the craziest things": INT Joan Kehlhof.

CHAPTER 17

194   "never, ever thought they would call the note": RTS testimony, *W. v. S.*

197   "He committed the oldest sin": *Business Week,* "How Bobby Sakowitz Took an Escalator to the Basement," 8-19-85.

197   "he said the press was 'negative'": *TM,* 12-85.

198   "cowboy, who's gonna pay it?" *People* interview of RTS by Ann Maier.

198   "called his uncle Alex Sackton": INT Sackton.

199   "he believed certain parts of the expansion program were ill-advised": OSW DEPO, *W. v. S.*

200   "viability of the corporation was virtually nil": Ibid.

201   "income of only $1 million": *HP,* 2-2-86.

202   "no payment from Robert was forthcoming": *OSW v. RTS.*

202   "Oscar charged that Robert 'lived off Sakowitz'": Ibid.

203   "peace seems to torment his soul": *HC,* 12-20-86.

204   "intervened in Oscar's lawsuit": INT Pat Hughes.

204   "Mecom shook his head. . . . 'If all I had to live on'": *TM,* 4-91.

205   "Douglas . . . was trying to block the merger": INT Joan Kehlhof.

206   "Bobby . . . bought these sewer rights": INT Toby Sackton.

206   "he did not seek his family's participation": *HC,* 10-5-91.

CHAPTER 18

208   "touted as the leader of the cult": Roger Hall DEPO, *W. v. S.*

209   "All women are selfish cunts": Ibid.

209   "He will buy everything for you": *VF,* "East Side Alien," Marie Brenner, 3-90.

211   "your soul's report card": INT Roger Hall.

212   "his life reading as 'amazingly accurate'": Douglas Wyatt DEPO, *W. v. S.*

212   "they met over tea at Frederick's apartment": Ibid.

212   "You see how terrible your families are?": *VF,* 3-90.

212   "Don't become a cock worshipper": Ibid.

213   "In Douglas's case, she was . . . brunette model": INT Roger Hall.

213   "he needed $20,000 to pay his taxes": Douglas Wyatt DEPO, *W. v. S.*

214   "sleeping on a straw mat . . . next to Frederick's bed": INT Roger Hall.

214   "Lynn purchased $70,000 worth of . . . gems": LSW DEPO, *W. v. S.*

214   "You incarnated as a Jew": Roger Hall DEPO, *W. v. S.*

216   "your friend Frederick died of AIDS": Douglas Wyatt DEPO, *W. v. S.*

216   "what he took to be a pass at him by Douglas": INT Roger Hall.

CHAPTER 19

218 "check *everything* with me": RTS testimony in *W. v. S.*

219 "we knew that Oscar had been having affairs": Ann Sakowitz DEPO, *W. v. S.*, 5-17-91.

220 "She called back and said . . . I did have to pay it": Ibid.

221 "like the Mario Puzo characters": INT RTS.

221 "no reason to deprive his family of the new home": Ibid.

221 "Robert agreed to give Oscar . . . $412,000": *HC*, 3-17-90.

221 "he reportedly paid his attorney $500,000": INT Berg. Note: Although the source of information on the $500,000 is David Berg, Berg was not Robert's lawyer in Oscar's suit against Robert.

224 "Douglas, however, insisted he . . . bring Susan Bearden": INT Roger Hall.

227 "'Last 9 days' said notices in the paper": *Houston Press*, 8-2-90.

CHAPTER 20

229 "But you're really Bob Lipman's son": INT Bill Teeter.

229 "Steve threw up his fists": INT Luke Fullen.

230 "once made love in the bathroom": *Globe*, 4-7-92.

230 "Lynn was horrified . . . I was expecting": Ibid.

231 "to be with the rhythms of the day": Ibid.

231 "Steve . . . became a Christian": INT Karen Fertitta.

232 "Fergie's car was seen outside Steve's . . . flat": *Fergie Confidential*, by Chris Hutchins and Peter Thompson, p. 176.

232 "Steve then took her to a comedy": Ibid., p. 177.

232 "She's a straight-up girl": *VF*, 4-91.

233 "riding horses through the olive groves . . . lounging comfortably on a swing": *Fergie Confidential*, p. 178.

233 "a cross between Bobby Ewing": *Tattler*, Christa D'Souza.

234 "Lynn checked herself into . . . the Hotel Plaza Athenee": *Fergie Confidential*, p. 187.

234 "dinner . . . for Steve and Dr. Ramzi Salman": Ibid., p. 181.

CHAPTER 21

236 "correct the president's image as a wobbly wimp": *TM*, 4-91, p. 217.

237 "makes the mistake of attacking [Iraq]": *Financial World*, 1-8-91.

237 "their chicken shit conflicts": *TM*, 4-91, p. 156.

237 "Guys like me like Iraq": Ibid.

238 "never bringing the oil to U.S. shores": *Wall Street Journal*, 3-11-91.

239 "sending subtle . . . signals": Ibid.

244 "clipping the columns of . . . Maxine Messinger": *TM*, 12-81.
245 "slaves of an Arab monarch": *TM*, 4-91, p. 126.
245 "You'd have thought I had AIDS": Ibid., p. 127.
246 "might starve them first": *Dallas Morning News*, 5-10-91, p. 18A.
247 "introducing himself . . . as 'Sarah's friend'": *Fergie Confidential*, p. 190.
247 "a report about Steve's party was filed at Scotland Yard": Ibid., p. 191.

CHAPTER 22

249 *"he's killed Oscar"*: INT Berg.
250 "six-figure flat fee that he had to borrow": Ibid.
250 "asked Douglas to get his mother . . . to buy the Eternal Values stones": Roger Hall DEPO, *W. v. S.*, 7-22-91.
250 "Roger called Lynn himself": Ibid.
251 "the biggest break of his life": INT Roger Hall.
252 "to fight Jews in government": *HC*, 9-1-91.

CHAPTER 23

257 "failure is the only thing I'm terrified of": *VF*, 4-91.
257 "shouldn't have settled the case with him": Ibid.
260 "Robert's wealth . . . $2 million": INT Berg.
262 "testicles of a brass monkey": *Houston Press*, 6-7-90.
262 "swore to punch Smith in the nose": INT Smith.

CHAPTER 24

269 "Robert had instructed him to do an inventory": INT Renken.
270 "If you testify, I'll destroy you": Ibid.
270 "basic Wyatt bulldog master plan": *Houston Press*, Tim Fleck, 10-3-91.

CHAPTER 25

274 "look like you're scared to death": INT Smith.
274 "Douglas had offered to settle": INT Berg.
275 "$99,433 annual salary": *HC*, 5-5-91, p. 1.
277 "Berg wanted minorities": INT Berg.
277 "going to have a coronary": INT Smith.
279 "good deals always fell in his pocket": OSW DEPO, *W. v. S.*
280 "felt as though he was back at Sakowitz": INT Berg.

CHAPTER 26

284 "She put the pain of testifying": INT Smith.

286 "go jump all over her": INT Andy Vickery.

288 "Ann cut short the length of her stay": INT Renken.

CHAPTER 27

293 "Berg had never prepared harder": INT Berg.

300 "Michelle's involvement . . . extended beyond merely covering the trial": INT Berg.

300 "we were out-lawyered": INT Trey Wyatt.

300 "Steve's phone call may have been premature": Ibid.

CHAPTER 28

302 "Gregory spent part of his . . . holidays": INT RTS.

303 "her 'big-time' jewelry": INT Jerry Zipkin.

305 "Berg would not charge Robert any further fee": INT Berg.

305 "Berg just the ammunition he wanted": Ibid.

305 "Michelle's first move . . . a call to Judge Gregory": Michelle Smith DEPO, *Robert Sakowitz v. Judge Pat Gregory*.

306 "She had discussed with him his Motion for a New Trial": Ibid.

307 "asking Gregory for a summary judgment": INT Andy Vickery.

CHAPTER 29

308 "I think she's trying to become much quieter": INT Robert Clark.

312 "Steve . . . knew . . . he would have to make a statement": INT Karen Fertitta.

315 "accused Berg of creating a sham issue": *HC*, 5-12-92.

315 "sent a settlement proposal to the Wyatts": INT Berg.

316 "lest someone say he gave in": INT RTS.

317 "his last chance to stop the case from being tried in October": INT Berg.

317 "Robert thinks that [if he resigns the trusteeship] and walks down the street": INT Smith.

318 "Berg feared that Judge Harmon might assume the case was settled": INT Berg.

319 "Oscar will 'try and trump up something in the future'": INT RTS.

319 "Gregory was indicted on state theft charges": *HC*, 3-16-93.

319 "Gregory provided . . . preferential treatment": *HC*, 3-10-93.

321 "an ice pick to chip him away from the tree": *HC*, 10-7-92.

321 "Beatty's bid . . . ran into strong opposition": *Dallas Morning News*, 3-12-93.

Bibliography

Newspapers and magazines are identified in the notes.

Blair, John M. *The Control of Oil.* New York: Pantheon Books, 1976.

Calder, Robert. *Willie: The Life of Somerset Maugham.* New York: St. Martin's Press, 1990.

Cordell, Richard. *Somerset Maugham.* Bloomington: Indiana University Press, 1969.

Curtis, Anthony. *Somerset Maughm.* New York: Macmillan, 1978.

Engler, Robert. *The Politics of Oil: A Study of Private Power and Democratic Directions.* New York: Macmillan, 1961.

Frantz, Joe, and David McComb. *Houston: A Student's Guide to Localized History.* New York: Teachers College Press, Columbia University.

Grimes County Historical Commission. *History of Grimes County.* Dallas: Taylor Publishing, 1982.

Hackett, Pat. *The Andy Warhol Diaries.* New York: Warner Books, 1989.

Harris, Leon. *Merchant Princess: An Intimate History of Jewish Families Who Built Great Department Stores.* New York: Berkley Books, 1980.

Hutchins, Chris, and Peter Thompson. *Fergie Confidential: The Real Story.* New York: St. Martin's Press, 1992.

Jacobson, Stuart E., and Jill Spaulding. *Only the Best: A Celebration of Gift Giving in America.* New York: Abrams, 1985.

Johnson, Arthur Menzies. *The Development of American Petroleum Pipelines.* Ithaca: Cornell University Press, 1956.

Josephson, Matthew. *The Robber Barons: The Great American Capitalists.* New York: Harcourt, Brace, 1934, 1962.

Kilman, Ed, and Theon Wright. *Hugh Roy Cullen.* Englewood Cliffs, N.J.: Prentice-Hall, 1978.

Konolige, Kit. *The Richest Women in the World.* New York: Macmillan, 1985.

Linsley, Judith, and Ellen Rienstra. *Beaumont: An Illustrated History.* Woodland Hills, Calif.: Windsor Publications, 1984.

Marcus, Stanley. *Minding the Store: A Memoir.* Boston: Little, Brown, 1974.

Matthews, Wilbur L. *San Antonio Lawyer.* San Antonio: Corona Publishing Company, 1983.

Montgomery, Ruth. *Aliens Among Us.* New York: G. P. Putnam's Sons, 1985.

Morgan, Ted. *Maugham.* New York: Simon and Schuster, 1980.

Nueces County Historical Society. *History of Nueces County.* Austin: Jenkins Publishing, 1972.

Ornish, Natalie. *Pioneer Jewish Merchants.* Dallas: Texas Heritage Press, 1989.

Quine, Judith Balaban. *The Bridesmaids: Grace Kelly and Six Intimate Friends.* New York: Pocket Books, 1989.

Richardson, Ann. *The Grand Homes of Texas.* Austin: Texas Monthly Press, 1982.

Robinson, Jeffrey. *Rainier and Grace.* New York: Atlantic Monthly Press, 1989.

Rosenberg, Leon Joseph. *Sangers': Pioneer Texas Merchants.* Austin: Texas State Historical Association, 1978.

Thompson, Thomas. *Blood and Money.* New York: Doubleday, 1976.

Tolbert, Frank X. *Neiman-Marcus, Texas.* New York: Henry Holt, 1953.

Acknowledgments

―――

T HIS IS NOT an authorized biography, but several family members were very helpful to me, and I want first to thank them. They are Robert T. Sakowitz, Alexander Sackton, Elizabeth Sackton, Toby Sackton, Margaret Sackton Rosan, Gaylord Johnson, Jr., and Dora Baum Axelrod. Most especially, I am grateful to Pamela Zauderer Bryan, for her many hours of family recollections and fascinating family photographs.

David Berg, the attorney representing Robert T. Sakowitz, was most generous, not only with his time and careful explanations of the facts and the law, but also with his files. Also helpful were Mr. Sakowitz's attorney James Patrick Smith and Douglas Wyatt's attorney Andrew Vickery.

Scores of Sakowitz employees gave me fascinating anecdotes and facts, but no one was more vital to my research or more generous with her time than longtime Sakowitz vice president Carol Waldrop, to whom I am grateful.

I conducted more than two hundred interviews in Houston, Dallas, San Antonio, Corpus Christi, New York, Pittsburgh, London, and Paris, with friends, business associates, and competitors of the Wyatt and Sakowitz families. I am grateful for information, which came in the form of either interviews or observations, from the following:

Jackie Pope Aldredge, Mortimer April, Tony Barbato, Harriet Bath, Harry Berkowitz, Bill Blass, Marvin Blumenfeld, Richard Branch, Richard Brown, Mary Ellen Carey, Mark Carnes, Jessie Mae Craig Chappell, Carolyn Clark, Robert Clark, Leonard Coleman, W. S. Conklin, Blair Corning, Neblett Davis, Audrey Del Rosario, Nigel Dempster, Leroy Denman, Johnnie Dodson, Jeff Dorrell, Gary Easterly, Michael Eastham, C. C. Eckhoff, Betty Ewing, Frenchy

Falik, Karen Fertitta, Norman Fiddmont, Bill Flemming, Luke Fullen, William Garrett, Bobbie Gee, Ed Gerlach, Judith Green, Mary Owen Greenwood, Chuck Griffin, Vince Guercio, Sue Harris, Richard "Racehorse" Haynes, June Hewling, Ester Marion Hoffenberg, Nancy Holmes, Raymond Howard, Bill Hudson, Patrick Hughes, Lyndon Johnson, Donna Neuhoff Josey, Jack Josey, Michael Judd, Joan Kehlhof, John Kilgore, Tamara Kinnie, John Kirksey, Bob Kramer, Kenneth J. Lane, Leonard Lauder, Lowell Lebermann, Nancy Lemmon, Betsy Levy, Judy Levy, Michael Levy, Albert Lidji, Martha Lidji, C. W. Lucas, Karen Lucas, Ann Maier, Camilla "Coco" Blaffer Mallard, Jack Manley, Betty Hughes Maples, Lawrence Marcus, Richard Marcus, Stanley Marcus, Tom Marsh, Mary Ann Maxwell, Marcia May, Boaz Mazor, Lasker Meyer, Peter Miller, Shel Mitelman, Sol Mitelman, Walter Moser, Robert Nemir, Paul Orth, Stewart Orton, Francisco Paco, George Parker, Jerry Patterson, Peggy Pepper, Mrs. V. C. Perini, John Astin Perkins, John Ratcliff, Val Renken, Charles Richard, Jim Richardson, Gregory Rodriguez, Timothy Coltman-Rogers, Marion "Ug" Rowe, Bobby Short, James Siros, Taz Speer, Donald Stone, Patty Taliaferro, John Taylor, Bill Teeter, Mike Tomlin, Philip Van Rensselaer, Donald Waugh, Buck Weirus, Marvin Wise, Frank Zachary, Christina Zilker, Jerry Zipkin.

In addition, I am greatly indebted to a number of librarians and researchers, including Sherry Adams at the *Houston Chronicle;* Phyllis Harvison at the Houston Public Library; Bruce Chabot at the *Corpus Christi Caller-Times;* Andy Apostolou and Mike Lee in London; researchers at *Women's Wear Daily* and *Town & Country;* Lee Brame at Corpus Christi's Nueces County District Court; Clark and Robert Whitten at the *Navasota Daily Examiner;* Casey Green at the Galveston and Texas History Center of the Rosenberg Library, Galveston; the helpful staffs of the Dallas Public Library, New York Public Library, and at the records warehouse of the Harris County Courthouse, and the Freedom of Information Act office in Washington, D.C.

I am especially grateful to my editor, Fredrica S. Friedman, for her outstanding judgment and her excellent editing. Every writer should be as fortunate as I have been with my editor.

Finally, I thank Leon Harris for his understanding during those nine months I lived in Houston researching this book, for his constant encouragement, and for his love.

Index